W9-CUJ-311

POLAND
AND THE WESTERN POWERS
1938–1939

STUDIES IN POLITICAL HISTORY

Editor: Michael Hurst

Fellow of St. John's College, Oxford

CHIEF WHIP: The Political Life and Times of Aretas Akers-Douglas 1st Viscount Chilston by Eric Alexander 3rd Viscount Chilston.

GUIZOT: Aspects of French History 1787–1874 by Douglas Johnson.

MARGINAL PRYNNE: 1660–9 by William M. Lamont.

LAND AND POWER: British and Allied Policy on Germany's Frontiers 1916–19 by H. I. Nelson.

THE LANGUAGE OF POLITICS in the Age of Wilkes and Burke by James T. Boulton.

THE ENGLISH FACE OF MACHIAVELLI: A Changing Interpretation 1500–1700 by Felix Raab.

BEFORE THE SOCIALISTS: Studies in Labour and Politics 1861–81 by Royden Harrison.

THE LAWS OF WAR IN THE LATE MIDDLE AGES by M. H. Keen.

GOVERNMENT AND THE RAILWAYS IN NINETEENTH CENTURY BRITAIN by Henry Parris.

THE ENGLISH MILITIA IN THE EIGHTEENTH CENTURY: The Story of a Political Issue, 1660–1802 by J. R. Western.

SALISBURY AND THE MEDITERRANEAN, 1886–96 by C. J. Lowe.

VISCOUNT BOLINGBROKE, Tory Humanist by Jeffrey Hart.

W. H. SMITH by Viscount Chilston.

THE McMAHON LINE: A Study in the Relations between India, China and Tibet, 1904–14; in two volumes by Alastair Lamb.

THE THIRD REICH AND THE ARAB EAST by Lukasz Hirszowicz.

THE ELIZABETHAN MILITIA 1558–1638 by Lindsay Boynton.

JOSEPH CHAMBERLAIN AND LIBERAL REUNION: The Round Table Conference of 1887, by Michael Hurst.

SOCIALISTS, LIBERALS AND LABOUR 1885–1914 by Paul Thompson.

POLAND AND THE WESTERN POWERS, 1938–1939 by Anna M. Cienciala.

DISRAELIAN CONSERVATISM AND SOCIAL REFORM by Paul Smith.

JÓZEF BECK

Foreign Minister of Poland, 1932-1939

POLAND
AND
THE WESTERN
POWERS
1938–1939

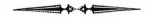

A Study in the Interdependence
of Eastern and Western Europe

by
ANNA M. CIENCIALA

LONDON: Routledge & Kegan Paul
TORONTO: University of Toronto Press

First published 1968
in Great Britain by
Routledge & Kegan Paul Ltd
and in Canada by
University of Toronto Press

Printed and Bound in Great Britain by
Bookprint Limited, London and Crawley

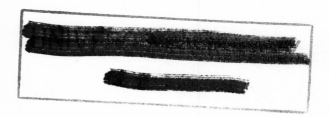

CONTENTS

PREFACE

THE object of this study is twofold. In the first place, the author seeks to explain the nature and historical roots of the problems facing Polish foreign policy in 1938–39 and the manner in which they were approached by the men who shaped and directed Polish diplomacy. Secondly, the author's aim is to illustrate the political interdependence in these years of Eastern and Western Europe. This interdependence hinged on the German problem. The attitude of France and Britain towards Poland and Eastern Europe as a whole was primarily a reflection of their policy towards Germany; at the same time, this policy was the decisive factor in the individual reactions of Germany's eastern neighbours to the threat of resurgent German power.

As far as Poland was concerned, she not only had to strive to avert the danger of German revisionism, the realization of which would have made her a vassal of Berlin, but she also had to consider the possibility of Soviet expansion at her expense. This study is, however, primarily concerned with Polish attempts to obtain security with regard to Germany and, in the period in question, this was the main objective of Polish diplomacy. In contrast to the intense diplomatic activity on the German sector, Poland's relations with the USSR were virtually in a state of 'cold war'. Nevertheless, the Polish government's aversion to any close co-operation with the Soviet Union was naturally a factor of great importance in its overall attitude towards the German problem, although it never led even to the consideration of an anti-Soviet alliance with Germany. Poland's relations with the smaller countries of Eastern Europe, particularly with Czechoslovakia, were primarily governed by the Western attitude towards Germany and the fear of any growth of Soviet influence in this area.

Since this is a study in diplomatic history, Polish domestic history has been touched upon only in so far as it had a bearing on foreign policy. This applies particularly to the criticism of the government's diplomacy by the leading parties of the opposition. Although Piłsudski seized dictatorial power in May 1926, Poland could not thereafter be called a totalitarian state. The government majority in Parliament, first the 'Non-Party Bloc of Co-operation with the Government', and subsequently the 'Camp of National Unity', did not eliminate the influence of the opposition on the political life of the country. Even after the opposition parties had boycotted the elections in protest against the constitution of April 1935, which gave virtually dictatorial powers to the President, they still retained a strong influence through their press. Since they were strongly in favour of co-operation with France and critical of the government's relations with Germany, and since their criticism was widely reflected in the public opinion of the country, the government was obliged to formulate its foreign policy with this factor constantly in mind.

This book originated as a doctoral thesis for Indiana University (1962), written under the guidance of Professor Piotr S. Wandycz who read the drafts and the final manuscript and whose valuable advice and comments have been of immeasurable help in my work.

The basic sources for this study are the published documents on Polish, German, British, and American foreign policy and unpublished Polish documentary material. At the time of writing, documents on French foreign policy were available only for the first few months of 1936, while the official Soviet documentary series had only reached the year 1927. The Italian diplomatic documents for this period had not yet been published. I trust, nevertheless, that the Polish documentation made available to me for this study is extensive enough to trace and elucidate Polish diplomacy in this critical period of European history. The interpretation of these documents is, of course, entirely my responsibility.

The gathering of the materials for this book involved travel and study in North America and Europe. It could not have been accomplished without the generous assistance of the Ford Foundation. The publication was made possible by a grant from the Social Science Research Council of Canada, using funds provided by the Canada Council, and by a grant from the Publications Fund of the University of Toronto Press. I should like to express my great appreciation for the aid given me by these institutions.

It is also a great pleasure for me to express my gratitude to the following institutions which gave me access to their archives and libraries: the General Sikorski Historical Institute, the Polish Research Centre, the British Foreign Office Library, and the Institute of International Affairs in London, England; the Hoover Institute and Library on War, Revolution, and Peace, Stanford, California, the National Archives, Washington, D.C., the Józef Piłsudski Institute of America, New York, and the curators of the archives of the former Polish Ministry of Foreign Affairs, Montreal, Canada; the Polish Ministry of Foreign Affairs, the Polish Institute of International Affairs in Warsaw, the Ossolineum Institute in Wrocław, and the Provincial Archives in Gdańsk, Poland.

Many friends and colleagues have taken the trouble to read and comment on my work. For this time-consuming labour and for the valuable advice I received, I should like to thank the following: Professors Charles L. Lundin and Robert F. Ferrell of Indiana University; Professor Harold I. Nelson and Dr. Bohdan Budurowycz of the University of Toronto; the readers of the Social Science Research Council of Canada, and Miss M. J. Houston and Miss M. L. Pearson of the University of Toronto Press. I should like to acknowledge gratefully the comments and advice of the late Dr. Titus Komarnicki, former Polish delegate to the League of Nations, minister to Switzerland, and Research Adviser in the Polish Institute and Sikorski Museum, London; Count Edward Raczyński, former Polish Ambassador in London; the late Count Michał Łubieński, former Chef de Cabinet to Col. Beck; General Wacław Stachiewicz, former Chief of the Polish General Staff, General Marian Kukiel, Director of the General Sikorski Historical Institute, London, and my father, Andrew M. Cienciala. For the maps, I am indebted to Professor Bogdan Zaborski of Sir George Williams University, Mr. G. J. Matthews of the Geography Department, University of Toronto, and Mr. Daniel Holdgreve of the University of Kansas. I should also like to thank Dr. Robert F. Byrnes, former Chairman of the Department of History and of the Centre for Russian and East European Studies at Indiana University, for his encouragement and support of this project.

A. C.

University of Kansas, 1967

ABBREVIATIONS

APEL	Archives of the former Polish Embassy, London (General Sikorski Historical Institute, London)
DBFP	*Documents on British Foreign Policy*, series 2, 3, 1933–1939
DDF	*Documents Diplomatiques Français*, series 2, vol. I, 1 January – 31 March 1936
DGFP	*Documents on German Foreign Policy*, series C, 1933–1937, series D, 1937–1945
DM	*Documents and Materials Relating to the Eve of the Second World War*, vols. I, II
Evénements	*Les Evénements survenus en France de 1933 à 1945: Temoignages et Documents recueillis par la Commission d'Enquête Parlementaire*, IX vols
FOL	Foreign Office Library, London
FRUS	*Foreign Relations of the United States, 1938–1945*
JCEA	*Journal of Central European Affairs*
MFA	Archives of the former Polish Ministry of Foreign Affairs deposited in the General Sikorski Historical Institute, London, England, and Montreal, Canada; archives of the Ministry of Foreign Affairs, Warsaw
	(a) Cyphers: collection of cypher letters and telegrams, London
	(b) Files:
	P–F Polish-French Relations
	P–G Polish-German Relations
	P–GB Polish-British Relations
NDHM	*New Documents on the History of Munich*
NYD	*New Yorsky Dennik*
PD I	*Polnische Dokumente zur Vorgeschichte des Krieges, Erste Folge*
PD II	*Polnische Dokumente zur Vorgeschichte des Krieges, Zweite Folge* (Microfilm)
PGD, Hoover	Photostats, German Documents, Hoover Institute and Library on War, Revolution and Peace, Stanford University, California

PWB	*Polish White Book: Official Documents Concerning Polish-German and Polish-Soviet Relations, 1933–39*
SC II	Referat: Śląsk Cieszyński, Zeszyt II (Report on Teschen Silesia, Book II), collection of documents compiled from archives of the former Polish Embassy, London; roneograph in the Polish Centre, London
SDNA	State Department files, National Archives, Washington, D.C.
Szembek MSS	Jan Szembek's Diary and Papers; manuscript deposited in the Polish Institute and Sikorski Museum, London
ZH	*Zeszyty Historyczne, Polski Instytut Spraw Międzynarodowych, Warszawa* (Historical Notebooks, Polish Institute of International Affairs, Warsaw, roneotype)

THE BACKGROUND, 1918—1938

DESPITE Poland's triumphant resurgence as an independent state in 1918, her existence was an extremely precarious one. Wedged in between two great powers who had in the past partitioned her between them, the new Poland lived under the constant threat of a renewed German-Russian alliance and of a revision of her frontiers which would leave her at the mercy of one or the other of her mighty neighbours.

The maintenance of Polish boundaries as constituted in the west by the Versailles Treaty, plebiscites, and decisions of the League of Nations, and in the east by the Treaty of Riga, was considered by all Polish governments and the vast majority of the population as the condition of Poland's independence. In the north-west, Poland had obtained direct access to the sea through the Free City of Danzig and Polish Pomerania, a neck of land better known by its German term, the 'Polish Corridor', since it separated East Prussia from the Reich. Originally Poland had claimed Danzig outright and also demanded the southern part of East Prussia which had a sizable Polish population. However, the British Prime Minister, Lloyd George, successfully pressed the Poles, Clemenceau, and Wilson to accept the Free City instead, while plebiscites were decreed for Marienwerder and Allenstein which in July 1920 voted for union with Germany.[1]

---

[1] For Polish demands, see Roman Dmowski, *Polityka Polska i Odbudowa Państwa* (Polish Policy and the Rebuilding of the State, 2nd ed., Warsaw, 1926), part V, *passim*, annexes X, XI. Roman Dmowski (1864–1939) was the leader of the National Democrats and favoured Polish autonomy within the Russian Empire between 1905–1916; later he became Chairman of the Polish National Committee and Polish delegate to the Paris Peace Conference. After Piłsudski's coup in 1926, his political activity was increasingly hampered and he spent the last years of his life in exile, returning to die in Poland. For disputes among the leaders of the Great Powers over Danzig, see *FRUS, The Paris Peace Conference* (Washington, D.C.,

Since Poland did not have full freedom of action in Danzig, which manifested its hostility by refusing to unload supplies during the Polish-Soviet war, the Polish port of Gdynia was built a few miles west of the Free City. In the south-west, the Poles had demanded the whole of the industrial region of Upper Silesia but Lloyd George had again successfully pressed for a plebiscite. The Poles staged three uprisings and the plebiscite, though it gave an overall majority vote for Germany, was not considered final. The League of Nations finally partitioned the region between Germany and Poland.[2]

The new frontiers left about one million Germans in Poland and about two million Poles in Germany. The Minority Treaties, however, were binding only on the new states so that Poland could never adequately protect the rights of her nationals in Germany. Germany remained bitterly unreconciled to the loss of her eastern territories to which she laid claim on ethnic, economic and historical grounds. From the ethnic point of view, the German claim held good only for Danzig, while in Posen, the Corridor and in Upper Silesia east of the river Oder, the population was preponderantly Polish even according to the Prussian censuses of 1900 and 1910. From the economic point of view, Posen and Upper Silesia had found their chief customers even before the war in Russian and Austrian Poland, while the port of Danzig possessed its natural hinterland in Polish territory, a fact proven in practice by the tenfold increase of Danzig tonnage between 1918 and 1928. Historically, the territories

---

1943), vol. IV, pp. 413–19, also Paul Mantoux, *Les Délibérations du Conseil de Quatre* (Paris, 1955), vol. I, p. 125. For a detailed discussion of Polish questions at the Peace Conference, see Titus Komarnicki, *Rebirth of the Polish Republic: A Study in the Diplomatic History of Europe 1914–1920* (London, 1957), part II, chap. II., *passim*, also Harold I. Nelson, *Land and Power: British and Allied Policy on Germany's Frontiers, 1916–1919* (Toronto, 1963), part III, chaps. VI, VII, *passim*.

[2] For Polish demands, see Dmowski, *Polityka Polska*. For the debates in the Supreme Council, see *FRUS, The Paris Peace Conference*, vol. VI, pp. 140–60, 303–4; Mantoux, *Les Délibérations*, vol. II, p. 423. For a discussion of the problem, see Komarnicki, *Rebirth of the Polish Republic*, and H. I. Nelson, *Land and Power*. For the plebiscites, see Sarah Wambaugh, *Plebiscites since the World War* (Washington, D.C., 1933), vol. I, pp. 208–12, 251, 258, 266. Of the total vote, 707,605 or 58 per cent was for Germany and 479,359, or 40.3 per cent for Poland. Of the German vote, 191,154 or 16 per cent was cast by 'outvoters', that is to say, voters born but no longer resident in Upper Silesia; *ibid.*, p. 250.

in question had been under Prussian rule only since the latter part of the eighteenth century, although the towns of Upper Silesia had had a German-speaking population since the Middle Ages. The most important point, however, was that these territories were essential for the economic development of the new Poland but not for the great industrial power of Germany, a fact which was recognized by almost all the allied experts in Paris. While ethnically Germany's claim to Danzig was incontestable, the question had another and far more important aspect which was crucial for Poland. Few people in Western Europe realized that for Germany the revindication of Danzig was inseparable from revindication of the Corridor. The retrocession of the Corridor, however, would have meant that Poland's access not only to Danzig but also to Gdynia would have run through German-held territory. This would have allowed Germany to apply economic pressure at will in order to subordinate Polish policy to her interests. It is only in this light that the Polish attitude toward the Danzig question can be fully understood.[3]

In the East, parts of Byelorussia and of East Galicia had been acquired as a result of the war of 1920. While these territories

---

[3] For the ethnic structure of Posen, East and West Prussia, and Upper Silesia, see the excellent *Handbooks* prepared by the Historical Section of the Foreign Office for the Paris Peace Conference under the general editorship of G. W. Prothero and published in London in 1920, nos. 45, 39 and 40 respectively. Using the Prussian censuses of 1900 and 1910, the compilers concluded that Posen was 77.4 per cent Polish with the exception of Bromberg (Bydgoszcz) and the German *Kreise* on the western border of the province; the northernmost part of West Prussia, which later formed part of the Corridor, was also preponderantly Polish as was the southern part of East Prussia. In Upper Silesia, east of the Oder, the population was said to be from 75 to 83 per cent Polish, the four major towns excepted; see *Prussian Poland*, pp. 5–8, 55; *East and West Prussia*, pp. 11–15; *Upper Silesia*, pp. 4–7. These findings are represented in a map supplement to the Handbooks, in maps 1 and 2, of Germany and Poland respectively, and drawn up for the War Office in December 1918. They correspond with J. Spett's *Nationalitätenkarte der östlichen Provinzen des Deutschen Reichs*, drawn on the basis of the 1910 census, and printed by Justus Perthes, Gotha, 1910; see Map I. For the export markets of Posen, see *Prussian Poland*, p. 51; for Danzig's need of the Polish hinterland, see *East and West Prussia*, pp. 42–3. For the prewar economic connection between Upper Silesia and Russian and Austrian Poland, see Etienne Mantoux, *The Carthaginian Peace, or the Economic Consequences of Mr Keynes* (Oxford, 1946), p. 77. For the opinion of American experts on Poland's need of Danzig and the Corridor, see David H. Miller, *My Diary at the Conference of Paris. With Documents* (n.d), vol. VI, document 441, p. 50.

were inhabited mainly by Byelorussians and Ukrainians, there was also a sizable Polish population, particularly in the Wilno and Grodno regions in the north and Lwów in the south.[4] Historically, these lands had been ruled by the Polish crown from the end of the fourteenth century to the partitions, but their value to the new Poland was primarily strategic since they pushed back the Russian frontier to a distance which made Soviet intervention in Polish life impossible.[5] Thus, territorial concessions in the east, as in the west, were, in the opinion of Polish statesmen and of the majority of the Polish people, equivalent to the establishment of foreign domination and the main task of Polish diplomacy was to prevent their realization.

The man who by his ideas and attitudes towards Poland's problems was to dominate her foreign policy, as he dominated her domestic policies, was Józef Piłsudski (1867–1935), the first Head of State, Commander-in-Chief, Marshal of the Army, and virtual dictator from 1926 until his death. Piłsudski's most trusted disciple in the sphere of foreign policy was Col. Józef Beck (1894–1944) who held the post of Foreign Minister from 1932 until 1939. Since Beck followed and built upon the

[4] According to the German census carried out in 13 districts of the Wilno-Grodno region, the Poles had an absolute majority in 7, a relative majority in one, and 30 per cent in 4 others; see T. Komarnicki, *Rebirth of the Polish Republic*, p. 193. The official Russian census of 1897 was strongly contested by the Poles and, in any case, covered all of Lithuania; see *Russian Poland*, Handbook no. 44 (London, 1920), pp. 19–24. In Galicia, the Austrian census of 1910 gave 4,672,000 as Polish-speaking out of a population of 8,025,600—this, however, included the preponderantly Polish region of Western Galicia. East of the San and Wisłoka rivers the Ukrainians formed 59 per cent of the population except for certain Polish districts; see *Austrian Poland*, Handbook no. 46 (London, 1920), pp. 9–10. For Polish demands and allied policy in 1919, see R. Dmowski, *Polityka Polska*, chap. VII, *passim*, and annexes X, XII; T. Komarnicki, *Rebirth of the Polish Republic*, part II, chaps. IV, V, *passim*. According to the Polish census of 1931, there were in Poland 3,222,000 Ukrainians, 1,219,600 Ruthenians (also Ukrainians), 989,000 White Ruthenians (Byelorussians), and 2,732,600 Jews; except for the latter, these were concentrated mainly in Eastern Poland. The German minority of 741,000 was located mainly in Western Poland. The total population in 1931 numbered 31,915,800, of which 21,993,400 were listed as ethnically Polish; see *Concise Statistical Yearbook of Poland 1938*, ed. E. Szturm de Sztrem (Warsaw, 1938), pp. 22–3. By 1939, it was estimated that the total population had grown to about 35,000,000.

[5] Józef Piłsudski, *Pisma Zbiorowe* (Collected Works), vol. VII, *Rok 1920* (The Year 1920, Warsaw, 1937), p. 147.

4

principles laid down by Piłsudski, it is necessary to bear in mind the latter's views on the main objectives of Polish diplomacy and the means by which they were to be achieved.

Piłsudski did not speak or write much on the subject of foreign policy; thus his ideas have been, and still are, subject to different interpretations. However, it is possible to deduce his main principles from scattered pronouncements and decisions made in his lifetime.[6] The cardinal point which emerges from such a study, and which was the backbone of his political thought, is the idea of independence. This belief, stemming from a fierce national pride and reaction to a past in which Poland had been merely the tool of other powers, gave a specific tone to his diplomacy and also to the diplomatic methods of Col. Beck. But this was not merely a romantic and sometimes arrogant code of behaviour; it was the result of long meditation on the nature of Poland's interests. In the sphere of foreign policy it was translated into the principle of 'equilibrium' between Poland's great neighbours, Germany and Russia, of an individual policy in East Central Europe, and of a refusal to serve as the obedient tool of even an allied power like France. Piłsudski believed that Poland, allied with France, should strive for good relations with both Moscow and Berlin without becoming the ally of either. He based this attitude on the belief that the disparity of power

[6] This analysis is based on the following works: Józef Beck, *Dernier Rapport: Politique Polonaise, 1926–1939*, ed. Mme J. Beck, M. Łubieński, W. Pobóg-Malinowski, T. Schaetzel (Neuchâtel, 1952, tr. as *Last Report*, New York, 1957); Jan Szembek, *Journal, 1933–1939*, ed. Léon Noël (Paris, 1952); see also *Fragmenty Dziennika Szembeka* (Fragments of Szembek's Diary), ed. Józef Chudek (Warsaw, 1956), and *Diariusz i Teki Jana Szembeka* (Diary and Papers of Jan Szembek), vols. I, II, ed. Tytus Komarnicki (London, 1964–1965). Szembek was Under-Secretary of State for Foreign Affairs, Nov., 1932–Sept., 1939. Juliusz Łukasiewicz, *Polska Jest Mocarstwem* (Poland is a Power, Warsaw, 1938) and *Polska w Europie w Polityce Józefa Piłsudskiego* (Poland in Europe in the Policy of Józef Piłsudski, London, 1944). Łukasiewicz was Minister, then Ambassador in Moscow, 1933–36, and in Paris, 1936–39; Tytus (Titus) Komarnicki, 'Piłsudski a Polityka Wielkich Mocarstw Zachodnich' (Piłsudski and the Policy of the Great Western Powers) *Niepodległość* (London, 1952), vol. IV, pp. 17–92. T. Komarnicki was the Polish delegate to the League of Nations, 1934–37, then Minister in Berne to 1940, underground delegate, France, 1942–3, Minister accredited to the Dutch government in London, 1944–45. The two major biographies of Piłsudski are by W. Pobóg-Malinowski, *Józef Piłsudski, 1867–1914*, 2 vols. (Warsaw, 1935), new edition, ed. K. Sawicki (London, 1964), and Anatol Muhlstein, *Le Maréchal Piłsudski 1867–1919* (Paris, 1939).

5

between Poland and either neighbour was too great to allow an alliance on equal terms. Such an alliance, in his opinion, would mean that Poland would become a vassal state to her ally and would also facilitate an agreement between her two hereditary enemies at her expense. Good relations with both, on the other hand, would give Poland a strong position in relations with other states.[7] In East Central Europe Piłsudski aimed at close co-operation with those states which shared common interests with Poland. Thus in 1921 he signed a defensive alliance with Rumania, operative in case of a Soviet attack on either country. His hopes that Poland would lead a Baltic bloc were frustrated by the Polish-Lithuanian dispute over Wilno (Vilnius); he therefore confined himself to good relations with Latvia and Estonia and set Polish diplomacy the task of preventing the Baltic States from falling under German or Soviet hegemony. As far as France was concerned, Piłsudski refused to subordinate Polish interests to Paris when he thought that they would not be well served; this was not only because he abhorred what he called the traditional Polish 'boot-licking' attitude towards everything Western but because he believed that Poland should always consider her interests first and, where possible, secure her objectives on the basis of her own strength.

It was this combination of personal characteristics and views on Polish interests which led Piłsudski to oppose the setting up of any 'Directorate' of Great Powers in Europe even if it included his allies. He rightly feared that such a directorate could dispose of Poland's interests without consulting her or against her own will. In the face of such a possibility he was ready to take individual and independent action to defend her interests.

Much has been written about Piłsudski's distrust of Russia. It has sometimes been seen as the determining factor in both his policy and that of Col. Beck;[8] it has been interpreted as the result of pro-German sympathies and of class-hatred for Soviet Russia.[9] The key, however, lies in Piłsudski's concept of in-

[7] Beck, *Dernier Rapport*, p. 5.

[8] 'It seems, indeed, that this almost instinctive and deep-seated mistrust of the USSR was the dominant feature of Polish foreign policy between the wars . . .'; Bohdan Budurowycz, *Polish-Soviet Relations, 1932–1939* (New York, 1963), pp. 190–91.

[9] This is the standard interpretation of Piłsudski's policy in postwar Polish

6

dependence and in his personal experience. From his education in Russian schools and his revolutionary past, he retained a deep conviction about the unchanging nature of Russian imperialism, whether aristocratic or proletarian, Tsarist or Soviet. His expectation of an imminent Soviet attack on Poland dictated his march into the Ukraine in 1920. It was not a fear which he held alone.[10] Even if it is assumed that Piłsudski was mistaken and that the Soviet government had no intention of attacking Poland, it must also be admitted that the Soviets reciprocated with an error of equally far-reaching consequences. The Red Army's drive into ethnographic Poland, the setting up of a Polish Communist government behind its lines, and the peace terms of August 1920 which would have reduced Poland to the status of a Soviet satellite[11] convinced the majority of the Polish population that the new Soviet Russia was merely the reincarnation of the old Tsarist imperialism, inimical to Polish independence. The frontier established by the Treaty of Riga in 1921 meant the end of Piłsudski's hopes to establish a Polish-Lithuanian-Bye-lorussian-Ukrainian federation.[12] It also meant that the Russian attempt to bring revolution to Europe had failed. The aim of Polish diplomacy was henceforth to maintain the eastern frontier, and to strive for good relations with Moscow but not to support its attempts to take an active share in European politics.

---

historiography; cf. Karol Lapter, *Pakt Piłsudski-Hitler* (Piłsudski-Hitler Pact, Warsaw, 1962), p. 204, *passim*, and Marian Wojciechowski, *Stosunki Polsko-Niemieckie, 1933–1938* (Polish-German Relations, 1933–1938, Poznań, 1965), p. 30. This is also the interpretation of Soviet historians; cf. P. N. Pospelov (ed.), *Istoriia Velikoi Otechestvennoi Voiny Sovetskovo Soiuza, 1941–1945* (History of the Great Patriotic War of the Soviet Union, 1941–1945, Moscow, 1960), vol. I, pp. 155, 159.

[10] General Hans von Seeckt noted in November 1919 that the Bolsheviks intended to start an offensive against Poland; see T. Komarnicki, *Rebirth of the Polish Republic*, p. 516. The German Foreign Ministry received confidential information in February 1920 that preparations were being made for a Soviet offensive to begin in March; see Josef Korbel, *Poland Between East and West: Soviet and German Diplomacy toward Poland, 1919–1933* (Princeton, 1963), pp. 28–9.

[11] Polish armed forces were to be limited to 50,000 men while the Soviet Union was to have 200,000 troops on the Polish border and the right of free passage; Poland was to be completely demobilized; the frontier was to follow the Curzon Line; texts in T. Komarnicki, *Rebirth of the Polish Republic*, pp. 670–3.

[12] See Marian K. Dziewanowski, 'Piłsudski's Federal Policy 1919–1921,' *JCEA*, vol. X (1950), no. 3, pp. 113–28.

At the same time neither Piłsudski nor Beck ever considered an alliance with Germany against the USSR.

Piłsudski's principle that Poland should pursue an independent policy was confirmed and strengthened by the attitude of the Western Democracies towards Germany. The cornerstone of Polish foreign policy was the alliance with France which was concluded in February 1921, and accompanied by a secret military convention.[13] It seemed at first as if France, by her alliance with Poland and, in 1924, with Czechoslovakia, had committed herself to the support of those two countries as a counterweight to Germany. However, it soon became apparent that Paris did not feel strong enough to pursue such a policy of 'containment' without the support of another Great Power. Since the United States had withdrawn into isolation, the only ally of such stature was Great Britain but she refused to underwrite French commitments in Eastern Europe. The Locarno treaties of 1925 were the omen of what was to be a gradual French retreat from the grand design of 1921 and 1924. Germany officially recognized her postwar frontiers in the west and France received an international guarantee of these frontiers with Germany; no such guarantee was, however, given to the frontiers set up in Eastern Europe. The arbitration treaties which Germany signed with Poland and Czechoslovakia and the Treaties of Mutual Guarantee which France concluded with her two allies[14] did not cancel the discrimination which had been established by Locarno between the boundaries of Eastern and Western Europe. Gustav Stresemann, the architect of Locarno, saw the agreements as giving Germany the possibility of revision in the East.[15] Moreover, a dispute began between Paris and Warsaw as to which alliance was valid, the pact of 1921, which provided for automatic bilateral assistance, or the agreement of 1925, according to which aid by one party to the other seemed

[13] For the texts of the alliance and military convention, see Piotr S. Wandycz, *France and Her Eastern Allies, 1919–1925: French-Czechoslovak-Polish Relations from the Paris Peace Conference to Locarno* (Minneapolis, 1962), appendices II and III, pp. 393–5.

[14] *Ibid.*, appendix VIII, pp. 401–2.

[15] *Les Papiers de Stresemann*, ed. Henry Bernhard (Paris, 1932), vol. II, p. 181. Stresemann planned this revision to include 'the recovery of unlimited sovereignty' over the Polish Corridor, Danzig, and Upper Silesia; see Zygmunt Gąsiorowski, 'Stresemann and Poland after Locarno', *JCEA*, vol. XVIII (1958), no. 3, p. 299.

dependent on the recognition of an act of aggression by the League of Nations. While successive French governments attempted to revise the military convention and alliance of 1921, all Polish attempts to obtain adequate security guarantees within such new agreements met with failure. The Polish government, therefore, continued to regard the treaties of 1921 as binding. Piłsudski was henceforth haunted by the need, as he put it, of restoring the balance between Eastern and Western Europe.[16]

Locarno did have one advantage for Poland, however, for by setting Germany on the path of good relations with France and Britain it averted the danger of a German-Soviet alliance as foreshadowed by the Rapallo Treaty of 1922. In the years from 1920 to 1925, the re-establishment of the 1914 frontier had been a frequent subject of discussion between Moscow and Berlin. It is true that the Soviet government made proposals for closer relations with Warsaw but these were seen as Moscow's 'Polish Card' in its relations with Berlin. Chicherin's proposal for a Non-Aggression Pact with Poland in September 1925 fell into this category. Immediately thereafter he proposed an alliance to Stresemann;[17] this was on the eve of the Locarno treaties. After Locarno, the Soviet Union displayed more interest in stabilizing relations with its neighbours. In February 1929, it signed a multilateral declaration on the model of the Briand-Kellogg Pact with Poland, Estonia, Latvia, and Rumania, denouncing war as an instrument of policy. The Japanese attack on Manchuria in 1931 brought the threat of war to Soviet Russia's eastern frontiers and stimulated her efforts to secure peace in the West. Piłsudski, too, welcomed the opportunity of ending the state of unrest which had prevailed on Poland's eastern borders and thus the two states signed a Non-Aggression Pact in July

[16] Beck, *Dernier Rapport*, p. 6. For a summary of Polish-French relations in the period 1928–1936, see the note in ed. T. Komarnicki, *Diariusz i Teki Jana Szembeka*, vol. II, pp. 10–17. For documents dealing with Franco-Polish negotiations in the period 1925–1932, see MFA (London), P–F, A.11/49/F, 1, 2.

[17] Chicherin told Ambassador Brockdorff-Rantzau that the non-aggression proposal was a manœuvre on the part of Russia as of Poland; Korbel, *Poland between East and West*, p. 222. G. Freund is of the opinion that the Soviet proposal to Poland was 'a blatant attempt to scare Stresemann with the threat of a Russo-Polish détente'; *Unholy Alliance: Russo-German Relations from the Treaty of Brest-Litovsk to the Treaty of Berlin* (London, 1957), p. 231. See also Beck, *Dernier Rapport*, p. 10. n. 1.

1932.[18] The Marshal was now in a stronger position to press for a stabilization of Poland's relations with Germany.

This task became more urgent than ever with the opening of the Disarmament Conference in February of the same year. The German government demanded equality of armaments before entering negotiations and made it clear that its agreement to any limitations would depend on the revision of its frontiers with Poland. There were increasing signs of readiness on the part of London and Paris to pay this price. French ministers warned their Polish colleagues that Poland should reach an accommodation with the Reich.[19] In January 1933, conversations took place between German officials on the one hand, and French and Belgian industrialists on the other. The task of the latter, who had the full support of their governments, was to explore the extent of German demands with regard to the Corridor and Upper Silesia.[20] The French Ambassador in Warsaw, Jules Laroche, told his German colleague, von Moltke, that in his opinion the Polish Corridor was not tenable in the long run. [21] Finally, on 17 March, Mussolini announced his project for a Four Power Pact the patent object of which was to obtain an agreement on armaments at the price of revising the *status quo* of 1919 in Eastern Europe. The presence in Rome of the British Prime Minister, Ramsay MacDonald, and the Foreign Secretary, Sir John Simon, at the time of the announcement was regarded in Poland as an indication that Mussolini had the blessing of Great Britain.

Piłsudski had made efforts to reach a *modus vivendi* with Gustav Stresemann but these had come to nothing in view of the latter's insistence that revision should precede any improvement in relations.[22] A new situation was created, however, with the appointment of Adolf Hitler as German Chancellor in January

[18] Text in *PWB*, no. 151 (New York, 1940).

[19] In October 1932, Pierre Cot, the French alternate delegate to the League of Nations, told Mr August Zaleski, the Polish Foreign Minister, that France must come to an agreement with Germany and, therefore, that Poland should give up Danzig and the Corridor; personal account by Mr Zaleski to the author, London, December 1958.

[20] *DGFP*, series C, vol. I., nos. 2, 18.

[21] *Ibid.*, no. 34.

[22] For an account of secret Polish-German conversations, see Z. Gąsiorowski 'Stresemann and Poland after Locarno', *JCEA*, vol. XVIII, no. 3, pp. 300, 314.

1933. At first the new Chancellor was as vociferous as his predecessors in stating German demands against Poland but Piłsudski decided to explore the new possibilities. On 6 March, he ordered the reinforcement of the Polish garrison on Westerplatte in Danzig where Poland had a munitions depot. There had been bad relations with the Senate which shortly before had abolished the mixed Harbour Police and replaced it with its own men. The Nazi Party was also gaining power in the city. Piłsudski meant his military demonstration to be a warning to Hitler and to Danzig, as well as to the Western Democracies.[23] He may also have approached France shortly afterwards with propositions for a joint preventive war against Germany.[24] What-

[23] The German Minister in Warsaw, Von Moltke, commented '. . . the sabre-rattling method, the fanaticizing of the population, the various warlike gestures of the last few weeks, and the exaggeration of the danger threatening from Germany, are important stage props of Polish policy in its fight against disarmament and revision'; *DGFP*, C, I, no. 180; see also Hans Roos, *Polen und Europa: Studien zur Polnischen Aussenpolitik, 1931–1939* (Tübingen, 1957), pp. 61–71.

[24] A considerable literature exists on this debatable question. Z. Gąsiorowski does not think there was any question of preventive war; 'Did Piłsudski attempt to initiate a Preventive War in 1933?' *Journal of Modern History*, vol. XVII (1955), no. 2, pp. 135–51; nor does Tadeusz Kuźmiński, 'Wokół Zagadnienia Wojny Prewencyjnej w 1933 roku' (On the Problem of Preventive War in 1933), *Najnowsze Dzieje Polski: Materiały i Studia z Okresu, 1914–1949* (Warsaw, 1960), vol. III, pp. 5–45, reprinted as chap. II, in his *Polska, Francja, Niemcy, 1933–1935* (Poland, France, Germany, 1933–1935, Warsaw, 1963). Marian Wojciechowski, *Stosunki Polsko-Niemieckie*. p. 31, thinks Piłsudski wanted to create an 'atmosphere' of preventive war as a means of pressure on Germany, but had no real intention of launching one. Roos, *Polen und Europa*, p. 77, thinks it likely that Piłsudski had a preventive war in mind, as does Józef Lipski, who was appointed Ambassador to Berlin in the summer of 1933: 'Przyczynki do Polsko-Niemieckiej Deklaracji o Nieagresji' (Contributions to the Polish-German Declaration on Non-Aggression), part II, *Bellona* (London, 1951), no. III, p. 11.
No documents specifically setting out such a proposal have been found. The secret mission of Senator Jerzy Potocki to Paris in April of 1933, discussed by Piotr S. Wandycz: 'Trzy Dokumenty: Przyczynek do Zagadnienia Wojny Prewencyjnej' (Three Documents: A Contribution to the Problem of the Preventive War), *Zeszyty Historyczne* (Paris, 1963), vol. 3, pp. 7–14, apparently had no connection with proposals for a preventive war. Wandycz notes that Paul-Boncour told him he had no recollection of this (*ibid.*). Józef Potocki, former Polish Ambassador in Spain and cousin of the Senator, wrote to T. Komarnicki in 1964, that as far as he knew, the Senator's mission was concerned with other matters, see: *Diariusz i Teki Jana Szembeka*, vol. II., pp. 3–4. Nevertheless, rumours to this effect were rife in 1933. In November, the head of the Polish News Agency in Berlin told Ambassador Phipps that Poland had made such a proposal to France in April of that year or earlier but had been rebuffed; *DBFP*, 2, vol. VI, no. 59. Secret soundings through military channels may have taken place, but documentary evidence is lacking.

ever the case may be, Hitler at least seems to have realized that there was some advantage in better relations with Poland. He was also advised to this effect by former Chancellor Brüning and by the Army.[25] As a result, on 3 May, a joint Polish-German *communiqué* was issued in which Hitler declared his intention of maintaining German relations with Poland within the limits of the existing treaties.[26] For all practical purposes this meant that Berlin would desist from its revisionist campaign against Poland.

It should be noted that before Piłsudski exerted pressure on Hitler to obtain the *communiqué*, he had explored the possibility of constructing a united front against Germany in alliance with Czechoslovakia. Polish-Czechoslovak relations had been marred almost from the beginning by territorial disputes and differences of outlook on foreign policy. The territorial dispute principally concerned the Duchy of Teschen which was economically important for its excellent coking coal from the Karvina mines and which had in its western region a preponderantly Polish population.[27] In November 1918, the Czechoslovak Council for the Duchy and the Polish National Council for Teschen agreed to divide the territory on ethnographic lines (see Map II). Piłsudski was ready to settle the matter through a mixed Polish-Czechoslovak commission and sent a letter to President Masaryk

---

The French government of the day was averse to the launching of a preventive war; Anatol Muhlstein, Counsellor at the Polish Embassy in Paris, reported in a letter of 17 April 1933 to Józef Beck, that Joseph Caillaux had said to him: 'Ne vous orientez pas vers la guerre. Ce pays ne marchera pas', *Diariusz i Teki Jana Szembeka*, vol. I, p. 12. Muhlstein noted that Daladier and Paul-Boncour had also expressed their fears regarding such a war. Whether these statements were made as the result of specific secret conversations of which no record was made, or as reactions to the prevalent rumours, cannot be verified. See also p. 267.

[25] Brüning wrote in a private letter to a Polish inquirer that in April and May 1933 German diplomatic sources reported Polish soundings in Paris for a preventive war and that he had pointed out this danger to Hitler; S. Sopicki, 'Przyczynek do Polskiej Akcji Prewencyjnej' (Contribution to the Polish Preventive Action), *Niepodległość* (London, 1952), vol. IV, pp. 169–70. Col. von Reichenau told Ambassador Phipps in November that Germany could not put up a successful resistance in case of a preventive war; *DBFP*, 2, VI, no. 60.

[26] *PWB*, no. 2.

[27] The Austrian census of 1910 gave the population of the Duchy as 426,700, of whom 54.85 per cent spoke Polish, 27.11 per cent Czech and 18.04 per cent German; see H. W. C. Temperley (ed.), *A History of the Peace Conference in Paris* (London, 1921), vol. IV, p. 351. The Polish population was concentrated in the counties of Teschen, Bílsko, and Fryštát; in Poland this area was known after 1919 as 'Zaolzie', or Trans-Olza.

to this effect.[28] The Czechs were, however, unwilling to forgo the Karvina mines and the territory, particularly since on 28 September, Foreign Minister Eduard Beneš had obtained French recognition for the historic boundaries of Bohemia which included the Duchy of Teschen. The French government seemed to be unaware that there was a dispute over the territory. When Czechoslovak troops arrived from France, Prague felt strong enough to occupy the region in January 1919. It was finally adjudicated to Czechoslovakia by the Great Powers as the result of the Spa Conference in July 1920, in which Poland agreed to accept the decisions of the Great Powers on the Danzig and Teschen questions in return for the promise of allied aid against Soviet Russia. The resentment felt in Poland was great and bitter. Although the Beneš-Skirmunt Pact of November 1921 foresaw the final settlement of territorial disputes by a mixed commission, this did not take place. In April 1925, Beneš and Skrzyński initialled a treaty of arbitration and conciliation for all disputes except territorial ones and a liquidation convention settling border delimitations and minority protection. A commercial treaty was also signed. Nevertheless, though relations between the two countries became closer they were never cordial.

Besides the territorial question there were also great differences of outlook in foreign policy. During the Polish-Soviet war of 1920, supplies for Poland were not allowed passage through Czechoslovakia and Czechoslovak statesmen made it plain that they looked on Russia as a potential ally and protector against Germany; to this end there was a desire for a common frontier with Russia which would run through Eastern Galicia. Furthermore, with the creation of the Little Entente in 1921, Czechoslovakia devoted its efforts to the prevention of Hungarian revisionism and did not wish to be involved in Polish quarrels with Germany and Russia. Both Masaryk and Beneš expressed the view that the Polish-German frontier could not be regarded as final and Beneš himself was resolutely averse to concluding a military convention or alliance with Poland.[29]

Despite this unhopeful record, the Polish Ministry of Foreign

[28] See Piotr S. Wandycz, *France and her Eastern Allies*, p. 81.
[29] *Ibid.*, pp. 336–7, 342.

Affairs showed great interest, in the face of growing German revisionism, in closer relations with Czechoslovakia. Soundings were made towards the end of 1932 and at the beginning of 1933 but led to no results since Czech observers, who had connections with the Polish opposition parties, were against the conclusion of any agreements with the Piłsudski government and preferred to wait for its overthrow. When the Polish Ministry decided at the beginning of March to work towards the opening of negotiations with Prague, the Czechoslovak minister in Warsaw, V. Girsa, wrote to Beneš that Beck was an inexperienced diplomat and did not possess 'the necessary spiritual qualities which would make such a discussion of equal value for both sides'. Beck, according to Girsa, was merely the instrument of Piłsudski who was himself hostile to Czechoslovakia and jealous of the respect paid to Masaryk and Beneš in Western Europe.[30] In this situation, no progress towards closer relations was possible. Indeed, on 13 and 18 March 1933, Beneš told the British Prime Minister and Foreign Secretary that he had refused Beck's proposal for an alliance against Germany.[31] After the announcement of Mussolini's project for a Four Power Pact, which met with a vigorous protest from Poland and the Little Entente, Beck planned to visit Prague to discuss common action. He cancelled his visit, however, when the Czechoslovak government, under French pressure, withdrew its unqualified opposition to the pact.[32] The Czechoslovak position on

[30] J. Kozeński, *Czechosłowacja w Polskiej Polityce Zagranicznej w Latach 1932–1938* (Czechoslovakia in Polish Foreign Policy in the Years 1932–1938, Poznań, 1964), pp. 48, 53. See also his article: 'Rokowania polsko-czeskie na tle Niebezpieczeństwa niemieckiego w Latach 1932–1933' (Polish-Czechoslovak Negotiations against the Background of the German Danger in 1932–1933), *Przegląd Zachodni* (Poznań, 1962), no. 2, pp. 253–75.

[31] On 13 March, Beneš told Sir John Simon that 'He had had a long talk recently with Mr Beck. He had told him that Czechoslovakia would not make an alliance with Poland against Germany, because he thought it would be very dangerous to give Germany clear cause for fearing encirclement'; *DBFP*, 2, IV, no. 298. Five days later, Beneš told Simon that he opposed Italian revisionist claims against Yugoslavia because these could lead to war in which Czechoslovakia would be involved and 'This would push her into the arms of Poland, and, as he had already told the British Ministers confidentially, he had already declined an alliance with Poland'; *DBFP*, 2, V, no. 43. There is no Polish record of such a conversation between Beneš and Beck but the two ministers did meet in Geneva on 26 January and 3 February; see Kozeński, *Czechosłowacja*, p. 53.

[32] In a memorandum on Polish-Czechoslovak relations written in June 1938,

14

relations with Poland in 1933, as later, was that 'in view of the great danger of a conflict over the Corridor, this type of alliance was unacceptable to us'.[33] President Beneš certainly wanted good relations with Poland; he offered a pact of 'eternal friendship' in 1933 and made later offers along these lines but he did not want an alliance.[34] The experience of 1933 confirmed Beck in his belief that Czechoslovakia could never be an ally of Poland and this must be borne in mind when considering his later policy towards Prague.

In the autumn of 1933, Piłsudski decided that the time had come to redress Poland's position in the European balance of power.[35] He might not have moved so quickly in consolidating good relations with Germany had the latter not left the Disarmament Conference and the League of Nations. As it was, his considerations on reaching an agreement with a revolutionary government which needed time to establish itself, and on the favourable fact that Hitler was an Austrian, not a Prussian, were reinforced by the opportune circumstance of Hitler's temporary diplomatic isolation. The Marshal therefore pressed the Führer for an agreement to stabilize Polish-German relations, and after a few months of negotiations the Polish-German Declaration on Non-Aggression was signed on 26 January 1934.[36] The agreement was valid for ten years. Piłsudski failed to obtain his major

---

A. Heidrich, the Czechoslovak delegate to the League of Nations, wrote that Beneš had desisted from his energetic opposition to the Four Power Pact project on being told by Paul-Boncour that such action might force his resignation and bring in a right-wing government in France which could easily reach an agreement with Germany; see K. Lapter, 'Współpraca Polski z ZSSR w walce z Paktem Czterech' (Polish-Soviet Co-operation in the Fight against the Four Power Pact), *Studia z Najnowszych Dziejow Powszechnych* (Warsaw, 1963), vol. III, p. 75.

[33] Another extract of Heidrich's memorandum cited by Stefania Stanisławska, *Wielka i Mała Polityka Józefa Becka* (The Great and Small Policy of Józef Beck, Warsaw, 1962), p. 12.

[34] For Beneš's account of his offers to Poland, see L. S. Namier, *Europe in Decay* (London, 1950), pp. 481–5. Ferdynand Kachánek, in his book *Beneš contra Beck: Reportaže a Dokumenty* (Beneš against Beck: Reports and Documents, Prague, 1938), p. 177, wrote that in 1933 Czech political circles knew that Poland would propose a military pact to Czechoslovakia. To avoid this, Beneš proposed a pact of friendship since this meant nothing, while a military pact would have been a pact for mutual aid in case of war and Czechoslovakia did not desire this; cited by Kozeński, *Czechosłowacja*, p. 54.

[35] Beck, *Dernier Rapport*, p. 29.

[36] *PWB*, no. 10, see also p. 267.

objectives which were an official German recognition of Poland's western frontier and of the Statute of the Free City of Danzig, but at least he felt that he had averted the possibility of revision by international agreement. According to an anecdote attributed to Piłsudski, the Marshal remarked that Poland had been removed from Germany's *hors d'œuvre* to her dessert.[37]

The Polish-German agreement met with violent criticism both at home and abroad. All the opposition parties, led by the National Democrats, the Socialists, and the Populists (Peasant Party), attacked the declaration pointing out the programme of *Mein Kampf* and expressing the fear that it would only help Germany to rearm. Fear was also expressed for Danzig which was by now completely under Nazi control. The Communist Party claimed that the pact marked the first step towards Polish co-operation with Germany against the USSR.[38] Press reaction in France was violent and the agreement was portrayed as betrayal by an ally. These criticisms were so often repeated that they finally gained the status of a political axiom; it is, therefore, worthwhile to analyse the pact in order to determine their validity.

The Polish-German Declaration of Non-Aggression was certainly a turning point in Polish foreign policy but it was by no means an abandonment of France, a resignation from independent policy, a factor in German rearmament, or an anti-Soviet move. Poland's previous alliances were specifically recognized. Piłsudski told Ambassador Laroche that Poland retained full freedom of action and that if France should initiate an active policy against Germany she could count on full Polish co-operation.[39] The Declaration did not open the way to German rearmament; France and Britain, without consulting Poland, had already agreed to the principle of equality in armaments in 1932 while Britain was definitely opposed to any action to stop the rearmament already in progress.[40] Nor did the

[37] Adam C. Rosé, *La Politique Polonaise entre les Deux Guerres* (Neuchâtel, 1944–45?), p. 46.
[38] See K. Lapter, *Pakt Piłsudski-Hitler*, pp. 179 ff.
[39] See Roman Debicki, *Foreign Policy of Poland, 1919–1939* (New York, 1962), p. 77.
[40] In 1933 the French government wished to confront the Germans with a *dossier* of breaches of the disarmament clauses of the Versailles Treaty. The idea

agreement mean that Poland was ready to co-operate with Germany against the USSR. Both Piłsudski and Beck realized that such a policy would be only to the advantage of Germany and that Poland could then at best hope to be a leading satellite of Berlin.[41] In any case, to mark his policy of maintaining good relations with both neighbours, Piłsudski sent Col. Beck in February on an official visit to Moscow where he was well received and in May the Polish-Soviet Non-Aggression Pact was extended to 1945. Finally, as far as Danzig was concerned, the nazification of the city by no means made it any more dependent on Germany than it had been before. The German treasury had subsidized the Danzig economy from the beginning in order to check the development of Polish interests, and the members of the Danzig administration were also members of the German civil service. On the contrary, for a short period between May 1933 and November 1934, there was a distinct improvement in the relations between the City and Poland. This was due to the policy of the first Nazi President of the Senate, Hermann Rauschning. Rauschning believed that good relations between Poland and Danzig would serve as a bridge to closer relations between Warsaw and Berlin and he had contributed to persuading Hitler to adopt the new policy towards Poland. He believed that at some time in the future Poland could be persuaded to accept revision at the price of compensation in the East. His policy, however, included the objective of making Danzig economically independent of the Reich and the preservation of a modicum of respect for democratic procedures. Albert Forster, the Nazi 'Gauleiter' for Danzig, persuaded Hitler that such a

was to demand a commission of inquiry and, if this was refused, to launch preventive action; *DBFP*, 2, VI, no. 5. The British reaction was that such a policy would lead to the breakdown of the League of Nations and might even bring about conflict between France and Britain; *ibid.*, no. 196. In October, Generals Weygand and Gamelin spoke of a preventive action through the occupation of the Rhine bridgeheads, but said that France would not move without at least the moral support of Britain; *ibid.*, V, no. 508.

[41] See B. Budurowycz, *Polish-Soviet Relations*, p. 192. For a detailed account of the negotiations, see Marian Wojciechowski, *Stosunki Polsko-Niemieckie*, chap. I, pp. 15–123, where he takes into account the readiness of France and Britain to agree to a revision of Polish-German frontiers. The conception of an eventual later exchange of Danzig and the Corridor for territories taken from Russia, put forward by Hermann Rauschning, first Nazi president of the Danzig Senate, cannot imply that Piłsudski himself considered this possibility, *ibid.*, pp. 117–18.

policy would lead to the 'polonization' of the City and Rauschning was forced to resign.[42]

The Polish-German Declaration should be seen as Piłsudski's
reaction to the growing danger of German revisionism and as an
example of his belief that Poland should pursue an independent
policy. There is no doubt, however, that a firm French attitude
towards Germany would have made the agreement unnecessary,
or would at least have led to the improvement of Polish-German
relations with the participation of France. It is ironic that in
November 1933, at the very time when Piłsudski began negotiations with Berlin, the French government approached the
Germans with the suggestion that they sign non-aggression pacts
with Poland and Czechoslovakia. The price for these pacts was
to be French consent to German rearmament.[43] It is difficult to
establish how serious these suggestions were or whether France
would have been ready to guarantee the pacts without the
support of Great Britain. In any case, it is doubtful whether such
an arrangement would have provided real security for Poland
and Czechoslovakia since it would at the same time have
sanctioned German rearmament. There is no evidence that the
French government communicated its proposals to its East
European allies.

Paris made one last attempt to create a security system linking
Eastern and Western Europe in Louis Barthou's proposed
'Eastern Locarno', put forward in 1934. Its object was to
guarantee the *status quo* in Eastern Europe by making the
Soviet Union its protector. Formally, the project envisaged a
Soviet guarantee for France's border with Germany and a
French guarantee for the western borders of the Soviet Union.
It was clear, however, that if the USSR was to come to the aid of
France, its armies would have to enter Eastern Europe. For
Warsaw, the pact involved the double disadvantage of drawing
it into a zone of Soviet influence and of destroying its new
relations with Germany. This would have meant the end of the
policy of 'equilibrium' between Moscow and Berlin. In any case,
Barthou was assassinated in October and his successor, Pierre
Laval, was no devotee of Franco-Soviet co-operation. Nor was

[42] See *DGFP*, C, I, no. 291, III, no. 224, IV, no. 123.
[43] *Ibid.*, II, nos. 54, 61, 62.

there any enthusiasm for an eastern pact in London, which showed no willingness to give its guarantee. The final upshot of Barthou's initiative was the signature of the Franco-Soviet alliance and of a Soviet-Czechoslovak alliance in 1935; in the latter case, Soviet aid to Czechoslovakia and Czechoslovak aid to the USSR was made dependent on the simultaneous aid of France. While Polish opposition to the Eastern Locarno project was a factor in its failure,[44] it was not decisive. Neither Poland, nor Czechoslovakia, nor, indeed, any other country in Eastern Europe was willing to accept Soviet protection while the attitude of London and Paris was at best half-hearted.

It has been suggested that had the Eastern Locarno project been realized it would have reduced the possibility of German expansion and favoured an anti-Nazi coalition.[45] This is, of course, a possibility but aside from the reservations of the East European states involved and the distrust existing between the Western Democracies and the Soviet Union, the real aims of Soviet policy are far from clear. While calling for collective security and warning Europe against Hitler, the USSR does not seem to have excluded the possibility of a reconciliation with the Reich. German diplomatic documents report repeated Soviet declarations of a desire for the re-establishment of the old relations, and of suggestions for a Non-Aggression Pact.[46] In

[44] Postwar Polish historiography assigns the major blame for the Pact's failure to Poland, though the ambivalent attitude of the French and the negative approach of Great Britain are also taken into account; see Jarosław Jurkiewicz, *Pakt Wschodni: Z Historii Stosunków Międzynarodowych w Latach, 1934–1935* (The Eastern Pact: From the History of International Relations in the Years 1934–1935, Warsaw, 1963), pp. 129–31. See also Budurowycz, *Polish-Soviet Relations*, chap. III, *passim*.
[45] Budurowycz, pp. 196–7.
[46] In October, 1933 Litvinov told the German Chargé d'Affaires that the Soviet government was, as in the past, always ready to negotiate with Germany in order to settle disputes and restore the old relations; *DGFP*, C. II. no. 12. Marshal Tukhachevsky, Deputy Commissar for War, more than once expressed the opinion that the Rapallo policy remained the most popular in the USSR and that the Red Army had great sympathy for the Reichswehr (no. 47). War Commissar Marshal Voroshilov hoped the old relations would be restored, as did the Chief of the General Staff, Marshal Yegorov (nos. 176, 181). In August 1934, the Italian Ambassador in Moscow, Attolico, reported Litvinov as saying that he would gladly re-establish friendly relations with Germany if the latter gave the Soviet Union real guarantees of non-aggression. He was also prepared, should the Eastern Locarno fail to materialize, to include Germany as a third party in the Franco-Soviet Pact (III, nos. 148, 156). In July 1935, two months after the signature of the Franco-Soviet Pact, David Kandelaki, head of the Soviet Trade Mission in

January 1937, the head of the Soviet Trade Mission in Berlin and a man close to Stalin, David Kandelaki, told Hjalmar Schacht, the German Minister of Economics and President of the Reichsbank, that the Soviet government was ready to negotiate with Berlin for an improvement of mutual relations and in the interests of general peace. Moscow was prepared to conduct these negotiations in secret if Berlin so desired. Hitler, however, rejected the offer, considering it a manœuvre on the part of the Soviet Union to strengthen its hand with France. He did add, though, that if and when the Soviet government should consolidate its position to one of absolute despotism based on the Army, Germany would certainly not miss the opportunity of re-establishing contact with the USSR.[47] Time can only tell whether there was any connection between the Red Army purges of 1937 and Stalin's abortive approach to Hitler. It is also impossible to say whether Litvinov's policy of collective security was a policy in its own right or a means of pressure on Hitler to return to the old alliance. In the same way, it is debatable whether the Soviet approaches to Germany were sincere or a means of putting pressure on France. In any case, they were most discreet. Whatever the case may be, the failure of an Eastern Locarno to materialize in 1934, or later, was not simply due to the refusal of Hitler's potential victims to accept Soviet protection.

The attitude of passivity toward violations of peace and of treaties which France and Britain adopted towards German conscription, Mussolini's invasion of Ethiopia, and Hitler's march into the demilitarized zone of the Rhineland became crystallized into the policy of 'appeasement' when Neville Chamberlain became Prime Minister of Great Britain in May

---

Berlin, expressed the hope that it might be possible to improve German-Soviet political relations (IV, no. 211). In October, Tukhachevsky told Ambassador Schulenberg, 'If Germany and the Soviet Union still had the same friendly political relations they used to have, they would now be in a position to dictate peace to the world' (IV, no. 383). In December, the Counsellor of the Soviet Embassy in Berlin, Bessonov, suggested that the Treaty of Berlin be supplemented by a bilateral Non-Aggression Pact between Germany and Russia. He said he thought this subject had been mentioned already in a private Soviet-German conversation early in the year (IV, no. 472).

[47] German microfilms cited by John Erickson, *The Soviet High Command: A Military-Political History 1918–1941* (London, 1962), p. 453.

1937. The aim of achieving a settlement with Germany was not new, but in his hands it assumed a clear sense of direction and a high moral purpose: the preservation of peace. The Prime Minister not only had a passionate hatred of war,[48] but he also sincerely believed that all disputes could be settled by negotiation. He rejected the alternative, intensive rearmament, out of hand. Chamberlain was completely attuned to the mood of the country which was pacifist and sympathetic to German protests against the Versailles Treaty. J. M. Keynes's famous criticism of the treaty, *The Economic Consequences of the Peace*, published in 1919, was merely the first of a whole school of thought. 'By the middle of the nineteen-thirties no one dared to say a word in favour of the peace-makers of 1919.'[49] Liberal and left-wing criticism of the treaty was complemented in the ruling circles by the traditional view of Eastern Europe as the natural zone of influence for Russia or Germany and which, at this time, favoured the latter. However, even during the course of the war, the British Cabinet had assumed that Germany would revive as a Great Power and the efforts of Lloyd George to strike a compromise between Polish and German claims were guided by this assumption. He considered the European equilibrium of 1919 to be a temporary one,[50] presumably to be rectified in due course by Germany in her own favour. The prevalent view on the German-Polish dispute among British statesmen was summarized in 1925 by Austen Chamberlain, then Foreign Secretary, when he wrote that for the Polish Corridor 'no British Government will or ever can risk the bones of a British Grenadier'.[51] It must be said to his credit, however, that, as early as April 1933, he openly opposed discussing the revision of the Corridor with Hitler.[52] His younger half-brother did not share this view, nor

[48] 'Neville's abiding hatred of war was born of the death in action of Norman Chamberlain'; Iain Macleod, *Neville Chamberlain* (London, 1961), p. 74.

[49] A. J. P. Taylor, *The Trouble Makers: Dissent over Foreign Policy, 1792–1939* (London, 1957), p. 169.

[50] H. I. Nelson, *Land and Power*, p. 377.

[51] Cited by Sir Charles A. Petrie, *The Life and Letters of the Right Hon. Sir Austen Chamberlain* (London, 1940), vol. II, p. 259.

[52] On 13 April 1933, Sir Austen Chamberlain said in the House of Commons, after condemning Nazism as the worst form of Prussian imperialism with the addition of racial savagery, 'Are you going to discuss revision with a Government like that? Are you going to discuss with such a Government the Polish Corridor?

was it shared by an increasing number of people, particularly in right-wing circles, who regarded the domination of Eastern Europe as Germany's birthright and a cheap price to pay for peace. This was also the view of the government. As early as December 1935, the Poles were told by an official of the Foreign Office that in a choice between purchasing peace or waging war with Germany, Britain would do all to secure the former and that London clearly envisaged the revision of the Polish-German frontier.[53] There were dissenting voices, but they went un-heeded. There were men in the Foreign Office who did not share the Prime Minister's optimism: Sir Anthony Eden, Sir Robert Vansittart, and William Strang all voiced disapproval of unilateral concessions to the dictators. Neville Chamberlain, however, often bypassed the Foreign Office and relied increasingly on the advice of those who sympathized with his own views.

The Prime Minister made his first approach to Hitler through

The Polish Corridor is inhabited by Poles; do you dare to put another Pole under the heel of such a Government?'; *Parliamentary Debates, House of Commons*, 5th Series, vol. 276, col. 2759.

[53] In December 1935, Ralph C. S. Stevenson, Deputy Director of the League of Nations Department in the Foreign Office, told members of the Polish delegation in Geneva that the British government wished for the reform of article 19 of the Covenant so that revision of frontiers should take place by a majority vote binding on the states concerned. He added that, having the choice of purchasing peace or waging war with Germany, Great Britain would bend all her efforts in the direction of peace; the House of Commons, said Stevenson, would never sanction British intervention for the maintenance of the *status quo* in Central or Eastern Europe, for example, in defence of the Corridor; see M. Wojciechowski, *Stosunki Polsko-Niemieckie*, pp. 210–12. For British opinion, see Martin Gilbert and Richard Gott, *The Appeasers* (London, 1963), p. 48 ff. For the inroads of German revisionist propaganda in British conservative circles, and particularly the skilful work of Margarete Gärtner, see D. C. Watt, *Personalities and Policies: Studies in the Formulation of British Foreign Policy in the Twentieth Century* (London, 1965), Essay 6, pp. 117–38. Gärtner gives her own interesting account of her public relations work for the cause of frontier revision, the war guilt question and reparations. This was carried out in close co-ordination with the German Ministry of Foreign Affairs and included aid and advice to some British historians and writers, e.g., to Sir Robert Donald for his book, *The Polish Corridor and its Consequences* (London, 1929), Col. G. S. Hutchison for his *Silesia Revisited* (London, 1929), William Harbutt Dawson for his article, 'Germany and the Corridor', *The Nineteenth Century and After*, vol. DCLVII, November 1931, pp. 671–84, and his book *Germany under the Treaty* (1933), and Sir Raymond Beazley's *The Road to Ruin in Europe, 1890–1914* (London, 1932); see Margarete Gärtner, *Botschafterin des Guten Willens* (Bonn, 1955), pp. 116, 160–11, 200–5, 214.

the intermediacy of Lord Halifax, then Lord President of the Council, in November 1937. Halifax expressly told the Führer that Great Britain did not regard the *status quo* of 1919 as immutable. Certain problems could be 'adjusted', provided this was done by peaceful means. As 'possible alterations', Halifax mentioned Danzig, Austria, and Czechoslovakia. He also expressed British readiness to discuss colonial questions in direct negotiations with Germany.[54] Chamberlain stated his views on the matter after the return of Halifax. He wrote in his diary of German ambitions:

> Of course they want to dominate Eastern Europe; they want as close a union with Austria as they can get without incorporating her in the Reich, and they want much the same things for the Sudetendeutsche as we did for the Uitlanders in the Transvaal.

He gave favourable consideration to concessions in Africa and, returning to Eastern Europe, noted:

> I don't see why we shouldn't say to Germany, 'give us satisfactory assurances that you won't use force to deal with the Austrians and the Czechoslovakians, and we will give you similar assurances that we won't use force to prevent the changes you want, if you can get them by peaceful means'.[55]

The aim of Polish foreign policy in the face of the rising tide of appeasement was a triple one: it had to prevent the conclusion of a 'New Locarno' at Poland's expense,[56] to maintain good

[54] *DM* (Moscow, 1948), vol. I, no. 1; also *DGFP*, D, I, no. 31. Lord Halifax wrote in his memoirs: 'On all these matters we were not concerned to stand for the *status quo* as of to-day, but were very concerned to secure the avoidance of such treatment as would be likely to cause trouble. If reasonable settlements could be reached with the free assent of those primarily concerned, we certainly had no desire to block them,' Earl of Halifax, *Fullness of Days* (New York, 1957), p. 188.

[55] Keith Feiling, *The Life of Neville Chamberlain* (London, 1946), p. 333. Lord Halifax, though in essential agreement with the Prime Minister, tempered his characteristically cautious judgment with a note of regret. In a personal memorandum he wrote, 'However much we may dislike the idea of Nazi beaver-like propaganda, etc., in Central Europe, neither we nor the French are going to be able to stop it, and it would therefore seem short-sighted to forgo the chance of a German settlement by holding out for something we are almost certainly going to find ourselves powerless to secure'; The Earl of Birkenhead, *Halifax: The Life of Lord Halifax* (London, 1965), pp. 373-4.

[56] Weizsäcker had informed the Counsellor of the Polish Embassy in Berlin, Lubomirski, of Halifax's suggestion that Great Britain would countenance a peaceful solution of the Danzig question in favour of Germany; Wojciechowski, *Stosunki Polsko-Niemieckie*, p. 362.

relations with Germany, and to keep the door open for closer relations with the Western Powers if they should show signs of taking a firm stand against Hitler. The task of maintaining good relations with Berlin was the most pressing and also the most difficult of these aims. Although Piłsudski estimated in 1934 that the greatest likelihood of an attack on Poland in the near future came from the Soviet side,[57] neither he nor Beck viewed the Declaration of Non-Aggression as a permanent solution of the Polish-German question. The government certainly did what it could to play down incidents and difficulties but the issue of Danzig remained an inflammatory one. For Beck it was certainly the thorniest problem in his foreign policy. On the one hand, Poland had been given no rights to station either troops or ships in Danzig,[58] nor could it send these without the consent of the High Commissioner of the League; on the other hand, any military move against the City entailed the breakdown of Polish-German relations. Polish economic and minority rights in Danzig were constantly violated and the main plank of opposition attacks on the government was the latter's apparent unwillingness to take a firm line in the Free City. Furthermore, Beck also had to keep in mind the increasing tendency in London and Paris to favour a withdrawal of the League mandate from Danzig rather than suffer repeated humiliation at the hands of the Nazis. The Polish Foreign Minister vigorously opposed such a step because it would create a vacuum in the Free City which would invite its annexation by the Reich.

In the face of these problems Beck tried to reduce tension in

[57] For the conference Piłsudski called in April 1934, to study the problem, see Szembek, *Journal*, pp. 2–3. The Army felt that Germany was the greatest threat to Poland, but Piłsudski did not think Germany's internal or military situation justified such an assumption for the immediate future. Furthermore, he assumed that in a conflict with Germany Poland would not be isolated because of her alliance with France, while in a war with the USSR she would stand alone; see General Fabrycy, 'Komórka Specjalna' (Special Section), *Niepodległość* (London, 1955), vol. V, pp. 217–20.

[58] Poland had the right to a *Port d'Attache* and a munition depot in Westerplatte with a limited garrison. The Supreme Council indicated Poland 'as the Power "specially fitted" to defend Danzig but without permitting her to make the military and naval preparations deemed essential by the Military and Advisory Commission to ensure the adequate defence of Danzig'; Ian F. D. Morrow, *The Peace Settlement in the German Polish Borderlands: A Study of Conditions To-day in the Pre-War Prussian Provinces of East and West Prussia* (London, 1936), p. 61.

Danzig but, at the same time, made it clear to Hitler and to the League Powers that Poland would not tolerate a unilateral solution in favour of Germany. He assumed correctly that the Führer did not wish for a showdown in Danzig. The Foreign Minister's policy can be illustrated by two actions over the Free ·City in 1935 and 1936. In 1935 the Danzig Senate, on the advice of Hjalmar Schacht, devaluated the Gulden and imposed currency restrictions, measures which it had no right to take without consulting Poland. While these steps were taken owing to German shortage of foreign exchange, and therefore a much restricted ability to subsidize Danzig, Schacht together with Forster and some high officials of the German Foreign Ministry hoped that this provocation would lead to Polish reprisals and these in turn to the annexation of Danzig by Germany.[59] Poland did, indeed, retaliate with economic counter-measures but Beck's determined warnings that the situation might lead to a conflict decided Hitler to end the crisis amicably. The matter was smoothed over in top-level discussions between Ambassador Lipski, Hitler, and Göring.[60]

In June 1936, another crisis arose, this time involving the High Commissioner of the League of Nations, Sean Lester. The officers of the visiting German warship, the *Leipzig*, omitted their usual courtesy visit to the High Commissioner, apparently because in the preceding year Lester had invited members of the Danzig opposition to the reception. By the same token, Germany insulted the League. The matter was brought before the League Council at the end of the month and rumours were thick that the occasion had come for the League to withdraw rather than suffer further humiliations. Beck found support in his opposition to this solution in Sir Anthony Eden, British delegate to the League and Rapporteur on Danzig affairs to the Council, who opposed any further weakening of the League. The Polish Foreign Minister was asked at his own suggestion to settle the matter by diplomatic negotiations with Germany. This he did, at the same time warning Hitler that any unilateral change of the

[59] See *DGFP*, C, IV, no. 215; also, *ibid.*, section on Poland and Danzig for April, May, June, July, pp. LVI–LXV, *passim*.

[60] *Diariusz i Teki Jana Szembeka*, vol. I, 7 Aug., 1935, pp. 343–46; Szembek, *Journal*, pp. 109–10.

Danzig Statute would cause conflict between two countries.[61] Hitler disavowed the violent speech of Senate President Greiser in Geneva and the matter was dropped. Sean Lester resigned and was succeeded by Dr. Carl J. Burckhardt, a Swiss historian and close friend of German Under-Secretary of State, Ernst von Weizsäcker. Beck knew, however, that the Danzig problem could not be stalled permanently. By the middle of 1937, when negotiations were in process between Warsaw and Berlin for an agreement to replace the Upper Silesian Convention, the Foreign Minister warned his colleagues that the time was not far off when the Danzig problem would have to be discussed with Berlin.[62] Beck tried to obtain an official German recognition of Polish rights in the Free City but desisted when Berlin showed no interest. A Polish-German Declaration on Minorities was signed on 5 November 1937, and Hitler gave Ambassador Lipski confidential confirmation of his recognition of Polish interests and rights in Danzig.[63] Luckily for Poland, the Führer was not yet ready for action.[64]

While working for the maintenance of good relations with Berlin, Beck also kept the door open for closer relations with France and Britain. When Hitler's troops invaded the demilitarized zone of the Rhineland on 7 March 1936, Beck told the French Ambassador, Léon Noël, that Poland was ready to fulfil her obligations to France.[65] While Beck did not expect the French to fight, his declaration was not an empty gesture. If fighting had broken out the whole international situation would have changed and Polish troops would have moved against Germany.[66] However, the French government made no use of

[61] Beck to Lipski, Geneva, 4 July 1936, MFA (London), P-G, 1936; *Diariusz i Teki Jana Szembeka*, vol. II, pp. 241–8, 457–81.
[62] Michał Łubieński (Beck's Chef de Cabinet) to Ambassador Edward Raczyński (London), 14 June 1937, MFA (Montreal), P-G, 1937.
[63] *PWB*, nos. 32, 33.
[64] In September he told Dr. Burckhardt, '. . . if the Danzig question were broached in earnest, then the Corridor question, the Sudeten-German question and the Austrian question would have to be opened simultaneously, and now was not the right time for that'; *DGFP*, D, V, no. 5, encl. 2.
[65] Beck, *Dernier Rapport*, p. 113; Léon Noël, *L'Agression Allemande contre la Pologne: Une Ambassade à Varsovie, 1935–1939* (Paris, 1946), p. 25; Szembek, *Journal*, 7 March 1936, p. 166; *Diariusz i Teki Jana Szembeka*, vol. II, 110 ff, 401–2.
[66] The Chief of the Polish General Staff, General Wacław Stachiewicz, told the Estonian Minister that if Germany attacked France, Poland would attack im-

the Polish offer and Foreign Minister Flandin even concealed it from his Cabinet.[67] At the meeting of the Locarno signatories in London later that month Beck pressed the French ministers for a discussion of the Franco-Polish alliance, for staff conversations, and for elucidation of the French position on the Military Convention of 1921.[68] His efforts met with failure but Franco-Polish relations were somewhat improved by the reciprocal visits of General Gamelin to Poland and of General Śmigły-Rydz to France in August and September respectively. The Śmigły-Rydz visit resulted in a French loan for Polish rearmament. It was also in 1936 that Beck had two important conversations with Sir Anthony Eden. During the Locarno meeting in March, the Polish Foreign Minister expressed the wish that Britain should not influence France to enter into any international agreement which might weaken the Franco-Polish alliance. On a second visit to London in November Beck restated this wish, adding that if Britain should be forced to go to the aid of France the extent of Polish engagement would not be unimportant.[69] In these moves as well as his stiff warnings on

mediately; *DDF*, 2, vol. I, no. 268. Marian Wojciechowski calls Beck's attitude in the crisis 'two-faced', analysing his motives as (1) to shift the centre of gravity of France's East European alliances from Moscow to Warsaw; (2) to use the Franco-Polish alliance as a lever to strengthen Polish-German relations; (3) to obtain a loan from France for Polish armaments; (4) to neutralize Noël's activity against Beck; *Stosunki Polsko-Niemieckie*, pp. 284, 290–1. Beck's attitude during the crisis can, however, bear a different interpretation. Assuming that France would not fight, he tried to use his declaration of loyalty as a springboard towards the clarification of Polish-French treaty relations. In his conversations with French statesmen in London in the latter part of March 1936, Beck proposed to reconstruct the basis of Polish-French relations, see: *Diariusz i Teki Jana Szembeka*, vol. II, p. 145.

67 Paul Reynaud, *La France a sauvé l'Europe* (Paris, 1947), vol. I, p. 356. General Gamelin, Chief of the French General Staff, claimed that he did not receive the telegram of the French Attaché Militaire in Warsaw; General Maurice Gamelin, *Servir* (Paris, 1948), vol. II, p. 213. According to Polish sources, however, the Polish Attaché Militaire in Paris informed the General of the Polish position; see Gustaw Łowczowski, 'Przymierze Wojskowe Polsko-Francuskie widziane z Attachatu Wojskowego' (The Franco-Polish Military Alliance as seen from the Office of the Attaché Militaire), *Bellona* (London, 1951), I–II, pp. 44, 46, and the same author's letter to the editor, *Bellona* (1960), IV, p. 310.

68 Conversation between Beck and Paul-Boncour, London, 15 March 1936, MFA (Montreal), P–F, 1936; also *DDF*, 2, vol. I, no. 445, *Diariusz i Teki Jana Szembeka*, vol. II, pp. 145, 408–10.

69 Conversation between Beck and Eden, London, 27 March 1936, and Summary of Conversations between Minister Beck and Sir Anthony Eden, London,

Danzig to the League Powers,[70] Beck followed Piłsudski's precept that Poland should be ready to co-operate if France decided to adopt a firm attitude towards Germany, but that she could not allow her interests to be decided upon without her consent, even by her allies.

As the year 1937 drew to a close, Beck had reason to believe that he had been successful in maintaining an independent policy and an equilibrium between the USSR and Germany. He knew very well that relations with Germany could be shattered at any moment by a crisis over Danzig, but he thought that Hitler still needed time and that in any case German expansion in a south-eastern direction rather than against Poland might go unopposed by the Great Powers. While relations with France were estranged and those with the USSR distinctly cool, Poland was not a satellite of Germany. Hitler himself realized that this was not the case. At a secret conference in November at which the Führer outlined his ideas on the future absorption of Austria and Czechoslovakia and a possible war with France and Britain, he was far from sanguine about Poland. His opinion was that

> Our agreements with Poland will remain valid as long as Germany's strength will remain unshakeable. Should Germany have any setbacks, then an attack by Poland against East Prussia, perhaps also against Pomerania and Silesia, must be taken into account.[71]

The fact that Hitler did not regard Poland as committed to German policy was both indicative of the state of Polish-German relations at the end of 1937 and of his policy toward Warsaw in

---

9, 10 November 1936, MFA (Montreal), P–GB, 1936; *Diariusz i Teki Jana Szembeka*, vol. II, pp. 340–1, 537–40.

[70] In a conversation with Delbos and Eden in Geneva on 29 September 1936, Beck warned that any attempts to solve the Danzig question which might worsen Polish-German relations or be at the expense of Poland, would be opposed by the latter. He obtained the agreement of both statesmen that there would be no solution of the Danzig question behind Poland's back and that she would not be left alone to face Germany, see Conversation of Minister Beck with Delbos and Eden, Geneva, 29 September 1936, APEL, Gdańsk, 1936. On 9 December 1937, Beck warned Delbos that if the League of Nations withdrew from Danzig, it would sign its own death warrant, that Poland would not accept any half-way solution but would defend her rights in the city, Szembek, *Journal*, p. 258.

[71] Hossbach Memorandum, 5 November 1937, *DGFP*, D, I, no. 19.

the future. Beck, for his part, looked sceptically at the likelihood of any Western engagement in Eastern Europe and prepared to safeguard Polish interests in any crisis which might arise. He knew well, however, that these interests would not allow him to seek the alliance of either Moscow or Berlin.

I

THE ANSCHLUSS

THE big question in diplomatic circles at the beginning of 1938 was whether the Führer would be allowed to proceed with his declared plan of uniting all German-speaking peoples outside the Reich with Germany. This would mean not only the Austrians but also the three million Germans of Czechoslovakia who were mostly concentrated in the northern, western, and southern mountain fringes of that state—the Sudetenland. It was not clear which country would be menaced first but soon Austria emerged as Hitler's immediate goal.

In 1919, the existence of an independent Austria had been considered a vital element of the balance-of-power in Europe. For this reason the union of Austria with Germany had been prohibited by the treaties of Versailles and St. Germain. It was on this assumption too that France had prevented a customs union between the two countries in 1931. Mussolini at first opposed the nazification of Austria because he feared that it would enable Hitler to extend his influence over the Balkans. Thus it was that in 1934 he averted a Nazi *coup* in Vienna by bringing Italian troops to the Brenner Pass. A year later, at Stresa, Great Britain, France, and Italy signed a resolution supporting Austrian independence.

By 1938, this situation had changed. The Duce, after his conquest of Abyssinia and his involvement in the Spanish Civil War, had drawn closer to Hitler in the Rome-Berlin Axis. France still proclaimed her support for an independent Austria, but since she could no longer depend on Italian co-operation and would make no move without British support, the decision on

Austria's fate lay in the hands of the British government. Chamberlain was not averse to the idea of an Anschluss while British public opinion saw the issue in ethnographic terms and was generally sympathetic to Germany.[1] Yet such a development would end not only Austrian independence but would also threaten that of Czechoslovakia and could have far-reaching consequences for the whole of Europe. In 1925, James Headlam-Morley, historical adviser to the Foreign Office, had proposed a British guarantee of the entire territorial settlement including East Central Europe. Considering the possible fall of Austria and Czechoslovakia, he wrote: 'This would be catastrophic, and, even if we neglected to intervene in time to prevent it, we should afterwards be driven to interfere, probably too late.'[2] Ten years later, Eden proposed a European pact of mutual assistance and advised firmness in defence of collective security.[3] Unfortunately, these were but voices in the wilderness.

The sympathetic British attitude towards the Anschluss was reflected in Poland, though here the underlying causes for it were different. As early as 1919, the leader of the National Democrats, Roman Dmowski, had suggested that the union with Austria could be used as compensation for Germany's loss of her Polish provinces. This idea, though rejected by the Polish Ministry of Foreign Affairs at least until 1933, was repeatedly echoed by certain writers and journalists, although with different motives and undertones. Outspoken proponents of close co-operation or even alliance with Germany, such as Władysław Studnicki, Stanisław 'Cat' Mackiewicz, and Adolf Bocheński, did not re-

[1] The opinion of the 'Cliveden Set', and by the same token of the inner circles of government, was expressed by Thomas Jones in a letter to an American friend: 'In this country we believed that Versailles Austria could not survive permanently'; *A Diary with Letters, 1931–1950* (London, 1954), p. 396. The Austrian Minister in London, Franckenstein, reported at the end of December 1937 that the right-wing press, represented by the *Daily Mail, Daily Express, Observer,* and *The Times,* generally supported German aims, *DGFP,* D, I, no. 274. The British Ambassador in Berlin, Sir Nevile Henderson, assured Fritz von Papen, German Ambassador in Vienna, in June 1937, that Britain fully understood the 'historical need' for a solution of the Austrian problem but that time was necessary to 'correct' the recalcitrant attitude of the French; *DGFP,* D, I, no. 228.
[2] Sir James Headlam-Morley, *Studies in Diplomatic History* (London, 1930), p. 184.
[3] Anthony Eden, *The Memoirs of Anthony Eden, Earl of Avon: Facing the Dictators, 1923–1938* (Boston, 1962), p. 199.

present any political groups but exerted a certain influence on right-wing circles. The first two welcomed the Anschluss and the consequent dismemberment of Czechoslovakia as a means of achieving a common Polish-Hungarian frontier and of building a strong barrier against the expansion of Russian power or influence in Europe. Studnicki, in his brilliantly written book, *System Polityczny Europy a Polska* (The European Political System and Poland), published in 1935 and translated into German the following year, propounded the view that such a development would pave the way to a powerful bloc in Eastern Europe in which Germany would have the first and Poland the second place. He assumed that Germany's domination of such a bloc would reconcile her to the loss of her Polish territories. Together with Mackiewicz he also envisaged the possibility of recovering Poland's former eastern provinces in a common war against Soviet Russia. Bocheński, in his book *Między Niemcami a Rosją* (Between Germany and Russia, published in 1937), went even further, suggesting that Poland's future lay in expansion to the east and hinting that the cession of certain territories to Germany was a small price to pay for German aid to this end.

The views of Piłsudski and Beck, despite certain superficial similarities with those of Studnicki and Mackiewicz, were not so clearly defined and did not constitute a definite programme. First, both the Marshal and the Foreign Minister consistently refused to discuss any possibility of military co-operation with Germany against the Soviet Union. They realized that such a policy would only redound to the advantage of Berlin. Second, they held that in any serious East European crisis Polish policy must adjust itself to the attitude of France and Great Britain. Their approach to the Austro-Czechoslovak problem was based on two factors of which the second was decisive. The first was distrust of Czechoslovakia and disbelief, strengthened after 1933, in any possibility of concluding an alliance with Prague; the second was the policy of the Great Powers. As early as 1931, Piłsudski had told the French Ambassador in Warsaw, Jules Laroche, that in his opinion the survival of both Austria and Czechoslovakia was dependent on the Great Powers.[4] At the

[4] Jules Laroche, *La Pologne de Piłsudski: Souvenirs d'une Ambassade, 1925–1935* (Paris, 1953), p. 74. This opinion was shared by Laroche. On the part of Piłsudski,

same time there was a tendency in Polish official circles to view German expansion in a south-eastern direction with some complacency since this was seen as a diversion of German revisionism from Poland. This short-sighted attitude resulted not only from a negative attitude towards Czechoslovakia and a miscalculation of the time which Hitler would need to digest his new conquests but also from the assumption that the Western Powers would not do anything to check him. It is ironic that Masaryk and Beneš had taken a similar stand towards the possibility of a revision of the Polish-German frontier in the previous decade. The link between these two mutually inimical attitudes was the assumption by each side that revision of the other's frontiers would not be opposed by the Western Democracies.

The progressive undermining of collective security in the early 1930's, the Polish-German Declaration of Non-Aggression, which was Piłsudski's reaction to this development, and the Western tendencies towards appeasement of Germany, which were becoming progressively more explicit after Chamberlain became Prime Minister of Great Britain, confirmed Beck in his favourable disposition towards a union of Austria with Germany. Nevertheless, his attitude towards further developments was strictly dependent on the policy of France and Britain. It cannot be said that his sympathy for the Anschluss was evidence of a crystallized programme of action to be carried out regardless of international developments. It is worthy of note that even President Beneš, whose country was most directly threatened, did not venture to offer Czechoslovak support to Vienna. On the contrary, towards the end of 1936, he had welcomed secret German overtures for a Non-Aggression Pact based on the Polish model and told the German emissaries on that occasion that he had nothing against German-Austrian 'co-operation'. In the following year, when Austria was desperately casting about for

---

this was a modification of his earlier attitude that neither Austria nor Czechoslovakia would survive and that the only important point was to know which would disappear first; Beck, *Dernier Rapport*, p. 9. In 1933, on the eve of Wysocki's departure as Ambassador to Rome, the Marshal told him that Mussolini was opposed to the Anschluss but Poland would be ready to 'sell' it provided she got a good price; see Wojciechowski, *Stosunki Polsko-Niemieckie*, pp. 374–5.

an escape from her approaching nemesis, the Czechoslovak President told the Austrian Foreign Minister, Guido Schmidt, that he had no inclination to stand up against Germany.[5] All other difficulties apart, an Austro-Czechoslovak, or Austro-Czechoslovak-Hungarian bloc could only have been created with French support. Thus the position of both Beck and Beneš was ultimately determined by the policy of France and consequently of Great Britain.

Surveying the political scene at the beginning of 1938, Col. Beck estimated that the whole of Central Europe lay at the mercy of Germany unless the important states, France and Britain, had the strength to adopt a more energetic policy.[6] If they did not do so, Beck's attitude, like Piłsudski's before him, was that Poland should follow the course of 'individual solutions' and pull what she could from the wreckage. Already in December 1936, reflecting on what Poland should do if France disintegrated as a power, he had drawn up a list of priorities. In such an event he thought of regaining the Trans-Olza territory from Czechoslovakia, obtaining a common frontier with Hungary by supporting her annexation of Subcarpathian Ruthenia, and of making Slovakia a buffer state under Polish protection. Other alternatives he then envisaged were the occupation of either Kaunas or Danzig.[7] In Beck's view, such a plan could only be realized if France was unable to protect Austria and Czechoslovakia. It would be the consequence of French weakness and essentially constituted a policy of 'compensation' in view of the likely expansion of Germany.

When it became evident that the Austrian crisis would not lead to a general state of flux in East Central Europe, Beck limited his aims and planned to use the situation in order to gain more

[5] Gerhardt L. Weinberg, 'Secret Hitler-Beneš Negotiations in 1936–1937', *JCEA*, XIX (1960), pp. 366–74. See also: *Der Hochverratsprozess gegen Dr. Guido Schmidt vor den Wiener Volksgericht* (Vienna, 1947), p. 54. Chancellor Schuschnigg's efforts, renewed in February 1938, to create an Austro-Czechoslovak-Hungarian bloc came to nothing, not only because of Hungarian revisionist claims against Czechoslovakia, but also because it was clear that France and Britain were unwilling to commit themselves to stand up for Austrian independence; see C. A. Macartney, *October Fifteenth: A History of Modern Hungary*, 1929–1945 (2nd ed.; Edinburgh, 1961), vol. I, pp. 205–6 and chap. 11, *passim*.
[6] Beck, *Dernier Rapport*, p. 141.
[7] Szembek, *Journal*, 21 December 1936, p. 220.

security in Polish-German relations and in particular to improve the state of affairs in Danzig. It was thus that the Free City came to be the prism through which the Foreign Minister viewed the Austrian crisis. The danger of an international settlement of the Danzig question in favour of Germany was as real as ever. Chamberlain regarded the Free City—like Austria and the Sudetenland—as the possible price of a peaceful adjustment. The new League High Commissioner in the Free City, Dr. Carl J. Burckhardt, reflected those views and did not have much faith in the durability of his post. He described it to his friend Ernst von Weizsäcker, the German Under-Secretary of State, as 'a slowly dying organ of a decadent institution', and he expected to be its last incumbent. Weizsäcker noted that '. . . Burckhardt considers natural the idea of a gradual release of the League of Nations from its obligations to guarantee the Danzig constitution'.[8] If the League withdrew its mandate Poland would be faced with the possibility of a German annexation of the Free City. Col. Beck had such a threat very much in mind in the early weeks of 1938.

The internal, as well as the international, situation of Danzig was such as to cause great anxiety to the Polish government. Both moderate and extreme Nazis wished for a return to the Reich at the earliest opportunity. The Polish Commissioner General reported that the only difference between the policy of the extreme Nazis, led by Gauleiter Albert Forster, and that of the moderates under Senate President Arthur Greiser was one of method. The senate group ostensibly desired as close a union with Berlin as possible without violating the Danzig Statute; Forster's followers called for a triumphant return to Germany. Tension had increased since the latter part of 1937 when, having liquidated all political opposition, the Gauleiter proclaimed that coexistence between the Free City and Poland was artificial and demanded total assimilation of the city with the Reich. This attitude was accompanied by constant attacks on Polish rights

---

[8] *DGFP*, D, V, no. 30. Burckhardt does not describe his own attitude towards the appointment in such terms but presents his acceptance of the post, on Weizsäcker's suggestion, as an effort to prevent a conflict over Danzig; see Carl J. Burckhardt, *Meine Danziger Mission, 1937–1939* (Munich, 1960), chap. III, *passim*.

in all sectors of Danzig life.[9] Such a state of affairs, combined with rumours of British willingness to give Germany satisfaction on this issue, was bound to cause considerable worry in Warsaw and influence its attitude towards the Austrian question.

The Polish Foreign Minister restated his position on Danzig in the first days of 1938. Speaking before the Foreign Affairs Committee of the *Sejm* (National Assembly) on 12 January, he said that regardless of any fluctuations in the international situation the maintenance of Polish rights in Danzig was a stable and inviolable factor in Polish foreign policy.[10] Beck's statement was aimed at two audiences: on the one hand, it was a warning to the Western Democracies and, on the other, it was an indication of his unaltered stand on Danzig aimed at Berlin where he planned to stop on his way to the forthcoming League of Nations session in Geneva. Apparently, Beck also tried to sound out Western intentions concerning Austria by speaking favourably of the Mussolini-Laval project of 1935 which had envisaged closer co-operation between Vienna and its neighbours.

On the two days following his declaration Beck paid a visit to the German capital. His aim was principally to discuss Polish-German relations and to investigate the possibilities for an agreement on the Danzig question. The German Ambassador in Warsaw reported that Beck's Chef de Cabinet, Michał Łubieński, had indicated that in return for the satisfaction of certain Polish economic requirements in Danzig Poland would be willing to make concessions in internal matters, subject always to the maintenance of the Statute.[11] Beck was apparently thinking in terms of an agreement between Poland and the Danzig Senate.[12] This was a project conceived to ward off the dangers inherent in a withdrawal of the League mandate. The Polish Under-Secretary of State, Jan Szembek, told the French Ambassador in Warsaw that, if the legal *status quo* of Danzig should be changed through the retreat of the League of Nations,

[9] The Commissioner General to the Foreign Minister, General Report for 1937, Danzig, 1 January 1938, APEL, Gdańsk, 1938.

[10] Beck, *Przemówienia, Deklaracje i Wywiady* (2nd ed., Warsaw, 1939), pp. 340-9.

[11] *DGFP*, D, V, no. 26.

[12] On 12 January, he told Szembek that if the conversation with Hitler went well, he might suggest an exchange of notes on Danzig in which he would declare readiness to reach an agreement with the Senate; Szembek, *Journal*, p. 268.

Poland could regulate her relations with the City by direct conversations with the Senate and added that France knew well who was behind that institution.[13]

While the Polish Foreign Minister hoped that the international situation might make Berlin willing to consider a new agreement on Danzig, the main interest on the German side was to investigate the possibility of securing Polish neutrality in the projected Anschluss. The views in Berlin did not, however, go beyond a disinclination to inflame the issue, and that was a long way from the hopes of Col. Beck. In a brief drawn up by the Director of Political Division V for the German Foreign Minister's conversation with the visitor, it was stated that the Danzig question was being used by Polish opposition circles against the government and that '. . . to confront Beck with coups of any kind would be likely to shake his position'. It was therefore suggested that Forster's demand for the display of the National Socialist flag in Danzig should not be pressed for the time being. With regard to Austria, it was noted that Poland was showing a tendency to support its independence. The author of the memorandum also remarked that the French alliance was still the cornerstone of Polish foreign policy and that the German government had to take this factor into account when dealing with Poland.[14]

Col. Beck had three important conversations during his brief visit to Berlin. On the first day he talked with the Foreign Minister, Baron Konstantin von Neurath, and with the Commander-in-Chief of the German Air Force, Field-Marshal Hermann Göring, who was also Hitler's special deputy for Polish affairs. Neurath did not seem anxious to discuss the eventual withdrawal of the League's High Commissioner from Danzig, a subject which the Polish Foreign Minister tried to use as an opening for the discussion of a new agreement on the Free City.[15] Neurath also remarked ominously that in view of

[13] *Ibid.*, 22 January 1938, p. 269.
[14] *DGFP*, D, V, no. 25.
[15] See Roos, *Polen und Europa*, p. 303, n. 72. In view of Szembek's entry of 12 January, Moltke's report of the same day, and also of Szembek's conversation with Noël on 22 January, it is clear that Beck wished to lead to the discussion of an agreement between Poland and the Danzig Senate. The Germans did not, or chose not to, understand his aims; see *DGFP*, D, V, no. 30.

Schuschnigg's 'obstinacy' an 'explosion' in Austria was not impossible. Beck declared that Poland had no particular interests in Austria, except those of an economic nature. Neurath in this conversation also gave Beck notice of German plans against Czechoslovakia, saying that the Czechoslovak 'appendix' would have to be cut out sooner or later.[16]

At lunch with Göring on the same day the Polish Minister again tried to raise the Danzig question. The Field-Marshal, however, evaded the issue by suggesting that Beck should receive Gauleiter Forster in order to liquidate the 'misunderstandings' over the Free City. He took care to inform his guest that Lord Halifax had shown an 'understanding' of Germany's plans for Austria. Halifax had been told that Germany would try to solve the problem peacefully, but that if this proved impossible she would solve it without asking anyone's permission. As for Italy, said Göring, she would not oppose German aims in Austria.

The Field-Marshal was quite as much, if not more, preoccupied with an eventual move against Czechoslovakia. He dwelt on the fact that he considered any French help to Prague as illusory, since the fortifications on Germany's western frontier would make such help extremely difficult at the time and impossible in the future. Simultaneously, he reassured Beck on the subject of Polish-German relations by saying the Germans realized that any severance of Poland from the sea would provoke the pressure of forty million people against Germany. This was a stock argument used to reassure the Poles since 1934, and did not have any particular value save that of indicating that Berlin did not envisage making an issue of the Danzig question for the time being. Göring did, however, vaguely state that in the future, if other 'compensations' were found for Poland in the East, Germany would want certain 'communication facilities' through the Corridor. Here again he tried to tempt the Polish Foreign Minister into showing some interest in such a bargain but Beck would not be drawn. Furthermore, Göring assured the Polish Minister that Germany would have full understanding for

---

[16] *DGFP*, D, V, no. 28; see also Conversation of Minister Beck with German Foreign Minister, von Neurath, 13 January 1938 11.30 to 13.00, Lipski to the Foreign Minister, Berlin, 13 January 1938, MFA (London), P–G, 1938.

Polish economic interests in Austria.[17] This was a matter of great importance for Poland since under a trade agreement she exported a considerable amount of coal to that country.

The most important conversation which took place during Beck's visit to Berlin was that which he had with Hitler on 14 January. The Chancellor set out to reassure his guest on the state of Polish-German relations. He emphatically reiterated the declaration which he had made on Danzig to Ambassador Lipski on 5 November 1937, to the effect that the Polish rights in the Free City would not be infringed and that the legal status would not be violated.[18] He also told Beck that he did not wish to make the latter's position in Poland more difficult by acceding to Forster's wish for the official display of the National Socialist flag in Danzig. When the conversation turned to Austria and Czechoslovakia, Hitler, like Neurath, intimated that Germany had designs against both countries.[19] The upshot of the Berlin conversations was thus a renewed German recognition, given in private, and not, as the Poles had wished, in public, of Polish rights in Danzig. Beck, for his part, hinted that Poland would not actively oppose the Anschluss. The Polish Minister was disappointed in his hopes of discussing a new settlement for the Free City, but at least he had the knowledge that Hitler was not interested in making an issue of Danzig in the near future.

In fact, Hitler had decided to do all that he could to calm Polish fears of a German move in this sector. His motive was to secure Polish neutrality in the approaching Austrian crisis. He told the visiting Yugoslav Prime Minister, Milan Stoyadinović, that the Corridor was a bitter pill for Germany but that it had to be accepted.[20] This was intended to be passed on in diplomatic circles and it was. The same line was followed at home. At the end of January the German Foreign Minister informed the Army that no 'surprises' were to be anticipated in Danzig from either the Polish or the German side.[21] This policy was im-

[17] *Ibid.*, Lipski's report on the Beck-Göring conversation; see also Wojciechowski, *Stosunki Polsko-Niemieckie*, pp. 375-7.

[18] See *PWB*, no. 34; *DGFP*, V, no. 18.

[19] *DGFP*, D, V, no. 29; extracts in *PWB*, no. 36; full Polish text in Lipski's report of 30 January, no. 16 above.

[20] *DGFP*, D, V, no. 163.

[21] *Ibid.*, no. 31.

D

mediately reflected in the Free City which demonstrated yet again its role as the barometer of Polish-German relations. The Polish Commissioner General reported at the end of the month that the first weeks of the new year saw an abatement of the National Socialist Party's anti-Polish propaganda, and that the Party instead began to proclaim that Danzig was a factor of political stability in Polish-German relations.[22] Thus, although Col. Beck had not gained his primary objective, the results of his visit were encouraging, not least from the point of view of the Polish position at the forthcoming League of Nations session in Geneva.

The fact that the League Council made no decision hostile to Poland's interests in Danzig in January 1938 was due not only to Hitler's anxiety for good relations with Warsaw but also to a modification of the British attitude towards this problem. This change, however, represented only the views of Foreign Secretary Anthony Eden, who was also the Rapporteur on the Danzig question to the League Council. Thus the British attitude on Danzig at the beginning of 1938 was a reflection of the deepening divergence of views on foreign policy between the Foreign Secretary and the Prime Minister of Great Britain.

An intimation of the new line of thought appeared in the conversations which took place at this time between the Polish Ambassador to London, Edward Raczyński, Col. Beck, and Winston Churchill on the one hand, and between Col. Beck and the British Foreign Secretary on the other. On 23 January 1938, before the meeting of the League Council, Churchill and Beck had a conversation in Cannes where they were both spending a short vacation; Beck was accompanied by Raczyński. Churchill told the Foreign Minister that both he and Eden approved of Beck's speech before the Foreign Affairs Committee of the *Sejm*. He told Beck that he thought the time unpropitious for reforming the League in the sense of further curtailing its responsibilities; this was a clear reference to the rumoured termination of the League mandate in Danzig. He also reiterated his distaste for dictatorships and stressed the growth of British and French armaments and the attitude of the United States, noting that

[22] Commissioner General to Foreign Minister, Danzig, 26 January 1938, APEL, Gdańsk, 1938.

time was on the side of the Democracies.[23] The only subject on which the two men disagreed was the role of the Soviet Union, which Churchill viewed as a potential counterweight to Germany.[24] A few days later, on 27 January, after Beck's departure for Geneva, Churchill made his motive in these conversations clear. He talked with Ambassador Raczyński and twice with emphasis repeated the question whether at the crucial moment Poland would stand by the Democracies. By way of reply Raczyński reminded Churchill of Beck's statement to Chamberlain in 1937 when the Polish Foreign Minister had told his host that Poland was the only country on the Continent capable of aiding Britain's friends in Europe.[25] Raczyński then pointedly asked Churchill what Great Britain would do in case of a conflict over Austria and, above all, over Czechoslovakia. Churchill replied that France would not fail to defend Czechoslovakia and would mobilize immediately in case of need, but that Britain herself was in a different position since she had no commitments in that part of Europe. He thought that Britain would not participate in the first stage of a conflict but that she would make her attitude known and might finally be drawn in. His reaction to Austria was negative; he merely said that the decision should belong to the population.[26] It was clear, then, that there was no prospect of British or French action on behalf of Austria.

At the meeting of the League Council in Geneva, Beck had an important conversation with Anthony Eden for which his talk with Churchill had in a sense prepared him. The two men exchanged ideas on Danzig and on the international situation in general. Beck openly told Eden that he had gone to Berlin in order to secure his position in case the League decided to withdraw its mandate from Danzig. He told the Foreign Secretary that he was well aware of the soundings which had been made for such a step. In the course of the conversation Eden took the same line as Churchill had taken at Cannes. He told Beck that he was authorized to give him information relative to British armaments,

[23] Edward Raczyński to Michał Łubieński, London, 12 February 1938, encl. I, APEL, P–GB, 1938.
[24] Beck, *Dernier Rapport*, pp. 127–8. Beck made an error of dates, placing this meeting in January 1937, instead of January 1938.
[25] *Ibid.*, p. 295, and n. 23.
[26] Raczyński, 12 February 1938, encl. II; see also n. 23.

that the state of the French Air Force was unsatisfactory, and that Anglo-American relations were generally closer than was believed. Beck responded positively to this approach. He reminded Eden of the statements he had made to him in 1936 and mentioned that during Foreign Minister Delbos's visit to Warsaw in December 1937, he had confirmed Poland's obligations to France. To give Poland the possibility of aiding her ally, however, said Beck, any new settlement in Europe should contain the necessary safeguards for the fulfilment of the Franco-Polish alliance. Finally, he asked Eden whether Great Britain could help Poland with heavy anti-aircraft artillery.[27] The statements of Beck and Raczyński in these conversations showed once again that Poland would welcome a firm policy on the part of the Democracies. Churchill and Eden obviously worked together in sounding out the Polish attitude.[28]

After talking to Eden Beck realized that he did not have to fear any British pressure for the withdrawal of the League from Danzig. The Polish delegate to the League, Dr. T. Komarnicki, reported that in Eden's opinion the maintenance of League obligations in case of a European war would help to draw out the conflict and contribute to both the moral and the material isolation of the totalitarian Powers.[29] The Committee of Three decided not to discuss the Danzig problem, and hence the report of the League High Commissioner was not published.[30] Thus the Danzig question remained in abeyance, largely because of Eden's desire to preserve the authority of the League of Nations.

Beck soon learned that the Foreign Secretary's views on the need for a stiffer policy were not shared by the rest of the British Cabinet. In the latter part of January the First Secretary of the British Embassy in Berlin, Ivone Kirkpatrick, revealed to the Director of the Polish News Agency (PAT) the outline of a British

[27] Beck, *Dernier Rapport*, pp. 294–5.
[28] 'In spite of my differences with the Government, I was in close sympathy with their Foreign Secretary'; Winston S. Churchill, *The Second World War*, vol. I, *The Gathering Storm* (Boston, London, 1948), p. 243.
[29] T. Komarnicki to the Foreign Minister, Cypher Letter no. 2, Geneva, 7 January 1938, APEL, Cyphers, 1938.
[30] The Danzig Question at the hundredth session of the League of Nations Council, Warsaw, 10 February 1938, APEL, Gdańsk, 1938. The Committee of Three was set up in July 1936 to deal with Danzig problems. It was composed of representatives of Great Britain, France, and Sweden.

project for agreement with Germany. The essential points of the proposal followed the lines of the Halifax-Hitler conversation of 19 November 1937. In return for an agreement on armaments and the entrance of Germany into some organization of European states, inducements were offered in the shape of colonies, British investments, and the extension of German influence in the Balkans. Indeed, according to Kirkpatrick, the British government would not object if Germany should even succeed France in 'some kind of leading role on the Continent'. The most important condition was that Germany should promise to behave 'decently' for at least eighteen months—the British government would not be able to proceed with colonial concessions in the face of an aroused public opinion. Ambassador Lipski believed that this project was intended to reach the ears of the German government.[31] Whether it was passed on or not, it was hardly likely to encourage the Polish government to support Austria.

In the meantime, Hitler and Ribbentrop became more impatient to carry out the Anschluss. Ribbentrop argued that speed and success in Central Europe would preclude any Western intervention[32] and in view of the attitude of the Democracies he was undoubtedly right. On 4 February the Führer cleared the decks for action by dismissing those statesmen and high army officers who were opposed to all risk of war. Blomberg was dismissed as Minister of War and Hitler took over that post himself. General Walter von Brauchitsch replaced General Werner von Fritsch as Commander-in-Chief of the Army. Ribbentrop replaced Neurath as Minister of Foreign Affairs. Göring later told Col. Beck that Hitler had been 'forced' to use measures of an internal nature in order to consolidate all the factors necessary for action against Austria.[33]

The ultimatum which Hitler presented to Austrian Chancellor Kurt von Schuschnigg at Berchtesgaden on 12 February, and the reaction of the French and British governments, proved to be a

[31] Lipski to the Foreign Minister, Berlin, 22 January 1938. MFA (London), P–G, 1938. There is no trace of this project in the German documents, while British documents for this period have not been published to date.

[32] *DGFP*, D, I, no. 93.

[33] Lipski to Łubieński, Berlin, 3 March 1938, MFA (London), P–G, 1938, encl.; extracts in Szembek, *Journal*, 23 February 1938, pp. 275–8.

dress rehearsal for the final absorption of Austria. France did, indeed, officially declare that she would support Austrian independence, and suggested to London that a joint Franco-British protest should be made in Berlin. But even this step was purely formal and was taken primarily for domestic reasons: to show the opposition parties of the Front Populaire that something had been done. Premier Camille Chautemps tried to justify French passivity to William C. Bullitt, the American Ambassador in Paris, by complaining that 'England has embarked on a policy of turning over Central and Eastern Europe to Germany in spite of her obligations to the League of Nations'.[34] The crisis deepened the differences of opinion on foreign policy which already existed in France. In the Chamber of Deputies a group led by former Foreign Minister, Etienne Flandin, advised reserve with regard to further French commitments in East Central Europe on the plea that France was isolated and had no British support there.[35] It was no wonder that French inquiries about German intentions towards Austria met with a rebuff from Ribbentrop who called the matter a 'German family affair'.[36]

Despite the lack of British support the French government turned to Poland. Suggestions were made for the establishment of closer Polish-Czechoslovak relations and Poland was in vague terms encouraged to play a great role in the regulation of the 'Danube Basin problem'. These suggestions were, however, accompanied by information that there was no Franco-British agreement on Austria, though attempts were being made to secure British help not only for Vienna but also for Prague. Speaking to the Polish Chargé d'Affaires in Paris, Feliks Frankowski, Delbos tried to put the blame for the crisis on the system of bilateral agreements, implying the Polish-German Declaration of Non-Aggression. Frankowski replied appropriately enough that if there was no unity among the signatories of the Stresa Conference then Poland could not be required to take a more decided attitude toward the Austrian question.[37]

[34] *FRUS*, 1938, I, pp. 25, 28.
[35] Feliks Frankowski to the Foreign Minister, Paris, 19 February 1938, Political Report, MFA (Warsaw), Polish Embassy, Paris, 1938.
[36] *DGFP*, D, I, no. 308.
[37] Frankowski to the Foreign Minister, Paris, 18, 19 February 1938, APEL, Cyphers, 1938; Wojciechowski, *Stosunki Polsko-Niemieckie*, pp. 378-9.

French warnings that, after Austria, Germany would turn against Czechoslovakia, Hungary, Rumania, and Poland lost much of their force by the admission that to counter German intervention in Austria, France and Britain could at most take purely diplomatic action.[38] In the light of such confessions, statements to the effect that Austrian independence was a canon of French foreign policy could not carry much conviction in Warsaw.[39]

The French government would not commit itself without British support and of that there was no sign. Hitler told Schuschnigg at Berchtesgaden, 'All that I do and will do in Austria and Czechoslovakia is in complete agreement with my conversation with Halifax.'[40] His claim was certainly confirmed by the attitude of the right-wing press in Great Britain. When the details of Hitler's ultimatum became known, *The Times* of 17 February proclaimed, 'Fundamentally, a close understanding between the two German states is the most natural thing possible. One of the least rational, most brittle, and most provocative artificialities of the peace settlement was the ban on the incorporation of Austria in the Reich.' With regard to other German aims in East Central Europe, *The Times* was also encouraging, provided they were accomplished in a peaceful manner. The British Prime Minister defined his stand by stating in the House of Commons that the League of Nations could not protect small states,[41] a clear hint that he would not approve a discussion of Austrian independence at Geneva. At the end of the month he declared that he did not consider the measures taken by the Austrian government after the Berchtesgaden meeting as a breach of Austria's obligations to maintain her independence, and that therefore the British government could not

[38] Frankowski to Foreign Minister, Paris, 4 March 1938, Cypher Letter no. 5, APEL, Cyphers, 1938.
[39] Cf., Noël's statement to Szembek on 8 March 1938, Szembek, *Journal*, p. 282. Wojciechowski interprets the French suggestions to Poland as insincere and motivated by the desire to delay German expansion but above all to disrupt Polish-German relations and thus subordinate Warsaw to Paris; *Stosunki Polsko-Niemieckie*, p. 379.
[40] The Polish Minister in Vienna, Jan Gawroński, reported that Schuschnigg was repeating this comment to foreign diplomats; Gawroński to Foreign Minister, Vienna, 16 February 1938, by Courier, MFA (Warsaw), Polish Legation, Vienna, 1938.
[41] *Parliamentary Debates, House of Commons*, 5th series, vol. 332, col. 227, 22 February 1938.

be called upon to act.[42] In his diary, however, he noted that Schuschnigg had been 'outrageously bullied by Hitler'.[43]

The Hitler-Schuschnigg interview only spurred Chamberlain's desire for reaching an agreement with Hitler before the threat of war again appeared over Europe. On 3 March, Ambassador Henderson transmitted to the Führer the suggestion that Germany should participate in a redistribution of territory in Africa. In return, Germany was urged to make a positive contribution to the establishment of peace and stability in Europe.[44] While trying to appease Hitler, Chamberlain also aimed at a settlement with Mussolini. Here he was at cross purposes with Eden who believed that the Duce should first give guarantees for withdrawing Italian troops from Spain. As a result, Eden gave up his office. During these conversations the Italian Ambassador in London reported that 'the British attitude to events in Austria has been, and I believe will remain, one of indignant resignation'.[45] The French attitude towards these developments was passive and petulant. The French Premier remarked to the American Ambassador in Paris that with the elimination of Eden, Cranborne, and Lord Vansittart, 'it seemed certain that England would be inclined to make increasing concessions to Germany'.[46] Mussolini, too, was in no mood to thwart Hitler. His Foreign Minister and son-in-law, Galeazzo Ciano, consoled himself with vague prospects of constructing an Italian-supported dam against the expansion of German influence in the Balkans.[47] It was clear that none of the Stresa signatories was willing to stand up for Austria.

Noting the reactions of the Great Powers to the Berchtesgaden ultimatum, Col. Beck concluded that the Anschluss was im-

[42] *Ibid.*, col. 730, 28 February 1938.
[43] Feiling, *Neville Chamberlain*, p. 337.
[44] *DM*, I, no. 3; *DGFP*, D, I, no. 138.
[45] *Ciano's Diplomatic Papers*, ed. Malcolm Muggeridge, tr. by S. Hood (London, 1948), p. 183.
[46] *FRUS*, 1938, vol. I, p. 27.
[47] On 17 February, Ciano noted, 'the bonds between Rome and Belgrade should be further strengthened and we must always bear in mind that Hungary and Poland are in a similar position . . . I think that we should forthwith study the question of an alliance with Yugoslavia. A horizontal Axis will make possible the existence of a vertical Axis;' *Ciano's Diary, 1937–1938*, tr. Andrew Mayor (London, 1953), p. 76.

minent.[48] Hitler made no attempt to hide his intentions from the Polish Ambassador in Berlin[49] and directed his efforts once more to the securing of Polish neutrality. In his speech to the Reichstag on 20 February, the Chancellor stated significantly that there were still ten million Germans beyond the frontiers of the Reich, but, to counteract any fears that this might include the German minority in Poland, he referred in a very friendly manner to Polish-German relations. He praised the memory of Marshal Piłsudski and declared that Poland respected the national character of Danzig, while Danzig and Germany respected Polish rights in the Free City.[50] In his speech Hitler omitted to recognize the independence of Austria, despite the express wishes of the Italians.

In the absence of opposition to Hitler's designs on the part of the Great Powers, Col. Beck prepared to enter into conversations with Germany on the price of Polish neutrality in the forthcoming Anschluss. When Göring told Beck during a visit to Warsaw on 23 February, that Hitler had set him the task of finding means of strengthening Polish-German relations, the Polish Foreign Minister answered that he saw two ways in which this could be done: an appropriate solution of the Danzig problem and the extension of the Polish-German Declaration of Non-Aggression of 1934. The Field-Marshal eagerly took up the second proposition and said that the Pact could be extended for twenty years, but he abstained from any comment on Danzig.

Beck assumed that the fall of Austria would sooner or later entail that of Czechoslovakia; he therefore raised this question in his conversations with Göring, saying that Poland was interested in a certain region of Czechoslovakia and would be concerned in the method of 'solving' that question. Göring immediately assured him that Polish interests in Moravská Ostrava would not be touched.[51] Since there was only a small Polish population

[48] Szembek, *Journal*, 16 February 1938, p. 274.
[49] Lipski to Foreign Minister, Berlin, 19 February 1938, MFA (London), P–G, 1938.
[50] Norman H. Baynes (ed.), *The Speeches of Adolf Hitler, April 1922–August 1939* (London, 1947), vol. II, pp. 1406–7.
[51] Lipski to Łubieński, Berlin, 3 March 1938, encl., MFA (London), P–G, 1938; the Polish text is in S. Stanisławska, 'Umowa Göring-Beck z 23 lutego 1938 roku' (The Göring-Beck Agreement of 23 February 1938), *Najnowsze Dzieje Polski*.

in that important industrial centre, the Field-Marshal probably used the suggestion as a bait to draw further comments from Beck; in this he was disappointed. Beck's aim in raising the question at all was simply to prepare the ground for achieving the main Polish objective in this area—the return of the Trans-Olza territory. If Germany was to turn immediately against Czechoslovakia and the Great Powers were passive, he did not want to be caught unprepared.[52] He obtained from Göring an assurance that in case of any German action against Czecho-slovakia Berlin would first consult Warsaw.[53]

On 12 March, German troops marched unopposed into Austria on the 'invitation' of the Nazi Minister of the Interior, Seyss-Inquart. As Hitler had foreseen, there was no opposition from France and Britain and after a diplomatic protest the Anschluss was recognized as a *fait accompli*. The Polish government now faced the problem of how to make the best use of the temporary disturbance of the international situation to further its own objectives.

In the hierarchy of Polish diplomatic goals at the beginning of 1938 Danzig ranked first and foremost. When the Polish Cabinet assembled in Warsaw on 12 March to consider what line of action to take, Marshal Śmigły-Rydz, speaking of the possible disintegration of Czechoslovakia, stated that in his opinion Poland should sell her neutrality to Germany in return for sub-stantial advantages in the Free City. The Marshal was perfectly aware of the danger that Germany might in time turn against Poland but he held that his country should continue her policy of good relations without, at the same time, blindly trusting her neighbour.[54] However, events moved too swiftly for any chance of success in Danzig. Col. Beck was in Italy at the time of the Anschluss. He had just completed a state visit to Rome when the

---

Materiały i Studia z Okresu 1914–1939 (Warsaw, 1960), vol. III., pp. 183–93; see also Józef Chudek, 'Rozmowy Beck-Göring z 23go lutego 1938r' (The Beck-Göring Conversations of 23 February 1938), *Sprawy Międzynarodowe* (Warsaw, 1960), no. 5, pp. 53–7.

[52] Szembek, *Journal*, 16 February 1938, p. 274. Wojciechowski points out that Beck's decision to enter into the talks with Göring was also motivated by fear of a new Four Power Pact which would isolate Poland; *Stosunki Polsko-Niemieckie*, p. 395.

[53] Szembek, *Journal*, 23 February 1938, p. 275.

[54] *Ibid.*, 12 March 1938, p. 289–90.

news of the crisis reached him at Sorrento where he was enjoying a brief vacation. Immediately after receiving the bulletin, he learned of a border incident between Poland and Lithuania in the course of which a Polish soldier had lost his life. Beck at once saw the possibility of utilizing the incident as a pretext to realize one of the secondary but perennial goals of Polish foreign policy —the establishment of diplomatic relations with Lithuania.[55] It thus came about that the Anschluss led to a change of relations between Warsaw and Kaunas.

For Col. Beck the establishment of relations with Lithuania was part of his 'Baltic policy' which aimed at the constitution of a Polish-Baltic-Scandinavian bloc, free of both German and Soviet influence. Both Piłsudski and Beck had made several attempts to open negotiations with Kaunas, but they had failed each time owing to the unwillingness of the Lithuanian government to envisage any step which might be construed as a recognition of the Polish annexation of Wilno.[56] Towards the end of 1937, Beck had authorized private soundings in Lithuania on the possibility of opening new negotiations. In February 1938, on the eve of the Anschluss, everything had been arranged for a meeting between a Lithuanian and a Polish delegation in Danzig. When, however, the Poles assembled in the Free City at the end of the month, the Lithuanian government suddenly called off the talks.[57] This incident, together with the uncertain

[55] Beck, *Dernier Rapport*, p. 149.

[56] In February 1938, the Latvian Foreign Minister, William Munters, told the Polish Ambassador in Rome, Dr Alfred Wysocki, that in 1936 he had made great efforts to arrange conversations between Beck and the Lithuanian Foreign Minister, Statys Lozaraitis. The conversations finally took place but the hostility of President Smetona prevented any concrete results. Munters told Wysocki that no one knew when German or Russian influence would become predominant in Kaunas and that Lithuania prevented the formation of a Baltic bloc; A. Wysocki, 'Pamiętniki, 1928' (Memoirs, 1938), typescript, p. 33 (Poland, Wrocław, Ossolineum).

[57] See the account of Stanislaw Schmidt published by T. Katelbach, 'Co poprzedziło polskie Ultimatum do Litwy' (What Preceded the Polish Ultimatum to Lithuania), *Kultura* (Paris, 1956), no. 4 (102), pp. 111–18. Franciszek Charwat, then Polish Minister in Riga, was in charge of the projected conversations. He told Szembek that Count Alexander Tyszkiewicz, who unofficially represented the Polish government in Kaunas, had remonstrated with Foreign Minister Lozaraitis against the suspension of the talks. Lozaraitis said that the talks were not possible in view of the sharp anti-Lithuanian trend in Poland. This was, of course, the Lithuanian point of view; Szembek, MSS, 1 March 1938.

international situation in mid-March 1938, prompted the course of policy on which Beck now proceeded to embark.

It became clear, even before the Foreign Minister's return to Warsaw, that the Polish government would make an issue of the frontier incident. On 14 March an interpellation was made in the Senate which called for the immediate establishment of relations between the two countries and for an official Lithuanian re-signation of all claims to Wilno. The Kaunas government, on the other hand, was determined to do all it could to avoid the establishment of diplomatic relations since it feared that their concomitant would be the final settlement of the Wilno dispute in favour of Poland. The Lithuanians appealed to the Great Powers but did not receive any support except from France. Ambassador Noël unofficially transmitted to the Polish govern-ment Lithuanian proposals to set up a commission for the in-vestigation of the border incident and hinted that Paris would be willing to mediate. He was rebuffed by Szembek who pointedly remarked that Col. Beck had twice protested against the attitude of certain French military and political circles towards Lithuania and gave as an example the close relations between the French and Soviet ministers in Kaunas.[58] The Poles suspected that French solicitude for Lithuania stemmed from the hopes of French military circles that Lithuania might provide a 'corridor' through which the Soviet Army could reach East Prussia in case of war with Germany.[59]

The Polish government may have originally intended to send a stiff ultimatum to Lithuania, demanding, besides the establish-ment of diplomatic relations, the conclusion of a minority treaty, a trade and customs agreement, and the deletion of the Wilno article from the Lithuanian Constitution.[60] If Warsaw had intended to make such demands, it soon decided to reduce them to a minimum. At a conference held after Beck's return to the capital on the night of 16 – 17 March, Szembek noted that the

[58] Szembek, *Journal*, 16 March 1958, pp. 293–5.

[59] Juliusz Łukasiewicz to Foreign Minister, Paris, 25 March 1938, Political Report, MFA (London), P–F, 1938.

[60] This version of the ultimatum was noted by General Jodl on 18 March 1938; see Roos, *Polen und Europa*, p. 310, n. 32. The same version was reported by Am-bassador Moltke from a newspaper confiscated by the Polish government; *DGFP*, D, V, no. 327.

Wilno question had been 'intentionally eliminated' from the text of the ultimatum.[61] The terms decided upon were limited simply to the establishment of relations between the two countries by 31 March. The Lithuanian government was given forty-eight hours to reply, and military measures were to be taken if the proposal were rejected. Polish troops were concentrated in the Wilno region.

The Polish move caught the Germans unawares, with their attention fixed on Austria. Ribbentrop did not welcome the reports of the first version of the ultimatum. He noted that a Polish annexation of Lithuania would eliminate the latter as a future 'object of compensation' for the Poles in return for the cession of the Corridor to Germany. He was of the opinion that in case of a Polish-Lithuanian conflict German troops should immediately occupy Memel; meanwhile, he decided that the Lithuanians should be pressed to accept Polish demands and thus avoid war.[62] On the same day orders were given to prepare for the occupation of Memel if Poland should move against Lithuania. At noon on 18 March directions for 'Case Memel' were complete and East Prussian units were in readiness positions.[63] At the same time Ribbentrop advised the Lithuanian Minister in Berlin to adopt a realistic policy towards Poland since Lithuania could not expect any help from Russia or anyone else.[64] When Ribbentrop learned the terms of the ultimatum, he told the Lithuanian Minister that 'the Polish terms were very moderate and ... we could only advise unconditional acceptance of the Polish proposal'.[65] The Soviet government also advised Kaunas to accept the Polish ultimatum on the grounds that, in case of conflict, a dangerous situation might arise which had to

[61] Szembek, *Journal*, 16–17 March 1938, p. 296; Beck, *Dernier Rapport*, p. 150; see also Budurowycz, *Polish-Soviet Relations*, p. 110, n. 63. Wojciechowski thinks that the modification of the ultimatum was due above all to French and British pressure, *Stosunki Polsko-Niemieckie*, p. 386. This was the opinion of Wincenty Witos, leader of the Peasant Party, then in exile in Czechoslovakia; it was based on information from opposition circles in Poland; see Wincenty Witos, *Moje Wspomnienia* (My Memoirs, Paris, 1965), vol. III, p. 435. Polish documents do not give the reason for the elimination of the article demanding that Lithuania recognize Wilno as belonging to Poland.
[62] *DGFP*, D, V, no. 329.
[63] See Roos, *Polen und Europa*, p. 314.
[64] *DGFP*, D, V, no. 328.
[65] *Ibid.*, no. 332.

be prevented.[66] This advice was given despite the fact that the acceptance of Polish terms meant a diplomatic defeat for Moscow which had always striven to foster the differences between Kaunas and Warsaw. The Lithuanian Attaché Militaire in Moscow bitterly told his German colleagues that his government had previously rejected repeated Soviet proposals for co-operation in military affairs and foreign policy.[67] In these circumstances, the Lithuanian government had no alternative but to accept the Polish ultimatum.

Polish diplomacy gained little in connection with the Anschluss. Although the agreement with Kaunas was an improvement over the former state of affairs, it came too late to be the stepping-stone to any Baltic bloc, particularly since the Scandinavian countries were committed to a policy of neutrality. In the sphere of German-Polish relations, Beck achieved nothing. There was no extension of the Polish-German Declaration of Non-Aggression; in fact, when Ambassador Lipski asked Ribbentrop about the prolongation of the agreement, the latter replied that he thought such a preterminal extension might weaken rather than strengthen it![68] No agreement was reached on Danzig. Furthermore, the Polish Commissioner General reported an increase in anti-Polish propaganda and renewed declarations for the return of the Free City to Germany, with an added demand for the Corridor. There were rumours of a plebiscite on the basis of which German troops would be called in.[69] Hitler had got his way so easily with Austria that he did not feel any necessity to make concessions to the Poles.

The government tried to make much of its achievement on the

[66] *Ibid.*, no. 339, encl. V. P. Potemkin, who was then Deputy Foreign Minister, claims that the Soviet Union threatened Poland with the abrogation of the Polish-Soviet Non-Aggression Pact if the Poles attacked Lithuania. This was to have influenced Warsaw in seeking a peaceful settlement; V. P. Potemkin (ed.), *Istoriia Diplomatii* (History of Diplomacy, Moscow, 1945), vol. III, p. 625. Wojciechowski repeats this statement; *Stosunki Polsko-Niemieckie*, p. 387. No documents have been published to support this claim, while the German documents show only Soviet protest against the form of the Polish demands. See also Budurowycz, *Polish-Soviet Relations*, pp. 110–11.

[67] *DGFP*, D, V, no. 338.

[68] *DGFP*, D, V, no. 34; also Lipski to Foreign Minister, 31 March 1938, MFA (London), P–G, 1938.

[69] Commissioner General to Foreign Minister, Danzig, 24 March 1938, APEL, Gdańsk, 1938.

Lithuanian sector. Public opinion, however, remained un-
impressed with the demonstrations organized by the Camp of
National Unity (OZN) which first called for an invasion of
Lithuania if it did not bow to Polish demands, and then proclaimed the brotherhood of the two peoples, once it had done so.
There was widespread anxiety over the danger of a German
annexation of Danzig. The supporters of closer relations with
France continued their criticism of the government. From their
point of view Poland could only find safety in solidarity with
Paris. The National Democratic Party, traditionally pro-French
and anti-German, gave the lead to this school of thought and its
statements found a deep echo in public opinion already pre-
disposed in this direction. The Army too feared German
expansion and earnestly desired a co-ordination of French and
Polish policy. General K. Sosnkowski, War Minister in 1920 and
1923, who had been pushed into the background after the *coup*
of 1926, expressed the fears of high Army circles when he told
Szembek that after the fall of Austria it would be the turn of
Czechoslovakia, Poland, and finally France.[70]

Col. Beck had no answer to these criticisms. He could not tell
the public that he had been trying to obtain German guarantees
for Polish rights in Danzig and had failed. He still hoped to
succeed. At the same time, he could not afford, nor did he wish
to provoke France into abrogating the Franco-Polish alliance by
publicizing the long-standing French willingness to see a
revision of the Polish-German frontier. The alliance with Paris,
however weak, still provided Poland with a valuable check on
Hitler. Moreover, if the international situation changed, Beck
knew that his country would have to align itself with France.
Meanwhile, he would try to seize what advantages he could. For
obvious reasons this was a policy which could not be explained
to public opinion either at home or abroad.

[70] Szembek, *Journal*, 23 February 1938, p. 275.

II

THE CZECHOSLOVAK
CRISIS: UNCERTAINTY
AND POSSIBILITIES

IN the Czechoslovak crisis, as in the Anschluss, Col. Beck's policy was ultimately dependent on the action of the Great Powers. France faced two alternatives and on her choice depended the policy of Poland: either she would betray her alliance with Czechoslovakia, in which case the latter would have to capitulate to Germany, or she would support Czechoslovak independence at the risk of a world war. Beck assumed that the Czechs would not fight, that the Western Democracies were unprepared, and that Soviet Russia would offer only symbolic protest. If this hypothesis turned out to be correct, he planned to press for certain Polish objectives in East Central Europe. If, however, the Western Powers should support Czechoslovakia, the Polish Foreign Minister was prepared to come in on the side of France and England for he held that in a world war Poland could never, even indirectly, be on the side of Germany. In this policy Beck had the full support of President Mościcki and of Marshal Śmigły-Rydz.[1]

---

[1] Beck, *Dernier Rapport*, pp. 162–3. Beck dates the formulation of this policy in the late summer of 1938, but it is clear that he acted on this assumption from the beginning of the Czechoslovak crisis. It is significant that for Beneš also the role of France had always been decisive. In December 1933, he told the Polish Minister in Prague that if war should break out between Germany on the one side and France and Poland on the other, he would not hesitate to support the latter; see Kozeński,

The fate of Austria did not predispose anyone to think that Czechoslovakia, although an ally of France, would find support in the West against Hitler. Assuming that there would be no British or French resistance to German aggression, Col. Beck hoped, as he had in February, that he could reach an agreement on Danzig and an extension of the 1934 Declaration of Non-Aggression but this time he also had broader objectives. He began an intensive preparation of public opinion at home and abroad for the realization of the Polish claim to Trans-Olza. Furthermore, realizing that if France resigned from all influence in the region there would be a temporary power vacuum in East Central Europe, Beck hoped to fill the gap with a new bloc of states—a 'Third Europe'. He owed his inspiration for this project to the first Foreign Ministers of the Republic. Prince Eustachy Sapieha and Erazm Piltz, respectively, thought in terms of a North to South bloc, and a bloc of the five victor states with the addition of Bulgaria and Hungary. The great Rumanian Foreign Minister, Take Ionescu, advanced a somewhat similar idea, but conceived the bloc more as an anti-Hungarian and anti-Soviet organization. These early plans came to naught because of disputes between Poland and Czechoslovakia on the one hand, and Rumania and Hungary on the other. Despite these precedents, Beck's conception of a 'Third Europe' was peculiarly his own. The new bloc was to stretch from the Baltic to the Black Sea, and perhaps to the Aegean as well; its corner-stone was to be a common Polish-Hungarian frontier and the close co-operation of these two countries was to assure its independence of both Germany and Russia. In connection with

---

Czechosłowacja w Polskiej Polityce Zagranicznej, pp. 70–71. Wojciechowski calls Beck's statement a 'decorative reinsurance' (*Stosunki Polsko-Niemieckie*, p. 417), but Beck at this time merely restated the axiomatic principle of Polish foreign policy held by Piłsudski before him.

The view of the Polish Ministry of Foreign Affairs of the impending crisis was also reported by the Hungarian Minister in Warsaw on 18 January 1938. Tadeusz Kobylański, Deputy Director of the Eastern Department, said he thought Prague would be forced to make far-reaching concessions to the Sudeten Germans. He expected this to lead to a new solution for the Hungarian and Slovak claims and would finally lead to the disintegration of Czechoslovakia; see Adam Magda, ed., *A Müncheni Egyezmény Létrejötte Es Magyarország Külpolitikája, 1936–1938*, Diplo-máciai Iratok Magyarország Külpolitikájához 1936–1945, vol. II (*The Coming of the Munich Agreement and Hungarian Foreign Policy, 1936–1938*, Diplomatic Documents for Hungarian Foreign Policy, 1936-1945, Budapest, 1965), doc., no. 104.

the Polish-Hungarian frontier, Beck thought that if Czechoslovakia lost her independence, Slovakia and Subcarpathian Ruthenia should be detached from Prague and not be allowed to fall under German domination.

In the early months of 1938 there were discussions in the Ministry of Foreign Affairs about a dual Slovak-Hungarian state or a federation of Slovakia, Czech territories, and Poland.[2] The idea of Slovakia as a buffer state under Polish protection had apparently lost ground.[3] In these ideas Beck went beyond Piłsudski's passive attitude of expectancy that Austria and Czechoslovakia would not survive in the long run, but even so, in his opinion, the realization of such plans could be envisaged only in the event of the disappearance of the independent Czechoslovak state and with it of all French influence in East Central Europe. It was not, however, a policy which the Foreign Minister intended to pursue regardless of the attitude of the Great Powers; on the contrary, he only deemed it mandatory if their passivity created a power vacuum in the area.[4]

Theoretically, the two alternative policies which Col. Beck envisaged for Poland, that is, support of France in a war, or the Third Europe, did not exhaust all the possibilities; there was also the question of an alliance or at least co-operation with Czecho-

[2] *Stanisławska, Wielka i Mała Polityka Józefa Becka*, p. 84.

[3] This concept had been noted by Szembek in December 1936; see *Journal*, p. 220. After the Hungarian state visit to Poland in February 1938, Beck stressed that he did not envisage the annexation of Slovakia by Hungary. If this should, nevertheless, take place, he saw it in the form of a very loose union with extensive autonomy; Szembek, MSS, 4 March 1938. This note qualifies the claim that Poland expected Hungary to 'come into possession' of Slovakia-Ruthenia; see C. A. Macartney, *October Fifteenth: A History of Modern Hungary 1929–1945* (Edinburgh, 2nd ed., 1961), part I, p. 208, which the author bases on information from Count Łubieński, former Chef de Cabinet to Col. Beck. In Beck's view, Subcarpathian Ruthenia was to come under unqualified Hungarian rule in order to create the Polish-Hungarian frontier. At the same time, Warsaw was interested in Hungarian pressure on the Slovaks in the direction of separatism.

[4] In view of the fact that Beck's plans for a Third Europe were strictly conditioned on the fall of Czechoslovakia, and, therefore, the withdrawal of French influence from Eastern Europe, the Hungarian Ambassador in Warsaw indulged in wishful thinking when he reported at the end of 1937 that Polish-Hungarian relations could be described as an 'unwritten treaty'; Macartney, p. 209. For Polish-Hungarian conversations until May 1938, see *A Müncheni Egyezmény*, nos. 160, 191, 200, 219, 236. It was only in September and October that exchanges of opinion became more frequent but co-operation was, for all practical purposes, limited to diplomatic action.

slovakia. Such a policy was supported by a large section of the opposition press. However, in 1938, the necessary preconditions for an alliance, or even for collaboration, did not exist. The dispute over Trans-Olza and the differences of outlook in foreign policy had accentuated the old aversion of both sides to support each other's interests. Polish attempts to conclude an alliance with Czechoslovakia during the 1920's and in 1933 had come to nothing. Thereafter, the policies of both countries reflected their adjustment to the Western appeasement of Germany. Though the Czechoslovak President expressed the desire for an improvement in relations, he did not, any more than in the past, envisage an alliance with Poland. In his view, such an act would entail commitments which might worsen his country's relations with the Soviet Union and Germany.[5]

Beck tried to balance the appeasement policy of the Western Democracies by maintaining good relations with Germany, while Beneš held to the principle that Czechoslovakia and the Little Entente could not act without French initiative and support. In consequence, Czechoslovakia and the other Little Entente states did not make any effort to prevent the Anschluss. Although relations between the two countries were burdened by the personal antipathy of Beck and Beneš for each other, this was not a decisive factor in Polish-Czechoslovak relations. In 1938, neither government envisaged the possibility of supporting the other without French aid, but both were ready to co-operate if France should decide to oppose Germany. A determined French policy of resistance to Hitler's ambitions, even at the risk of war, was the only practical means of cementing the rift between Poland and Czechoslovakia and of constructing an effective check to Germany in East Central Europe. The French government, however, had no intention of moving without Great Britain, while Chamberlain envisaged an agreement with Germany giving the latter East Central Europe as her sphere of influence. Thus, at the beginning of the Czechoslovak crisis, a

---

[5] '. . . Czechoslovakia, by allying herself with Poland, would have taken on all the risks and disadvantages and all the inevitable effects on her relations with Russia and Germany. . . . If Czechoslovakia did not want a military alliance with Poland, this was because she did not want to undertake any commitments towards a state which had so many unsettled disputes to resolve, both with Germany and with Russia'; Hubert Ripka, *Munich: Before and After* (London, 1939), p. 427.

divided group of small states faced the military might of Hitler's Germany with little prospect of support from the Western Democracies.

Hitler's choice of the slogan of self-determination as a weapon against the Czechoslovak state was a piece of brilliant strategy cloaking his aggressive designs with a 'moral' justification. There was a widespread belief in Britain that if the ethnographic principle had been the basis of the Peace Settlement of 1919, the Germans too had a right to make use of it for their own benefit. The slogan also had the merit of providing a convenient moral basis for Neville Chamberlain's projected agreement with Germany.

It is true that the incorporation of three million Germans in Czechoslovakia had not been in keeping with President Wilson's principle of self-determination, but in 1919 there had been no objection to the Czech claims on the part of the other Great Powers. Lloyd George, who had so vigorously opposed the cession of Danzig and Upper Silesia to Poland, had not demanded a plebiscite in the Sudetenland. At the Peace Conference, Beneš had asked for, and obtained, the 'historic boundaries of the Crown of Bohemia' in the West, with their predominantly German fringe areas. For the new Czechoslovak state, this region was not only of great strategic importance as a natural boundary with Germany and Austria, but was also an economic necessity in view of its highly developed industries. By 1938, the north and north-west fringes of Bohemia contained not only a heavily fortified defence system on the model of the Maginot line but provided almost all the lignite supply and most of the manufactured goods on which the country's foreign trade depended.[6] After the Anschluss the fortifications had been out-flanked in the south-west, but they could still provide at least a temporary line of defence. Moreover, it was clear to Prague that self-determination for its German citizens, in the sense in which Hitler meant it, would be equivalent to political and economic

[6] The Head of the Economic Department in the German Foreign Ministry noted on 21 September 1938, '. . . it appears that the greater part of the manufactured goods industry of the Czechoslovak Republic, which is primarily dependent on export and most sensitive to crises, is located in the Sudeten German area'; *DGFP*, D, II, no. 556.

dependence of the whole country on Germany and would be a prelude to the disintegration of the Czechoslovak state.

Hitler fully realized the strategic significance of Czechoslovakia and it was this factor and not ethnic considerations which was decisive in his plans. He considered the liquidation of the Czechoslovak state, with its French and Soviet alliances, as a necessary preliminary to the realization of his plan of expansion. He did not hide his views from France. As early as 1935 he had intimated to French statesmen that he found the Franco-Czechoslovak alliance objectionable.[7] In November 1937, he had already decided that the destruction of Czechoslovakia would be necessary as a preliminary step to any struggle with France.

The German Chancellor had a perfect instrument with which to work towards 'self-determination' of the Germans in Czechoslovakia in the shape of the *Sudetendeutsche Partei* (Sudeten German Party, SDP). The SDP, under the leadership of Konrad Henlein, had been organized in 1933 to replace the Sudeten National Socialist Party which had been dissolved on government orders. From 1935, if not earlier, the new party obtained considerable support both from the German Ministry of Foreign Affairs and from the Nazi Party.[8] The SDP programme postulated autonomy for the Germans of the Sudetenland, and more vaguely, for all the Germans of Czechoslovakia. It was indicative of Hitler's long-term plans that Henlein courted British public opinion from 1935 onwards, making four trips to London in the period 1935–38. The SDP leader spoke in the Royal Institute of International Affairs, where he made a good impression, and also had conversations with important personages in the Foreign Office and Parliament.

At the end of March a programme of action was drawn up by the SDP leaders and Hitler. The demands were to include self-government for the Sudetenland, a law for the protection of

[7] Pierre Laval already at this time flirted with the idea of obtaining an agreement with Hitler at the expense of France's allies in East Central Europe. He allowed his friend, Count de Brinon, Chairman of the Franco-German Friendship Society, to conduct private conversations with Hitler in 1935. Hitler told de Brinon that he looked forward to a 'peaceful revision of frontiers'; Ferdinand de Brinon, *Mémoires* (Paris, 1949), pp. 30–1.

[8] See Boris Celovsky, *Das Münchener Abkommen von 1938* (Stuttgart, 1958), p. 115.

minorities, the recognition of German as a state language equal to Czech, municipal elections and, most significant of all, a demand for changes in the foreign policy of Czechoslovakia. It was agreed to proceed in such a way as to make the acceptance of these demands by Prague difficult or impossible, and thus to avoid giving the impression abroad that a compromise solution could be found. The Reich government was to eschew any visible support for the SDP in order to make the whole question appear in the light of a dispute between the German minority and the government in Prague. Simultaneously, the SDP was also to follow a policy of political co-operation with the other minorities of Czechoslovakia. As this well-planned machinery swung into action, Hitler began to meditate on the military steps which he foresaw as a conclusion of the dispute. Speed was an essential element in these calculations for it was estimated in Berlin that only if victory were achieved within four days of the beginning of operations could a European war be avoided.[9]

Col. Beck took the first steps towards publicly formulating his policy in the face of the approaching crisis in a speech before the Foreign Affairs Committee of the *Sejm* on 12 January 1938. He declared then that any decision made by Czechoslovakia in favour of one of her minorities, if not applied to the Polish minority, would be regarded by Poland as an unfriendly act.[10] He confirmed this stand on 21 March, in an interview with Ward Price of the *Daily Mail* in which he said that the Poles living under Czech rule had the same rights to local autonomy as the Sudeten Germans. This was a policy of 'playing it safe', for it was clear that the solution eventually reached in the Sudetenland would have to be sanctioned by France and Britain. At the same time, Beck registered his claim for the equal treatment of Polish interests and made use of the widespread public sympathy for the fate of the Poles of Trans-Olza. The concomitant of this policy was the co-operation of the Union of Poles in Czechoslovakia with the SDP. On 29 March the Polish Deputy from Trans-

[9] *DGFP*, D, II, no. 133. For Henlein's programme, announced as the 'Eight Points' at Karlovy Vary (Karlsbad), on 24 April 1938, and for a detailed account of the crisis, see R. G. D. Laffan, 'The Crisis over Czechoslovakia, January to September 1938' in *Survey of International Affairs, 1938* (Oxford, London, 1951), vol. II, and B. Celovsky, *Das Münchener Abkommen*.

60

Olza, L. Wolf, demanded autonomy for the Poles of this region in a speech before the Czechoslovak Parliament.

To superficial observers, another pointer in Polish policy towards Czechoslovakia was the Hungarian state visit to Poland in February. The Regent, Admiral Horthy, accompanied by his Foreign Minister, Kálmán Kánya and the latter's Chef de Cabinet, Count István Csáky, held a series of talks with Beck and other members of the Polish government. These contacts, however, resulted in mutual disappointment. The Poles could hardly welcome Horthy's advice that they give up Danzig and the Corridor to Germany, and there seemed to be a personality clash between Kánya and Beck. While the visit was covered with much flourish in the press, no agreement was reached on a common course of action.[11]

Another sign of strain in Polish-Czechoslovak diplomatic relations was the Polish note to Prague on 22 March, accusing Czechoslovakia of tolerating the anti-Polish activities of the Communist Party and of *émigré* Polish Communists and other political refugees. Warsaw demanded that Prague should declare what steps it intended to take against the 'agencies of the Comintern'.[12] The real motive of this note, though apparently an act of co-operation with Germany, lay in Beck's attempts to avoid commitment for or against the Axis. After Italy had joined the Anti-Comintern Pact in the autumn of 1937, Poland had also been sounded out. Such a step, however, would commit her to the Fascist bloc, while the rejection of an invitation to support the Axis would carry the risk of antagonizing Berlin. Thus Beck's note to Prague represented his established policy of independent action,[13] while at the same time he tried to discount his attitude towards Czechoslovakia in the realm of Polish-German relations.

It seemed at first as if Beck's policy would reap dividends in Berlin. While Hitler was laying his plans, he took great care to assure the Poles on the issues of Danzig and of the German

[10] Beck, *Przemówienia*, p. 343; *Dernier Rapport*, p. 159.
[11] See Szembek, *Journal*, 5–9, 11 February 1938, pp. 270, 274; see also Macartney, *October Fifteenth*, p. 209.
[12] Stanisławska, *Wielka i Mała Polityka Józefa Becka*, pp. 86–7.
[13] *Ibid.*, pp. 89–90.

minority in Poland. Once the initial exhilaration over the Anschluss had passed, the Danzig Senate published an official denial of reports in the foreign press that decrees had been issued on the annexation of the Free City by the Reich, or that negotiations were in progress on this subject with Poland. At the end of April the Polish Commissioner General reported Ribbentrop's statement to Dr. Burckhardt that Germany did not desire any complications with Poland over Danzig. That problem, said the German Foreign Minister, did not exist for Germany; the separation of East Prussia was painful but Germany understood that Poland had certain vital interests which had to be respected.[14] Hints were once more thrown out as to the extension of the Declaration of Non-Aggression[15] and care was taken not to raise friction on minority questions.[16] In the first half of May, Gauleiter Forster of Danzig paid a visit to Poland during which he behaved in a very conciliatory manner and expressed his admiration for Polish culture and the Polish state.[17] By means of these demonstrations of friendship Hitler tried to induce the Polish Foreign Minister to commit himself on a policy towards Prague. Col. Beck, however, would not give the Führer this satisfaction; his own policy ultimately depended on that of London and Paris.

The official policy of France was expressed in repeated declarations of support for the independence of her Czechoslovak ally, but behind the scenes there was timidity and discord. The

[14] Commissioner General to Foreign Minister, Danzig, 28 April 1938, APEL, Gdańsk, 1938.

[15] When Hitler visited Rome at the beginning of May, he told the Polish Ambassador there, Dr. Alfred Wysocki, that he was willing to extend the 1934 agreement; DBFP, 3, I, no. 19. On 6 May, Ribbentrop told Ciano that the Corridor would have to be accepted for an indefinite period; Ciano's Diary 1937–1938, p. 113.

[16] The German census of 1938 was being prepared, not on the basis of the mother-tongue, but on the declaration of 'belonging to a people'—'Volkstumzugehörigkeit'. This principle left the way open for pressure on the Polish minority in Germany. On 26 March 1938, the Polish Ambassador protested against this principle; note by Weizsäcker, PGD, Hoover, ser. no. 878. Göring issued instructions that the census should not be carried out in German Upper Silesia, which had the largest Polish population in Germany, before the end of December 1938; copy of memorandum for the President of the State Statistical Office, Berlin, 30 April 1938, ibid.

[17] 'Forster's Visit to Poland, May 9–17, 1938,' MFA (Warsaw), Political Department, Section of International Organizations, 13 June 1938.

French General Staff did not consider that direct aid was possible while the Cabinet was divided on the question whether France should risk war with Germany. The organization of the French Army was such that a general mobilization was estimated to take two weeks or more by which time Czechoslovakia was expected to be overrun. French aircraft production in the spring of 1938 was down to forty planes per month, as against an estimated German production of two hundred and fifty. Soviet aid was discounted because of the well-known Polish aversion to any passage of Soviet troops, while Rumania, even if she agreed to it, had only one railway line available for troop transport between Czechoslovakia and the USSR. In any case, it was thought that, owing to purges, the Red Army was not capable of offensive action. The General Staff therefore held that the utmost France could do in case of war would be to man the Maginot Line.[18] These views were shared by Léon Noël, French Ambassador in Warsaw.[19]

While the military leaders were unwilling to risk war, Georges Bonnet, who became Foreign Minister in April, was determined to avoid it at all costs. He based his policy on the principle that without British support French aid to Czechoslovakia would be suicidal.[20] It is true that the Foreign Minister had to combat the pressure of some members of his Cabinet, who stood for an uncompromising support of Czechoslovakia, but not even they dared deny that British support for France was absolutely essential. Bonnet skilfully used this argument against them and he had the support of the right-wing benches in the Chamber of Deputies and of French public opinion. Already at the beginning of March, the Czechoslovak Minister in Paris, Stefan Osuský, reported that the idea of fighting for Czechoslovakia was very

[18] Minutes of the Permanent Committee of National Defence, 15 March 1938, cited by Gamelin, *Servir*, II, pp. 322–8.

[19] Noël advised Bonnet at this time that, in view of the international situation and the French lack of armaments, France was not capable of defending Czechoslovakia; Noël, *L'Agression Allemande contre la Pologne*, p. 198. The French were also at this time pressing Hungary to co-operate diplomatically with Paris in return for a future revision of Hungarian frontiers; see the report of the French office of the Hungarian Revision League in Paris, 6 February 1938, on the declaration of Jean Mistler, chairman of the Foreign Affairs Committee of the French Chamber of Deputies, *A Müncheni Egyezmény*, doc. no. 109.

[20] *FRUS*, 1938, I, p. 39.

unpopular in France.[21] In this state of affairs, French declarations of support for Prague had little value and presented a façade which was easily penetrated by Berlin.

In making French aid to Czechoslovakia dependent on the support of Great Britain, Bonnet was asking for the impossible and he knew it. Neville Chamberlain had made his lack of interest in East Central Europe quite plain at the time of the Anschluss and he was determined to reach an agreement with Berlin. He rejected the concept of a 'Grand Alliance' between Britain and France against Hitler on the grounds that Czechoslovakia would be overrun before aid could reach her while Great Britain was in no position to obtain a swift victory over Germany. On this hypothesis, as early as 20 March, Chamberlain noted, 'I have therefore abandoned any idea of giving guarantees to Czechoslovakia. . . .' Three weeks later, however, he told the American Ambassador, Joseph Kennedy, that the British government 'were thoroughly convinced that Germany was in no position as regards resources and reserves to go to war'.[22] It seems debatable whether, in fact, military considerations were decisive for Chamberlain's policy. In refusing to commit Great Britain to the support of Czechoslovakia, he acted on the assumption that Germany could be appeased by the satisfaction of her 'justified' grievances. In this he had the support of public opinion and of the majority of his Cabinet. This was also the view of the British Ambassador in Berlin.[23]

In keeping with the decision he had made, Chamberlain firmly rejected French requests for a British commitment to France on Czechoslovakia. For the same reason he also refused a Soviet proposal, made on 18 March, for a conference of the USSR, France, Great Britain, and Czechoslovakia to study possible means of averting aggression. On 24 March, he made a public declaration of policy in the House of Commons in which

[21] *DM*, I, no. 4.

[22] Feiling, *Neville Chamberlain*, pp. 347–8; *FRUS*, 1938, I, p. 44.

[23] Henderson wrote to Chamberlain on 21 March 1938: 'I can see every moral ground for a war to save the world from Germany's policy of the use of naked force; but I cannot see that we are on good moral ground . . . if we make war to compel three and a half million Sudeten Germans to remain inferior subjects of a Slav state. If we won the war, we should have to redraw the frontiers of Czechoslovakia, so as to leave the mass of the Sudeten outside them'; *DBFP*, 3, I, appendix I, p. 621.

he rejected the possibility of a British guarantee of Czechoslovak independence on the ground that this would take the power of decision for peace or war out of the hands of the British government, and that Britain could not commit herself in an area which was not vital to her interests. He attempted to offset the effect of this announcement by warning that if a war did break out it would most probably not be confined to those who had assumed obligations.[24] In this way, the British Prime Minister hinted vaguely at the possible involvement of Great Britain in a European conflict over Czechoslovakia.

It was not surprising that at a conference between the Prime Ministers and Foreign Ministers of France and Great Britain, held in London on 28 and 29 April, the French failed to obtain a promise of British support in case of a Franco-German war over the Czechoslovak state. Premier Daladier, who, in contrast to Georges Bonnet, was sincere in pressing for a British guarantee, realized that only a firm Franco-British policy could avert war and gain the support of the states of East Central Europe against Germany. With remarkable insight into the realities of the international situation, he told his British colleagues that

> war could only be avoided if Great Britain and France made their determination quite clear to maintain the peace of Europe by respecting the liberties and the rights of independent peoples. If we were to act accordingly and show that we were ready to take action to save the independence of Czechoslovakia, after she had made such concessions as we considered necessary to the German minority, then . . . an improvement would take place in the European situation. Only then could we expect to see Yugoslavia . . . and perhaps even Poland change their present attitude and give us their support in the cause of peace If, however, we were once again to capitulate when faced with another threat, we should then have prepared the way for the very war which we wished to avoid.[25]

[24] *Parl. Deb. H. C.*, 5, vol. 333, col. 1405.
[25] *DBFP*, 3, I, no. 194. Daladier's opinion was widely shared in Eastern Europe, even if with certain modifications. Already in March, Premier Stojadinović told the U.S. Minister in Belgrade that, with the aid of Italy, Germany was the most powerful state in Europe, but that if Italy, Great Britain, and France should present a united front, Germany could do nothing; Report of Minister in Belgrade to Secretary of State, 12 March 1938, SDNA, Poland, 1938, doc. file note 7600, 62/362, telegram no. 29.

However, Chamberlain and Halifax were deaf to this appeal. The upshot of the conversations was the decision that the two governments should exert the utmost pressure on Prague in the direction of concessions to the SDP. France was to play the chief role with relation to her ally, while Great Britain was to exercise a restraining influence on Berlin. The failure of such a strategy could be foreseen from the start. A high official of the British Foreign Office gave a succinct evaluation of this policy:

> In diplomacy, the word soon gets passed around; and the ambivalence of our policy in trying to deter the Germans from armed action by pointing to the probability of British intervention, and to discourage the Czechs from fighting by hinting at its improbability, was not long concealed.[26]

The month of April also witnessed some interesting developments in Czechoslovak policy towards Poland. Neither President Beneš nor the Czechoslovak minister in Warsaw, Dr. Juraj Slávik, believed that any agreement with Poland was feasible as long as Col. Beck was Minister of Foreign Affairs.[27] It was natural from this point of view that Prague should be interested in the views of the Polish opposition parties as to the possibility of improving relations with Prague. To investigate this matter Beneš decided to make use of Dr. Václav Fiala, a well-known writer on Polish affairs whose book had been translated into French and published in Paris in 1936 as La Pologne d'Aujourd'hui. Fiala visited Poland in April and held extensive conversations with the leaders of the National Democratic, Socialist, Populist, and Christian Democratic Parties. He also spoke with Prelate Zygmunt Kaczyński, director of the influential Catholic Press Agency and friend of Generals Władysław Sikorski and Kazimierz Sosnkowski who were both known to be critics of Col. Beck.

Fiala's long report to President Beneš gives an interesting insight into the attitudes of the leaders of the opposition, many of

---

[26] Strang, *Home and Abroad* (London, 1956), p. 134.
[27] 'As long as there is no change of regime in Poland and as long as Beck directs Polish foreign policy, there is no hope for Polish-Czechoslovak agreement, or for a sincere alliance with France, or for Poland's departure from her policy of serving German interests,' wrote Slávik on 26 March 1938; see Stanisławska, *Wielka i Mała Polityka Józefa Becka*, p. 101 (translation A.C.).

whom confidentially expressed views which they did not proclaim in the press. The spokesmen for the National Democrats told Fiala that though they thought Polish interests were in the long run incompatible with German aims, they realized that France was weak and that Eastern Europe was in danger of becoming a bargaining counter between the Western Powers on the one hand, and Germany and Italy on the other. To counter this danger, they spoke of creating a neutral bloc which was similar to Beck's concept of a 'Third Europe' except that Czechoslovakia was to keep her frontiers with only minor territorial changes. These changes were to include the return of the Polish Teschen district as well as certain concessions to Hungary. At the same time, all the leaders, with the exception of Stanisław Stroński, felt that Czechoslovakia should abrogate her alliance with the Soviet Union and recognize the predominant influence of Poland. There was also talk of the desirability of a Czechoslovak 'gesture' in the Trans-Olza territory.

In his conversation with M. Rataj, who represented the moderate wing of the Populist Party and who formulated its foreign policy, Fiala noted similar views. Rataj said that the Czechoslovak alliance with the Soviet Union created a negative impression in Poland. He thought that Poland could remain neutral in a European conflict and that she was too weak to embark on a quarrel with Hitler. 'If I were to become Foreign Minister today,' remarked Rataj, 'I would not really be able to act differently from Beck.' The only difference would be that Polish neutrality towards Czechoslovakia would change from a hostile to a benevolent one. However, under the influence of the government's radio and press campaign on the Trans-Olza question, Polish public opinion had grown increasingly cool towards Czechoslovakia. The only factor which could bring about a change would be an 'effective gesture' by Prague. Fiala commented that this meant the return of the Teschen district to Poland.

The leader of the Polish Socialist Party, M. Niedziałkowski, did not differ from the views expressed by the other opposition leaders. He thought that Beck's policy of sitting on the fence to gain time would not have much success, for France had grown cooler towards Poland while the USSR took an unfriendly attitude. But he was unable to suggest anything to improve Polish-Czechoslovak relations other than 'an effective gesture on Trans-Olza' which would give the opposition the right arguments against the anti-Czech policy of the regime.

According to Fiala, the greatest awareness of the dangers of Beck's policy was displayed by the loose political group known as the 'Front Morges'. Its representative in conversations with Fiala was Prelate Zygmunt Kaczyński, who also claimed to speak for the Polish generals. This claim was accepted by Fiala and Beneš, but there is no evidence of its validity. Kaczyński's statement that General Sosnkowski was the real master of the Army was fantastic. Nevertheless, some of his assertions in the name of that General may well have represented the latter's views on relations with Czechoslovakia. The Prelate stated that Sosnkowski and his followers would gain the support of public opinion if Prague returned the Teschen district to Poland, made certain frontier corrections in Spiš and Orava, and regulated some tariff questions. In return, they would offer a military alliance against Germany. They might even accept the Czecho-slovak-Soviet alliance, but this would require some technical preparation, for neither they nor anyone else would agree to the flooding of Poland by Soviet troops in case of war. Finally, Kaczyński repeated the same demand as the other spokesmen— the return of Trans-Olza. Fiala concluded his report to President Beneš with a pessimistic evaluation of the chances for an improvement of Polish-Czechoslovak relations if the opposition parties should come to power or gain some influence on the making of Polish foreign policy:

> All concessions in the matter of Trans-Olza are considered in Poland as a 'first stage', after which will come the demand that we should return the Teschen district, and this independently of whether Polish-German relations will be better or worse.
> . . . The decisive factor is that even those who in Poland are the most objective in stating that both sides are culpable in the worsening of Polish-Czechoslovak relations, are decided and in complete agreement that the key to the solution lies in the hands of Prague.[28]

[28] For Fiala's report, see Stanisławska, pp. 110–11, 113, 114, 116–18, 120, 125. The Front Morges took its name from the Swiss estate of former President Ignacy

The ideas of the Polish opposition leaders had thus evolved to a position which was hardly distinguishable from that of Col. Beck.[29] Though they promised improved relations, co-operation, or even military alliance, they asked, in fact, for the cession of the Polish territories of Trans-Olza. From the Czechoslovak point of view the price would not justify the gains. Prague held that such a sacrifice might be in vain, 'since Poland could not risk exposing herself openly against Germany'.[30] The decisive factor in Czechoslovak policy was in any case the attitude of France. The British Minister in Prague reported that Czechoslovakia would fight only if assured of immediate French aid, but the Czechs knew very well that France would not take such a step without the consent of Great Britain.[31]

While Fiala was carrying out his mission in Warsaw, Beneš embarked on an official effort to improve the atmosphere of Polish-Czechoslovak relations. He instructed Dr. Juraj Slávik, the Czechoslovak Minister in Poland, to prepare a project to this end. While the President did not want an alliance with Poland,[32] he was anxious to obtain better relations which would facilitate the demilitarization of the Polish-Czechoslovak frontier. However, Beneš did not have any concrete proposal in mind. He instructed Slávik in mid-April that his aim in seeking a better

---

Jan Paderewski where, in February 1936, General Władysław Sikorski proposed a form of political co-operation by the leading opposition parties. Finally, the Front consisted of the Christian Democrats led by Wojciech Korfanty, and the National Labour Party led by Karol Popiel. In 1937, this party was fused with the Labour Party of General Józef Haller. The leading political parties did not enter the Front; see Władysław Pobóg-Malinowski, *Najnowsza Historia Polityczna Polski, 1863–1945* (The Most Recent Political History of Poland, 1863–1945, London, 1956), vol. II, pp. 604–5.

[29] The Communist Party of Poland constituted the sole exception to this rule and even then it demanded an improvement of conditions in Trans-Olza. It had no influence on Polish opinion and was dissolved by Stalin some time in 1938. No date for the dissolution has been established.

[30] Ripka, *Munich*, p. 426. Ripka noted that a French Cabinet Minister told him in the spring of 1938 that Czechoslovakia should be willing to sacrifice the Teschen region in return for Polish friendship.

[31] Basil Newton, British Minister in Prague, wrote as early as 15 March that Britain should not support France over Czechoslovakia, for, 'should war come, nothing that we or France could do would save Czechoslovakia from being over-run'; *DBFP*, 3, I, no. 86.

[32] Ripka, *Munich*, p. 427.

'atmosphere' was to furnish proof of his good will to the Great Powers, who had urged him to co-operate more closely with Poland, and also to satisfy his critics at home. At best, he hoped that his predictable failure would lay the blame for bad relations at the door of Warsaw.[33] At the end of April, Slávik began to act. The objective in the first stage was to improve economic, cultural and sporting relations between the two countries. The concessions which Beneš was willing to make were, as he knew, sufficient to tempt neither Col. Beck nor the opposition. He was prepared to co-operate with Poland against Communist activity, and not permit Communist refugees from Poland to organize propaganda against that country in Czechoslovakia.[34] He also offered to make a declaration to the representatives of the Polish minority that they would receive the same concessions as any other minority in Czechoslovakia. These were not, however, unconditional concessions, but were dependent on a 'friendly change of Polish policy'.[35] With such proposals, Beneš knew that there could be little chance of success. It is possible that the Czechoslovak President counted on French support to obtain a somewhat better position with regard to Poland without having to pay the price which he knew to be mandatory for any real co-operation. In any case, he received the full diplomatic support of both France and Britain for his project.

Slávik began his diplomatic action on 30 April by visiting the Deputy Premier, Eugeniusz Kwiatkowski, who was known for his sympathy with Czechoslovakia and his interest in trade between the two countries. In this conversation Slávik proposed an extension of trade relations, the redirecting of Czechoslovak export trade from Hamburg to Gdynia, an air-agreement and the visit of a Czechoslovak trade delegation to Poland.[36] Not the smallest factor in the choice of Kwiatkowski as the first personage to be officially acquainted with Slávik's mission was the know-

[33] Juraj Slávik in *NYD*, 14 February 1958. In a series of short articles citing his reports and instructions, Slávik recounted his mission in Poland. See also Stanisławska, *Wielka i Mała Polityka Józefa Becka*, p. 102.

[34] This had already been stated in the Czechoslovak note of 12 April, in answer to the Polish 'Anti-Comintern' note of 22 March; *ibid.*, p. 93.

[35] Slávik, *NYD*, 15, 28 February 1958.

[36] Stanisławska, *Wielka i Mała Polityka Józefa Becka*, p. 108; Szembek, *Journal*, 30 April 1938, p. 305.

ledge of that minister's known differences of opinion with Col. Beck on foreign policy.[37]

Franco-British diplomatic support for the Czechoslovak *démarche* was immediately forthcoming. When Ambassador Noël had discussed the matter with Slávik in Prague at the end of April, he had already assured him that French diplomatic support would be formulated to look, not like a demand for Polish aid to Czechoslovakia, but for Polish aid to France in case of a conflict.[38] On 1 May, the French and British governments began a concerted action to obtain Polish diplomatic cooperation in their agreed policy of counselling restraint to Germany and to secure an improvement of Polish-Czechoslovak relations.

The main burden of persuading the Poles to agree to this policy fell on France. To this end, Foreign Minister Bonnet applied a mixture of cajolery and veiled threats. He told Ambassador Juliusz Łukasiewicz that Prague would have to accept any conditions put to it by Great Britain and France. Bonnet said that both London and Paris were surprised by Warsaw's attitude of passivity and reserve towards Czechoslovakia. The Democracies, stated the French Foreign Minister, wished to secure Polish co-operation in the restraining *démarche* planned by the British government in Berlin, or at least an attitude on the part of Poland such that Germany could not count on her support in the event of negotiations. Bonnet brought pressure to bear on the Ambassador by remarking ominously that France, having an alliance with Great Britain and sure of securing better relations with Italy, could really afford to lose interest in the affairs of Central and Eastern Europe. She would not do so, however, continued Bonnet, for she considered any new German expansion there as dangerous for peace.[39] For the Polish government there was more than the hint of a threat in these words, for it was well aware of the strong political trend in France towards a complete withdrawal from commitments in East Central Europe.[40]

[37] Prelate Kaczysńki told Fiala that Kwiatkowski might be Premier in a new government and even a future President of Poland; Stanisławska, p. 109 .

[38] Slávik, *NYD*, 22 February 1958.

[39] Łukasiewicz to Foreign Minister, Paris, 1 May 1938, cypher letter no. 8, APEL, Cyphers, 1938.

[40] Anatol Muhlstein, counsellor at the Polish Embassy in Paris, told Szembek

While the British and French Ambassadors supported the Czechoslovak *démarche* in Warsaw, Lord Halifax also spoke to the Polish Ambassador in London. He put forward a formal proposal for Anglo-Polish co-operation to prevent the Czechoslovak problem from becoming the cause of an armed conflict. It is important to note that, at this time, both the British Foreign Secretary and the British Ambassador in Warsaw assured the Polish government that British action in Prague aimed to influence that government to grant concessions not only to the Germans but also to the other minorities of Czechoslovakia. They expressed the hope that it would be possible for Poland to settle her differences with that country. Col. Beck responded cautiously to these advances. He promised to give objective consideration to the Czechoslovak proposals but he declined to commit himself to the defence of that state, and he enumerated Polish grievances against Prague—the treatment of the Polish minority, Comintern activity in Czechoslovakia, and transit difficulties.[41]

With the way thus prepared by French and British diplomatic action, Slávik saw Col. Beck on 4 May, and was received by him in a markedly friendly manner. The Polish Foreign Minister welcomed Slávik's declaration that the Polish minority would enjoy the concessions granted to any other minority, and did not comment on the hints that this was conditional on a change of Polish policy. The conversation proved to be the high point of Polish-Czechoslovak relations in 1938, but it did not change them. The only concrete achievement of the joint efforts of Prague, London, and Paris was Beck's declaration to Ambassador Kennard that Poland would not initiate a crisis, and that to Ambassador Noël stating that she would not make Czechoslovakia's position more difficult. However, the Polish Foreign Minister warned Noël that France could not demand of Poland a guarantee for the integrity of Czechoslovakia.[42] It was difficult indeed to expect that Poland should expose herself to

---

that such a development was imminent; Szembek, *Journal*, 23 March 1938, pp. 298–9.

[41] Beck to Raczyński, Warsaw, 3 May 1938, cypher telegram no. 28, Raczyński to Beck, London, 4 May 1938, cypher telegram nos. 30, 31, APEL Cyphers, 1938; see also *DBFP*, 3, I, no. 175.

[42] Slávik, *NYD*, 5 March 1958.

friction or conflict with Germany without any positive offer of aid from the West. The American Ambassador in Warsaw, Drexel J. Biddle, commented that unless France and Britain undertook part of the responsibility for the policy they advocated and gave adequate assurances for Polish security, 'I do not believe that Poland could be expected to "stick out her neck" in initiating a movement entailing the protection of Czechoslovakia.'[43]

The policy of France and Britain was, however, not that of protecting Czechoslovakia, but of exerting pressure on her to make the maximum concessions to the SDP and thus to avoid any risk of war. On 12 May, the British and French ministers in Prague conveyed to the Czechoslovak government the advice that it should even go beyond the proposed 'Nationalities' Statute', and, if need be, abandon the concept of a national state.[44] At the same time, Lord Halifax instructed Ambassador Henderson to inform the German government of the Franco-British advice to Prague and to request German co-operation in the form of exerting influence on the SDP towards a peaceful settlement. Henderson was simultaneously instructed to repeat, if necessary, the threat of a possible British involvement if a conflict should break out. In transmitting the instruction, Halifax expressly warned the Ambassador that 'you should not in any conversation, official or private, let the impression be created that we and others should certainly sit by in all circumstances'.[45] Such a policy had little chance of success, for the knowledge of Franco-British pressure on Prague was bound to encourage Berlin rather than restrain it. Moreover, Henderson's personal sympathy for the German cause made him the least likely diplomat to threaten Berlin with the dire consequences of the use of force. Finally, British policy could not have been aided by an article widely publicized in the American and Canadian press and assumed to have been 'inspired' by Chamberlain, to the effect that the cession of the Sudetenland to Germany would be the best solution to the problem.[46]

[43] *FRUS*, 1938, I, p. 497.
[44] *NDHM* (Prague, 1958), no. 12; see also: *DBFP*, 3, I, no. 166.
[45] *DBFP*, 3, I, appendix I, p. 627.
[46] *New York Herald Tribune, New York Times, Montreal Star*, 14 May 1938.

Beck's attitude towards Czechoslovakia hardened as he perceived that Franco-British policy towards that country continued along the lines of pressure for further concessions. His friendly tone towards Slávik, his receptive attitude to British proposals for co-operation, and the toning down of the Polish pro-government press in the first days of May were all the result of uncertainty as to the decisions reached in London at the end of the previous month. But now, not only could he see, from the Western press, which way the wind was blowing, but he also had detailed information. On 11 May the Polish Minister in Prague, Casimir Papée, was informed extensively by the Czechoslovak Foreign Minister, Kamil Krofta, of the demands made upon the latter's government by London.[47] As a result, the pro-government press resumed its attacks on Czechoslovakia for her treatment of the Polish minority in Trans-Olza. Whatever hopes Beneš might have nursed of strengthening his position with regard to Poland were lost. Moreover, in the second part of May the Sudeten problem plunged Europe into a nerve-racking crisis.

In the light of Chamberlain's set policy, it is not surprising that his reaction to the events between 19 and 21 May should have been wholly negative. On 20 May the Czechoslovak government mobilized one class of reservists, ostensibly because of German troop movements along the borders. No such movements could be detected, but the mobilization coincided with communal elections in Czechoslovakia and may have been intended to check possible SDP terrorism.[48] It is also possible that President Beneš wished to test the reaction of his French ally and of Great Britain to the risk of war. British reaction took the form of a repetition to Berlin of the warning made at the time of the Austrian crisis, that there was no certainty as to which Powers might eventually become involved if a war broke out, but, at the same time, of a warning to France that she could not expect Britain to co-operate with her in defending Czechoslovakia. The French government was informed that it would obtain im-

---

[47] Stanisławska, *Wielka i Mała Polityka Józefa Becka*, pp. 148–9.

[48] *NDHM*, no. 13. Krofta wrote to Fierlinger, the Czechoslovak Minister in Moscow, that the Henleinists could not carry out their plans; Zdenek Fierlinger, *Ve Službách ČSR* (In the Service of the Czechoslovak Republic, Prague, 1951), vol. I, p. 91.

mediate assistance if France were attacked, but that 'if the French Government were to assume that His Majesty's Government would at once take joint military action with them to preserve Czechoslovakia against German aggression, it is only fair to warn them that our statements do not warrant any such assumption'.[49]

Although Bonnet was aware of the attitude of the British government, he used the crisis as an opportunity to exercise pressure on Poland. He suggested to Ambassador Łukasiewicz that the Polish government should warn Germany, as the British had done—but not the French—of the consequences of a war. The French Foreign Minister attempted to use the Soviet Union as a lever by proposing that, if Poland came out actively on the side of France and Britain, he would see to it that the role of the USSR in a possible conflict with Germany would be adjusted to Polish requirements. He asked Łukasiewicz to transmit two questions to Col. Beck: whether Poland would be willing to execute a *démarche* in Berlin similar to that of Great Britain, and what he intended to do if an armed conflict broke out between Britain and France on the one hand, and Germany on the other.[50]

Col. Beck's first reaction to the French suggestion was that the *démarche* proposed by Bonnet was inconceivable, for it would mean the end of the Polish policy of 'equilibrium' between the two camps, and bring Poland into immediate conflict with Germany. As he was leaving on a state visit to Sweden he left instructions that if Ambassador Noël were to repeat Bonnet's questions, he should be told that no decision could be taken in the absence of the Foreign Minister and that, in any case, the Franco-Polish alliance was a purely defensive one.[51] He then, however, changed his mind and sent a highly significant instruction to Łukasiewicz. The instruction consisted of six points, two of which—the second and sixth—proclaimed respectively that a Polish *démarche* in Berlin would constitute a

[49] *DBFP*, 3, I, no. 271.
[50] Łukasiewicz to Foreign Minister, Paris, 22 May 1938, cypher telegram no. 50, APEL, Cyphers, 1938; Łukasiewicz to Foreign Minister, Political Report, 27 May 1938, MFA (London), P–F, 1938.
[51] Szembek, *Journal*, 22 May 1938, p. 311.

'unilateral obligation' for Poland not foreseen by the Franco-Polish alliance, but that Poland was always ready, as on 7 March 1936, to fulfil her treaty obligations and would welcome friendly discussions of all 'new phenomena'. In reply to Bonnet's question on Polish policy in case of war, Beck answered that a wider conflict would create a new situation in which the Polish government would reserve its freedom of decision.[52]

It is interesting that in the meanwhile (on 23 May), an article by Augur (Poliakoff) in the London *Evening Standard* claimed that Beck had told Ambassador Moltke that if Britain and France should defend Czechoslovakia, the Polish Army would be at their side. The article was obviously 'inspired', perhaps by the French government, to force a Polish declaration of policy. Beck reacted by ordering the Polish Embassy in London to deny in the press that any such interview had taken place. Augur's article, appearing at the same time as Bonnet's note to Beck, looked suspiciously like part of the same diplomatic manœuvre.

The Polish Foreign Minister's answer to Bonnet was the first sign on his part of a wish to engage in conversations with the French government on the subject of Czechoslovakia.[53] Bonnet's reaction to Beck's initiative of 24 May was, however, entirely negative. In reply to the message, he told Ambassador Łukasiewicz that in his opinion a Polish *démarche* in Berlin would not constitute a unilateral obligation; he also said that he did not consider the problem of the Polish minority in Czechoslovakia to be analogous to that of the German and he believed that Polish

---

[52] Beck to Łukasiewicz, Berlin, 24 May 1938, cypher telegram no. 12, APEL, Cyphers, 1938. The Polish text was published by Łukasiewicz in 'Sprawa Czechosłowacka w roku 1938 na tle Stosunków polsko-francuskich' (The Czechoslovak Problem in 1938 against the Background of Polish-French Relations), *Sprawy Międzynarodowe* (London, 1948), no. 6–7; Sir Lewis Namier published an English translation, *In the Nazi Era* (London, 1952), p. 185, where, however, the six points are given in a slightly different order.

[53] He had rejected French attempts to discuss the matter in 1935–37. As late as April 1938, he had also rejected a suggestion made by Ambassador Łukasiewicz that the time had come for such conversations. He justified his attitude by the argument that the new Daladier Cabinet would not last very long; Beck to Łukasiewicz, 22 April 1938, MFA (London), P–F, 1938. Beck's aversion to such discussion had been based in large part on his resentment against successive French governments for refusing to discuss a clarification of the Franco-Polish alliance.

claims could be settled after the 'bigger' problem had been solved.[54]

It is very likely that what Beck had in mind in his proposals of 24 May was some *quid pro quo* on the part of France in return for Polish diplomatic co-operation with respect to Germany and possibly a change of policy towards Czechoslovakia. On 26 May, Łukasiewicz commented that Poland had now the opportunity to restore closer relations with France and Britain[55] and Col. Beck may have hoped that he could clarify the interpretation of the Franco-Polish alliance and reach some understanding with both France and Britain on the Czechoslovak problem. Even Ambassador Noël drew Bonnet's attention to the fact that neither the alliance of 1921 nor the Mutual Assistance Pact of 1925 obliged Poland to aid France in case of a German attack on Czechoslovakia.[56] If Franco-Polish conversations had been seriously undertaken as a result of Beck's suggestion, these problems could have been discussed and a basis for co-operation might have been found. Bonnet, however, had no wish for the type of co-operation which might involve a guarantee of aid to Poland and Czechoslovakia. He not only rejected Col. Beck's initiative in May 1938, but also obliterated all traces of it in his memoirs.[57] Beck was so discouraged by the French reply that he

[54] Łukasiewicz to Foreign Minister, Paris, 28 May 1938, Political Report, MFA (London), P–F, 1938; see also *DM* I, no. 11.

[55] Łukasiewicz to Foreign Minister, Paris, 26 May 1938, cypher telegram no. 52, APEL, Cyphers, 1938.

[56] Georges Bonnet, *Défense de la Paix* (Geneva, 1946), vol. I, pp. 137–8.

[57] In his memoirs, Bonnet omits points 3 and 6 of Beck's instruction of 24 May, which dealt with the Polish Foreign Minister's reservation of a free hand in case of a wider conflict and his willingness to discuss new phenomena; cf. the text in Bonnet, p. 132, and Namier, *In the Nazi Era*, p. 185. Namier commented: 'The Polish offer, for what it was worth, was first torpedoed by Bonnet the statesman, and next obliterated by Bonnet the historian' (p. 186).

Three historians have recently commented on Beck's move. Boris Celovsky calls his proposals insincere and his reference to the Polish position in the Rhineland crisis a trick; *Das Münchener Abkommen*, p. 236. Hans Roos interprets the note of 24 May as Beck's attempt to secure his position in any eventuality, since he could not afford to be in the German camp in case of war; Roos, *Polen und Europa*, pp. 330–1. Wojciechowski interprets Beck's note as a 'bluff' and an attempt to play for time without committing himself; *Stosunki Polsko-Niemieckie*, p. 412.

None of these authors considers the possibility that Beck might have been willing to co-operate with France in return for a clarification of Franco-Polish relations. Even if he had merely wished to sound Bonnet on his position towards Czechoslovakia, his proposals committed him, in case of acceptance, to a mutual

instructed Łukasiewicz to drop the matter, despite the latter's report that the advisers at the Quai d'Orsay—unlike Bonnet— had grasped the intent of the Polish proposals and were eager for conversations.[58] Beck justified his attitude on the grounds that he did not consider the situation ripe for any basic 'straightening out' of Polish and French policy in Eastern Europe.[59]

In surveying the first phase of the Czechoslovak crisis, two questions arise: whether Beck's policy contributed decisively to worsen the situation of Prague and whether any other Polish government could have acted more constructively. In the first case, it should be noted that Beck's demand that the Polish minority in Czechoslovakia should be granted the same con- cessions as the German was recognized in principle by Prague and London, though not by Paris. Thus, although Beck's policy was essentially unfriendly to Czechoslovakia, it was not the decisive factor in the deepening crisis. The decisive factor here was the concerted policy of Paris and London to press Beneš in the direction of further concessions to the Sudeten Germans. In the second case, the leaders of the Polish opposition parties could only offer Prague an improvement in relations at the cost of territorial cessions to Poland and, in the case of the National Democrats, to Hungary as well. The prospective reward for such concessions varied from a more friendly attitude towards Czechoslovakia to the prospect of a military alliance. Beneš, however, apparently thought that he had nothing to gain from

---

discussion which might have had far-reaching consequences. It is true, of course, as Roos states, that Beck realized he could not be on the side of Germany in case of war but that was an established principle of Polish policy. At the time he did not fear war; if he had, he would not have set out on his state visit to Scandinavia. Stanisławska interprets Beck's move as a part of his policy of equilibrium between Germany and the Western Democracies, and also as a desire to keep open the possibility of intervention in Czechoslovakia when the situation allowed it; *Wielka i Mała Polityka Józefa Becka*, pp. 188–9.

[58] Łukasiewicz to Foreign Minister, Paris, 8 June 1938, cypher telegram no. 57, cited in Józef Chudek, 'Rozmowy Bonnet-Łukasiewicz w okresie przedmonachij- skim' (The Bonnet-Łukasiewicz Conversations in the Pre-Munich Period), *Sprawy Międzynarodowe* (Warsaw, 1958), no. 6, pp. 69–78, and also in Łukasiewicz, 'Sprawa Czechosłowacka', p. 43 (see n. 52).

[59] Beck to Łukasiewicz, 9 June 1938, cypher telegram no. 64, cited in 'Rozmowy Bonnet-Łukasiewicz' (see n. 58).

such sacrifices unless he obtained not only the support of Poland but also that of France.

Beck, despite his negative attitude, kept the door open for adjustment to a possible change in French and British policy. When this did not take place at the beginning of May, and when he was rebuffed by Bonnet at the end of the month, he was confirmed in his belief that Poland would have to continue the policy of non-commitment both to Germany and to the Western Democracies. While it is obvious that the chief beneficiary of this policy was Hitler, it is doubtful whether any other policy was possible. There was no agreed interpretation of the Franco-Polish alliance, France and Britain were exerting pressure on Beneš toward further concessions, and the Czechoslovak President in any case was no more willing than in the past to enter into an alliance with Poland. In these circumstances, any Polish government, with or without Beck, would, in giving diplomatic support to Prague, have risked a conflict with Germany. At the same time there was just as much sympathy in France and Britain for German claims to Danzig and the Corridor as there was for 'self-determination' in the Sudetenland. Ambassador Biddle reported from Warsaw in mid-June that Polish officials were ever mindful of the possibility of Germany turning her aggressive intentions against Poland.[60] Thus, a shift of policy in Warsaw might well have resulted in the shifting of the crisis from Czechoslovakia's western borders to Danzig, while neither Beck nor Beneš was willing to risk a conflict with Hitler without a guarantee of French aid.

There remained, of course, the Soviet Union. Several factors, however, barred the way to any co-operation between the USSR and Poland. First of all, it was clear that to aid Czechoslovakia Soviet troops would have to march through Poland; neither Rumania nor the Baltic States could provide an adequate land bridge and the communications necessary for mass troop movements, even had they been willing to do so. Not only Beck but all sectors of Polish opinion were violently opposed to such a

[60] Biddle to Secretary of State, 15 June 1938, SDNA, Poland, 1938, doc. file 7600 62/384, telegram no. 102. Wojciechowski interprets the attempts of France and Britain to draw Poland into diplomatic co-operation with them as motivated by the desire to end good Polish-German relations and draw Hitler into a new Four Power Pact; *Stosunki Polsko-Niemieckie*, p. 403.

possibility, and also to any such passage through Rumania, since Soviet troops could thus cut Poland's communications with her southern ally and the rest of the Balkans.[61] Furthermore, the West did not consider the Soviet Army capable of offensive action owing to the raging purges which decimated the higher ranks of the armed services. This opinion, together with distrust of Soviet aims and the continued desire for an agreement with Hitler, led to the failure of Litvinov's suggestions to Bonnet at the end of May that staff talks be held between France and the USSR. Finally, Beneš himself was averse to holding military talks with his Soviet ally without express French approval, and this was not forthcoming.[62] Thus, from all points of view, Polish military co-operation with the USSR was not feasible, while diplomatic support for the Soviet Union's friendly attitude towards Czechoslovakia would have entailed the risk of turning Hitler's anger against Poland. Matters were not made any easier by the violent anti-Polish campaign in Soviet papers and charges of Polish espionage liberally used in the purge trials.[63]

[61] For Beck's opposition to Soviet transit through Poland or Rumania, see Budurowycz, *Polish-Soviet Relations*, pp. 115–17.

[62] A Soviet military mission visited Czechoslovakia in March but no decisions seem to have been made; *NDHM*, no. 6. When in April the Soviet Union proposed negotiations between the Czechoslovak, French, and Soviet General Staffs, the Czechoslovak government replied that it must wait for French initiative; see Czechoslovak documents cited by Václav Král, 'Československo a Mnichov' (Czechoslovakia and Munich), *Československý Časopis Historický*, vol. VII, no. 1 (1959), p. 42. For the same version, see also *Istoriia Velikoi Otechestvennoi Voiny Sovetskovo Soiuza, 1941–1945*, vol. I, p. 146. For a general discussion of the Czechoslovak crisis in post-war Czechoslovak articles, see Vladimir Sojak (ed.) *O Československé Zahraniční Politice w Letech 1919–1939* (On Czechoslovak Foreign Policy in the Years 1919–1939, Prague, 1956), chap. VI, *passim*.

[63] Budurowycz, *Polish-Soviet Relations*, p. 107.

III

THE CZECHOSLOVAK CRISIS: WESTERN PRESSURE AND POLISH ADJUSTMENT

JUNE–12 SEPTEMBER 1938

THE Czechoslovak mobilization of 20 May initiated the second phase of the crisis, during which the 'Sudeten German' problem evolved from an apparently internal question into an international issue. In this phase the British and French governments continued to exert growing pressure on Prague to make concessions to the SDP, until London decided to take the matter into its own hands by sending a 'mediator', thus recognizing that the question could not be settled between Prague and Henlein. The German government, on the other hand, pursued its set policy of standing aside while the SDP maintained an inflexible position on its Eight-Point programme. Although the events of 20 – 22 May did not alter Hitler's plans to hold his hand until 1 October,[1] the SDP grew bolder. Henlein told a correspondent of the *Daily Mail* at the end of May that he saw three possible solutions to the 'Sudeten German' problem:

[1] On 28 May, at a conference on Operation Green, he repeated his statement of 20 May that only irreversible developments in Czechoslovakia or some favourable and unique opportunity in the European situation would make him act before 1 October; *DGFP*, D, II, no. 221; Celovsky, *Das Münchener Abkommen*, pp. 217–18. Later, in his speeches of 12 November 1938 and 30 January 1939, Hitler was to claim that the Czechoslovak mobilization had decided him to 'deal' with Czechoslovakia; this was clearly an *ex post facto* argument aimed at world opinion.

autonomy, plebiscite, or annexation by Germany.[2] When the next phase of SDP strategy was discussed in Berlin, Henlein suggested that if the Czechoslovak government yielded to all his demands, it should be faced with a request to change its foreign policy—for this it could never grant.[3]

In this intermediate stage of the crisis, Poland was the object of continued French and British pressure to abandon her negative attitude towards Czechoslovakia in favour of support or benevolent neutrality, while she was simultaneously subjected to German promises and pressures in the sphere of Danzig and minority problems. The task of Polish diplomacy was to watch the Western Democracies carefully for any signs of a more determined attitude, not to risk a conflict with Germany, and to continue preparations for a 'Third Europe' in case Czechoslovakia should finally be abandoned to Hitler.

French policy towards Poland moved along the lines traced by Bonnet during the crisis of 20 – 22 May, and, as before, it was devoid of any far-sighted objectives. Indeed, while the French Foreign Minister tried to obtain a statement of policy from the Polish government, he also contemplated the abrogation of the Franco-Polish alliance. Ambassador Noël, however, advised Bonnet against such a step, pointing out that it would throw not only Poland but also Rumania into the arms of Germany.[4] The French Ambassador in Warsaw concentrated his efforts on obtaining a statement of Polish policy on Czechoslovakia from Marshal Śmigły-Rydz, whom he had long credited with serious differences of opinion from Col. Beck. Noël tried to obtain from Śmigły-Rydz a restatement of his alleged declaration in 1936, that Poland would never attack Czechoslovakia or find herself opposing France in the event of war. Śmigły-Rydz, however, showed no inclination to commit himself on this question, probably because he suspected that the French government might use such a declaration as a lever on Poland. Noël's impression from his conversation with Śmigły-Rydz was that if Germany successfully invaded Czechoslovakia, Poland could be expected to take Trans-Olza in order to prevent its falling into

[2] *Daily Mail*, 25 May 1938.
[3] *DGFP*, D, II, no. 327.
[4] Bonnet, *Défense de la Paix*, I, p. 138.

German hands. He thought that Poland would remain neutral if more extensive hostilities should develop, or choose the side most favourable to her interests.[5]

In June, the French Foreign Minister belatedly responded to Beck's initiative of 24 May but only in order to use it for his own ends. In return for a formal declaration that Poland would not attack Czechoslovakia, Bonnet hinted that he might oppose closer Franco-Soviet relations. What is more, despite his earlier statement to Łukasiewicz, that the problem of the Polish and German minorities in Czechoslovakia could not be considered on the same level, he informed the Polish Minister that the French Ambassador in Prague had been instructed to advise the Czechoslovak government that the Polish minority should simultaneously be granted the same rights as the Sudeten Germans. He also asked for a Polish recognition of the League of Nations Covenant, which obligated each member to come to the aid of the victim of aggression.[6] In a further elaboration of his offer, Bonnet promised that in return for 'positive results' in conversations on East Central Europe, France would limit the role of the USSR as an eventual ally and even obtain guarantees for Poland in this matter. These proposals did not have much effect on Beck, since it was a well-known fact that the Soviet Union did not enter into the calculations of either London or Paris. The only concrete result of the Bonnet-Łukasiewicz conversations was the French recognition of Warsaw's claim that the Polish minority in Czechoslovakia should obtain the same concessions as the German minority.

When Bonnet found himself balked of an official Polish statement of policy, he decided to obtain it by a subterfuge. He instructed Noël to ask Beck for a written confirmation of a declaration which, he asserted, had been made to him by Łukasiewicz, namely, that Poland would not attack Czechoslovakia and that she would carry out her obligations under the League of Nations Covenant. At the same time, he tried to obtain from Łukasiewicz a declaration of Poland's attitude of

---

[5] For accounts of the Noël–Śmigły-Rydz conversation of 3 June 1938, see *DBFP*, 3, II, no. 375; Bonnet, *Défense de la Paix*, I, pp. 139–40.

[6] Łukasiewicz to Foreign Minister, Paris, 11 June 1938, cypher telegram no. 58, APEL, Cyphers, 1938.

non-aggression towards Czechoslovakia, on the basis of an alleged statement made by Śmigły-Rydz to Noël on 3 June.[7] Neither the Marshal nor Łukasiewicz had, of course, made any such statement. Bonnet's aim in this manœuvre was simply to tie Beck down by an exchange of notes.[8] The Polish Foreign Minister saw through the stratagem and refused Noël's request to this effect.[9] A few days later he explained his refusal by saying that it was not customary for the Polish government to commit itself on a policy in an inflexible fashion, and he expressed his surprise that the French government wished for such an exchange of notes in view of the exhaustive conversations which had taken place in Paris. He hoped that a 'contact amical' with France would be maintained, and said that he did not plan to break with the League of Nations. When Noël seized upon this statement and asked what harm there would be in making such a declaration in writing, Beck angrily retorted that 'such a question put him in the position of a Gentleman who is asked to declare in writing that he does not cheat at cards'. In partial explanation for this outburst, he told Noël that he did not know what use the Czechoslovak government might make of such a declaration, thus giving the Ambassador a hint of Polish suspicions as to the purity of French intentions.[10]

While the Polish Foreign Minister carefully avoided any commitment to France on Czechoslovakia, he also avoided any commitment to Germany. In mid-June, Ambassador Lipski brought a reply to Göring's proposal, made at the time of the May crisis, that Poland, Germany, and Hungary should apply economic pressure to Czechoslovakia. Lipski transmitted the message that his government did not consider such action desirable because combined Polish and German economic pressure on Czechoslovakia might have undesirable international, economic, and political consequences.[11] Göring was

---

[7] Bonnet prints Noël's account of his conversation with Śmigły-Rydz on 3 June 1938, in which no such statement was made; see n. 5; see also Noël, *L'Agression Allemande contre la Pologne*, p. 217.

[8] Bonnet admits this was his aim, Bonnet, *Défense de la Paix*, I, p. 165.

[9] Szembek, *Journal*, 8 July 1938, p. 324; see also Beck to Łukasiewicz, 8 July 1938, cypher telegram no. 47, APEL, Cyphers, 1938.

[10] Note on the Conversation of Minister Beck with Ambassador Noël, 16 July 1938, MFA (London), P–F, 1938.

[11] *DGFP*, D, II, no. 255.

also unsuccessful in his attempts to obtain a statement of Polish policy on Czechoslovakia. A few days after Lipski's announcement of Polish reluctance to apply economic pressure, Göring reassured Lipski that Germany recognized Polish interests in 'a certain region of Czechoslovakia', and that she had no revisionist claims against Poland. He also said that the solution of the Sudeten German problem would be the end of German aspirations in Europe, whereupon Germany would turn her attention to colonial problems.[12] Lipski made no reply to these advances beyond restating the Polish attitude of 23 February, when Beck had declared his interest in a 'certain area' of Czechoslovakia, and requested that he be consulted in any German action against that country.[13]

As a result of Beck's non-committal policy, the German government was somewhat worried about the Polish attitude towards Czechoslovakia. Towards the end of June, a German Foreign Office memorandum counselled that everything should be done to avoid war, since it was to be feared that in a general conflict Poland would also have to be dealt with, and the later this would be, the better.[14] Moltke's reports from Warsaw were not very encouraging. He reported on 1 July that while the Polish Foreign Minister was hostile towards Prague and would most probably not support France in a conflict, he could not be relied upon to attack Czechoslovakia. The Ambassador thought, therefore, that Germany might make certain concessions to influence Poland in the right direction, such as the extension of the 1934 agreement, a solemn guarantee for the western frontier, and a binding assurance on Teschen or a recognition of Polish interests in Lithuania and in the Ukraine. Even then, concluded Moltke, Poland would act only in her own interests and could not be counted upon to hold to her side of the bargain in a serious situation.[15] While the views of Moltke and the experts of the Wilhelmstrasse on Poland were not at all sanguine, German military plans drawn up at the beginning of July actually took into account the possibility of a Polish attack against East

12 Lipski to Foreign Minister, Berlin, 19 June 1938, MFA (London), P–G, 1938.
13 See *supra* chap. I, pp. 47–8, n. 51, 52.
14 *DGFP*, D, II, no. 259.
15 *Ibid.*, no. 277; cf. Noël's opinion, *supra* n. 5.

Prussia.[16] Thus Beck's policy of 'balance' and non-commitment to either side did produce uncertainty as to Poland's attitude in Berlin. This by itself could have helped the Western Powers if their aim had been to exercise a realistic pressure on Hitler instead of merely seeking a face-saving procedure for the surrender of Czechoslovakia.

While Beck refused to commit himself, he also continued preparations for the eventual disintegration of Czechoslovakia by elaborating his plans for a Third Europe. Moltke noted that Beck's Baltic policy aimed to weld the Baltic States into a 'cordon sanitaire' under Polish leadership.[17] This was correct in the sense that, for Beck, the Baltic States constituted one of the two basic elements for a Third Europe, the other being the common frontier with Hungary. He considered that the 'bridge' between Poland and the western states lay through the Baltic and Scandinavia rather than through 'the artificial combination' of the Little Entente.[18] The importance of this concept in his policy can be seen from the fact that he did not postpone his visit to Sweden despite the May crisis. In June, July and August 1938, he paid official visits to Riga, Copenhagen, Tallinn, and Oslo.

Beck's chief object in the Baltic was to bring about a Scandinavian-Baltic-Polish Entente based on the powerful support of the British Navy. He saw the need for such support in order to

---

[16] The Strategic Order of 7 July 1938 spoke of holding out on the Eastern fortifications and in East Prussia until troops could be moved up after the defeat of Czechoslovakia; *DGFP*, D, II, no. 282. The head of Hungarian Military Intelligence, Col. Andorka, reported on 27 June that during his visit to Berlin he had offered General Tippelskirch and Admiral Canaris his services in the development of Polish-German military relations. He was told, however, that these were not friendly and that Germany would energetically develop its espionage action in Poland; see *A Müncheni Egyezmény*, no. 252.

[17] Moltke, 1 July 1938, *DGFP*, D, II, no. 277.

[18] Beck, *Dernier Rapport*, p. 154. Biddle reported on 4 May 1938, with reference to Beck's forthcoming visit to Scandinavia, that 'undoubtedly in the back of his mind is that long cherished hope, envisaging Poland's assuming the predominant role in a neutral area between Germany and the Soviet Union. . . . Beck is now becoming more sanguine in his desire to lay the foundation for a neutral zone in time to block Hitler's aim to make this area a bastion of Hitlerism *vis-à-vis* the Soviet'; SDNA, Poland, 1938, documentary file note 7600. 62/380, despatch no. 469. The chief of the Eastern Department in the Polish Ministry of Foreign Affairs, T. Kobylánski, told Col. Andorka at the end of June that Poland's ultimate objective was the creation of a north-south security belt in Eastern Europe; see *A Müncheni Egyezmény*, no. 252.

prevent the weak Baltic States from falling under the sway of either Germany or the USSR and he hoped also to persuade the Scandinavian States to abandon their policy of neutrality.[19] He did his best to convert the British government to this point of view but there is no evidence that it was even considered. At the end of June the Foreign Minister told Ambassador Kennard that Polish interests in the Baltic were not only the result of tradition but that they were dictated also by the desire to strengthen the stability of that region. He particularly asked the Ambassador to repeat his words to Lord Halifax and expressed the hope that the Foreign Secretary would understand this policy.[20] He expounded the same point of view to Duff Cooper, the First Lord of the Admiralty, when the latter visited Gdynia and Danzig at the beginning of August 1938 on a pleasure cruise. At this time Beck went a step further and suggested joint Polish-British support of the Baltic States as long as these pursued an independent policy.[21] Duff Cooper took no notice of this suggestion, however, and seems to have considered his visit to Gdynia and his talks with Beck as rather annoying,[22] while to his wife, the Polish Foreign Minister appeared as 'a colourful freak', and the cheering Poles surrounding the British yacht seemed to her as remote as the little men in the Bayeux tapestry.[23] Apart from Duff Cooper's lack of understanding, Beck's hopes of British support in the Baltic were doomed in any case—there was no place for them in the framework of appeasement. Far from desiring to strengthen Poland in the Baltic, the British government made no secret of its opinions on Danzig. At the League of Nations Council meeting in May, Lord Halifax had told Burckhardt that he considered

[19] The Counsellor in the U.S. Embassy in Warsaw, Winship, reported on 1 July 1938 that the visits of Gen. W. Stachiewicz, Col. Jaklicz, and Capt. Horach to Riga, Tallinn, and Helsingfors, while officially only a return of courtesy calls, were widely commented in the Polish press as steps towards military *rapprochement* with the Baltic and Scandinavian States; SDNA, Poland, 1938, documentary file note 7600, dispatch no. 569.

[20] Beck to Raczyński, 30 June 1938, cypher letter no. 15, APEL, Cyphers, 1938.

[21] Conversations between Col. Beck and Duff Cooper in Gdynia, 8 July 1938, cited by Roos, *Polen und Europa*, p. 335.

[22] He described his visits to Gdynia and Danzig as 'minor annoyances'; Duff Cooper (Viscount Norwich), *Old Men Forget* (London, 1954), p. 223; see also Burckhardt, *Meine Danziger Mission*, p. 173.

[23] Lady Diana Cooper, *The Light of Common Day* (London, 1959), pp. 227–8.

Danzig and the Corridor as the most harmful decisions of the Versailles Treaty. This statement was duly reported to Berlin.[24]

In the southern part of the projected Third Europe the major aim of Polish policy was to establish a common frontier with Hungary in Subcarpathian Ruthenia. After a short period, during which efforts were made to organize a group of patriots in this region who would co-operate with Poland, this policy was abandoned in favour of its annexation by Hungary.[25] In Slovakia, the Polish government gave a certain amount of support to the autonomist movement and cultivated relations with Father Andrej Hlinka's Slovak People's Party. Karel Sidor, editor of the party newspaper and a leading Slovak Deputy to the Parliament in Prague, served as intermediary between Warsaw and Bratislava. Polish support for Hlinka's autonomist demands was particularly strongly demonstrated at the end of May on the occasion of a visit to Poland by a delegation of American Slovaks on their way to Czechoslovakia. The delegates carried with them the original copy of the famous 'Pittsburgh Manifesto' which they were to present to their native land on the twentieth anniversary of its signature by Thomas G. Masaryk. Hlinka's party made use of the manifesto as a propaganda slogan by interpreting it as a promise of self-government which had not been kept by the Czechoslovak republic.[26] The Polish government, by means of official receptions for the delegation, speeches, and newspaper coverage, manifested its hearty support for Hlinka's demands. Thus the visit of the Slovak delegates was

[24] *DGFP*, D, V, no. 37, encl.

[25] When Col. Tadeusz Schaetzel had been Head of the Eastern Department of the Polish Foreign Ministry, he had pursued a policy of building up a Ruthene group independent of Russian ideological leanings to co-operate with Poland. This attempt failed and in 1938 the Polish government decided to hand its agencies in the region over to Hungary; letter of M. Chałupczyński (former Polish Consul in Bratislava) to Gen. I. Modelski, Angers, 31 May 1940, General Sikorski Historical Institute, London, Commission of Inquiry into the Causes of the Catastrophe of September 1939.

[26] The Pittsburgh Convention, signed on 30 June 1918 by Thomas G. Masaryk, the representatives of the Slovak League, and other organizations, foresaw a unified Czechoslovakia and a separate administration for Slovakia; see R. W. Seton-Watson, *A History of the Czechs and Slovaks* (London, 1943), p. 306; text in J. Lettrich, *History of Modern Slovakia*, New York, 1955, annex no. 5, pp. 289–90.

turned into a political demonstration of Polish sympathy for an autonomous Slovakia.[27]

Beck's views on the fate of Slovakia, in case of a disintegration of the Czechoslovak state, seemed to crystallize in June. He then apparently gave serious consideration to the incorporation of the province in Hungary, though with an extensive autonomy, a possibility he had only reluctantly considered in March. On 17 June, Count Janos Eszterházy, leader of the Hungarian minority in Czechoslovakia, outlined to Count Szembek the Budapest plans for the creation of an autonomous Slovakia within the borders of Hungary. Eszterházy suggested that Poland should be a guarantor for the Hungarian annexation of Slovakia, together with Germany and Italy. He apparently counted on German and Italian support in this matter, for he told Szembek that, during Hitler's visit to Italy, Ciano had spoken to him of the desirability of a Warsaw-Budapest-Belgrade-Rome Axis, parallel to the Rome-Berlin Axis.[28] It is evident that a tacit agreement was reached between Warsaw and Budapest on the subject of Slovakia at this time. At the beginning of July the Hungarian Ambassador in Berlin, Dome Sztojáy, told Göring that, aside from territory populated by persons of Polish origin, Poland would at most demand from Czechoslovakia minor frontier rectifications along the old Hungarian boundary.[29]

Col. Beck's projects for a Baltic Entente supported by Britain, and for a new power bloc in the Balkans supported by Italy, were based on reasonable assumptions. If Great Britain were to be

[27] See Roos, *Polen und Europa*, p. 323, and Celovsky, *Das Münchener Abkommen*, pp. 229–330.

[28] Szembek memorandum of 17 June 1938, M-Akten, cited by Roos, *Polen und Europa*, p. 341; see also the account of the Beck-Eszterházy conversation of 27 June, in *A Müncheni Egyezmény*, no. 250.

[29] *DGFP*, D, II, no. 284. At this time, Beck remarked that with regard to Czechoslovakia the Germans did not want to commit themselves either to Hungary or to Poland. The Foreign Minister stated that Poland could not go further than the Germans but had to watch them closely. The instruments of Polish policy were to be the Polish minority in Czechoslovakia and Slovak autonomy; Szembek, MSS, 6 July 1938. Also in July, Szembek visited Bucharest and talked with Foreign Minister Comnène about improving Rumanian-Hungarian relations and on the subject of Soviet passage through Rumania and Czechoslovakia. On this last point Comnène assured Szembek that Rumania would never allow it; Wojciechowski, *Stosunki Polsko-Niemieckie*, p. 429.

persuaded to commit herself at all this seemed more likely in the sphere of sea power than in any other, and it was British sea power which was needed to keep the Baltic free of German control, a state of affairs which Britain might be expected to desire in case of war. It also seemed reasonable to suppose that Germany, and, in particular, Italy,[30] would support a new Balkan bloc which would be based on close co-operation between Poland and Hungary. In any case, Beck's projected Third Europe did not constitute a dogmatic policy to be followed regardless of international developments. He regarded it as an alternative system of power relations in Eastern Europe in case the Czechs should be abandoned by their ally and fall under the domination of Germany. For this reason he avoided any commitments to either side and carefully followed the evolution of Franco-British policy towards Czechoslovakia.

After the May crisis the British government decided to concentrate all its efforts on finding a peaceful solution to the Czechoslovak problem. The right-wing press continued to favour the SDP demands and even supported the analogous demands of the Polish and Hungarian minority groups. The guiding principle of this policy was the desire to avoid all risk of war. As the *Daily Telegraph* of 8 June 1938 put it, perhaps not without a touch of sarcasm, 'Anything which can be got without a shot being fired can count upon the agreement of the British.' The leading articles in *The Times* became frankly pro-German.[31] An article on 3 June supported the attitude of W. R. Matthews, Dean of St. Paul's, who advocated the cession of the Sudetenland to Germany. Whether officially inspired or not, the article reflected the views already expressed in the article of 14 May.[32] Lord Halifax was obliged to send a formal denial to Prague that

[30] During his state visit to Italy in March 1938, Beck observed that Mussolini was interested in cautiously building a bulwark against German penetration into the Danubian and Balkan regions. Beck and Ciano had agreed to co-operate in an effort to improve relations between Rumania and Hungary, Poland being responsible for the former and Italy for the latter; see Debicki, *Foreign Policy of Poland*, p. 113.

[31] *History of The Times* (London, 1952), vol. IV, part II, p. 920.

[32] The authors of the *History of The Times* (p. 924) think this conceivable but unlikely. Celovsky thinks it inconceivable that Geoffrey Dawson, the editor-in-chief, should not have consulted Chamberlain first; *Das Münchener Abkommen*, p. 263. For the article of 14 May, see *supra*, ch. II, p. 73.

The Times represented in this instance the official views of the government. At the same time, however, the Foreign Secretary asked the French government to apply pressure on Prague by a threat to 'reconsider' the French attitude towards the Franco-Czechoslovak alliance.[33] There was also some thought of settling the matter by an international conference. The French Ambassador in Berlin, André François-Poncet, suggested to Henderson that France, Great Britain, and Germany should meet together and agree on the neutralization of Czechoslovakia, giving their guarantees to Prague in return for the surrender of its alliances. This proposal, which foreshadowed the final settlement, was, however, rejected by Halifax, on the grounds of the British aversion to commitments and guarantees, and by Ribbentrop, who opposed settlement by conference.[34]

Up to mid-June, British policy towards Prague had been one of pressure on Beneš to grant concessions to the SDP, but, at the same time, of giving no support to any programme put forward by the President for fear that any retreat would involve London also.[35] When the situation showed no improvement, the British government proceeded to embark on a policy of indirect commitment by the policy of 'mediation'. The idea of employing a mediator between Prague and the SDP had already been mooted at the time of the May crisis when Halifax had suggested it to the Czechoslovak Ambassador in London, Jan Masaryk. The Foreign Secretary had at that time also proposed that Prague's alliances with France and the USSR should be replaced by an international guarantee of Czechoslovak neutrality.[36] This development in British thinking was well known to the Polish government, for Chamberlain communicated part of the new line of thought to the Polish Ambassador. At a luncheon in the Polish Embassy, Chamberlain asked Raczyński whether the

[33] *DBFP*, 3, I, no. 354.

[34] *Ibid.*, nos. 381, 387, 391, *passim*; *DGFP*, D, II, no. 264.

[35] Writing about his mission to Prague at the end of May, Lord Strang, then Head of the Central Department in the Foreign Office, says: 'We did not . . . want to get into the position of endorsing Dr Beneš's plan (however good it might be) and then have to run away from it because the Germans rejected it and became violent again'; Lord Strang, *Home and Abroad*, p. 133, n. 2.

[36] *DBFP*, 3, I, no. 315. Celovsky believes that Halifax was thinking of a guarantee to be given by the neighbouring states; *Das Münchener Abkommen*, p. 268, n. 2.

neutralization of Czechoslovakia might not provide the basis for an understanding with Germany. At the same time, he reaffirmed his aversion to the granting of any automatic guarantees.[37]

The British decision to confront President Beneš with 'mediation' was carried out on 20 July. The British Minister in Prague, Basil Newton, advised Beneš to accept the proposal—or face the possibility of a British publication of his refusal if the negotiations with the SDP should break down. The proposal came as a great shock to the President[38] because he realized that a mediator would tie his hands and leave the final decision to London and Berlin. Under pressure from Paris, however, he accepted the suggestion on 23 July and this allowed Chamberlain to announce in the House of Commons on 26 July the mission of Lord Runciman as the answer to a 'request' by the Czechoslovak government. The announcement was naturally welcome in Berlin where it was known that the neutralization of Czechoslovakia and the cession of the Sudetenland were already envisaged by the British Prime Minister.[39]

The Polish government reacted to the announcement of the British mission by expressing the hope that Runciman would emphasize to Prague the necessity of serious and equal treatment for all the minorities, including the Poles. The Polish Chargé d'Affaires in London was instructed to say that any discrimin-

[37] Raczyński to Foreign Minister, London, 14 June 1938, cypher telegram no. 26, APEL, Cyphers, 1938.

[38] Newton reported that 'He seemed greatly taken aback and much upset, flushing slightly, and hardly recovering his full equanimity by the end of the conversation which lasted over two hours'; *DBFP*, 3, I, no. 521.

[39] At the end of June, Helmuth Wohlthat, one of the directors of the Economic Department of the German Foreign Ministry, talked with Sir Horace Wilson, a close adviser of Chamberlain. Wohlthat's impression was that the British government would accept the incorporation of the Sudetenland in Germany; *DGFP*, D, II, no. 269. The Hungarians were also aware of the British attitude towards Czechoslovakia. On 15 July the head of the Foreign Minister's Cabinet, István Csáky, reported a conversation with the Foreign editor of *The Times*, Kean. Kean said that Hungary, through her good relations with Italy, might help Great Britain to reach an agreement with that country. As for Germany, Chamberlain was ready to recognize German claims to colonies and a British-German agreement would facilitate German expansion eastwards. Csáky had the impression that the British government would not protest against a German takeover of Czechoslovakia if this were done with due respect to outward forms; see *A Müncheni Egyezmény*, no. 265.

ation with regard to the Polish minority would lead to a worsening of Polish-Czechoslovak relations.[40] Although the Polish Chargé d'Affaires reported Lord Halifax as saying on 27 July that concessions made to the German minority should be extended to the Poles and Hungarians also,[41] the British government failed to grant the Polish request. The Chargé d'Affaires was informed that, if Lord Runciman were to undertake any action for the Polish minority, it would have to be on the invitation of the Czechoslovak government and of the minority itself.[42] This was, of course, the last thing which Beck desired, for it would have made the settlement of his claims in Czechoslovakia dependent on Prague and London; he therefore beat a hasty retreat.[43] A few days later Mr. Strang assured the Polish representative that Lord Runciman would consider the interests of the Polish minority,[44] but in the end London refused to undertake any such obligations to Poland on the grounds that 'the British government had only a certain amount of influence in Prague and it was important to reserve this influence for use in immediate and serious cases'.[45] In fact, this was not the reason, for Bonnet had long ago assured Łukasiewicz that Prague would have to accept whatever London and Paris proposed. The real motive for the British refusal to press the claims of the Polish minority as well as the German was the position of the French government, which was hostile to any prospect of territorial changes in Czechoslovakia beyond those considered inevitable.

The problems which the Polish Foreign Minister had to envisage during the Czechoslovak crisis were not confined to

[40] Beck to Chargé d'Affaires in London, 26 July 1938, cypher telegram no. 52, APEL, Cyphers, 1938.

[41] Chargé d'Affaires to Foreign Minister, London, 30 July 1938, Political Report, APEL, P–GB, 1938.

[42] Chargé d'Affaires to Foreign Minister, London, 1 August 1938, cypher telegram no. 57, APEL, Cyphers, 1938.

[43] Beck instructed the Chargé d'Affaires, tongue in cheek, to say that if the Polish government had misunderstood the role of Lord Runciman as part of the British intervention to maintain peace, then the Polish *démarche* should be considered as not having taken place; Beck to Chargé d'Affaires in London, Oslo, 5 August 1938, cypher telegram no. 1, APEL, Cyphers, 1938.

[44] Chargé d'Affaires to Foreign Minister, London, 9 August 1938, cypher telegram no. 59, APEL, Cyphers, 1938.

[45] Halifax to Norton (British Chargé d'Affaires in Warsaw), 12 August 1938, *DBFP*, 3, II, no. 612.

uncertainty as to the ultimate action of the Western Democracies; he also had to face a war of nerves with Germany. Berlin strove to obtain a declaration of Polish policy in an eventual conflict by the dual method of courtship and menace. This war of nerves was nowhere more apparent than in Danzig. Here, as Himmler remarked to Burckhardt, Gauleiter Forster and President Greiser complemented each other: the one pushed while the other acted as a brake.[46] There were declarations of friendship on the one hand, and 'whisper propaganda' on the other, which propagated the slogan of the return of the Free City to Germany and threatened an inevitable war with Poland.[47] When Goebbels visited Danzig at the end of June for the festivities of the *Danziger Gaukulturwoche* (the Danzig District Culture Week), he told the youth of the City that they belonged to the Führer and were witnesses to the German character of the City.[48] In mid-July the suspicions of the Polish government were aroused on the occasion of Forster's visit to London. There were fears of an agreement on Danzig at the expense of Polish interests. As it happened, Forster was unable to see any member of the British government. He only spoke with Churchill, and there is no mention in Churchill's memorandum of any proposals on the Free City.[49] Rumour was nevertheless rife that a plebiscite might be proposed, and Ambassador Raczyński reported to Beck that Great Britain would probably take no action in Danzig if the Senate managed to keep a cloak of legality over its activities.[50]

In the City itself the situation grew tense. At the beginning of August the Senate suddenly broke off negotiations which had been going on for one and a half years and were on the point of finalization. At one stage on 22 July, Beck told Burckhardt that Danzig had become the test-case of Polish-German relations and that Polish policy would be influenced by the manner in which

[46] Commissioner General to Foreign Minister, Danzig, 24 May 1938, APEL, Gdańsk, 1938.

[47] Commissioner General to Foreign Minister, Danzig, 21 June 1938, APEL, *ibid*.

[48] Commissioner General to Foreign Minister, Danzig, 28 June 1938, APEL, *ibid*.

[49] Churchill's memorandum on his conversation with Forster, 14 July 1938, is to be found in *DM*, I, no. 13.

[50] 'Forster's Visit to London,' Raczyński to Foreign Minister, 22 July 1938, Political Report, APEL, P–GB, 1938.

Berlin handled the question. If Hitler put pressure on Poland, said the Polish Foreign Minister, she would reply with counter-pressure.[51] Beck well knew that his words would be reported in Berlin. It was in character with his whole policy that, even at this stage, when relations with France were as bad as ever, he should have warned Hitler against using force in Danzig. Throughout the summer Beck had to contend with German pressure on the Free City.

The other sensitive sphere in German-Polish relations was the minority question and here the Germans also kept up an insidious tension. In the spring of 1938, the *Volksdeutsche Mittelstelle* (Central Office for Germans Abroad) directed its efforts to the ending of the split between the German parties in Poland and to the unification of these parties into one organization. The leader of the National Socialist *Jungdeutsche Partei* (Young Germans' Party), Senator Wiesner, made a speech in Poznań on 1 May, in which he outlined a programme of demands somewhat reminiscent of Henlein's 'Eight Points'.[52] The work of unification stalled, due to the personal rivalries of the German leaders in Poland, but these developments were bound to cause anxiety to the Polish government. What is more, at the beginning of July the German Ambassador in Warsaw again took up the old project of setting up a mixed commission on minorities[53]—a proposal which the Polish government had always evaded since it would have put minority problems outside its direct control.

As the summer drew to a close and the Führer's October deadline approached, Berlin again sounded Warsaw on its attitude towards Prague in an eventual conflict. In a report of 11 August the Polish Ambassador wrote that Göring and other members of the more radical wing of the Party did not believe in a peaceful settlement of the Czechoslovak question; what was more, added Lipski, the British seemed resigned on this matter. Ambassador

---

[51] Burckhardt, *Meine Danziger Mission*, pp. 163–4.

[52] Wiesner demanded that the Polish government grant the German minority its own schools and allow German teachers to teach there; that it give employment to Germans and orders to German enterprises; that it protect the German state of possession and the rights of the German minority with reference to the state and nation; see *Sprawy Narodowościowe* (Warsaw, 1938), no. 3, p. 304. Since the Germans already had their own schools, Wiesner's demands probably envisaged complete control and an increase in their number.

[53] *DGFP*, D, V, no. 48.

Henderson had said that if Lord Runciman failed to bring about an agreement, and if the fault lay with the Czechs, then the Germans would be quite right in claiming that force was the only solution. Göring at this time made a new advance to Lipski. At a reception given for the Italian Air-Marshal, Italo Balbo, the German Field-Marshal told Lipski that the time had come for a discussion of closer Polish-German relations. He suggested that both countries suspend espionage activities against each other and exchange information on the Soviet Union and Czechoslovakia. On this occasion, Göring repeated his earlier offers of German help in case of a Polish-Soviet conflict and denied rumours of German plans to take the Ukraine, remarking that he knew Poland had certain interests there. He told Lipski that the Sudeten German affair was nearly drawing to its close and that the time was nearing when consultations and decisions between Warsaw and Berlin would be necessary.

The Polish Ambassador's reply to these advances was non-committal. The only new element in his answer was one already known to Berlin, that of the common Polish-Hungarian frontier. But Lipski did not have much faith in German assurances on this question, for he told the Hungarian Ambassador that he feared Polish and Hungarian interests might be disregarded in the settlement of the Czechoslovak problem, and that both should secure their interests ahead of time. Sztojáy expressed agreement but emphasized Hungary's need for Polish help and declared his fear of possible Yugoslav and Rumanian opposition to Hungarian expansion. Lipski concluded his report with the remark that, unless Beneš accepted the SDP demands for equal national status with the Czechoslovaks and for territorial autonomy, he would be abandoned by Great Britain and France and would have to face the Reich alone. A peaceful solution was all the more unlikely since the American Ambassador to Berlin, who had just returned from Prague, reported that President Beneš would not agree to the SDP demand for territorial autonomy.[54]

[54] Lipski to Foreign Minister, 11 August 1938. See Józef Chudek (ed.), *Wrześniowy Kryzys Czechosłowacki w Raportach Ambasadora Lipskiego* (The Czechslovak Crisis of September in the reports of Ambassador Lipski), *ŻH*, 7 (Warsaw, 1958), doc. I; English text in *DM* I, no. 15.

The official Polish reply to Göring's proposals of 11 August was contained in an instruction sent to Ambassador Lipski two days later. He was directed to insist on autonomy for Slovakia and to sound out Berlin on its attitude towards Hungary; finally, he was also to mention the situation in Danzig. Any new German proposals were to be taken 'ad referendum', and the Ambassador was also to see if there was any desire on Göring's part for a personal conversation with Beck. The Polish Foreign Minister suggested that this could take place on his way to Geneva on 7 September.[55] As for Göring's suggestion that espionage activities might be suspended, Beck thought that Lipski might mention on some appropriate occasion the possibility of a mutual cessation of the practice of using the minorities for political and other activities harmful to their respective governments.[56] In this way, the Polish Foreign Minister reacted in a typical manner to the German advances, with suggestions along the lines of his Third Europe project, and with an attempt to obtain a better position on the minority question.

The second conversation between Göring and Lipski took place on 24 August. On the German side, it marked another attempt to discover the Polish plan of action in an eventual conflict over Czechoslovakia, while on the Polish side the aim was to ascertain the attitude of Berlin towards Hungary and the extent of German willingness to come to some agreement on Danzig. It should be borne in mind that the conversation took place against the background of a rapidly worsening situation in Czechoslovakia and of the decreasing likelihood of any Western support for that country against Germany. Lord Runciman's mission had not brought the conflicting sides any nearer. Göring set out to impress Lipski with the impossibility of British and French aid for Czechoslovakia. He pointed out that the British Air Force would not be ready for battle before the end of 1939,[57] while the British Fleet, though powerful, was awaiting

[55] Łubieński to Lipski, Warsaw, 23 August 1938, typed note, MFA (London), P–G, 1938.
[56] Beck to Lipski, Warsaw, 23 August 1938, handwritten note, MFA (London), P–G, 1938.
[57] Göring was, if anything, too optimistic about the RAF. According to plan 'K', the RAF was to have a total striking force of 1,360 planes by March 1941,

the completion of new ships. Göring then spoke of the great fortifications being constructed on Germany's western frontier opposite the Maginot Line; he also stated with assurance that Mussolini would mobilize if France did, so that Paris would have to face a war on two fronts. The Field-Marshal told Lipski that General Vuillemin, the Commander-in-Chief of the French Air Force, had told him that the French-Czechoslovak alliance could come into play only through the League of Nations, and then only if Czechoslovakia were declared the victim of unprovoked aggression. This, Göring cynically assured Vuillemin, would never happen. On the contrary, he told Lipski that Germany would be attacked or 'provoked' by Czechoslovakia, for example, by an 'incident' in the Sudetenland. In connection with Czechoslovakia, Göring pointedly remarked that he did not agree with the British advice to wait nor with the belief that all could be settled with time. He did not see how Czechoslovakia could make any real concessions, owing to the large minorities within the state.[58]

Lipski, in replying, confined himself to the directives which he had received from Warsaw and tried to discover the extent of German support for Hungarian plans. On this point Göring was quite explicit. While the German government had no agreement with Budapest, it expected the Hungarians to move against Czechoslovakia after the Germans. If Hungary did not stir, said Göring, this would be inconvenient for Berlin, since the Czechoslovak Army could then retreat into Slovakia. The Field-Marshal said that the Yugoslav Prime Minister had agreed to let Hungary have a free hand against Prague. In any case, Göring expected Poland and Hungary to arrange the action between them and he agreed glibly that Slovakia should have an extensive autonomy, whether it was annexed by Poland or by Hungary. From the Field-Marshal's remarks it was clear that Germany did not intend to give any direct military aid to Budapest in any action by the latter, although such action was apparently desired by Berlin.

---

while the estimated German figure for 1938 was 1,350. Britain was almost three years behind Germany in aircraft production; see Sir John Slessor, *The Central Blue: Recollections and Reflections* (London, 1956), p. 184.

[58] Ambassador Lipski's conversation with General Field-Marshal Göring, 24 August 1938, ZH, 7, doc. III.

Göring reassured Lipski of German readiness to extend the 1934 agreement for twenty-five years and, for the rest, made vague allusions to recognizing Polish interests in the Ukraine. It was significant that he held out prospects of a major settlement between Berlin and Warsaw only after the solution of the Czechoslovak crisis. Then Germany would by 'an act in great style' show that definite stabilization had been reached, and Poland would also benefit. He simply noted Lipski's allusion to Polish difficulties in Danzig, but he was more expansive on the subject of minorities. He even remarked that since the Polish-German frontier was recognized—which, as far as Germany was concerned, it was not—there might be a transfer of populations. This remark must have been a manœuvre either to avoid the discussion of final recognition for Poland's western frontier or to encourage the Poles in the belief that Berlin was ready to grant the much desired recognition. In conclusion, Göring expressed his readiness to meet with Col. Beck on 6 or 7 September.[59]

On the basis of his conversation with Göring on 24 August, Lipski estimated that Polish neutrality was important for Germany and that the time was therefore ripe for putting forward formal demands for a 'positive' solution of the outstanding problems in Polish-German relations. He suggested that Poland should ask for an extension of the agreement of 1934 and for a German declaration on the frontier with Poland analogous to those made with regard to Alsace-Lorraine and the German frontier with Italy. The Polish Ambassador took care to stress that he was not thinking in terms of an immediate and public Polish-German declaration, for this would be undesirable in view of Poland's relations with the Western Powers, but of a *pactum de contrahendo* which could be revealed at a suitable moment.[60] He was thinking of defining the price of Polish

---

[59] *Ibid.* Göring's non-committal remarks on Hungary were due to the failure of Hitler's attempt to obtain a guarantee of Hungarian co-operation in a war against Czechoslovakia; see Macartney, *October Fifteenth*, I, pp. 238–48. Admiral Horthy refused to commit himself without German military aid which Hitler was unwilling to give. One of the reasons may have been the Führer's dislike of the prospect of a common Polish-Hungarian frontier. He may have wished to limit Hungarian co-operation to the seizure of the Magyar districts of Slovakia. Horthy, for his part, was afraid of being tied to Germany in case of a European war.

[60] Lipski to Łubienski, Berlin, 26 August 1938, MFA (London), P–G, 1938.

neutrality. At the same time, steps were taken to discuss the possibility of Polish-Hungarian co-operation. Lipski talked with the Hungarian Regent who was on a state visit to Germany. Horthy emphasized the sincere relations between the two countries and hoped that they would soon achieve a common frontier. He told the Polish Ambassador to inform his government that he would soon send a 'trustworthy' person to Warsaw to discuss the situation.[61] It is clear from this conversation that no plans for concerted military action by the two countries had been made.

The Czechoslovak crisis began to enter its decisive stage at the end of August and the beginning of September 1938, when it became patently obvious that Lord Runciman's mission had failed in the face of the intransigence of the SDP. The British government therefore put increasing pressure on President Beneš. Newton bluntly told the President that in the event of war Czechoslovakia would be overrun and that she would not regain her frontiers of 1919 even if the outcome were to be a victory for France and England.[62] In London, Lord Halifax told the American Chargé d'Affaires that the Sudeten German question 'would be a most dubious issue on which to wage a war'. The British Foreign Secretary indicated that in his opinion the Sudeten grievances were soundly based, although in speaking of Hitler he thought that to all intents and purposes he was dealing with a madman.[63] At the same time, the British made it clear to Berlin in confidential conversations that the matter was now one of decision by mutual agreement. In London, Sir Horace Wilson, a close confidant of Chamberlain, told the German Chargé d'Affaires, 'If we two, Great Britain and Germany, come to an agreement regarding the settlement of the Czechoslovak problem, we shall simply brush aside the resistance that France and Czechoslovakia herself may offer to the decision.'[64] The same line of argument was pursued by Ambassador Henderson

---

[61] Ambassador Lipski's conversation with the Regent of Hungary, 24 August 1938, *ibid.* It is interesting in this connection that in his report of 26 August to Łubieński, Lipski wrote that he had confidential information to the effect that the Hungarians were not ready to move against Czechoslovakia alone but would follow the Poles if they did so; see *supra* n. 60.

[62] *DBFP*, 3, II, no. 758.   [63] *FRUS*, 1938, I, p. 550.

[64] *DM*, II, no. 7.

in Berlin when he told Weizsäcker that 'it was a question of forcing the unreliable Beneš to make a comprehensive offer to Henlein and tying him down to a public statement so that he could no longer evade the issue'.[65] In Paris, the Germans received the same assurance as in London. Bonnet openly told the German Ambassador that 'if Mr Beneš would not accept Lord Runciman's verdict, France would consider herself released from her engagements to Czechoslovakia'.[66] The French Foreign Minister did not stop at this, but spoke of a 'continued peaceful development by revision of the peace treaties and an understanding with France and Great Britain'.[67]

Lord Runciman did not conceal the policy of his government from Beneš. He told the President that if the choice were to be made between Henlein's 'Eight Points' and war, he was to be under no illusion as to British preference.[68] Beneš thereupon presented to the SDP leaders, on 5 September, his 'Fourth Plan' in which he virtually conceded all the demands embodied in Henlein's programme by proposing that Czechoslovakia should be divided into cantons as nationally homogeneous as possible.[69] The SDP, however, faithful to its strategy of never reaching agreement, broke off negotiations on the pretext of an 'incident' which took place in Moravská Ostrava on 7 September. On the same day *The Times* proposed in its leading article that the best solution of the Sudeten problem would be the cession of this territory to Germany.[70] In view of the British attitude towards this question, the article was not surprising, nor was it the first such proposal to be made.[71] Nevertheless, the article of 7 Septem-

---

[65] *DGFP*, D, II, no. 419.   [66] *DBFP*, 3, II, no. 747.
[67] *DGFP*, D, II, no. 422.   [68] *DBFP*, 3, II, no. 753.
[69] The first plan put forward was in the form of a projected Nationalities Statute which had been sent to London at the end of April and found inadequate. The second plan was the Nationalities and Language bill, rejected by the SDP on 28 July. The third plan was presented at the end of August and also rejected; its core was the proposition to reorganize Czechoslovakia into twenty nationally homogeneous cantons.
[70] *The Times*, 7 September 1938. The *History of The Times*, vol. IV, part II, p. 931, claims that Dawson's decision to publish the article was taken independently of any consultation with the government. From the correspondence between Henderson and Halifax, however, it is clear that the idea had long been current in Cabinet circles.
[71] It had already been suggested in the article published in the Canadian and American press on 14 May.

ber was the most decided formulation so far of British willingness to cede the disputed territory to Germany. Despite official denials, it reflected accurately enough the stand of the Cabinet on the matter. Almost from the outset of the Runciman mission, such a solution had been foreseen in one form or another. Indeed, in mid-August, Halifax wrote to Runciman that if his mission should end in failure, two possible suggestions could be made in order to avert war—a conference or a plebiscite—and, of these two, a conference was judged preferable.[72] The idea of a Great Power conference, which had been originally suggested by the French Ambassador in Berlin, François-Poncet, was taken up by Henderson at the beginning of September. The British Ambassador envisaged a conference of Germany, France, Great Britain, and Czechoslovakia, possibly with Poland and Hungary as 'observers', though he thought it preferable to deal without them.[73] Thus, at the beginning of September, the crisis was inexorably moving towards its final dénouement.

As the situation in Czechoslovakia grew more tense, Berlin was still in a state of uncertainty as to Polish policy. At the end of August, Weizsäcker noted: 'Poland is on the alert and wants to keep all roads open for herself', and 'The only certainty is that, in event of war, Poland will not permit the Russians to set foot in their country.'[74] Similarly, in German military calculations the only favourable assumption regarding Warsaw was that a neutral Poland would restrict possible Soviet action in the Baltic region.[75]

German uncertainty as to Polish policy resulted in a temporary cessation of pressure on the Danzig sector and in minority problems. This relief was also partly due to the strong anti-German feeling in Poland which manifested itself in public demonstrations. Patriotic anti-German songs were sung in front of German consulates, German goods were boycotted, and criticism of Beck's policy appeared in the opposition press. Even the conservative Wilno paper, *Słowo*, directed by Stanisław 'Cat' Mackiewicz, who had always supported good relations

[72] *DBFP*, 3, II, no. 643.   [73] *Ibid.*, no. 771.
[74] *DGFP*, D, II, no. 409.
[75] Extended Case Green, 25 August 1938, *International Military Tribunal: Nazi Conspiracy and Aggression* (Washington, 1946), vol. III, doc. no. 375–PS, p. 282.

102

with Germany, now accused the Polish Foreign Minister of failing to obtain corresponding advantages from Berlin in return for Poland's friendly attitude.[76] Mackiewicz aptly summarized Beck's dilemma by asserting that Polish policy was a riddle: abroad, Poland was considered an ally of Germany, while at home public opinion believed that Germany was the historic foe of Poland. He noted that Poland was estranged from France and Britain, and that she had received nothing from Germany in return for her benevolent attitude towards German expansion. Furthermore, Mackiewicz desired Polish-German co-operation with a view to great aims in the East and thought that Poland could mediate between the Western Democracies and Germany, but Beck's policy of non-alignment with ideological blocs had brought none of these advantages, while the much advertised re-establishment of relations with Lithuania had not improved Poland's international position by one inch. In 1935, wrote Mackiewicz, he had suggested that a Polish-German *condominium* should be established in Danzig to replace the League mandate; instead, Poland had not only been denied any economic concessions in the Free City but instead of a *condominium* there was unquestioned German domination.[77]

While the so-called 'Germanophiles' criticized Beck for not obtaining compensations for Poland in return for her favourable attitude towards Germany, the rest of the non-official press warned against the danger of the German *Drang nach Osten.* The Christian Democratic *Polonia* noted the ominous formation of a 'Pomeranian Legion' on the model of the Austrian and Sudeten legions. It also pointed to the increasingly vocal slogan in Danzig of 'Zurück zum Reich' and suggested that a new government was needed in Poland to cope with the situation. As for Polish-German relations, declared the *Polonia,* a proof of German good will would be a declaration on the Polish-German frontier analogous to that given by Hitler to Italy. The same paper warned on 2 September that, if Czechoslovakia fell to Germany, the latter would be greatly strengthened by gains in

[76] *DGFP*, D, V, no. 53.
[77] *Słowo*, 20 August 1938; see *Opinia Polska wobec Mnachium w Świetle Prasy* (Polish Opinion on Munich in the Light of the Press, ed. Barbara Ratyńska, Warsaw, 1959), *ZH*, 9, pp. 1–3.

population, territory, armaments factories, and geographical position; Poland, on the other hand, would be threatened on her Carpathian frontier in the south, while any German drive to the south or into the Ukraine would encircle her completely. Moreover, if Poland decided to take Trans-Olza at the time of a German attack on Czechoslovakia, she would be automatically involved in a war with France and Britain. Finally, the chances of a common front with Hungary after a German victory in Czechoslovakia were slim since Budapest was already under the sway of the Rome-Berlin Axis. The Socialist *Robotnik* stressed that Poland must defend the justified rights of her minority in Czechoslovakia but she must also understand that a German annexation of that country would be dangerous to her. The paper suggested negotiations with the Czechs on that subject since such a step would not further Nazi aims.[78]

It is no wonder, in view of press opinion, that the German Ambassador in Poland expressed the fear that anti-German feeling might restrict the government's freedom of action on important issues.[79] In view of the uncertainty of Polish policy and of the anti-German feeling in the country, Hitler reverted to the old stand-by of ordering a temporary cessation of pressure on Warsaw. Hostile German press comment was suppressed.[80] The Führer asked Admiral Horthy to refrain from advising Poland that she should return the Corridor to Germany.[81] At the end of the summer the German government was feeling anxious about the conduct of Warsaw as the climax of the Czechoslovak crisis drew near. Beck, for his part, was preparing to press Germany for the compensation which he was accused of not having demanded earlier, compensation which he had in fact demanded but which he had failed to obtain. The Foreign Minister was more acutely aware than any of his critics of the need to balance German expansion by safeguarding Poland's vital interests, but, unlike them, he also knew that this was an extremely difficult and delicate task, the success of which depended on the development of the international situation.

[78] Ratyńska, pp. 16–17, 34, 37–40, 59.
[79] *DGFP*, D, V, no. 53.
[80] Szembek, *Journal*, 6 September 1938, p. 332.
[81] *DGFP*, D, V, no. 52. Horthy had already proposed this to Beck during his state visit to Poland in February.

At the beginning of September, Berlin again showed an active interest in Polish plans. On 5 September, Göring raised Lipski's suggestion, made on 24 August, of a talk with Col. Beck. He declared that he wished to give the Polish Foreign Minister 'some explanations of the greatest importance', and affirmed German willingness to go far to satisfy Polish wishes.[82] Beck, however, decided to avoid such a meeting before the League of Nations session in September, since he felt that such a visit might give the appearance of commitment to Germany. He expressed instead readiness to see the Field-Marshal after 20 September, perhaps at his estate at Rominten, as Göring had suggested.[83]

In the first week of September, events brought about a development in Beck's policy towards Germany. The tension in Czechoslovakia was approaching boiling point and any new incident threatened to lead to war. The Polish Foreign Minister decided that the time had come to press Berlin for information as to the concessions it would be willing to make on the outstanding issues in Polish-German relations. Ambassador Lipski was instructed to sound out Göring and Ribbentrop on this subject at the Party Conference which was to be held in Nuremberg on 7 – 12 September.

Lipski's efforts to carry out his mission were fruitless. He tried to bring up the subject of Danzig by telling Göring that certain 'international elements' hoped to use the City as an instrument for poisoning Polish-German relations. Göring, however, averted discussion by saying that he had telephoned Gauleiter Forster and had told him that Danzig must not complicate relations between Poland and Germany. He also repeated the old assurances that Germany had no revisionist claims against Poland. Ribbentrop likewise refused to take up Lipski's hints for a discussion of the Free City. On the contrary, the German Foreign Minister even employed a veiled threat by telling Lipski that he would work for Polish-German interests only as

[82] Lipski to Foreign Minister, Berlin, 6 September 1938, MFA (London), P–G, 1938.
[83] Łubieński to Lipski, 5 September 1938, by courier, *ibid.* It should be noted that while on 24 August Göring did not seem over-anxious to meet Beck, on 5 September the roles were reversed. It cannot, therefore, be said that the Polish government was at all times more anxious to hold such a meeting than the Germans; for the latter opinion see J. Chudek, *ŻH* 7, p. 6.

long as Beck held to his policy, and that 'small problems' should be solved in a 'friendly' manner.[84]

The result of Lipski's Nuremberg conversations showed that Berlin was not yet ready to make any concessions on the major problems in Polish-German relations. Beck's dilemma was that he could not exercise sufficient pressure on Germany to attain his aims. In these circumstances, the Polish Foreign Minister had to accept the German rebuff and hope that if the Sudeten problem led to an isolated German-Czechoslovak conflict he could then obtain his *desiderata* from Hitler. Thus the second phase of the Czechoslovak crisis closed on the same note for Poland as the one on which it had begun.

[84] The Conversations of Ambassador Lipski in Nuremberg, 7–12 September 1938, MFA (London), P.-G, 1938.

IV

THE CZECHOSLOVAK
CRISIS: THE BETRAYAL AND
ITS CONSEQUENCES

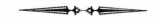

12 SEPTEMBER – 1 OCTOBER 1938

IN mid-September, Col. Beck faced a diplomatic task of great complexity. If, as he assumed, France and Britain should abandon Czechoslovakia, he had to try to gain some advantages in Polish-German relations, particularly in Danzig; furthermore, he was committed by his demands for equal treatment of the Polish minority in Czechoslovakia to follow them to their logical conclusion and obtain whatever should be given to the Sudeten Germans. Last but not least, he would have to strive for a common Polish-Hungarian frontier as the basis of his 'Third Europe' project. He could not, however, commit himself to any plan of co-operation with the Germans since a sudden reversal of Franco-British policy would automatically involve a ninety-degree turn in the policy of Warsaw. In these circumstances, the Polish Foreign Minister's policy towards Czechoslovakia was closely attuned to Franco-British policy towards Germany. Each new stage in negotiations between London, Paris, and Berlin was therefore followed by a new stage in Polish-Czechoslovak relations.

The third and final phase of the Czechoslovak crisis opened with Hitler's speech of 12 September at the end of the Party Congress in Nuremberg. The Führer cunningly combined a threat to intervene in favour of the Sudeten Germans with the statement that he had no quarrel with France and with a favourable comment on Polish-German relations. He served an official warning, however, on the Democracies when, speaking of the Sudeten Germans, he threatened: 'I can only say to the representatives of these democracies that this *does* concern us, and that if these tortured creatures can of themselves find no justice and no help they will get both from us.'[1]

Hitler's speech of 12 September was immediately followed by fighting and staged 'incidents' in the Sudetenland, whereupon Lord Runciman decided that his mission had come to an end. This was not an unexpected conclusion for the British Prime Minister, who had already, at the end of August, decided on a course of action if things should come to a really bad pass. On 3 September he noted:

> I keep racking my brains to try and devise some means of averting a catastrophe, if it should seem to be upon us. I thought of one so unconventional and daring that it rather took Halifax's breath away. But since Henderson thought it might save the situation at the eleventh hour, I haven't abandoned it, though I hope all the time it won't be necessary to try it.[2]

What Chamberlain was, in fact, considering, was a personal interview with Hitler. There were thoughts of such a meeting on the German side also, for Göring had told Henderson on 8 September that 'Hitler and Chamberlain must meet'.[3] Thus, when disturbances took place in the Sudetenland and the SDP again broke off negotiations with Prague, Chamberlain decided to carry his 'daring' project into action. On 13 September he sent a telegram to Ribbentrop proposing an interview with Hitler. He informed the Cabinet of his step afterwards.[4]

The French Foreign Minister, who had also anticipated the

---

[1] Norman H. Baynes, *The Speeches of Adolf Hitler, April 1922–August 1939* (London, 1947), vol. II, p. 1490.

[2] Feiling, *Neville Chamberlain*, p. 357.

[3] Henderson apparently worked for such a meeting together with Sir Horace Wilson. On 9 September, Henderson wrote to Wilson that the moment for 'X' had not yet come; presumably 'X' stood for Chamberlain's proposal to meet Hitler; *DBFP*, 3, II, appendix I, p. 647.

[4] 'So I sent the fateful telegram and told the Cabinet next morning what I had done'; Feiling, *Neville Chamberlain*, p. 363.

failure of the Runciman mission, took steps to obtain coverage for himself in the decisions which he intended to make. On 10 September he asked the British Ambassador to transmit to Lord Halifax a question of great importance. What would the British answer be if France should say, 'We are going to march, will you march with us?' The British Foreign Secretary gave the expected reply that

> while His Majesty's Government would never allow the security of France to be threatened, they are unable to make precise statements of the character of their future action, or the time at which it would be taken, in circumstances that they cannot at present foresee.[5]

Thus, the British government maintained its position of not giving commitments to France on Czechoslovakia. If Bonnet had needed any decisive argument to convince his colleagues in the Cabinet that France could not aid her ally, he now had it. The British Ambassador in Paris reported that the Foreign Minister 'seemed to be genuinely pleased at the negative nature of your reply to his question.'[6] He had also asked for and received a copy of the British statement of 22 May 1938, to the effect that France could not expect Britain to undertake joint action with her to preserve Czechoslovakia from German aggression. He told Phipps that 'he had found it useful with certain bellicose French Ministers.'[7]

Despite the firm decision of both London and Paris not to be involved in a conflict with Germany, Lord Halifax asked Ambassador Raczyński on 13 September whether the two governments could count on Polish support in case of war. He also asked whether Col. Beck could undertake a diplomatic *démarche* in Berlin in order to exercise a 'moderating' influence in the German capital.[8] Like Bonnet, however, Halifax offered no prospect of aid to Poland, should the action he asked of her lead to complications with Germany. Bonnet, for his part, was

[5] *DBFP*, 3, II, no. 843.   [6] *DBFP*, 3, II, no. 843, footnote.
[7] *Ibid.*, no. 855.
[8] Raczyński to Foreign Minister, 13 September 1938, cypher telegram no. 68a, and 14 September, cypher telegram no. 1; in Józef Chudek (ed.), *Wrześniowy Kryzys Czechosłowacki 1938r. w Raportach Ambasady R. P. w Londynie* (The September Czechoslovak Crisis of 1938 in the Reports of the Polish Embassy in London, Warsaw, 1958), *ŻH*, 8, docs. V, VI.

at this time so overcome by fear of war that Ambassador Phipps commented: 'His Excellency seems completely to have lost his nerve and to be ready for any solution to avoid war.'[9]

At Berchtesgaden, where Chamberlain arrived on 15 September, Hitler told him that if Great Britain accepted the principle of self-determination in the case of the Sudeten Germans, he, on his side, would be prepared to discuss its application. It was soon agreed that the result of such application would be the detachment of the Sudetenland from Czechoslovakia. Chamberlain assured Hitler that he personally agreed that cession would be the best solution, but that he would have to consult his Cabinet before giving a formal reply. When, however, the Prime Minister asked whether the annexation of the Sudeten territories would mark the end of all German demands on Czechoslovakia, Hitler introduced a new element. He said that similar demands would be made by the Poles, the Hungarians, and the Slovaks, and that in the long run it would be impossible to ignore them. He took care, nevertheless, to stress that he was not the spokesman for those peoples, thus giving Chamberlain to understand that he would not be too insistent on the matter.[10]

When Chamberlain returned to London from Berchtesgaden, all signs seemed to point to a speedy solution of the crisis by means of a plebiscite. On 15 September, Mussolini, in the official paper, *Popolo d'Italia*, published an open letter to Runciman proposing that he advise President Beneš to grant plebiscites not only to the Sudeten Germans but to all the other nationalities of Czechoslovakia who should ask for it. In these circumstances, Col. Beck acted in conformity with his established policy of demanding for the Polish minority equal treatment with the German. Polish diplomatic action proceeded in conjunction with Hungary, on the basis of a very loose 'Gentlemen's Agreement' between the two countries.[11] In its *démarches* made in London on 16 Septem-

---

[9] *DBFP*, 3, II, no. 852.

[10] *DGFP*, D, II, no. 487; for Chamberlain's account see *DBFP*, 3, II, no. 895, and Feiling, *Neville Chamberlain*, pp. 366–68.

[11] The proposal for such an agreement came from the Hungarian Minister in Warsaw, András Hory; Szembek, *Journal*, p. 332. Beck told Szembek that he wanted the text to be flexible and rather general and asked him to tell Hory that the Polish government looked on it merely as a statement of its position but that it could be expanded later; Szembek MSS, 9 September 1938. The agreement signed

ber,[12] and in Paris on the following day,[13] the Polish government officially demanded that if a plebiscite were granted to the German population of Czechoslovakia, it should be simultaneously held for the Polish minority. The Polish Foreign Minister warned London that, if the application of the plebiscite were not simultaneous, grave tension would ensue between Poland and Czechoslovakia. Łukasiewicz transmitted the same message to Georges Bonnet. The Ambassador stressed the significance of the problem from the point of view of Franco-Polish relations, the policy in East Central Europe, and the necessity of eliminating the question which had poisoned the atmosphere between Poland and Czechoslovakia for twenty years. He thus left Bonnet in no doubt that Poland would insist on territorial concessions from Prague. The French Foreign Minister, however, evaded any commitments, merely assuring Łukasiewicz that the promise which had been already made to Poland—the equal treatment of her minority with the German—would be carried out. He asked that Poland have confidence in the word of London and Paris, and not make it impossible for them to obtain Czechoslovak agreement to the solution of the Sudeten

---

on that day was very vague. It read: 'Le gouvernement de la République de Pologne et le gouvernement de la Hongrie constatant la communauté de leurs intérêts dans les régions de l'Europe Centrale et désireux de maintenir une coopération politique efficace ont décidé dans le cas où l'un des deux Etats le jugerait nécessaire de se concerter au sujet des decisions qui seraient à prendre en vue d'harmoniser leur politique'; see *A Müncheni Egyezmény*, no. 320. Col. Andorka reported on 12 September that the chief of the Polish General Staff, General W. Stachiewicz, had told him that at the moment there was no necessity for Polish-Hungarian military conversations; *ibid.*, no. 331. Beck's attitude was that Poland could offer Hungary only diplomatic support in her claims; Szembek MSS, 13 September 1938. On 15 September he telephoned Lipski that Poland and Hungary both supported plebiscites in all parts of Czechoslovakia; *ZH*, 7, doc. VIII. The only time at which Beck departed from his policy was on 16 September when he proposed that, if Hungary were determined to pursue its objective by force if necessary—Poland would be ready to conclude a political and military alliance with her. On 20 September, however, he told the Hungarian Minister that the time for such an alliance was past; see *A Müncheni Egyezmény*, nos. 354, 369; Macartney cites the Polish proposal in *October Fifteenth*, I, p. 255. Beck's proposal of 16 September probably reflected the fear that Hitler and Chamberlain would settle the Czechoslovak problem without allowing for the establishment of a common Polish-Hungarian frontier.

[12] *DBFP*, 3, II, no. 5; *ZH*, 8, doc. VII.
[13] Łukasiewicz to Foreign Minister, 17 September 1938, MFA (London), P–F, 1938; 18 September, cypher telegram, no. 3, APEL, cyphers, 1938.

problem, which, he averred, would not be easy.[14] This was not a very convincing argument in the light of Bonnet's previous confident assertion that Prague would have no choice but to accept whatever France and Britain should propose.

The Polish government's demand for a plebiscite for its minority in Czechoslovakia was a logical consequence of its established policy in the crisis, and was undertaken quite independently of any suggestions made to this effect by Berlin. On the afternoon of 15 September, when Chamberlain was in Berchtesgaden, Beck informed Ambassador Lipski by telephone that he would aim by all possible means to include a plebiscite for Trans-Olza in any general programme for the solution of the Czechoslovak problem. In order to give weight to this statement, he stressed that Poland would not shrink from threats if these proved necessary.[15] It was not until the following day that Lipski had a conversation with Göring, who suggested that Poland should categorically demand a plebiscite in the territory inhabited by a Polish population. This suggestion was, of course, unnecessary, in view of Beck's independent decision to pursue such a course of action.[16]

The day following the Chamberlain-Hitler conversations in Berchtesgaden, Lipski made a determined attempt to elicit from the German government some response to Polish *desiderata*. In a conversation with Göring, he again brought up the project which had been aired on the eve of the Anschluss and in the Nuremberg conversations—the extension of the Declaration of Non-Aggression of 1934. More important than this were two

[14] Łukasiewicz to Foreign Minister, 17 September 1938, cypher telegram no. 78; in Józef Chudek (ed.), *Wrześniowy Kryzys Czechosłowacki 1938r. w. Raportach Ambasadora Łukasiewicza* (The September Czechoslovak Crisis of 1938 in the Reports of Ambassador Łukasiewicz, Warsaw, 1960), *ŻH*, 10, doc. III; also printed in J. Chudek, 'Rozmowy Bonnet-Łukasiewicz w Okresie przedmonachijskim,' *Sprawy Międzynarodowe* (Warsaw, 1958), no. 6, pp. 69–78.

[15] Lipski received this message on 15 September at 16.40 hrs.; see *ŻH*, 7, doc. VII.

[16] The editor of *Wrześniowy Kryzys Czechosłowacki, ŻH*, 7, p. 5, suggests that Polish demands for a plebiscite were perhaps the result of Göring's advice to Lipski. However, docs. VII and VIII show that Beck sent the instructions for this demand independently of the Lipski-Göring conversation. Wojciechowski, *Stosunki Polsko-Niemieckie*, p. 443–4, notes the instructions were sent twenty minutes before the Hitler-Chamberlain talk began in Berchtesgaden and a few hours before Beck obtained Lipski's report on the results of this conversation.

other points put forward by the Ambassador: a demand for a German declaration recognizing the Polish-German frontier as final, and a clear confirmation, in writing, of the Chancellor's declaration of 5 November 1937 on Danzig—which he had repeated to Beck on 14 January 1938.[17] Göring did not register any opposition to the proposed declaration on the frontier, but remarked, on Danzig, that it was a matter which should eventually be settled by mutual consent after the solution of the Czechoslovak question. He not only failed to give any promises to Poland but touched briefly on the subject of a motor highway through the Polish Corridor which would link Germany with East Prussia.[18] This highway or *Autobahn* project had been sporadically mentioned by the Germans since 1935;[19] together with hints as to possible conflicts on minority issues, it constituted an excellent means of diplomatic pressure on Poland. There was no reason for Hitler to be anxious about Warsaw since he already had Chamberlain's assent to the annexation of the Sudetenland. Thus Beck's attempt to obtain a response to his demands from Germany failed for a second time within a month, and for the third time in the course of the year. In order to keep Polish and Hungarian hopes high, however, Hitler professed to stand for the demands of their minorities also. In an interview with Ward-Price, published in the *Daily Mail* on 17 September, he declared: 'To set an intellectually inferior handful of Czechs to rule over minorities belonging to races like the Germans, Poles and Hungarians, with a thousand years of culture, was a work of folly and ignorance.'[20]

The British government now faced the problem of giving its

[17] The main points of the declaration of 5 November 1937 were: there was to be no change in the legal and political situation in Danzig; the rights of the Polish population there would be respected; Polish rights in the City would not be impaired; *PWB*, no. 36.

[18] Lipski to Foreign Minister, 16 September 1938, *ZH*, 7, doc. XIV.

[19] Hitler mentioned the project to Lipski on 22 May 1935, but qualified it then as a 'premature' idea which might perhaps be realized in fifteen years' time; he mentioned an extra-territorial railway link as well; *PWB*, no. 19. In November 1936, Łubieński showed Szembek the report of a conversation between Göring and Lipski in which the former had said that in return for compensation to be given to Poland on another plane Hitler envisaged an Autobahn through Polish territory and the organization of German trains through Pomerania under Polish control; Szembek, *Journal*, p. 214.

[20] Baynes, *Speeches*, II, p. 1503.

official assent to Hitler's demands. On his return to London, Chamberlain heard from Lord Runciman an opinion identical in principle with, though different in extent from, the one he had heard in Berchtesgaden.[21] Runciman's recommendations combined the SDP demands with suggestions which had been entertained for some time in London.[22] It is also possible, in view of Runciman's close contacts with President Beneš, that the latter had himself indicated that he would not oppose the cession of certain frontier districts as a sacrifice necessary for the continued existence of a united and independent Czechoslovakia.[23]

Against the background of a tense international situation,[24] the French and British ministers met for consultations in London on 18 and 19 September. The debate turned on what territories should be ceded to Germany and whether a plebiscite should be

[21] Lord Runciman's report was published on 21 September, but he had already reported to Chamberlain at the Cabinet meeting held on 16 September.

[22] Runciman suggested that 'the frontier districts should at once be transferred from Czechoslovakia to Germany'. For the remaining districts where the Germans did not constitute a majority, Runciman recommended local autonomy on the lines of Beneš's Fourth Plan. A special commission and an International Peace Force were proposed to survey the transfer of territory; *The Runciman Report: Correspondence respecting Czechoslovakia*, September 1938. Command Papers, no. 5847, London, 21 September 1938; also *DBFP*, 3, II, appendix II, pp. 675 ff.

[23] Hubert Ripka denies that Beneš had made any such suggestions; *Munich: Before and After*, pp. 85–6. Léon Blum, however, declared after the war that a friend had brought him a map of the territories which Beneš was willing to cede and that this map was transmitted to Daladier on the eve of the latter's departure for London on 18 September, *Evénements* (Paris, 1947–49), vol. I, p. 256. According to Czechoslovak documents published by the German government in 1942, Stefan Osuský, the Czechoslovak Minister in Paris, reported, on 19 September, that it had been decided in London to make territorial cessions, especially since the French Ambassador in Prague had telegraphed on 17 September that Beneš had proposed to him the cession of the Sudetenland to Germany; Friedrich Berber (ed.), *Europäische Politik 1933–1939: Im Spiegel der Prager Akten* (Essen, 1942), p. 123. It is curious that in a conversation with Halifax on 2 May, Jan Masaryk, the Czechoslovak Minister in London, told the Foreign Secretary that in 1919 Lloyd George had 'forced' the Sudetenland on a reluctant Czechoslovak government; *DBFP*, 3, I, no. 166. Beneš himself denied that he had made any suggestions as to cession of the Sudetenland; Edvard Beneš, *Mnichovské Dny* (Munich Days, 2nd edition, Ustav Dr Edvarda Beneše, London, 1958), pp. 7–7b.

[24] On 17 September, Henlein announced the formation of a 'Sudetendeutsche Freikorps' in Germany, where he had escaped after Hitler's speech at Nuremberg. Hitler had told Chamberlain of Henlein's demands for the cession, not only of the frontier districts, but of all territories where 50 per cent or more of the population was German; Celovsky, *Das Münchener Abkommen*, p. 343. Duff Cooper wrote: 'The Prime Minister seemed to expect us all to accept that principle [self-determination] without delay'; *Old Men Forget*, p. 230.

held in the remaining parts of the country. Daladier's military advisers had told him that Germany could crush Czechoslovakia in a few days, before the French offensive could even begin,[25] and he told Chamberlain that he thought Prague might agree to cede part of the Sudeten territory. The French Premier was, however, opposed to plebiscites. He stressed that France needed Czechoslovakia in order to obtain relief from German pressure. Daladier fought hard to obtain a promise from Chamberlain that Britain would join in an international guarantee for what remained of Czechoslovakia after territorial cession. It is difficult to see how he imagined that a neutralized and truncated Czechoslovakia could still be a counterweight to Germany in the East, but in any case, he at last obtained Chamberlain's assent to British participation in the projected guarantee. The British Prime Minister thus departed from his principle of no commitments on Czechoslovakia in return for Daladier's consent to the principle of territorial cession to Germany. It was agreed that an International Commission should be organized for the transfer of territories where over 50 per cent of the population was German. Czechoslovakia was to be neutralized and her former alliances replaced by an international guarantee in which Britain was to participate. France and England were to exert pressure on Prague to accept this solution as final.[26] The French Cabinet, however, divided as it was between fervent supporters of the Czechoslovak alliance and equally fervent appeasers, gave its consent only to the presentation of the demands in Prague and not to their enforcement. Nothing was decided with regard to policy in case of a refusal.[27]

The French and British governments sent their demands to Prague on 19 September. President Beneš at first attempted to temporize, apparently hoping for a crisis in the French Cabinet which would bring his supporters to power. While discussing the situation with the Soviet Minister in Prague, S. Alexandrovsky,

[25] General Gamelin together with Generals Georges and Billotte were of the opinion that a French offensive could not get under way before the fifteenth or twentieth day after the General Mobilization had been proclaimed. Georges expressed the majority opinion in Cabinet and Army circles when he said that a French offensive could not be envisaged except within the framework of a coalition; *Evénements*, II, p. 33.

[26] *DBFP*, 3, II, no. 928.   [27] Bonnet, *Défense de la Paix*, I, p. 243.

he received a report from Paris to the effect that six ministers of the Cabinet had threatened to resign because of their disagreement with the London decisions. Alexandrovsky reported that Beneš told him: 'There will be a Cabinet crisis, the keynote being loyalty to the alliance with Czechoslovakia.'[28] Encouraged by this news, Beneš instructed Prime Minister Hodža to ask such a question of the French government as would put the issue before it in the sharpest light. Hodža asked the French Ambassador, De Lacroix, whether France would intervene in case of war between Germany and Czechoslovakia; the Ambassador telegraphed to Paris for a definitive answer. The resignations for which Beneš had hoped did not, however, take place. Bonnet dealt with the telegram alone, without calling the Cabinet, and presented it only the next day with the explanation that Prague had asked the question as a means of saving face with the Czechoslovak population.[29]

Beneš also turned to the second ally of Czechoslovakia, the Soviet Union. He asked Alexandrovsky whether the USSR would help his country in either of two possible cases: if France also helped, or if Czechoslovakia had to fight alone. It was only on 21 September, when Beneš knew that he had lost his case in Paris, that the Soviet Minister brought the answer. The first message was unsatisfactory, but the second purported to promise Soviet assistance even if Czechoslovakia fought alone, provided she notified the League and informed the Soviet Union.[30] Whatever Soviet intentions may have been,[31] Beneš

---

[28] *NDHM*, no. 36.

[29] For Bonnet's version see *Défense de la Paix*, I, pp. 248–50. In Delacroix's version, Hodža told him that France would not march and that if a telegram were received confirming this assumption, Beneš would give in to the Franco-British proposals; *Evénements*, II, p. 268. Daladier also interpreted the message as a face-saving gesture on the part of Beneš; *ibid.*, I, p. 34.

[30] Benes, *Mnichovské Dny*, pp. 86, 88.

[31] Soviet documents give a somewhat different version of the Beneš-Alexandrovsky conversations from that given in *Mnichovské Dny*. Instead of the two alternatives as recorded by Beneš, the Soviet document states that Beneš asked: (a) whether the Soviet Union would help if France also helped, and (b) whether it would aid Czechoslovakia as a member of the League of Nations; *NDHM*, no. 36. According to *NDHM*, the Soviet Union, on 20 September, promised its assistance as a member of the League if Beneš asked the League Council to apply articles 16 and 17 of the Covenant; *ibid.*, no. 38. It is noteworthy that, on 21 September, Fierlinger telegraphed Foreign Minister Krofta from Moscow to the effect that, if

was not willing to accept Soviet aid alone.[32] When he was informed that France would not aid Czechoslovakia as the latter refused the demands of 19 September, he accepted them on 22 September and the Hodža Cabinet resigned. In Paris, the friends of Czechoslovakia offered their resignations in protest, but were persuaded to withdraw them by Daladier's plea that all reservists were being called up and that preparations were being made for war.[33] Chamberlain could now fly back to Germany with the 'consent' of Prague to cede the territories with a German majority and to give up its alliances.

The situation created by Hitler's demands to Chamberlain and the sending of the Franco-British proposals to Prague called

---

France changed her attitude and came to the help of Czechoslovakia, the whole Soviet army would march; *Mnichov v Dokumentech* (Munich in Documents, Prague, 1958), vol. I, no. 92. The discrepancy between the account of Beneš and the Czech and Soviet documents may be due to the fact that Beneš wrote his memoir during World War II and expected to publish it. At this time he already considered good Czechoslovak-Soviet relations as absolutely necessary for the future security of his country. He took pains to stress that the USSR was the only state to stand by Czechoslovakia in 1938; *Mnichovské Dny*, p. 88. In any case, Litvinov, speaking at Geneva on 23 September, officially denied that Czechoslovakia had asked for Soviet aid independently of France and also suppressed the fact that his government had given a conditional promise of assistance; *ibid.*, no. 51. The official Soviet version is that Beneš wanted to find some excuse for his 'policy of capitulation' by seeking a negative answer to his question about Soviet aid. According to Soviet historiography, an affirmative answer was given on 20 September, promising Soviet aid even independently of France and Britain, provided Czechoslovakia decided to resist aggression. All interpretations which cast doubt on Soviet intentions are classed as 'falsifications of history'. Among these is Boris Celovsky's work, *Das Münchener Abkommen von 1938*, in which he expressed the opinion that the USSR had no interest in saving Czechoslovakia; this is singled out as a book by a 'former Sudeten Fascist'; see *Istoriia Velikoi Otechestvennoi Voiny Sovetskovo Souiza, 1941–1945*, I, p. 147.

[32] In his *Mnichovské Dny*, Beneš explained his rejection of isolated Soviet aid on the grounds that (a) such an action would have confirmed Hitler's accusation that Czechoslovakia was a Bolshevik outpost; (b) that France and England would have adopted a 'wait and see' attitude, thus giving Bonnet an 'alibi' for his policy of betrayal before French public opinion, and Poland and Hungary an excuse for their policy; (c) acceptance of isolated Soviet aid would have facilitated a Nazi-Soviet war, which, Beneš averred, was desired by the West, and with it the possible defeat of the USSR; pp. 89–90. Finally, in view of the negative attitude of Poland and Rumania to the transit of Soviet troops, Beneš feared that Soviet help might be limited to the type given by Russia to the Spanish Republic, and that would have been insufficient if Czechoslovakia fought Germany without English and French aid; p. 93.

[33] Paul Reynaud, *La France a sauvé l'Europe* (Paris, 1947), vol. I, pp. 562–3.

for another attempt on the part of Beck to elucidate Polish-German relations. On 20 September, when the Western proposal was being considered in Prague, Hitler invited Ambassador Lipski down to Berchtesgaden. He explained his invitation on the grounds that if Czechoslovakia should accept his demands he would not be able to reject a settlement, even if the whole Czechoslovak problem were not solved thereby. In these circumstances, he told Lipski that he wished to discuss the means of settling the problems relating to Poland and Hungary. He had already seen the Hungarian Prime Minister, Béla Imrédy, and the Chief of the Hungarian General Staff with this purpose in view.

The Polish Ambassador came prepared to carry out a mission of great importance. Like Beck, he thought it imperative for Poland that the Czechoslovak crisis should not end merely in the annexation of the Sudetenland by Germany—which would only strengthen the latter—but that the final solution should include a frontier correction at least in Trans-Olza, a common Polish-Hungarian boundary and a satisfactory arrangement in Slovakia. Such a solution, wrote Lipski on 18 September, would be desirable only if the Western Powers did not intervene and if there should be only a localized conflict—not a world war.[34] On the following day, he was instructed to raise all these points with Hitler.[35]

[34] Lipski to Foreign Minister, 18 September 1938, German translation from the original in *PD*, II, Microfilm H, 1682, FOL.

[35] Minister Beck's Instruction to Ambassador Lipski, 19 September 1938, *ZH*, 7, doc. XXI. Wojciechowski prints the instruction in full and calls it the 'quintessence' of Beck's policy during the Czechoslovak crisis. He claims that Beck's aim throughout the crisis was to support the dismemberment of Czechoslovakia, hence the formulation, on 19 September, of the Polish desire to obtain Teschen Silesia and access to Bohumin (Oderberg). From Beck's mention that Polish troops would be ready for action on the Czechoslovak border on 21 September, Wojciechowski deduces that though Beck did not believe in the eventuality of war, he was ready to enter it, if need be, on the side of Germany; *Stosunki Polsko-Niemieckie*, p. 456. Though Wojciechowski does not state it expressly in this context, it is clear that he means Polish participation in a war between Germany and Czechoslovakia; there is certainly no evidence that Beck envisaged such participation on Germany's side if France and Britain should aid Czechoslovakia. The instruction of 19 September simply indicates that in view of the results of the Chamberlain-Hitler meeting in Berchtesgaden, Beck was adjusting his policy to the existing situation, that is, since France and Britain were apparently abandoning Czechoslovakia, he intended to register his claim for Teschen Silesia and a common Polish-Hungarian frontier. Polish troops were ready to move if London and Paris agreed to a plebiscite for the

In his conversation with Hitler at Berchtesgaden, Lipski divided the Polish *desiderata* into three parts. To begin with, in the first official formulation of Polish claims in Czechoslovakia, the Ambassador said that Poland was interested in territory which covered little more than the districts of Teschen and Fryštát and access to the important railway junction of Bohumin (Bogumin, Oderberg). Second, Lipski said that Poland saw the best location for the Polish-Hungarian frontier in Subcarpathian Ruthenia and advanced the argument of a Polish-Hungarian 'dam' against the USSR. Third, Lipski repeated the proposals he had already made to Göring: an agreement on Danzig, a declaration recognizing the Polish-German frontier as final, and an extension of the Declaration of Non-Aggression of 1934.

The Führer's reaction to Lipski's proposals was discouraging. He would not commit himself on the frontier with Hungary. As for the Polish claims in Czechoslovakia, he merely repeated the old assurances about aid in case of a Polish conflict with the USSR and advised the Poles not to move before the German occupation of the Sudetenland. He was even less forthcoming on Danzig. In his opinion, the 1934 agreement was sufficient. He agreed on the desirability of a final recognition of the Polish-German frontier, but in the same breath mentioned the *Autobahn* and railway and said that these could be built in the Corridor on a strip of territory thirty miles wide. When the conversation took this turn, Lipski did not think it wise to pursue it any further. The only positive result of this otherwise negative exchange of views was Hitler's assurance that he would not give his guarantee to Czechoslovakia until Poland and Hungary had given theirs; this promise was, however, as much in his own interest as in theirs. Thus, once again, Beck's attempt to obtain advantages in German-Polish relations as the price for Polish benevolent neutrality resulted in failure.[36]

Sudetenland but not for Teschen Silesia. On 28 September, as Wojciechowski himself notes, Polish military action to secure Teschen Silesia, in case of a localized German-Czechoslovak conflict, was considered a possibility (p. 477), but there is no evidence for his statement (p. 456) that Beck had made up his mind on this by 19 September. A special army group was not formed before 23 September; see further, n. 94.

[36] Ambassador Lipski's Report to Minister Beck, 20 September 1938, *ZH*, 7, doc. XXIII; English text in *DM*, I, no. 23.

While he pursued his aims on the sector of Polish-German relations, Col. Beck likewise kept in step with developments in the Czechoslovak crisis by adjusting his policy to the Anglo-French decisions. On 19 September, the day on which the Western proposals were presented in Prague, Polish ambassadors in the chief capitals of Europe formally put forward the demand that the principle applied to the German minority—this time territorial cession—should also be applied to the Polish minority. The notes stated that otherwise the tension between the two countries would continue. Parallel *démarches* were carried out by the Hungarian ministers.[37] In his conversation with Łukasiewicz, on 20 September, Bonnet told the Ambassador that the Polish declaration would be favourably considered by the French government in future negotiations but that, for the time being, the Sudeten problem would have to be settled first. He informed Łukasiewicz of the Anglo-French proposals which had been sent to Prague and expressed the opinion that the latter would have to accept them. Łukasiewicz, for his part, remarked that he doubted whether the Czechs would, after making concessions to the Sudeten Germans, be willing to make any others. He concluded that Poland had confidence in France and Britain and was opposed to the domination of Czechoslovakia by either Germany or the USSR.[38] The latter was an allusion to the Soviet-Czechoslovak alliance. The upshot of the conversation was that France opposed the simultaneous settlement of the German, Polish, and Hungarian claims.

After the Czechoslovak government had accepted the Franco-British demands on 21 September, Warsaw again took a step forward in its policy towards Prague. The Polish minister in the

[37] *DBFP*, III, no. 20; Raczyński to Foreign Minister, 19 September 1938, *ŻH*, 8, doc. XVIII; also, Note for the Ambassador's conversation with Minister Bonnet, 19 September 1938, MFA (London), P–F, 1938. As before, Beck avoided giving any commitments of military aid to Hungary. On the same day he instructed Arciszewski to tell the Hungarian Ambassador, who was insisting on a statement whether Poland would act in case of a conflict, that there were two possibilities: either Hungary would act herself, or observe events and take what she could. In the second case, it was difficult for Poland to help; as far as the first was concerned, Budapest must present some detailed plans. Hory answered that the Hungarian aim was a common frontier with Poland and to achieve this, close co-operation and perhaps an alliance was absolutely necessary. Beck avoided the issue; Szembek, MSS, 19 September 1938.

[38] *ŻH*, 1c, doc. V; also in 'Rozmowy Bonnet-Łukasiewicz', see n. 14.

Czechoslovak capital, Kazimierz Papée, handed a note to the Prague government on the evening of 21 September. The Polish note reminded Prague of its promise not to discriminate against the Polish minority, and informed it that Poland expected an immediate and analogous decision, with respect to territories which had a predominantly Polish population, to that applied to the Sudeten Germans. In other words, Warsaw now demanded territorial cession. Since the Czechoslovak government accepted cession of the Sudeten territory, the Polish government abrogated part III of the Polish-Czechoslovak convention of 1925, which concerned the Polish minority in Czechoslovakia.[39] In his conversation with the Czechoslovak Deputy Minister of Foreign Affairs, Papée implied that Prague would do well to make a gesture of 'voluntary' cession of Trans-Olza as reparation for the injustice done in 1919, and thus definitively 'regulate' relations between the two countries.[40] In London and Paris, Polish ambassadors delivered notes on the same day, demanding equal treatment for the Polish minority and declaring that if the Polish demand were not accepted, Warsaw would reserve its eventual collaboration in the settlement of the Czechoslovak problem.[41] Thus Beck's policy towards Prague ran parallel to the London decision on the cession of the Sudetenland.

The Polish demand, although its merits had been recognized as valid earlier in the crisis, was unwelcome to Britain and France. They claimed that the extension of the principle of territorial cession to Poland and Hungary might hamper their efforts in obtaining a final settlement of the Sudeten problem. Halifax and Bonnet repeated their earlier pleas that the Polish government refrain from complicating the situation. Halifax implied to Raczyński that the Polish government could, at the appropriate time, make use of Article 19 of the League Covenant

---

[39] The Polish note was sent by telephone on 21 September, at 17.00 hrs., Polish text in SC II; English text in Lewis Namier, *Europe in Decay*, pp. 285–6. It was not sent as a result of the Lipski-Hitler conversation of 20 September, as alleged by Keith Eubank, *Munich* (Norman, Oklahoma, 1963), p. 185, nor did Hitler in that conversation promise to help the Poles against the Czechs—only against an attack by the USSR.

[40] Namier, *ibid.*

[41] *DBFP*, 3, III, no. 20, encl. no. 1. The Polish note to the French government is included in Łukasiewicz to Foreign Minister, Paris, 21 September 1938, MFA (London), P–F, 1938.

to realize its wishes.[42] Bonnet suggested to the Polish Ambassador in Paris that Polish interests could be taken care of after Czechoslovakia had received its international guarantee. Łukasiewicz replied that if the Polish government took no action after its demands had been ignored by France and Britain, the Poles might be under the impression that Poland had obtained Trans-Olza from Hitler. But, said Łukasiewicz, the Polish government would not allow this to happen, and the Polish people would know that it received the territory from its own government and Army. In the face of this warning, Bonnet only said that the Polish *démarche* in Prague of 21 September would enable him to support Polish demands there.[43]

While the Polish ministers were energetically putting forward Polish demands in London and Paris, the government in Warsaw stepped up its press campaign demanding the return of Trans-Olza to Poland. With very few exceptions—among them the Christian Democratic *Polonia*—the Polish press supported the government's demands for territorial cession. The National Democratic leader, Stanisław Stroński, reminded the public of the fact that the Paris Peace Conference had originally decided on a plebiscite in Teschen, Spiš, and Orava but that at the Spa Conference the Polish government had been forced to accept the decision of the Great Powers on this as on other matters and that the Conference of Ambassadors had finally decided in favour of Czechoslovakia. He recalled the words of Paderewski that no Polish government would be able to convince the Polish nation that justice had been done. Stroński aligned himself with government policy when he wrote that no one could expect to see Poland stand idly by and agree to a solution of the Sudeten German problem without acting on behalf of its own minority in Czechoslovakia. He added, however, that France and Britain wished to maintain an independent Czechoslovak state and that this should also be Polish policy. Unlike the Christian Democrats, who counselled persuasion, Stroński rejected Franco-British advice that Poland should wait until the Sudeten

[42] *DBFP*, 3, III, no. 20; Raczyński to Foreign Minister, 21 September 1938, *ZH*, 8, doc. XIII.

[43] Łukasiewicz to Foreign Minister, 22 September 1938, *ZH*, 10, no. VII; also 'Rozmowy Bonnet-Łukasiewicz' telephonogram no. 83, see n. 14 above.

question was settled. Mackiewicz wrote that Poland could not defend the Czechoslovak *status quo* because Czechoslovakia formed the buckle of the Franco-Czech-Soviet alliance which should be broken and replaced by a common frontier with Hungary.[44] In the face of the popular feeling on the justice of Polish claims, the opposition parties had no alternative but to support them, although their attitude to Czechoslovakia was otherwise friendly and sympathetic.

September 22 saw a further move in the appeasement of Hitler when Chamberlain flew for his second interview with the Führer, bearing with him the Czechoslovak 'agreement' to the cession of predominantly German territories. Hitler stunned the Prime Minister by declaring that these concessions were no longer satisfactory, and demanding that the Czechoslovaks should evacuate the Sudetenland between 26 and 28 September and that the region should be occupied by German troops on 1 October. The Chancellor said, furthermore, that Germany would only give her guarantee to the new Czechoslovak state if Italy and all the neighbours of Prague would also grant theirs; this meant, of course, that Polish and Hungarian claims would have to be satisfied.[45] In view of these new demands, the international situation again grew tense. In the afternoon of 23 September, while Chamberlain was still at Godesberg, the British and French ministers in Prague withdrew their previous advice against mobilization and the Czechoslovak government duly proclaimed it on the evening of the same day. At his second interview, in the afternoon, Chamberlain obtained, however, the apparent concession that the deadline for meeting German demands should be 1 October, instead of 28 September, and that Hitler would make no move so long as negotiations were in progress—unless, of course, some 'incident' took place. The German territorial demands were handed to the Prime Minister in the form of a memorandum with a map attached, showing the zones of immediate and later occupation. He flew back to London, still determined to achieve a peaceful solution of the

[44] Stroński in *Kurier Warszawski*, 19, 20, 23 September; *Słowo*, 26 September 1938, in B. Ratyńska, *Opinia Polska wobec Monachium w Świetle Prasy*, pp. 108–9, 114–15, 137, 151.
[45] *DGFP*, D, II, no. 562; *DBFP*, 3, II, no. 1033.

crisis if Hitler could be persuaded to accept some 'orderly method' of transferring the Sudeten territory.[46]

In this uncertain situation, the Polish government began troop concentrations on the Polish-Czechoslovak frontier on 22 September. The move elicited protests from Britain, France, and finally the USSR, but Col. Beck brushed aside all diplomatic interventions. When the British Ambassador asked the Polish Foreign Minister for an assurance that Poland had no aggressive intentions towards Czechoslovakia, Beck curtly replied that he saw no cause for giving formal assurances since Poland had received none from Britain.[47] In his letter to Ambassador Raczyński, Beck also stressed that he did not think it useful to discuss Polish security measures since Poland ought to be the judge in such matters.[48] Halifax advised Ambassador Raczyński against the use of force or threats against Czechoslovakia, warning him of the growing tide of public opinion against Poland.[49] His words seemed to be borne out by a speech given previously on 21 September by Lord Winterton, Chancellor of the Duchy of Lancaster and member of the Cabinet, in which he warned the states bordering on Czechoslovakia against putting forward demands which had not been discussed between Hitler and Chamberlain. He declared that such demands would not have the support of the British government.[50] This was, however, not the official attitude, for Halifax informed the British Minister in Budapest that Lord Winterton's speech should not be

[46] Lord Templewood claims that the 'four Ministers' (Chamberlain, Halifax, Simon, and Templewood, then Sir Samuel Hoare) decided the new demands were unacceptable; Viscount Templewood, *Nine Troubled Years* (London, 1954), p. 312. According to the unpublished Diary of Sir Alexander Cadogan, however, Chamberlain was for total surrender, while Sir John Simon commented that it was only a matter of 'modalities'. Halifax changed his mind on the following day, 25 September, and opted for a refusal of Hitler's terms, see The Earl of Birkenhead, *Halifax: The Life of Lord Halifax* (London, 1965), pp. 399–401.

[47] *DBFP*, 3, II, no. 1024; Beck to Polish ambassadors in London, Paris, Berlin, Rome, 23 September 1938, SC, II.

[48] Letter of the Foreign Minister to the Ambassador in Great Britain, 23 September 1938, APEL, P–GB, 1938; also *DBFP*, 3, III, nos. 34, 45.

[49] *ŻH*, 8, doc. XIV. For Raczyński's report of this conversation and of the conversations in London between 13 and 23 September, see his Political Report, 23 September 1938, *ibid.*, doc. XV.

[50] Raczyński to Foreign Minister, Political Report, 23 September 1938, *ibid.*, doc. XVI.

considered as an authoritative statement of government policy.[51] Thus there seemed to be some wavering in the British Cabinet on the question of Polish and Hungarian claims.

Aside from French and British interventions, Poland also had to face some pressure from the Soviet Union. The Soviet protest of 23 September, against Polish troop concentrations on the Czechoslovak border, was the first and only direct Soviet intervention in Warsaw during the entire course of the Czechoslovak crisis. The Soviet note protested against the Polish concentrations and warned that if these were not denied, and if Polish troops should cross the border and occupy Czechoslovak territory, the Soviet Union would be obliged to abrogate the Non-Aggression Pact of 1932.[52] Col. Beck sent a sharply worded reply stating that defence decrees were an affair of the Polish government which was not obliged to explain them to anyone, and that the Polish government knew the text of the agreements it had made. He also expressed surprise at the Soviet *démarche* since Warsaw had not ordered any military measures to be taken on the Polish-Soviet frontier.[53]

The Soviet note to Poland was not written on the initiative of the Kremlin, but on the request of Prague, and was so interpreted by Col. Beck;[54] it naturally, therefore, influenced his attitude toward President Beneš in a decidedly negative fashion. It was apparent that the President was following a double policy of trying to exert pressure on Warsaw through London, Paris, and Moscow, and, at the same time, of expressing willingness to negotiate with Poland. On 22 September, he told General Ludvik Krejči, the Chief of the General Staff, General Jan Syrový, the Inspector General of the Armed Forces, and Foreign Minister, Dr. Kamil Krofta, that he was considering an approach to Poland in order to obtain her benevolent neutrality in the conflict which threatened. All three agreed enthusiastically to this suggestion and pressed him to take such a step—even if this should be at the cost of territorial cession to Poland. Beneš told

[51] *DBFP*, 3, III, no. 43.

[52] Chargé d'Affaires in Moscow to Foreign Minister, 23 September 1938, SC, II.

[53] Chargé d'Affaires in Moscow to Foreign Minister, 23 September 1938, 16.10 hrs., *ibid*. See also Budurowycz, *Polish-Soviet Relations, 1932–1939*, pp, 122–23.

[54] Beck, Circular to Polish Missions, 23 September 1938, SC II. See also n. 56.

them that he would write a letter to this effect to President Mościcki.[55]

The Czechoslovak President did indeed write a letter to President Mościcki on 22 September, but he did not despatch it for another four days. In the meanwhile, he instructed the Czechoslovak Minister in Moscow, Zdenek Fierlinger, to request the Soviet government to exert a restraining influence on Poland.[56] This resulted in the Soviet note to Warsaw on 23 September. At the same time, Beneš asked for the intervetion of France and Britain,[57] and met with full support there.

Whether Beneš seriously considered territorial cession or not, his intention was interpreted in Paris as one of putting pressure on Poland to change her policy, and was eagerly seized upon by Bonnet. In his memoirs the French Foreign Minister presents Beneš's move as inspired by France in order to force Poland to aid Paris in protecting Czechoslovakia.[58] Ambassador Noël was instructed to protest against the Polish troop concentrations. He received a significant reply from Marshal Śmigły-Rydz who declared that, if Czechoslovakia gave an immediate and formal recognition of Polish claims, there would be no question but that Poland would remain neutral in a German conflict with Czechoslovakia.[59] It was thus clear that if President Beneš really wanted Polish neutrality, he had only one step to take. A recognition of Polish claims at this time, moreover, no longer constituted a dangerous precedent since Prague had already recognized the principle of territorial cession with respect to the Sudetenland.

However, matters were complicated by Beneš's apparent hope that a change of government in Poland might improve his situation with respect to the territorial cession envisaged. There

[55] Beneš, *Mnichovské Dny*, p. 37.

[56] Beneš, *Mnichovské Dny*, pp. 93–4. Fierlinger asserts that he drew Potemkin's attention to Polish troop concentrations without instructions from Beneš and that the Soviet note to Poland followed; Z. Fierlinger, *Ve Službách ČSR*, I, p. 154. Soviet sources claim the demand was made by the Czechoslovak Foreign Minister; see *NDHM*, no. 49.

[57] Beneš, *Mnichovské Dny*, pp. 93–4.

[58] Bonnet, *Défense de la Paix*, I, p. 258. Noël takes the credit for inviting Beneš to agree to the cession of the western part of Teschen but mentions a change of Polish policy as a 'hope' and not as a condition for such a concession; Noël, *L'Agression Allemande contre la Pologne*, pp. 232–3.

[59] Bonnet, *Défense de la Paix*, I, annexe IV, pp. 363–4; see also *DBFP*, 3, III, no. 38.

was little prospect of success in this direction. General Sikorski told the Czechoslovak minister in Warsaw that the opposition was doing everything possible to 'check Beck's policy of getting Poland in on Germany's side in case of war', but that Czechoslovakia had to make some 'gesture' to help them against the Foreign Minister.[60] It must have been plain to Beneš from such declarations that only a preliminary recognition of at least part of the Polish claims could lead to any modification of Polish policy, whether the government was in the hands of Col. Beck or of the opposition. Both the French and the British ambassadors believed that such a concession on the part of Prague was mandatory, and Kennard, for his part, thought that it would lead to a change in the Polish government.[61] Beneš, however, delayed sending his letter, pending the results of his diplomatic pressure on Poland and the clearing of the international situation.

September 25 marked another stage in the development of the Franco-Czechoslovak action with regard to Poland. Prague rejected the Godesberg memorandum which had been forwarded from London, and in the evening French and British statesmen met again in the British capital to discuss the situation. Daladier held to his former position that there should be no plebiscites in Czechoslovakia, and proposed that the Democ-

---

[60] Slávik, *NTD*, 31 June 1958. At the beginning of August, General Sikorski asked General Marian Kukiel to visit Wincenty Witos, the leader of the Populist Party, who had crossed to Czechoslovakia to escape a prison sentence and was living in Frydek. Witos told Kukiel that, if he had a mandate to negotiate, he would be able to obtain nearly all the Polish demands in return for a pact of eternal friendship and alliance. He had some support, he averred, in Prague. This support probably came from Hodža who was in sympathy with Polish claims and whose views differed radically from Beneš; letter of General Kukiel to author, London, 5 May 1958. Witos, in his diary, mentions meeting General Kukiel at Zlín (now Gottwaldov) on 19 August 1938, but the entry contains nothing about the possibility of Witos's mediation between Warsaw and Prague. There are, however, two mentions of a conflict between Beneš and Hodža in September and these may possibly have concerned Polish-Czechoslovak relations; see Wincenty Witos, *Moje Wspomnienia* (My Memoirs, eds., St. Kot and Fr. Wilk, Paris, 1965), vol. III, pp. 456, 460–61.

[61] Kennard wrote on 23 September that he would not support Polish claims and urge the British government to press Czechoslovakia to accept them, 'if I did not feel that the immediate offer of the line agreed in 1918 as the Polish-Czechoslovak frontier would enormously strengthen the hands of those Poles who did not wish to see their country committed by force of circumstance to the German side'; *DBFP*, 3, III, no. 40.

racies should stand by their proposals of 19 September. Chamberlain, Halifax, and Sir John Simon, on the other hand, worked for the acceptance of the Godesberg memorandum by France. They mercilessly exposed French weakness by insistently asking exactly what military action France would take in case of war. From Daladier's defensive replies, it could be gathered that he did not intend to do anything besides concentrating French troops on the Maginot Line. He did mention that the German defences, in particular the Siegfried Line, were still far from complete and therefore vulnerable,[62] but it was clear that the French Army was not prepared to march. General Gamelin was summoned from Paris and arrived in London on the following day. He told the British statesmen that he was optimistic as to the chances of Czechoslovak resistance and that if the Army could make a stand in northern and southern Moravia, it might save itself. Much would, therefore, in his opinion, depend on Poland; if she entered the field as an ally, Gamelin thought that an eastern front could be constructed.[63]

Daladier eagerly seized upon Gamelin's assertion and also on a statement made by Halifax to the effect that President Beneš had sent a courier with proposals to Warsaw, and that a common Franco-British démarche should be made in the Polish capital that no further aggression would be tolerated against Czechoslovakia. Daladier alleged that the French government had in its possession a written statement made by Śmigły-Rydz in 1936, to the effect that he would never permit the Polish Army to attack Czechoslovakia. He suggested that Beneš had intimated to the French Cabinet that if Poland gave a guarantee not to attack Czechoslovakia 'he would be prepared to consider the cession of Teschen and to make a public declaration to this effect'.[64] He therefore demanded that France and Britain exercise a 'brutal pressure' on Warsaw to demand from it, in return for Teschen, not only neutrality but also a benevolent attitude towards Czechoslovakia.[65] While these conversations were going on in

[62] Ibid., 3, II, no. 1093 (p. 528).   [63] Gamelin, Servir, II, p. 352.
[64] DBFP, 3, II, no. 1096 (pp. 538–40).
[65] Evénements, I, p. 35. According to Jean Zay, Daladier had told the French Cabinet before the London talks that Prague would agree to consign 70,000 Poles in Czechoslovakia to France for future restoration to Poland; Jean Zay, Carnets Secrets, ed. Philippe Henriot (Paris, 1942), p. 13. If this information is correct, it

London, Bonnet wrote to Noël on 25 September that, if Poland engaged herself formally and precisely to leave the German camp, the cession of Teschen could be quickly arranged; this message was transmitted to President Beneš.[66] Nevertheless, on the same day a Czechoslovak note was received in Warsaw in answer to the Polish note of 21 September. The Czechoslovak note stated that the Polish minority could only receive equal treatment with the German if it remained within the boundaries of the Czechoslovak state.[67]

Preceded by the Soviet note of 23 September, by the Franco-British *démarches*, and the Czechoslovak note of 25 September, the letter which Beneš had written to President Mościcki was finally delivered in Warsaw on the evening of 26 September. The Polish government had been eagerly expecting it and negotiations for its delivery had been conducted by President Mościcki's son, who was Polish Ambassador in Brussels. On 25 September, Szembek told Slávik that the Polish government would welcome the letter and that special arrangements had been made for the pilot's landing, for all communications had been cut between the two countries. He warned the Czechoslovak Minister, however, that the letter could not be considered as an official answer to the Polish note of 21 September.[68]

President Beneš's letter, delivered four days after it had been written, differed from the Czechoslovak official note of the day before. Beneš was still unprepared to agree to immediate cession of territory to Poland but he suggested that a solution could be based on frontier rectification.[69] Foreign Minister Krofta explained to Minister Papée in Prague that the Czechoslovak government was willing to enter into immediate 'negotiations' with Warsaw in order to reach a real understanding.[70] Simultaneously, a joint Franco-British note was handed to Col. Beck

---

would indicate that Beneš had put the question of territorial cession to Poland in French hands to use as Paris thought fit.

[66] Bonnet, *Défense de la Paix*, I, pp. 258–9.

[67] Beck, *Dernier Rapport*, p. 163; for text of the Czech note, see Namier, *Europe in Decay*, p. 288, and report of Kennard on 26 September, in *DBFP*, 3, III, no. 54.

[68] Szembek, *Journal*, 25 September 1938, p. 339.

[69] Text of the letter in Beck, *Dernier Rapport*, pp. 342–3, and Namier, *Europe in Decay*, p. 288.

[70] Namier, *ibid.*

by Ambassador Kennard. The note stated that the British and French governments had learned of the Czechoslovak government's readiness to accept territorial cession in order to solve the Teschen problem, provided the Polish government, for its part, undertook the engagement to adopt an attitude of benevolent neutrality towards Czechoslovakia. Both governments expressed the hope that Poland would give her agreement to the Czechoslovak proposal, and drew her attention to the responsibility which she would bear if she engaged by force or by political means in any action hostile to Czechoslovakia.[71]

President Beneš's letter of 22 September, and the Franco-British note of 26 September, were not the reply which Warsaw had expected from Prague. In Paris Ambassador Łukasiewicz had asked his friend Ambassador Bullitt to transmit to the Secretary of State an appeal to the United States government asking it to persuade France and Britain to give Poland a common frontier with Hungary and 'rely on Poland, Hungary and Yugoslavia to resist the German advance in Eastern Europe'. He also asked the American Ambassador to repeat this statement to the Quai d'Orsay and stressed the point that Poland would only take Teschen and eastern Slovakia if German troops crossed the Czechoslovak border.[72] On 26 September Bullit reported, whether correctly or not it is hard to say, that Łukasiewicz had expected Bonnet to return from London 'with the Teschen district on a platter to him as a gift for Poland'. In his disappointment, reported Bullitt, the Polish Ambassador had said that the London conference would not change anything and that Poland would take Teschen when she wished. Any gift of this territory, said Łukasiewicz, would mean something only if it were made, not to 'purchase' Polish neutrality, but as a recognition of the conditions necessary for real peace in Eastern Europe.[73] Thus, at this juncture Beck made it doubly clear that Polish territorial claims merited satisfaction before a final agreement could be reached on Czechoslovakia.

In view of his expectations and plans, it is not surprising that

[71] *DBFP*, 3, III, no. 53, annex; also *DBFP*, 3, II, no. 1102.
[72] *FRUS*, I, 1938, p. 651. Bullitt made an error in his report; the Polish government had no plans to take Eastern Slovakia, but desired small frontier rectifications.
[73] *Ibid.*, p. 664.

Beck found the Czechoslovak President's letter and the official note from Prague disappointing as well as contradictory. He told Kennard that the Czechoslovak answer was unsatisfactory and even represented a regression, although he modified this remark to the extent of admitting that Beneš's letter had prevented a final rupture and allowed negotiations to continue.[74] President Mościcki wrote a short answering letter to Beneš expressing the hope that an agreement would be quickly reached between the two countries, but emphasizing that the first step should be a 'courageous decision' on territorial questions which had made any amelioration of the atmosphere between Poland and Czechoslovakia impossible for almost twenty years.[75] On 27 September, Papée was instructed to transmit to Krofta a note proposing the immediate conclusion of an agreement to regulate the problem of Czechoslovak territory inhabited by a predominantly Polish population. Poland proposed the immediate cession of territories inhabited by an undisputed Polish majority, their occupation by Polish troops, and agreement for a plebiscite to be held in territories with a strong percentage of Polish population. Papée asked for a speedy reply and informed the Czechoslovak Foreign Minister that he had full powers to negotiate the agreement at any time.[76] At this point the British government, at least, seems to have abandoned any plans of putting pressure on Beck to change his policy. Halifax instructed Newton to tell the Prague government that it should cease all 'diplomatic manœuvring' and give an immediate undertaking through diplomatic channels to negotiate the cession to Poland of territories inhabited by a Polish majority. The British government, added Halifax, was ready to offer its mediation.[77]

While the British government seemed to envisage a settlement of Polish claims in favour of Warsaw, France made one more attempt to use the issue as a means of pressure on the Polish

[74] *DBFP*, 3, III, no. 53.
[75] Beck, *Dernier Rapport*, pp. 343–4; Namier, *Europe in Decay*, pp. 290–1.
[76] Beck to Lipski, 27 September 1938, *ZH*, 7 doc. XXXV; Namier, pp. 291–3; *DBFP*, 3, III, no. 57. Wojciechowski notes that, although the Polish demands were made in Prague after Hitler's speech on 26 September, the note was sent without prior consultation with Berlin; *Stosunki Polsko-Niemieckie*, p. 472.
[77] *DBFP*, 3, III, no. 55.

government to change its policy. General Gamelin wrote a personal letter to Marshal Śmigły-Rydz, reminding him of his alleged declaration in 1936 that Poland would never find herself in a camp opposed to France, and warning him that this would happen if she took Teschen by force. The Chief of the French General Staff added that he was convinced the matter could be solved directly between Poland and Czechoslovakia. It appears more than likely that Gamelin's letter contained a veiled threat of leaving Poland to the mercies of the Soviet Union.[78] The Soviet Attaché Militaire in Paris had said on 26 September that the USSR had thirty divisions and cavalry units massed on the frontiers of Poland. Marshal Klimentii Voroshilov instructed the Attaché to declare that Soviet tanks and most of the Air Force were ready for intervention in the 'West.'[79] Such an intervention would also have settled accounts with Poland. In an earlier conversation the Attaché had not concealed from Gamelin Soviet hopes, that if Poland co-operated with Germany and seized Teschen, the Soviet Union would use the occasion to take its revenge. There was no mention of any Soviet attack on Germany.[80] In May the French Ambassador in Moscow had already specifically assured the Soviet government that, in such a case, France would not stand by Poland.[81] Nothing came of these deliberations, however, since France and Britain did not resolve to march against Germany and the Soviet Union was not willing to risk war with Hitler by forcing a passage through Poland and Rumania to help the Czechs.[82] Marshal Śmigły-Rydz answered Gamelin in a dignified letter in which he rejected the French General's suggestion that he had undertaken any unilateral obligations with regard to Czechoslovakia in 1936, and pointedly

[78] Gamelin does not give the text of this letter, though he does give the text of the one he simultaneously sent to General Syrový, but he says 'As far as Poland was concerned, if she attacked Czechoslovakia in order to take Teschen, and if we at the same time envisaged supporting Czechoslovakia, Poland could find herself our adversary and we would have nothing to do but let Russia attack her'; Gamelin, *Servir*, II, p. 356 [author's translation].

[79] *Ibid.*, p. 352; also *NDHM*, nos. 53, 54.

[80] Gamelin, p. 348.

[81] R. Coulondre, *De Staline à Hitler: Souvenirs de deux Ambassades, 1936–1939* (Paris, 1950), p. 152.

[82] Litvinov himself denied that the USSR would take such action in his conversations with Bonnet on 2 and 11 September; Bonnet, *Défense de la Paix*, I pp. 199–200.

reminded him of the Polish attitude towards France in March of that year.[83] So ended the last French attempt to effect a change of Polish foreign policy towards Czechoslovakia—without any guarantee of French support.

The Polish-Czechoslovak exchange of notes on 26 and 27 September took place in a tense international situation. After Prague had rejected the Godesberg memorandum, Hitler made a speech on the evening of 26 September leaving the decision for peace or war to President Beneš. Chamberlain still hoped for a peaceful solution and he sent Sir Horace Wilson to deliver at letter to this effect on the afternoon of the twenty-sixth. After the speech, tension mounted, and there was even a *communiqué* by the Foreign Office that, in case of German aggression agains Czechoslovakia, France would carry out her obligations and Britain and the Soviet Union would support her. The *communiqué* was, at least in part, inspired by Lord Halifax.[84] The Prime Minister himself made a conciliatory speech expressing the hope that Hitler would accept the Franco-British proposals and save Europe from bloodshed. On 26 September, Sir Horace Wilson again saw Hitler and repeated the warning that Britain would help France if Czechoslovakia were attacked. Hitler secretly mobilized five divisions, placing them in readiness positions on the Czechoslovak border, while Britain took the portentous step of mobilizing the Fleet. The question on the evening of 27 September was, then, whether Hitler would provoke war over a question of timing—for agreement had been reached on the principle of cession—or whether some compromise could be reached at the last moment.

In this tense atmosphere, Ribbentrop again approached Lipski on 26 September with the aim of eliciting information on Polish plans with regard to Czechoslovakia. He told Lipski that

[83] Gamelin says he received the letter after the Munich Conference; *Servir*, II, p. 357. From a copy of the Śmigły-Rydz letter, it appears that it was written between 27 and 29 September; MFA (London), P–F, 1938.

[84] The Earl of Birkenhead writes that on the second day of the Anglo-French Conference, 26 September, Chamberlain, on the urging of Halifax, declared he would try once more to reach a settlement by negotiation but also warned Hitler that if France fulfilled her treaty obligations, Britain would come to her aid. 'This assurance was, thanks to Lord Halifax, expressed in stronger terms in a Foreign Office statement on the evening of 26 September and made public the next day'; *The Life of Lord Halifax*, pp. 402–3.

he foresaw two possibilities: either the Czechoslovak government would finally accept the Godesberg memorandum and then, suggested Ribbentrop, German and Polish representatives could meet to discuss further steps on Polish and Hungarian claims, or, if Prague refused, Germany would be forced to march. In the latter case, the German Foreign Minister wanted to know whether Poland would also march. To the first alternative Lipski answered that Col. Beck would be willing to meet the Chancellor for discussions, but to the second he replied that he could express no opinion since the matter was for the Polish government to decide. Speaking for himself only, he said that, if Czechoslovakia rejected the Polish demands, Poland might use force whether the Germans marched or not. He passed over in silence Ribbentrop's suggestion that it might be a good idea to establish contact from the operational point of view. Thus, while the Polish Ambassador made it clear that Poland would pursue her interests in Czechoslovakia, he did not commit himself on the question which was of the greatest interest to Ribbentrop: whether Poland would be ready to march against Czechoslovakia at the same time as Germany.[85]

As the situation grew worse, Lipski was again invited for a conversation with Ribbentrop and State Secretary Weizsäcker on the evening of 27 September. The German Foreign Minister expressed confidence that Great Britain would exert great pressure on Czechoslovakia to accept the German terms. Lipski informed the Germans of what they knew already—the delivery of the Polish note in Prague demanding the cession of territories with a preponderantly Polish population. Weizsäcker, who had before him a German General Staff map of Czechoslovakia, suggested that on the next day the Polish Attaché Militaire should, with a member of the German General Staff, establish a demarcation line so as to avoid collision between Polish and German troops. To this the Ambassador replied with reserve that the extent of Polish and German political interests in Czechoslovakia should be established first. It was agreed that the matter would be discussed again the next morning. Ribbentrop pressed his point however, and asked Lipski again whether

---

[85] Ambassador Lipski's report to the Foreign Minister, 26 September 1938, *ŻH*, 7, doc. XXXIV; English text in *DM*, I, no. 32.

Poland would march if Czechoslovakia rejected German demands and was militarily crushed; he remarked that if Germany were to occupy the whole of Czechoslovakia, it would be useful to establish a clearer definition of Polish and German political and military interests in that country. He specifically requested the Ambassador to ask Warsaw for instructions on this point. From this request it is clear that the Polish government had not given the Ambassador powers to negotiate on military or political co-operation against Czechoslovakia.[86]

While Poland was faced with German proposals for military co-operation against Prague, another problem arose in connection with her interests in Czechoslovakia. On 27 September, the day of the second Ribbentrop-Lipski conversation, the French Attaché Militaire in Warsaw showed the Polish government the German map attached to the Godesberg memorandum. On this map, Bohumin, to which Lipski had already laid claim in his conversation with Hitler on 20 September, was included in the region marked for immediate German occupation. What is more, a large part of the territory north-east of the Orava river, in which Poland was interested, was included in the region marked on the German map for a plebiscite.[87] The British Ambassador also pointed out the German demands to the Polish government.[88] The German claims conflicted with the Polish objectives not only in Bohumin but also in the territories which Poland envisaged for annexation and plebiscites.[89] The German government was well aware of Polish *desiderata*, having been informed of them by Lipski on 19 September, and by the reports of the German Ambassador in Warsaw.[90] It is noteworthy that

[86] Ambassador Lipski's report to the Foreign Minister, 27 September 1938, *ŻH*, 7, doc. XXXVI; English text in *DM*, I, no. 33; also *DGFP*, D, II, no. 644.

[87] Łubieński to Lipski, 27 September 1938, letter sent by plane, MFA (London), P-G, 1938.

[88] Note on the conversation of Minister Arciszewski with the British Ambassador, Mr. Kennard, 27 September 1938, APEL, P-GB, 1938.

[89] On 23 September, Beck had sent Lipski an outline of Polish territorial claims in Czechoslovakia. The maximum claims A, included Trans-Olza, the industrial centres of Vitkovice and Moravská Ostrava, and the southern part of the Frydek district; version B was the same but excluded the southern part of Frýdek; version C stipulated Trans-Olza only; Beck to Lipski, 23 September 1938, MFA (London), P-G, 1938; see Map II.

[90] On 24 September, Moltke reported on the economic importance of the Karvina coalfield and of Moravská Ostrava to Poland. He also mentioned Polish

already, on 20 September, the Italian Ambassador in London had given Raczyński a veiled warning of German intentions by asking whether Berlin was not putting forward demands on Czechoslovak territory in which Poland had an interest.[91] Judging from the fact that the German government did not show the Godesberg map to the Poles,[92] but that Warsaw had learnt of it from the French Attaché Militaire and the British ambassador, it is evident that, at least in one sector, the Germans hoped to face the Poles with a *fait accompli*.

Col. Beck reacted very strongly to the revelations of the Godesberg map. This explains his stiff instruction to Lipski that the whole problem should be clarified 'in order to avoid a political or, worse still, a military conflict between us and the Germans'. Lipski was instructed to use map C[93] and also to show the Polish map which had been sent to Prague. He was to refer to his conversation with Hitler on 20 September. For his own information, the ambassador was told that Polish troops were ready to move after the outbreak of a German-Czechoslovak conflict.[94] In Warsaw, the Polish Foreign Minister told Moltke that he hoped no clash would occur between Polish and German interests in the territories claimed by Poland.[95]

As a result of this instruction, Polish and German maps were compared when Lipski saw Weizsäcker at noon on 28 September. From the comparison it was seen that the German 'red' line, denoting immediate occupation, entered the Bohumin region

claims to Bohumin and demands for frontier corrections in Spiš and Orava; *DGFP*, D, II, no. 588.
[91] Raczyński to Foreign Minister, 20 September 1938, *ŻH*, 8, doc. XI.
[92] Lipski reported on 24 September that Weizsäcker had given the excuse that he did not have the map since it had been drawn up at Godesberg; *ŻH*, 7, doc. XXX (p. 74).
[93] Beck referred to version C of 23 September; see n. 89.
[94] This referred to the case of a localized conflict. A special army group had been formed on 23 September; see 'Samodzielna Grupa Operacyjna Śląsk: Sprawozdanie z Działania Grupy, 1938' (Independent Operational Group Silesia: Account of Action, 1938, unpublished typescript, Józef Piłsudski Institute of America, New York, N.Y.). The preparations were made *ad hoc*. Beck mentions that Piłsudski, as early as the autumn of 1934, had worked out a plan for army operations to recover Trans-Olza in case Czechoslovakia disintegrated or capitulated to Germany; in 1938, however, it appeared that this plan had been lost, *Dernier Rapport*, pp. 83–4.
[95] *DGFP*, D, II, no. 652.

and included that town, while the proposed German plebiscite line entered the region which the Poles had marked for their own proposed frontier with Czechoslovakia. Lipski put the main emphasis on Bohumin and claimed that Hitler had given his 'silent assent' on this point during the Berchtesgaden conversation of 20 September. When Weizsäcker tried to temporize by saying that he would have to find out why Bohumin had been included in the German 'red' line district, Lipski told him that the matter would have to be settled on that very day. He also showed the State Secretary the map which the Polish government had sent on the previous day to Prague, according to which a plebiscite was to be held in part of the Frydek region. The German line of immediate occupation also entered this territory.

On the evening of the same day, Lipski and Counsellor Lubomirski had another conversation with Weizsäcker. The State Secretary told Lipski that the German government had agreed to retract its 'red' line from the territory of Bohumin and agreed that this region should be included in the proposed Polish frontier with Czechoslovakia. Moravská Ostrava was to be left for decision by plebiscite. With regard to Western Frydek, Weizsäcker proposed an eventual plebiscite to decide whether the region should belong to Poland, Germany, or Czechoslovakia. Finally it was agreed that the German government should take no decisions as to plebiscites in this region without consulting Poland. Lipski told Weizsäcker that, in case of Polish military entry into Czechoslovakia, the Polish 'proposed frontier' would be regarded as the boundary for the Polish sphere of occupation.[96] Thus, on 28 September, the Germans conceded the Bohumin region to Poland and promised consultation on eventual plebiscites in the regions of Frydek and Moravská Ostrava.[97]

The conversation on the evening of 28 September was held when the danger of war had already passed. Hitler's sudden

---

[96] Lipski to Foreign Minister, 28 September 1938, *ŻH*, 7, doc. XXXVIII; *DGFP*, D, II, no. 666.

[97] This was the result of Polish pressure, for such an arrangement had been suggested by Beck in an instruction sent by plane to Lipski, dated Warsaw, 28 September 1938, 12.40 hrs.; MFA (London), P–G, 1938.

decision to hold a conference was not the result of the military threats of the Democracies, but of their willingness to grant further concessions and of his own realization that the German people was not ready to fight. After Chamberlain had proposed the idea of a conference to Berlin and to Prague, he worked feverishly on a plan of concessions which would satisfy the Führer and at the same time maintain the appearances of legality. He proposed that the towns of Aš (Asch) and Cheb (Eger), which lay outside the Czechoslovak fortifications, should be ceded and occupied by German troops on 1 October, while an International Commission was to demarcate a zone to be occupied between 1 and 10 October. Finally, a conference was to take place to draw up the new frontiers and to guarantee the neutralized Czechoslovak state. The members of the conference were to be Germany, Czechoslovakia, France, and Great Britain.[98] Chamberlain sent this project to Berlin and Prague on the evening of 27 September. At the same time, Halifax warned President Beneš that, if the latter did not accept Hitler's terms by 2 p.m. on 28 September,

> That must result in Bohemia being overrun and nothing that any Power can do will prevent this fate for your own country and people and this remains true whatever may be the ultimate issue of a possible world war. His Majesty's Government cannot take the responsibility of advising you what you should do but they consider that this information should be in your hands at once.[99]

When Hitler showed interest in Chamberlain's plan, the latter assured him that agreement could be reached within one week, and sent instructions to Prague that, if the new proposal were rejected, there would be no alternative but the invasion and partition of Czechoslovakia. France was prepared to make even more extensive concessions[100] and Mussolini, on British prompting, suggested a conference. In view of these facts, Hitler postponed the mobilization and issued invitations to Chamberlain, Daladier, and Mussolini to meet him on 29 September at Munich. Since the Democracies had conceded everything he wanted, it was difficult, as he later admitted to a confidant, to

---

[98] *DBFP*, 3, II, no. 1140.   [99] *Ibid.*, no. 1136.
[100] *Ibid.*, nos. 1138, 1151, 1154, 1177, 1193, *passim*.

take the initiative in hostilities; moreover, the German people was not morally prepared for a war in 1938.[101]

Czechoslovakia was not officially represented at the Munich Conference and she was informed only *post facto* of the decisions which had been taken. The terms—the occupation of certain territories on 1 October, and the subsequent occupation of other territories where 50 per cent of the population was German— were transmitted to Prague with a curt comment to the British Minister: 'You will appreciate that there is no time for argument; it must be a plain acceptance.'[102] Beneš, at the last moment, turned again to the Soviet Union with the question as to what Moscow's attitude would be if he should reject the Munich decisions and fight. The Soviet Minister, Alexandrovsky, however, did not hurry to send the message and a few hours after Beneš had put this question, the Czechoslovak government decided to capitulate.[103] Neville Chamberlain thought that he had achieved his main objectives; he had saved peace and he considered that the way for an improvement of Anglo-German relations was open.[104] At Munich, after the Conference, he obtained Hitler's signature to a declaration that the two governments should consult each other in the future and returned to London to be acclaimed with delirious joy as the saviour of peace. Daladier, returning to Paris, was also, much to his surprise, accorded a great ovation.

The Munich Conference, which marked a severe diplomatic defeat for France and Britain, was also a defeat for Col. Beck. Poland was not invited, despite the fact that her interests were directly involved and had been, moreover, recognized as valid by France and Britain. Furthermore, the claims of Poland and Hungary were relegated to a later settlement, ignoring their demand for equal treatment with the Germans. Despite

[101] *The Diaries of Martin Bormann*, tr. 'Hitler m'a dit', *Figaro*, Paris, 5 and 8 December 1958.

[102] *DBFP*, 3, II, no. 1225.

[103] According to Soviet documents, Beneš put the question to Alexandrovsky on 30 September at 9.30 A.M. and asked for an answer by 7 P.M. Alexandrovsky, however, did not send the message immediately but went to 'check' on the situation with the President's First Secretary, Jan Smutny. While there, he heard at 11.45 A.M. that Beneš had accepted the Munich decisions and that no answer from the Soviet government was necessary; *NDHM*, nos. 57 and 60.

[104] Strang, *Home and Abroad*, p. 146.

Mussolini's pleading for Warsaw and Budapest, he could only obtain the decision that if Polish and Hungarian claims were not satisfied within three months, another Four Power Conference would be called. The fact that the international guarantee was made dependent on the satisfaction of Poland and Hungary, only meant that Hitler had found a convenient means of blocking the guarantee and not that he supported the claims of Warsaw and Budapest.

The Munich Conference confronted the Polish Foreign Minister not only with a snub but also with the apparent failure of his whole policy. Of all the objectives which he had set himself to gain from the Czechoslovak crisis—a Polish-German agreement on Danzig, the extension of the Declaration of Non-Aggression, German recognition of Poland's western frontier and the recovery of Trans-Olza—none had been attained. Even the Polish-Hungarian frontier had not materialized, since Hungary did not dare to move against Czechoslovakia in order to annex Subcarpathian Ruthenia. Despite repeated pleas, Budapest had been unable to obtain a German guarantee of its frontier with Yugoslavia[105] and the fear of Rumanian and Yugoslav action outweighed the desire for conquest and even Italian promises of support.[106] In the last stages of the crisis, Hungary was further intimidated by Rumanian diplomatic action to prevent her expansion at the cost of Czechoslovakia.[107] Faced with the failure of his policy with respect to Germany and Hungary, Beck decided to proceed at least with the recovery of Trans-Olza, the most publicized of Polish demands.

The Polish Foreign Minister's first move after the announce-

[105] See *Survey of International Affairs, 1938*, vol. II, pp. 291–98. In August, Hitler offered the Hungarians a military alliance but this was not considered by them as a sufficient guarantee against the danger of attack from Rumania and Yugoslavia (p. 297); see also Macartney, *October Fifteenth*, I, chap. 12, for Hungarian policy in September.

[106] In Rome, Ciano told Ambassador Wieniawa-Długoszowski that a common frontier had to be obtained between Poland and Hungary, linking them with Yugoslavia and Italy; Wieniawa-Długoszowski to Foreign Minister, Rome, 20 September 1938, in Józef Chudek (ed.), *Z Raportów Ambasadora Wieniawy-Długoszowskiego* (From the Reports of Ambassador Wieniawa-Długoszowski) (Warsaw, 1959), *ZH*, 6, doc. IV.

[107] Lipski to Foreign Minister, 23 September 1938, *ZH*, 7, doc. XXVI; N. Petresco-Comnène, *Preludi del Grande Dramma: Ricordi i Documenti di un Diplomatico* (Rome, 1947), pp. 98–137, also Macartney (n. 105).

ment of the Munich Conference was an attempt to obtain a voluntary Czechoslovak agreement to Polish demands outside the conference from which he had been excluded. In the early afternoon of 29 September, when the Great Power discussions were already in progress, the Polish Minister in Prague called on Deputy Foreign Minister Ivan Krno to 'make a last appeal' for a Czechoslovak answer to the Polish note of 27 September. Papée asked for a reply on the same day if possible. According to the Polish Minister, it was 'inevitably necessary that a solution of the Polish-Czechoslovak dispute should be reached outside of the scope of the Munich Conference'.[108] The Prague government, however, did not react to this appeal. A reply was only sent on the next day, when Beneš had accepted the dictates of Munich.

Failing to receive any response to his request, Beck decided to employ the threat of force. His main objective was to manifest a protest against the Four Power decisions taken at Munich without Polish participation. He stated his twofold aim in the instruction which he drew up for Papée. In his opinion, the Polish-Czechoslovak quarrel had two aspects: the first concerned the recovery of territory to which Poland had a right, and the second involved Poland's attitude towards the new Europe which was emerging and the manner in which it would be governed.[109] The Czechoslovak reply to Beck's message of 29 September arrived in Warsaw on 30 September after Czechoslovak acceptance of the Munich terms was known, and the decision to employ the threat of force had already been made. The note only confirmed the Polish Foreign Minister's resolve that the dispute should be settled on Poland's own initiative. The Czechoslovak government suggested, not the immediate cession which Poland had demanded, but a settlement by negotiation within the time limit of three months allotted by the Munich Conference for the satisfaction of Polish

---

[108] Namier, *Europe in Decay*, pp. 296–7. Macartney cites Count Łubieński, Beck's Chef de Cabinet at this time, as being of the opinion that if the Czechs had granted the Polish demands before the conference 'Poland would, even at that last hour, have turned round against Germany'; *October Fifteenth*, I, p. 272. This may perhaps have occurred earlier in the crisis, but there was very little likelihood of it as late as 27 September, unless, of course, Czechoslovakia would have simultaneously offered military resistance to Germany.

[109] Beck to Papée, 30 September 1938, *in Sprawy Międzynarodowe* (Warsaw, 1958), no. 2, pp. 115–16; also Beck, *Dernier Rapport*, pp. 166–7.

and Hungarian claims. A mixed Polish-Czechoslovak commission was proposed to draw up the transfer procedure, beginning its work on 31 October, and completing the transfer by 1 December. The note also asserted that the French and British governments were willing to give their guarantee for the offer.[110]

The Czechoslovak note, when it arrived in Warsaw, was judged as dilatory and unsatisfactory.[111] Not only was Warsaw unaware of any Western guarantee for the Czechoslovak offer, but there seemed to be a misunderstanding between the Democracies and Prague on the settlement of the Polish claims. French and British enquiries were made in the Czechoslovak capital asking why the dispute with Poland had not yet been settled. To this question Beneš answered that he felt the strategic Teschen–Bohumin railway could not be handed over to the Poles until it was certain that there was no danger of war.[112] Another reason given for the delay was that there were important Czechoslovak fortifications in the territories claimed by Poland.[113] In the late afternoon, Beck despatched his instructions to Papée. The ultimatum which the Polish Minister handed to Krofta a few minutes before midnight on 30 September stipulated that part of Trans-Olza was to be evacuated in twenty-four hours from noon 1 October, and that the transfer of the remaining territory should be effected within ten days. The Czechoslovak government was given twelve hours in which to answer, that is, until noon 1 October.[114] Beneš attempted to

[110] Namier, *Europe in Decay*, pp. 294–5.

[111] Szembek, *Journal*, 30 September 1938, pp. 342–3.

[112] *DBFP*, 3, III, no. 66. Bullitt reported from Paris on 30 September that Bonnet was going to telephone to Prague urging Beneš to accept the Polish demands; SDNA, Poland, 1938, documentary file note 76of. 62/1341.

[113] *DBFP*, 3, III, no. 88.

[114] Namier, *Europe in Decay*, pp. 297–8; *DBFP*, 3, III, no. 101, annex II. It is misleading to state that Beck despatched the ultimatum after being assured of German neutrality; see Keith Eubank, *Munich*, p. 225. Lipski's message on the favourable attitude of Berlin reached Warsaw after the decision to send the ultimatum had been made; see M. Wojciechowski, *Stosunki Polsko-Niemieckie*, p. 485. It was only on the evening of 30 September that Beck informed von Moltke of the ultimatum and asked whether Poland could count on the benevolent neutrality of Germany in a Polish-Czechoslovak conflict. He also said that he did not expect the Soviet Union to move against Poland, but asked nevertheless whether in such a case Germany would take a friendly attitude. To Moltke's question whether Polish troops would move in if the Czechs rejected the ultimatum,

gain time by appealing for French and British mediation, but finally accepted the Polish ultimatum. On 2 October, Polish troops marched into Trans-Olza occupying Western Teschen and Fryštát.

The return of these Polish territories met with the whole-hearted enthusiasm of the press, though there were, of course, differences in approach and interpretation. The papers support-ing the government stressed the 'triumph' of Col. Beck's policy and the 'inevitable' fall of Czechoslovakia. The opposition press welcomed the return of Teschen but hoped for a sincere co-operation with Prague and warned against German expansion. There was a general feeling that France and Britain had shown themselves unable or unwilling to stand up to Hitler. The supporters of co-operation with Germany expressed disappoint-ment that Poland's gains had not been greater. The Socialist *Robotnik* saw the Anschluss and the annexation of the Sudeten-land as merely steps towards the attainment of German hege-mony in Europe. Stanisław Stroński, writing in the National Democratic *Kurier Warszawski*, asked what role France and Britain intended to play in East Central Europe: that of under-takers or specialists in amputation? Stanisław Mackiewicz was gloomy because he felt that Poland, in failing to obtain a common frontier with Hungary, could not now be a counterweight to Germany. In general, however, the press supported the govern-ment's policy to an extent which had been unknown since the pre-1934 era.[115]

Beck answered that this had not yet been decided. The German answer to Beck's questions was not given till the Polish deadline to the Czechs had elapsed at noon 1 October. Berlin promised benevolent neutrality in case of a Polish-Czechoslovak conflict and a more benevolent attitude if Poland were in conflict with the USSR. This answer was received in Warsaw shortly before Prague accepted the ultimatum. Wojciechowski interprets Beck's inquiries to Berlin as a test to see whether the Germans would be ready to discuss the old Polish proposals on regulating relations between the two countries, i.e., the recognition of the frontier and the status of Danzig; *ibid.*, pp. 487–92. This interpretation may be correct since Beck had stated more than once that he did not believe in the possibility of active Soviet inter-vention and since, after the Prague government had accepted the results of the Munich Conference, there was no likelihood of Czechoslovak resistance to the Poles.

[115] *Robotnik*, 3 October 1938; *Kurier Warszawski*, 2 October 1938; *Słowo*, 3 October 1938, in B. Ratyńska, *Opinia Polska wobec Monachium*, pp. 204–5; pp. 190–3; pp. 206–8. Wojciechowski gives the government's need to gain popular support on the eve of elections as one of the motives for the occupation of Trans-Olza; *Stosunki*

October 2 1938, marked the end of a chapter in Polish foreign policy. Except for a few areas in which plebiscites were to be held, the long and bitter Polish-Czechoslovak dispute was at an end.[116] The most important aspect of the event was not, however, the rectification of an old injustice, but the fact that it was the natural consequence of the Western betrayal of Czechoslovakia at Munich. Beck's move was based on his fundamental assumption that if France and Britain abandoned the Czechs, Poland would have to compensate herself by attaining some of the long-standing objectives in her foreign policy. Further, he hoped to obtain Hitler's official recognition of the Polish-German frontier and of the Statute of the Free City of Danzig; also he saw the Polish-Hungarian frontier as the basis of a new bloc of states in Eastern Europe which would be capable of resisting further German expansion. Finally, he intended by his unilateral move against Czechoslovakia to manifest his protest against the setting up of a 'directorate' of Great Powers which would decide on matters concerning Poland without consulting her. In this respect he was faithful to Piłsudski's policy of opposing all attempts by the Great Powers to run European affairs.

But, it may be asked, what did Poland really gain in the last phase of the crisis? Was Beck's policy justified or were there other realistic alternatives? There was no new agreement in Polish-German relations, while the return of two districts in Trans-Olza hardly compensated Poland for the extension of German power and influence. While Beck had been right in assuming that the fate of Czechoslovakia would be decided by the Western Powers, he was soon proved wrong, as Chamberlain was proved

---

Polsko-Niemieckie, p. 494. Kozeński states that the occupation played an important role in avoiding an explosion of anti-German sentiments in Poland and strengthened Beck's position in the country; *Czechosłowacja w Polskiej Polityce Zagranicznej*, p. 289. Both agree, however, that this was a motive of secondary importance. Wojciechowski stresses Beck's anti-Czechoslovak and anti-Soviet attitude and his desire to regulate Polish-German relations, while Kozeński emphasizes the role of Anglo-French appeasement; Wojciechowski, pp. 493–5; Kozeński, p. 289.

[116] Poland received 1,871 sq. km. of Teschen Silesia (total territory: 2,282 sq. km.). This territory was rich in coal and steel production. The Polish government did not at this time put forward demands for territory in Spiš and Orava because it did not wish to alienate the Slovaks; Kozeński, *Czechosłowacja w Polskiej Polityce Zagranicznej*, p. 287.

wrong, in not realizing that the balance of power would be altered to the sole advantage of Germany. Moreover, his forceful method of dealing with Prague was harmful to Poland because her action was interpreted abroad not as an independent step but as an act of robbery in collusion with Hitler. This policy led to such denunciations of the Poles as the famous verdict of Winston Churchill:

> We see them in 1919, a people restored by the victory of the Western Allies . . . Now, in 1938, over a question as minor as Teschen, they sundered themselves from all those old friends in France, Britain and the United States . . . We see them hurrying, while the might of Germany glowered up against them, to grasp their share of the pillage and ruin of Czechoslovakia.[117]

Seen against the background of Anglo-French policy towards Prague, this condemnation is too harsh and does not take into account all the elements involved. The forceful annexation of Trans-Olza was not dictated by mere greed, nor was it a factor in the fall of Czechoslovakia but a consequence of the Western surrender of the Sudetenland to Germany.[118] Moreover, in Beck's policy it was an instrument in his relations with Berlin and a step towards a new alignment in Eastern Europe. The Western Powers, for their part, had not been trying to safeguard Czechoslovakia's security and independence. Their attempts to gain Polish co-operation were dictated only by the fervent wish to settle the Sudeten question without war. The cession of the Sudetenland, however, meant the end of Czechoslovakia as an independent state. Furthermore, in the course of the crisis both Paris and London had recognized the validity of Polish claims, though they hoped to relegate them to later negotiations. Even so, in the last few days before Munich they had exerted pressure on President Beneš to proceed with territorial cession as a price for Polish neutrality in case of war. Once the danger had passed

[117] Winston S. Churchill, *The Gathering Storm* (Boston, London, 1948), p. 323.

[118] Kozeński writes that while Beck did not oppose co-operation with France if the latter were threatened by Germany, it could not escape his notice, especially in the Czechoslovak crisis, that the French statesmen had no wish to stand up to Germany and subordinated themselves to the British policy of appeasement. It was this policy, in his opinion, which led to the fall of Czechoslovakia and later of Poland, although the occupation of Trans-Olza cannot be wiped off the pages of history books; *Czechosłowacja*, p. 289.

and Poland herself realized her demands, she was labelled as the jackal of Germany.

It is impossible to predict what would have happened if Poland and Czechoslovakia had made a united stand against Hitler in 1938. This might have prevented the dismemberment of Czechoslovakia, or the war might have broken out a year earlier, probably with the same results as in 1939. In any case, in the circumstances of 1938, there were only three ways in which a united Polish-Czechoslovak front could have been created. First, a Western guarantee of Czechoslovak independence, given at an early stage of the crisis, as Daladier had suggested in April, and backed by assurances of military support, would certainly have aligned Warsaw with Prague. Second, an early concession by Beneš of even a part of Trans-Olza to Poland might have brought about a change of government in Warsaw and an alliance between the two countries, or at least have forced the existing government to give Czechoslovakia diplomatic support. Third, if Beneš had decided to resist Hitler by force of arms and had thus precipitated a world war, Poland would have been forced to come in on the side of France and Czechoslovakia. It was Beck's firm opinion, as it had been Piłsudski's, that in a war between France and Germany, Poland could not find herself in the German camp. However, the first possibility was not realized because Chamberlain refused to give a guarantee to Czechoslovakia while there was still time, and France would not help the Czechs without British support. In the second case, President Beneš decided against any territorial cessions, preferring to wait as long as possible in the hopes of a change of policy in Paris. In the third case, the President would not embark on a war since it was his unwavering belief that Czechoslovakia could not risk conflict with Germany without the support of France.

It is difficult to say what the course of events might have been if, soon after Piłsudski's death, a government made up of the opposition parties had come into power. The National Democrats, the Populists, and the Socialists had all been very critical of the Polish-German Declaration of Non-Aggression of 1934, but their leaders were also unaware of the extent to which French foreign policy had become subordinated to that of Great Britain. If, nevertheless, such a government had abrogated the declaration, this would have had the effect of directing German revisionism once more against Poland. While this situation would certainly have driven Warsaw towards Prague there is no certainty that Beneš would have been any more willing than he had been earlier to ally himself with his northern neighbour without a guarantee of French aid. In any case, the leaders of the opposition, and the National Democrats in particular, were making the same demands of Czechoslovakia in 1938 as Beck and, like him, envisaged Czechoslovak concessions to Hungary and the creation of an East European bloc in which Poland would play the dominant role. It seems most likely that the last chance for an alliance between Poland and Czechoslovakia existed in 1933.[119]

Some Polish historians suggest another solution. According to this view, the only alternative for Poland in 1938 was to join the alliance system linking the USSR, France and Czechoslovakia. Such a step, it is claimed, would have checked German expansion even if France had continued her ambivalent policy.[120] This suggestion seems to lack a sense of reality. Quite apart from the fact that no sector of Polish public opinion, except for the politically insignificant and virtually non-existent Communist Party, was willing to envisage the passage of Soviet troops through Poland, Soviet aid to Czechoslovakia was conditional on the simultaneous aid of France and neither Prague nor Moscow was anxious for close co-operation without the fulfilment of this condition.[121] Since French aid to Prague was also

[119] Kozeński points out that not only Beck's predecessors but Beck himself had fruitlessly tried to obtain an alliance with Czechoslovakia and that before Hitler's coming to power the obstacles were on the Czech side; *ibid.*, p. 288. It is curious that he does not mention in his book Beneš's declarations to Simon and MacDonald in March 1933, after Hitler had come to power, that he had rejected Beck's proposal of an alliance against Germany; *DBFP*, 2, IV, no. 298, and V, no. 43.

[120] Stanisławska, *Wielka i Mała Polityka Józefa Becka*, pp. 209–10.

[121] Wojciechowski states that in 1938 the USSR could not have risked an isolated conflict with Germany and claims that Poland played no small part in preventing the Soviet Union from intervening in Czechoslovakia; *Stosunki-Polsko-Niemieckie*, pp. 468, 496. However, Batowski notes that the Soviet Union made no proposals to Poland for co-operation in the defence of Czechoslovakia and challenges the claim that Poland had rejected such a proposal, *Kryzys Dyplomatyczny w Europie*, p. 155, n. 61. Stanisławska notes that there is no evidence of Soviet plans to march through Poland to Prague, *Wielka i Mała Polityka Józefa Becka*, pp. 97–8. All three authors agree that Beck's anti-Soviet attitude played an

decisive for Beck's attitude towards the latter, it is clear that, in 1938, the surest way of preventing Munich would have been a Western guarantee for the independence of Czechoslovakia.

As it was, the British Ambassador in Warsaw, who had always been a sharp critic of Col. Beck, had to concede that Poland was in no position to risk Hitler's ire. Commenting on the Polish Foreign Minister's policy during the crisis, Kennard summarized the realities which Poland had to face in 1938:

> I feel that though Poland has from our point of view acted in an unhelpful and even unscrupulous manner, her Foreign Minister had to look at the situation from the realistic standpoint of a long and indefensible Western frontier, cut off from direct help from the Western Powers and psychologically antagonistic to the third possible ally, namely Soviet Russia.[122]

He might have added that it was not only the lack of direct aid but the obvious reluctance of France and Britain even to threaten Germany with an attack in the West which ultimately decided the course of Beck's policy towards Czechoslovakia.

It is clear that Polish diplomatic co-operation with London and Paris in 1938 would not have saved Czechoslovakia, but would have smoothed the way to the cession of the Sudetenland and probably reopened the Polish-German question. The decisions of Munich were the consequence of long-established policy assumptions with regard to Eastern Europe, and were considered as a step to further concessions. On the day of the Conference, Bonnet openly told the British ambassador: 'we must make up our minds to proceed gradually to a peaceful revision of many existing frontiers in Europe, as the Treaty of Versailles has collapsed.'[123] The Powers which had made the peace settlement of 1919 were now its undertakers. After Munich it looked, indeed, as if 'Europe, like an artichoke, was about to be eaten, leaf by leaf.'[124]

---

important part in Moscow's abstinence from intervention, but none considers that the USSR was prepared to risk a war with Germany.

[122] *DBFP*, 3, III, no. 206.

[123] *Ibid.*, II, no. 1206.

[124] Joseph Paul-Boncour, *Entre Deux Guerres* (Paris, 1946), vol. III, p. 115.

V

THE AFTERMATH OF MUNICH
AND THE FAILURE OF
THE 'THIRD EUROPE'

THE settlement of German and Polish claims in Czechoslovakia created the impression in Western Europe that
Berlin and Warsaw had acted in harmonious co-operation. This
was, of course, far from being the case, as has been seen in
connection with the delimitation of Polish and German
territorial claims, and there was again to be disagreement as to
their implementation. A controversy arose over Bohumin and
though this was soon settled Col. Beck had all the more reason
to pursue his plans for building a Third Europe. Another factor
which confirmed the Polish Foreign Minister in this course was
the policy of France which now set out to secure an accord with
Germany on her own account.

The first problem which arose in Polish-German relations after
Munich was the settlement of the Polish claims to the town of
Bohumin. Although on the eve of the Munich Conference, State
Secretary Weizsäcker had assured the Polish Ambassador that
the German line of 'immediate occupation' would be withdrawn
from this region according to the Polish request, a certain
reluctance to part so easily with the town became apparent on
the German side. The main reasons for this *volte-face* were not
economic, strategic, or demographic, although Bohumin was a
very important railway junction and had a considerable German

population.[1] The motive for the German change of attitude was the desire to use Bohumin as a bargaining counter for other territories where German claims might be disputed by Poland. Thus on 3 October, Weizsäcker noted that the Poles were to be told that the inclusion of Bohumin in the Polish zone presented Germany with a 'new situation', and Under-Secretary Woermann proceeded to inform Counsellor Lubomirski of this fact on the next day.[2] Lipski protested very strongly against the assertion that the Polish request had confronted Germany with a new situation, and advised his government that a speedy occupation of the town should be envisaged.[3]

The dispute over Bohumin seems to have been engineered by the Wilhelmstrasse in co-operation with Göring, for Hitler declared on 5 October that he was not interested and would not haggle with Poland over one town.[4] In the meanwhile, the leaders of the German minorities in both Teschen and Bohumin appealed against the inclusion of these towns in Poland. Dr. Harbich, the leader of the Germans in Teschen, was at the last moment dissuaded from appealing to the British, French, and Japanese ambassadors to remind them of a project mooted in 1919 for a three-way plebiscite in that area. Weizsäcker told him curtly that the Teschen question had been settled.[5] From the very fact that Dr. Harbich entertained such a plan, it may be conjectured either that the Germans had had some intention of demanding a mixed administration for Teschen, or that the local minority leaders were unaware of Berlin's recognition of Polish claims to Trans-Olza. In any case, neither Harbich nor Pfizner, the leader of the Bohumin Germans, could understand the final decision on those two towns.[6]

The dispute over Bohumin was probably connected with German interest in Moravská Ostrava and fear that Poland

---

[1] According to the Austrian census of 1910, the population of Bohumin and the surrounding region was composed of 6,615 Poles, 1,322 Czechs, and 7,810 Germans. The Czechoslovak census of 1930 estimated that there were 2,303 Poles, 10,831 Czechs, 6,908 Germans.

[2] DGFP, D, IV, no. 17.

[3] Lipski to Foreign Minister, Berlin, 4 October 1938, cited by Józef Chudek in 'Sprawa Bogumina w dokumentach polskich' (The Bogumin Question in Polish Documents, Sprawy Międzynarodowe, Warsaw, 1958), no. 9, pp. 109–14, and ŽH, 7, doc. XLVII.

[4] DGFP, D, V, no. 62.   [5] Ibid., no. 63.   [6] Ibid.

might lay claim to this important industrial centre. As early as February 1938, Göring had tried to use Moravská Ostrava as a bait to draw Beck out on Polish plans in the Czechoslovak crisis, and he mentioned the matter again to Lipski on 1 October, expressing his surprise that Poland had not demanded the town. The Field-Marshal had then suggested that since there would eventually be a plebiscite in the Polish section of the Frydek region,[7] and since one would be held by Germany in the Moravskà Ostrava region, some understanding might be reached. He stressed, however, that these were his own views and should not be treated as official.[8] Göring's ulterior motives in this proposal can be deduced from his remark to Weizsäcker on 4 October, that the south and south-eastern corner of Silesia must become German and that if a dispute arose over this territory with Poland, some deal might be made over Danzig; otherwise it would be best to leave the region to Czechoslovakia.[9] It seems, therefore, that Göring was very anxious to obtain Moravská Ostrava for Germany, and thought that either Bohumin or Danzig might be used as a counter towards such a settlement.

The Polish government took a stiff attitude towards this manœuvre. Col. Beck instructed Lipski that preparations were being made on the Polish side to occupy the Bohumin railway station with Polish railwaymen, as a preliminary to occupation by the Army.[10] The German ambassador in Warsaw was either ignorant of Hitler's decision on the matter, or pretended to be. He told Lipski on 6 October that he had been instructed not to discuss the matter in Warsaw but had been called to Berlin in order to help to solve the dispute.[11] He bent all his energies to obtain what could be had from the cession of the town to Poland. After a favourable reception by Lipski of his proposals on the Oder–Danube canal, German management of the Berlin–

---

[7] This had been foreseen in the Polish ultimatum to Czechoslovakia.

[8] Lipski to Foreign Minister, 1 October 1938, ZH, 7, doc. XLV.

[9] *DGFP*, D, V, no. 58. Wojciechowski interprets the Bohumin wrangle as an attempt by the Germans to initiate discussions with Poland on the lines of settling other territorial issues in favour of Berlin. He thinks that the unsigned instruction to Woermann on 3 October (see n. 2 above) was issued by Hitler; *Stosunki Polsko-Niemieckie*, p. 500.

[10] Beck to Lipski, 6 October 1938, cypher telegram, APEL, Cyphers, 1938.

[11] Lipski to Foreign Minister, 6 October 1938, ZH, 7, doc. XLVIII.

Breslau–Vienna railway on the sector which would run through Polish territory, and a guarantee for the German minority in Bohumin,[12] he returned to Warsaw to put these demands before Szembek. The Polish Under-Secretary of State assured Moltke that the German *desiderata* would be given favourable consideration.[13] The dispute was finally settled on 8 October by an agreement between the two countries.[14] Two days later, Polish troops occupied Bohumin. For internal consumption, the Polish press asserted that the occupation had been necessitated by the formation of German shock troops in the town.[15] Göring's hopes that Bohumin would serve as a counter for Polish agreement to the cession of Moravská Ostrava to Germany, were not realized but neither were Polish hopes of obtaining the northern Frydek region and the industrial centre of Vitkovice. On 11 October, Warsaw demanded from Prague the cession of those areas which had been envisaged for a plebiscite in the ultimatum of 30 September.[16] Berlin prevented the realization of these demands. On 12 October, Weizsäcker told Lipski that if Poland was interested in Moravská Ostrava and Vitkovice, Germany would demand a plebiscite in the region; it was therefore agreed that these territories should stay with Czechoslovakia.[17] Thus the first test of Polish-German relations after Munich was not settled without distrust and friction, while a clash of interests in the Moravská Ostrava and Vitkovice region resulted in the retention of these regions by Prague.

Because of the temporary friction with Germany Beck redoubled his efforts to build a Third Europe, the first step to which was a common frontier with Hungary. When Slovakia became a virtual German protectorate on 6 October, the only territory which could serve for the Polish-Hungarian boundary was Subcarpathian Ruthenia and Col. Beck laboured hard to achieve the annexation of this region by Hungary. This project, however, encountered formidable obstacles.

Budapest began the action by demanding on 3 October that

[12] *Ibid.*   [13] Szembek, *Journal*, 7 October 1938, pp. 346–7.
[14] *DGFP*, D, V, no. 66.   [15] *Ibid.*, no. 68.
[16] Szembek, *Journal*, 11 October 1938, pp. 351–2; *DBFP*, 3, III, no. 212; *DGFP*, D, V, no. 69, *passim*.
[17] *DGFP, ibid.*; Lipski to Foreign Minister, 12 October 1938, MFA (London), P–G, 1938.

Czechoslovakia should make a 'symbolic' cession of two towns in the frontier region and asked also for a conference to discuss Hungarian claims in Slovakia. The Polish official press loudly supported Hungarian claims in Subcarpathian Ruthenia and pressed for Slovak autonomy.[18] In her hour of need, Hungary turned to Poland for help. On 5 and 6 October, discussions on this subject took place in Warsaw with Count István Csáky, Chef de Cabinet for Foreign Minister Kálmán Kánya. Csáky told Col. Beck that Hungary agreed to Slovak autonomy—a matter in which she had no choice since it was proclaimed on 6 October and recognized by Germany. From the map which Csáky showed the Polish Foreign Minister it appeared, nevertheless, that the Hungarian idea of an autonomous Slovakia involved considerable territorial concessions to Hungary. Budapest desired the southern and eastern parts of Slovakia with its chief towns, Bratislava and Košice, as well as Subcarpathian Ruthenia. Not content with this, Csáky also stated that Hungary might eventually lay claim to the southern slopes of the Carpathians which had a Slovak population but whose economic ties lay, he asserted, with Hungary.

The main object of Csáky's visit to Warsaw was to obtain a promise of Polish aid in the Hungarian occupation of Subcarpathian Ruthenia, or rather, in view of Hungarian fears of an attack by Rumania and Yugoslavia, to persuade the Poles to undertake the task themselves. Beck refused to listen to this plea, pointing to the Soviet troop concentrations on the Polish eastern border and the absence of sufficient 'moral' motivation for the use of force in the existing situation. He did, however, promise diplomatic support, and in particular undertook the task of obtaining Rumanian consent to Hungary's plans in Subcarpathian Ruthenia. It was agreed that Bucharest should be offered as a bribe the Rumanian villages in the eastern tip of the region.[19] The real motive for Beck's refusal to engage the Polish

[18] *Dobry Wieczór*, 5 October 1938; *Gazeta Polska*, 6, 7, 8 October; *Kurier Poranny*, 8 October.

[19] J. Jurkiewicz, 'Węgry i Polska w okresie kryzysu czechosłowackiego 1938r' (Hungary and Poland during the Czechoslovak Crisis of 1938, *Sprawy Międzynarodowe*, Warsaw, 1958), no. 7/8, pp. 70–71. There is no evidence on the Polish side that at the beginning of October Beck was pressing Kánya 'almost hourly' to march into Slovakia; Macartney, *October Fifteenth*, I, p. 276, n. 2. The Polish

Army lay, not in any fear of the Soviet Union, but in the fact that such a move might provoke conflict with Berlin.

The German Ambassador in Warsaw warned his government that Poland would continue her independent policy and direct her main efforts to secure for herself the position of the dominant state in Eastern Europe. On 6 October, he reported:

> Even the demand for a common frontier with Hungary in the last resort pursues the objective of establishing more firmly the policy which is justified outwardly as a defence against Bolshevism but which actually aims at an expansion of the Polish sphere of influence and has as its goal to bring eastern states that border upon Russia together into the 'neutral European security zone'—a plan which is directed primarily against Soviet Russia but in which fears of German expansion also play a part.[20]

Beck's project incurred the opposition of Berlin—in itself a recognition of the check which a Third Europe might constitute to German expansion. The High Command of the Army informed the Foreign Ministry on 6 October that 'the creation of a

---

Foreign Minister summed up his attitude in a declaration to the Hungarian Ambassador on 2 October, by saying that: 1. the Polish government did not cease to be interested in Hungarian claims with respect to Czechoslovakia and continued its benevolent attitude; 2. it continued its interest in the Czechoslovak problem and considered that a final solution could not be reached without the participation of Poland; 2 October 1938, Szembek MSS. After Csáky's visit, Szembek sent a circular telegram to key Polish Embassies stating that the Hungarians had formulated a programme of incorporating territories inhabited by a Hungarian population and of creating a common frontier with Poland in Subcarpathian Ruthenia. He noted that if and when this programme were realized, Poland would take a benevolent attitude; 7 October 1938, APEL, cypher telegram no. 85, Cyphers, 1938. Three days later, Beck expressed dissatisfaction with the Hungarian lack of decision and refused Kánya's request that Poland send diversionary troops to Subcarpathian Ruthenia; 10 October 1938, Szembek MSS. The Hungarian military attaché reported from Warsaw on 10 October that the Polish General Staff had decided to send in regular soldiers in mufti to carry out sabotage action and volunteer patrols in Mukačevo and Užhorod; A Müncheni Egyezmény, no. 501. However, it is doubtful whether any action actually took place at that time since on 15 October the Chief of the Polish General Staff declared that, with regard to Hungary's project of submitting her claims to another Four Power Conference, the Polish volunteers would not be sent; ibid., no. 536. On 18 October the Hungarian military attaché reported that the beginning of Polish volunteer action had been ordered; ibid., no. 556. It is doubtful whether it amounted to anything, however, since the head of Hungarian Military Intelligence reported on 28 October that the total Polish volunteer force numbered 53 men; ibid., no. 601.

[20] DGFP, D, V, no. 64.

compact bloc of succession states on Germany's eastern frontier, with lines of communication to south-east Europe, will not be in our interest'. The Polish-Hungarian frontier was also declared undesirable for military reasons. As for Slovakia, the High Command stressed that it should not be separated from Prague, but should remain under German influence within the frontiers of Czechoslovakia.[21] The Political Department of the Ministry of Foreign Affairs was of the same opinion and advised against any orientation of an autonomous Slovakia towards Poland even more than towards Hungary since 'The addition of Slovakia to the Polish economic sphere might put considerable difficulties in the way of German economic expansion towards the South-east.' As far as Subcarpathian Ruthenia was concerned, it was considered hardly viable without outside support, though its existence as an independent state would have the advantage of providing a nucleus for a German-dominated Greater Ukraine of the future. The Political Department also opposed the orientation of an independent Subcarpathian Ruthenia towards Poland or Hungary because 'A common Polish-Hungarian frontier would thereby be created, which would facilitate the formation of an anti-German bloc.'[22] Berlin was thus definitely hostile to any attempt on the part of Beck to construct a Third Europe. The proclamation of Slovak autonomy, and its immediate recognition by Germany on 6 October, was the first manifestation of this attitude. In view of German hostility, the implementation of Beck's project automatically became dependent on the support of one of the Western Democracies or of Italy. This support, however, was not forthcoming.

The Polish Foreign Minister found no interest in his plan in either London or Paris, despite the favourable attitude to it of Ambassador Kennard. The British Ambassador's opinion on this matter at the beginning of October was that

> we should carefully consider how far it is in our interest that Czechoslovakia as a whole should pass under German influence or whether a Slovakia in the Polish or Hungarian orbit might not in the long run be an obstacle to German penetration.[23]

[21] *Ibid.*, D, IV, no. 39.
[22] Memorandum by the Director of the Political Department, 7 October 1938, *ibid.*, no. 45.   [23] *DBFP*, 3, III, no. 141; see also no. 156.

In this connection, Kennard also stressed Poland's Ukrainian problem. With four million Ukrainians, he wrote, Poland could not be expected to favour an autonomous Subcarpathian Ruthenia which could form the nucleus of an independent Great Ukraine.[24] From Budapest, Sir George Knox reported: 'The common frontier is in fact regarded here essentially as a short cut to the Rome-Warsaw Axis which was originally conceived as embracing Rumania.' Knox, however, did not think that such an axis would actually constitute a barrier to German penetration because of the weakness of Hungary and, what was more important, because of Italy's reluctance to oppose Germany in this part of the world.[25] This was also the point of view which prevailed in London. The British Minister in Budapest was therefore instructed to tell the Hungarian government that Great Britain felt 'morally bound' by her guarantee to Czechoslovakia and to warn the Hungarians to keep calm and avoid making any harsh demands.[26]

In view of the disinterest of London and Paris, Rome seemed to be the only Power whose aid could ensure the establishment of the common frontier. Italian support for this project, however, continually vacillated. Mussolini was torn between the desire to check German expansion into the Balkans, and the fear of antagonizing Germany; yet, if he did nothing, he feared that Hungary might become a bridge for German penetration into the Adriatic. Ciano even considered the possibility that Hungary, with German support, might lay claim to Fiume.[27] Furthermore, Italy feared to displease Yugoslavia, in whom she saw a potential

[24] *Ibid.*, no. 206.

[25] *Ibid.*, no. 168.

[26] *DGFP*, D, IV, no. 47. At the same time, a Hungarian journalist in London, Iván Hordossy, reported on 2 October that Lord Rothermere, a well-known champion of Hungarian revisionism, advised the use of violent means to realize Hungarian demands; see *A Müncheni Egyezmény*, no. 447. Rothermere received a hero's welcome when he arrived in Budapest in November; see his book, *My Campaign for Hungary*, London, 1939, chap. XIII. Horthy appealed to Neville Chamberlain in a personal letter of 8 October, in which he wrote that Sir Austen Chamberlain had told him in 1935 ' "Keep quiet now, I promise you, when the right moment will come, England will help you" ... I kept quiet and waited for the right moment to come'; *A Müncheni Egyezmény*, no. 486. Chamberlain did not answer till 28 October, when he expressed the hope that a settlement would be reached; *ibid.*, no. 603.

[27] *Ciano's Diary 1937–1938*, 4 October 1938, p. 173.

ally in the Balkans.[28] For these reasons, Rome displayed caution. The Italian Ambassador in Berlin, Bernardo Attolico, told Lipski that Rumanian agreement was essential for the solution of the problem of Subcarpathian Ruthenia.[29] The Italian Ambassador in Warsaw, however, told Moltke that Poland's plans of building a north-south axis in the Danube region would sooner or later be bound to clash with German and Italian interests there.[30] In Rome, though Ciano assured the Polish Ambassador of Italian diplomatic and press support, Wieniawa-Długoszowski reported voices which advocated a federal system for Czechoslovakia.[31] It was typical of the instability of Italian policy that despite earlier reservations on supporting Hungary, once Hungarian-Czechoslovak negotiations began on 9 Octobber, Mussolini instructed Ciano to bring pressure on Prague to cede to Hungary the Slovak areas which had a clear Hungarian majority.[32] The Hungarian Minister in Rome even told Ciano that Mussolini had expressed the opinion that Hungary should mobilize.[33]

The Hungarian negotiations with Czech and Slovak delegates which began in Komárno on 9 October, broke down four days later owing to the exorbitant demands of Budapest which managed to provoke the opposition of both the Czech and the Slovak negotiators. On the same day, 13 October, the Hungarian government informed Warsaw that it was considering an appeal to the Munich Powers to settle the dispute. Col. Beck reacted with an angry instruction to the Polish Minister in Budapest, Leon Orłowski, that if the Hungarians took such a step, Poland would disinterest herself from the whole affair.[34] The way to any

[28] *DGFP*, D, IV, no. 26.
[29] Lipski to Foreign Minister, 6 October 1938, cypher telegram no. 23, APEL, Cyphers, 1938.
[30] *DGFP*, D, V, no. 67.
[31] Wieniawa-Długoszowski to Foreign Minister, 11 October 1938, cypher letter no. 6, APEL, Cyphers, 1938.
[32] *Ciano's Diary 1937–1938*, 12 October 1938, p. 176.
[33] *Ibid.*, 13 October 1938, p. 177. Ciano offered one hundred Italian planes which could fly to Budapest to support an attempt to realize Hungarian objectives by military action. He made the offer on 5 October, and repeated it on 10 and 14 October; see *A Müncheni Egyezmény*, nos. 497, 530.
[34] Szembek, *Journal*, 13 October 1938, p. 354; see also *A Müncheni Egyezmény*, nos. 524, 527.

isolated Hungarian action was barred, in any case, by the threat of a Rumanian-Yugoslav action in the rear and by the veto of Hitler himself. The Führer told Darányi, a former Prime Minister of Hungary who was visiting Germany, that if a conflict broke out, Hungary would stand completely alone. He also told Darányi that the advantages of a Great Power Conference would be doubtful since the Powers were most likely to support Czechoslovakia.[35]

While Berlin was doing all it could to discourage any Hungarian action, military or diplomatic, Rome reverted to its policy of surreptitious support for Budapest. Mussolini favoured the project of a Great Power consultation on two conditions: the implementation of the Anglo-Italian agreement of 16 April, and the participation of Poland.[36] He suggested that the Conference take place in Brioni.[37] In this manner, with the participation of Poland and Italy, there would have been a good likelihood of attaining the much desired Polish-Hungarian frontier. Hitler, however, 'advised' the new Czechoslovak Foreign Minister, František Chvalkovský, to solve the question by direct negotiations with Hungary, and Mussolini thereupon abandoned his support for a Great Power Conference, suggesting German-Italian arbitration instead.[38] At the same time, to cover up the traces of his former action, he instructed Ciano to inform Berlin that Italy did not favour the Polish-Hungarian frontier. Ciano, although only a few days earlier he had feared a strong Hungary as a possible threat to Italian power in the Adriatic, noted that he would have been very glad to see Hungary and Poland knit together and that he feared further 'surprises' for Italy. He disliked the idea of direct Czechoslovak-Hungarian negotiations 'on the German model' and noted, somewhat inaccurately, 'this is the first time we have allowed ourselves to be taken in and I am not at all pleased.'[39] Since neither France nor Great Britain seemed interested in pressing for a Great Power Conference,[40]

[35] *DGFP*, D, IV, no. 62.   [36] *Ciano's Diary 1937–1938*, 11 October 1938, p. 176.
[37] *DGFP*, D, IV, no. 60.   [38] *Ibid.*, nos. 63, 64.
[39] *Ciano's Diary 1937–1938*, 15 October 1938, p. 178.
[40] Halifax told Raczyński on 17 October that in view of renewed negotiations between the interested parties on Hitler's initiative his government did not foresee any intervention on its part; Raczyński to Foreign Minister, 17 October 1938, cypher telegram no. 95, APEL, Cyphers, 1938. Bonnet told Łukasiewicz that since

and since there was little hope for fruitful Czechoslovak-Hungarian negotiations, the project for German-Italian arbitration seemed to have the best prospects. Such a solution, however, was the one which Col. Beck wished to avoid.

In the face of Hungary's failure to attain her ends by direct negotiations with Czechoslovakia, and her fear to take matters into her own hands,[41] Beck set himself energetically to the task of obtaining Rumanian consent to an eventual Hungarian annexation of Subcarpathian Ruthenia. On 18 October, Polish ambassadors in the chief capitals of Europe were informed that Poland aimed to obtain Rumanian co-operation 'so as not to hamper Hungarian revindications,'[42] and that this was to be accomplished by persuading Bucharest to claim the eastern tip of Subcarpathian Ruthenia. Michał Łubieński, Beck's Chef de Cabinet, was sent to Budapest to co-ordinate Polish diplomatic action with the Hungarians. The official aim of his mission was to stabilize Hungarian-Rumanian relations but, in fact, Łubieński apparently tried to persuade the Hungarians to annex Subcarpathian Ruthenia or, at least, to deter them from appealing to the signatories of the Munich Conference.[43] The Polish

---

Hungary had renewed negotiations and Mussolini had withdrawn the proposition for a conference of Foreign Ministers of the Great Powers, the French government had nothing to propose; Łukasiewicz to Foreign Minister, 18 October 1938, *ibid.*, cypher letter no. 17; see also *DBFP*, 3, III, no. 213.

[41] Ambassador András Hory, handing Szembek the Hungarian note of 15 October 1938, which demanded a speedy settlement, said the Hungarian Army was not so well equipped as the Czech and that there were fears of a Czech bombardment of Budapest; Szembek, *Journal*, 15 October 1938, p. 356.

[42] Szembek to Polish Embassies and Legations abroad, 18 October 1938, APEL, Cyphers, 1938.

[43] On 22 October, Szembek talked to Łubienski after his return from Budapest. Łubienski said that the Hungarians had made difficulties and that it had finally been decided that Horthy should write to Hitler asking for the evacuation of Subcarpathian Ruthenia by Czechoslovak troops; Szembek MSS, 22 October. The 'difficulties' apparently referred to the Polish plea that Hungary should annex Subcarpathian Ruthenia; see Macartney, *October Fifteenth*, I, p. 295. The Poles were very anxious to establish the common Polish-Hungarian frontier and knew this would not take place if the Hungarian claims were settled by German-Italian arbitration. On 29 October, the Hungarian Minister reported from Warsaw that Łubienski urged Hungary to annex Subcarpathian Ruthenia. The Hungarian Foreign Minister, however, told the Polish Minister in Budapest on the same day that only after the return of the former territory of upper Hungary would pressure be put on Subcarpathian Ruthenia; see *A Müncheni Egyezmény*, nos. 608, 611.

Foreign Minister himself decided to travel to Galaţi for a personal interview with King Carol.[44]

In his conversations with the King and the Rumanian Foreign Minister, N. Petresco-Comnène, Beck held out the inducement of a part of Subcarpathian Ruthenia and elaborated his project for a 'bloc of five states' capable of making a stand against both Germany and the USSR.[45] King Carol seemed disposed toward a relaxation of tensions with Hungary, but argued that Germany was exercising pressure against the creation of a Polish-Hungarian frontier, and intimated that Göring was opposed to the idea. Petresco-Comnène rejected the project on the ground of Rumania's obligations to the Little Entente and the likelihood of French opposition to any further German expansion at the cost of Czechoslovakia. Another objection was that the Polish-Hungarian frontier would cut Rumania off from Czechoslovakia, her main arms supply.[46]

Comnène's opposition to Beck's plans was not new; he had already opposed the cession of Subcarpathian Ruthenia to Hungary before Munich and he now stiffened his attitude.[47] He found support for his position in Paris, despite the fact that the French government was informed of the anti-German purpose of the common frontier.[48] Bonnet attributed the failure

[44] Beck asserts that an invitation had been extended by Franassovici, the Rumanian Ambassador in Warsaw; *Dernier Rapport*, p. 172. The Ambassador transmitted it on 15 October, Szembek MSS. It is clear, however, that the Polish Foreign Minister had intimated that such an invitation would be welcome; see Henryk Batowski, 'Le Voyage de Joseph Beck en Roumanie en Octobre 1938', Institut Polonais des Affaires Internationales, *Tirage à part de l'Annuaire polonais des Affaires Internationales* (Warsaw, 1959–1960), p. 149, n. 7; Polish version, 'Rumuńska Podróż Becka w październiku 1938 roku', *Kwartalnik Historyczny* (Warsaw, 1958), vol. LXV, no. 2, pp. 423–39.

[45] N. Petresco-Comnène, *Preludi del Grande Dramma (Ricordi e Documenti di un Diplomatico* (Rome, 1947), p. 295. The five states were: Poland, Hungary, Rumania, Yugoslavia, and Bulgaria.

[46] Beck to Lipski, 20 October 1938, cited by H. Batowski, 'Le Voyage de Joseph Beck,' pp. 152–4. Full text in MFA (London), P–G, 1938; also 22 October 1938, Szembek MSS.

[47] He informed the Italian Chargé d'Affaires in Bucharest that Rumania would not agree to the cession of Subcarpathian Ruthenia to Hungary for ethnographic, strategic, economic, and political reasons. He also expressed the belief that Czechoslovakia would make a recovery; Beck to Rogier Raczyński (Polish Minister in Bucharest), 21 October 1938, cypher telegram no. 96, APEL, Cyphers, 1938.

[48] General Dentz, Deputy Chief of the French General Staff, told the British Chargé d'Affaires in Paris that the Polish Attaché Militaire had informed him of

of Beck's mission to the influence of the Quai d'Orsay.[49] Although her role was not one of decisive importance, France undoubtedly played some part in Beck's discomfiture. There seemed to be only one person in the entourage of the King who shared the Polish Foreign Minister's views. Prince Frederick of Hohenzollern-Sigmaringen, the King's uncle, suggested to Beck that if the situation became more difficult Poland should call a conference of Hungarian, Czechoslovak, and Rumanian representatives. In such circumstances, the Prince thought that Rumania would adjust herself to the Polish position.[50] This interesting suggestion was never taken up by Poland.

When it was clear that attempts to gain Rumanian consent had failed, the Hungarian government, on 21 October, tentatively put forward the idea of a German-Italian arbitration of its dispute with Czechoslovakia.[51] Probably in the hope of some prospect for attaining the common frontier in the future, Budapest suggested that Germany and Italy should arbitrate on its demands for the towns of Nitra, Bratislava, and Košice in Slovakia, while German-Italian-Polish arbitration should be applied to the Hungarian claims to Užhorod and Mukačevo in Subcarpathian Ruthenia.[52] Although Italy was in favour of this plan, she as usual hesitated to commit herself.[53] Ribbentrop indicated strongly that he was opposed to the arbitration project on the flimsy plea that neither Budapest nor Prague would be satisfied with the result, and that Germany and Italy would have to use force to carry out the decisions.[54] Faced with determined

---

the necessity of erecting a common Polish-Hungarian frontier to contain the German *Drang nach Osten*; see *DBFP*, 3, III, no. 189.

[49] He wrote that King Carol and Comnène had French support in refusing Beck's proposals; *Défense de la Paix*, I, p. 328. The German embassy in Paris noted with surprise that the French press opposed the Polish-Hungarian frontier and rejoiced over Beck's failure in Bucharest, although the common frontier could have been to France's advantage in hindering German expansion in the South-East, FOL, 631/252306.

[50] Beck to Lipski, 20 October 1938, cited by H. Batowski, 'Le Voyage de Joseph Beck', see n. 44.

[51] *DGFP*, D, IV, no. 77, encl. 2.   [52] *Ibid.*, no. 80.

[53] Ciano noted on 21 October that Mussolini advised 'feeling the pulse of Germany before Poland is invited'. According to Ciano, von Mackensen 'made a particularly wry face on the idea of bringing in Poland, which was completely new to him'; *Ciano's Diary 1937–1938*, pp. 180-1.

[54] *Ibid.*

German opposition, Mussolini's half-hearted attempts to support Poland and Hungary collapsed again. Scared by a French press campaign which invested the common frontier with a definite anti-German flavour, the Italian Dictator instructed Ciano to take a definite stand against the Hungarian claim to Subcarpathian Ruthenia.[55]

After his failure in Galați, Col. Beck decided to work at least for the inclusion of Poland in an eventual Great Power arbitration, and instructed Ambassador Lipski to see Göring and, if possible, Ribbentrop in order to discuss the matter. The Field-Marshal angrily rejected the Rumanian imputations that he was opposed to the Polish-Hungarian project. He even told Lipski that if Germany and Italy agreed, he saw nothing against a Hungarian annexation of Subcarpathian Ruthenia. He stressed, however, that these were his personal views and should not be considered as official. In reply, Lipski told Göring that Poland wished to be consulted before Germany undertook any action on Subcarpathian Ruthenia.[56]

In view of the attitude of the High Command and the Ministry of Foreign Affairs, Göring's declarations can be interpreted only as an attempt to exercise a restraining influence on Poland at a juncture when joint Polish-Hungarian military action would not have been convenient for Germany. The proposals which Ribbentrop put to Lipski three days later, on 24 October, with regard to Danzig and the Corridor, should be seen in the same light. The Polish Ambassador, having been instructed to see Ribbentrop concerning Hungarian demands, pursued him to Berchtesgaden.[57] After Lipski had mentioned Poland's desire to participate in an eventual arbitration if this were decided upon, Ribbentrop, 'in strict confidence', revealed his reasons for inviting the Ambassador for the conversation. He stated then that in a 'general settlement' between Germany and Poland Danzig would have to return to the Reich, and an extra-territorial highway and railroad should be built through the

---

[55] *Ibid.*, 24 October 1938, p. 182.

[56] Lipski to Foreign Minister, 21 October 1938, by plane, MFA (London), P–G, 1938.

[57] The initiative was Polish. In his report of 21 October, Lipski wrote that he would do everything possible to see Rippentrop, even, if necessary, follow him to Munich; *ibid.*

Polish Corridor to connect Germany with East Prussia. When the conversation had taken this turn, Lipski dropped the topic of Polish participation in an arbitration of Hungarian claims. From later developments on this subject, it is clear that Ribbentrop was not seriously thinking at that moment of applying pressure on Poland for the return of the Free City and the construction of the highway. The German Foreign Minister was probably encouraged to bring up these questions by the forthcoming Franco-German declaration which he expected to sign at the beginning of November. His main purpose on 24 October, however, was to hold the Poles in check over Subcarpathian Ruthenia. Thus the conversation served both as a brake to any possible Polish designs of helping Hungary, and as a lever to keep the Poles out of an eventual German-Italian arbitration. Nevertheless, it was an omen of things to come and marked a turning point in Polish-German relations.[58]

The Hungarian government finally decided to make a formal application for German-Italian arbitration on 25 October, and was joined in this plea by Slovakia. For a week the proposition hung fire before Berlin finally gave its assent. Hungary and Italy still hoped that Poland would be included among the arbitrators. During Ribbentrop's visit to Rome which followed, Ciano referred to Italian sympathy for the Hungarian-Polish cause by reminding the German Foreign Minister that when the Prince of Hesse had brought forward Hitler's suggestion of a Four Power Conference a month before, Mussolini had accepted, with the proviso that Italian-British relations had first to be settled and that Poland should be included. Ribbentrop evaded the issue by saying that the situation was different from what it had been a month before. It was evident from Ciano's remark, and from his support of the Hungarian claims to Košice, Užhorod, and

---

[58] Conversation with the Foreign Minister of the Reich, Grand Hotel, Berchtesgaden, 24 October 1938, MFA (London), P–G, 1938; extracts in *PWB*, no. 44 and Szembek, *Journal*, 24 October 1938; German version in *DGFP* D, V, no. 81. The German objectives in this conversation were outlined in a note by Weizsäcker on 22 October, in which he suggested to Ribbentrop that, in return for a Polish-Hungarian frontier, Germany should ask for compensation in Danzig and Memel; *ibid.*, no. 85. For a discussion of the significance of the conversation for Polish-German relations see chap. VI of this book and Wojciechowski, *Stosunki Polsko-Niemieckie*, pp. 520–30.

Mukačevo—a claim officially supported in Berlin by the Poles[59]—that Italy wished to change the *status quo* in favour of Budapest,[60] and ultimately of Warsaw.

Germany's task of excluding Poland from the arbitration was facilitated not only by the violent opposition of Rumania[61] and the indecision of Italy but also by the continued disinterest of Great Britain[62] and the opposition of France. It was not surprising, therefore, that Berlin felt strong enough to tell Warsaw on 31 October that, after consultation with Rome and Budapest, the suggestion for the inclusion of Poland in the arbitration had been dropped.[63] It was decided that Ciano and Ribbentrop should sit in judgment on the Hungarian and Czechoslovak dispute at Vienna on 1 November. Poland was thus slighted by Germany for the second time within a month; first, she had not been invited to Munich, and now she was excluded from Vienna. For the second time, Germany broke her promise to consult Poland over Czechoslovakia.

When news reached Warsaw on 31 October that the arbitration was to take place in Vienna on the following day, Beck lost no time in manifesting his independence of the arbitrators by taking parallel but independent action in the same way as he had done on 30 September. Ultimatums were sent to Prague and Bratislava demanding frontier rectifications in the most important Carpathian and Tatra passes, in particular, Jablonka Pass, and in the districts of Spiš and Orava.[64] The Polish demands were accepted on the same day and it was agreed that delimitation commissions should be set up to fix the new frontier. Thus, once again, the Polish Foreign Minister escaped the fate of having his demands adjudged by other Powers. A secondary

[59] On 22 October, Ambassador Lipski again emphasized Polish interest in Subcarpathian Ruthenia and stated that Poland supported Hungarian claims to Užhorod and Mukačevo and for the rest favoured an autonomous region associated with Hungary; *DGFP*, D, V, no. 80.

[60] *Ibid.*, IV, no. 400.

[61] On 28 October, the Rumanian Chargé d'Affaires in Berlin asked on behalf of Petresco-Comnène that 'as a sign of friendship' Germany should oppose the Polish-Hungarian frontier; *ibid.*, V, no. 90.

[62] If anything, Great Britain was opposed to the inclusion of Poland in a Great Power Conference; *ibid.*, IV, no. 91.

[63] *Ibid.*, no. 98.

[64] *Ibid.*, V, nos. 93, 94; *DBFP*, 3, III, nos. 241, 242.

motive for Beck was, as ambassador Kennard put it, 'to have something as a set-off in case he does not attain a common frontier with Hungary'.[65]

The Vienna award of 1 November[66] once more overrode Polish-Hungarian plans for a common frontier, though it by no means put an end to them. The award made to Hungary verified Polish fears that the possibility of a semi-independent state in Subcarpathian Ruthenia was not to be excluded. Dr. Augustin Vološyn, leader of the National Ukrainian faction, organized a government in Hust based on the 'Karpatska Sič,' a militia formed on 8 November and headed by two leading members of the OUN (Organization of Ukrainian Nationalists). On 22 November, Slovakia and Subcarpathian Ruthenia became autonomous provinces.

Despite the Vienna decisions, Poland and Hungary did not give up hope of a common frontier, thus contesting the finality of the award, and they made their aims known in the European chancelleries and the press. The Polish Foreign Minister told Moltke menacingly that the population of Subcarpathian Ruthenia would soon express its desire for a plebiscite,[67] thereby taking up a tactic which had been rejected earlier when the objective had been the outright cession of that region to Hungary. The Hungarians, on the other hand, pinned their hopes to the possibility of creating disorders in the new province so as to justify military intervention. This plan found only vacillating support in Rome which, as before, favoured Budapest but feared Berlin.[68] Warsaw, too, despite hopes of Italian help,[69] found Rome chary on the matter. Not even the conferment on Ciano of the Order of the White Eagle, the highest Polish decoration,

[65] *DBFP, ibid.*, no. 243.

[66] Hungarian claims to Nitra and Bratislava were rejected but Slovakia lost Rimavská Sobota, Rožnáva, and Košice; in Subcarpathian Ruthenia, Užhorod and Mukačevo were given to Hungary; R. W. Seton-Watson, *A History of the Czechs and the Slovaks*, pp. 374–5; Macartney, *October Fifteenth*, I, p. 302.

[67] *DGFP*, D, V, no. 100.

[68] Ciano advised the Hungarian Foreign Minister, Kánya, against 'disorders' and intervention and told the Hungarian Ambassador, Villani, in Rome, 'I am particularly anxious that the Germans should not believe that we are playing a double game and that it is at our instigation that the Hungarians are throwing oil on the flames'; *Ciano's Diary 1937–1938*, 11 November 1938, pp. 193, 196.

[69] Beck told Szembek that Italy was clearly in favour of a common frontier; Szembek, *Journal*, 4 November 1938, p. 371.

could elicit a helpful attitude. The Italian Foreign Minister told the Polish Ambassador that if Germany should desire Italy to put pressure on the Hungarians to cease their agitation in Sub-carpathian Ruthenia, Italy would have to comply. Wieniawa-Długoszowski reminded Ciano of his 'whispered words' at the time of the Vienna Award 'that after the towns the rest would come of itself', but the Italian Foreign Minister replied evasively that if the Hungarians had taken action when the time was ripe, the matter would have been settled.[70]

Hungary, for her part, did not have the courage to take matters into her own hands and tried, despite all clear signs of German opposition, to obtain the fiat of Berlin for her ambitions. The only result was a blunt rebuff. The Regent's declaration that, in the event of an 'explosion' in Subcarpathian Ruthenia, Hungarian troops would march in met with a warning that Czechoslovakia 'would not endure such action', that Germany would not give Hungary any support and that she considered the action to be 'inopportune'. The German press was instructed not to publish any information on incidents in Subcarpathian Ruthenia. This time, despite the German attitude and his own previous vacillation, Mussolini appeared ready to take radical steps in support of Budapest. When the Hungarian government notified him on 20 November that it planned to take action within twenty-four hours,[71] Mussolini sent his good wishes and promised the despatch of one hundred Italian fighter planes to defend Budapest from a possible Czech attack.[72] At the last moment, however, the Duce wavered and informed Hitler at short notice of the impending Hungarian action, whereupon the

---

[70] Wieniawa-Długoszowski to Foreign Minister, 18 November 1938, cypher letter no. 7, APEL, Cyphers, 1938. Beck's opinion is borne out by Hungarian documents which show that until 28 October 1938 Ciano and Mussolini supported the concept of a common Polish-Hungarian frontier through a Hungarian annexation of Subcarpathian Ruthenia, even after the Germans had expressed opposition to this project; see *A Müncheni Egyezmény*, nos. 120, 368, 456, 480, 519, 533, 598. The Italian offers of air support were made with this object in mind; see supra n. 33.

[71] *DGFP*, D, IV, nos. 118, 122, 126, and 128, *passim*.

[72] The Regent informed the German Minister in Budapest of the Italian offer a few days after the venture had been vetoed in Berlin; *ibid.*, no. 139. Ciano had already made the same promise to Hungary in case of a Czechoslovak attack on 5 October; *Ciano's Diary 1937–1938*, p. 173.

Führer issued an express veto to the Hungarians.[73] Mussolini beat a hasty retreat and assured Hitler that he would join him in a *démarche* in Budapest if the German leader desired it.[74] The Polish-Hungarian project was thus foiled for a third time. The Germans made a token effort to assuage Polish discontent by communicating to Warsaw their note to Budapest and by asking whether Poland would join in the German *démarche* advising the Hungarians not to take any action 'for the time being'. Beck turned this proposal aside on the ground that Poland had not participated in the Vienna arbitration, and that she did not consider the solution reached there on Subcarpathian Ruthenia as satisfactory. He refused to be mollified by Ribbentrop's denial of all rumours of German plans for a Great Ukraine with a nucleus in Subcarpathian Ruthenia, and by Moltke's statement that Polish demands for a cessation of Ukrainian broadcasts from Vienna had been complied with. The Polish Foreign Minister also warned the Ambassador that Poland would deal with Subcarpathian Ruthenia herself, if that region should prove troublesome to her.[75]

The bitter fruits of the failure of the Polish-Hungarian project began to appear in December, when the UNDO (Ukrainian National Democratic Organization) deputies in the Polish *Sejm* demanded autonomy for south-eastern Poland (the former Eastern Galicia) and Volhynia.[76] Germany, meanwhile, continued to support the Ukrainian independence movements which had their headquarters in Vienna and Bratislava. Beck blamed the failure of his plans on Hungary's tortuous and cowardly policy[77] while the Hungarians declared that, if they had been in Poland's position, they would have annexed Subcarpathian Ruthenia.[78] It is possible that if Beck had moved at the time of the Munich Conference, or immediately after it, to federate with Slovakia or to protect its autonomy, he might have paved the way to the Hungarian absorption of Subcarpathian

[73] *DGFP*, D, IV, no. 128. [74] *Ibid.*, no. 129.

[75] The Minister's conversation with Ambassador von Moltke, 22 November 1938, MFA (London), P–G, 1938. Moltke's account of the conversation gives the gist but not the trenchant tone of the Polish version; see *DGFP*, D, V, no. 104.

[76] See Roos, *Polen und Europa*, p. 375.

[77] Szembek, *Journal*, 22 November 1938, p. 378.

[78] *Ibid.*, 15 October 1938, p. 356.

Ruthenia, and thus to the realization of the common frontier. The Polish Minister did not, however, take such action since it might have led to conflict with Germany. Moreover, even if he had chosen such a course, the common frontier would not of itself have sufficed to check German expansion. For Poland and Hungary to play such a role, they needed the support of at least one Great Power, and of that there was no sign. Great Britain did nothing, although Lord Halifax gave passing consideration to the possibility that a common Polish-Hungarian frontier 'might strengthen Poland and Hungary in their desire to retain sufficient independence to avoid becoming vassals of Germany'.[79] Mussolini, although he would have liked to see a check to German expansion in the Balkans, was restrained by his fear of antagonizing Berlin and by his plans for conquest in Albania and North Africa where he would need German support. The failure of the common frontier project was, in fact, seen as a defeat in Rome, but a defeat on a sector of secondary importance.[80] Finally, France was opposed to the plan on the official plea that Czechoslovakia was still a factor in international politics. Ironically enough, Rumanian opposition to the Polish-Hungarian frontier did not strengthen Czechoslovakia, but led to the closer dependence of Bucharest on Berlin, to which Rumanian politicians turned in their obsessive fear of Hungarian aggrandizement.[81] French policy too was dictated by other considerations than those of supporting the amputated Czechoslovak state.

The immediate aim of French foreign policy after the Munich Conference was to obtain an agreement with Germany on the model of the Anglo-German declaration on consultation which was signed by Chamberlain and Hitler on 30 September. The significance which such an agreement had for France was, however, very different from its meaning for Great Britain. For the British government the declaration was a continuation of its policy of disinterest in East Central Europe, while for France it signalled a further withdrawal from this region.

[79] *DBFP*, 3, III, no. 226.

[80] Wieniawa-Długoszowski to Foreign Minister, 1 December 1938, *ZH*, 6, no. VIII.

[81] See *DGFP*, D, V, nos. 227, 234, 237, 239.

A Franco-German agreement, with all the implications it carried for policy towards East Central Europe, had long had its supporters in France but it was only after Munich that Bonnet felt the time ripe for such a course and he envisaged further revision of the Versailles Treaty with equanimity. The same trend of thought prevailed in London. The United States Ambassador at St. James's, Joseph Kennedy, reported at the beginning of October that Lord Halifax did not think a war with Germany would be justified, unless she interfered directly with the British Dominions. According to Kennedy's report, Halifax had said that Britain and France intended to strengthen their air defences so that nobody could 'get fresh with them' and

> after that, to let Hitler go ahead and do what he likes in Central and South Eastern Europe. In other words, there is no question in Halifax's mind that reasonably soon Hitler will make a start for Danzig, with Polish concurrence, and then go for Memel, with Lithuanian concurrence, and even if he decides to go into Rumania it is Halifax's idea that England should mind her own business.[82]

Thus the Foreign Secretary's attitude towards further German expansion in Eastern Europe was based on the assumption that it would encounter no local resistance. It was of great importance for the future that if this hypothesis proved incorrect there would be room for a different policy on the part of Great Britain.

Encouraged by the indifference of London towards further German aggrandizement, Bonnet lost no time in working for a Franco-German agreement. The first move was made by Ambassador André François-Poncet on 13 October, when he elaborated in Berlin a proposal for a joint declaration. He suggested that the declaration should consist of three parts: a Non-Aggression Pact, a consultation agreement, and an agreement on currency questions.[83] Berlin welcomed the French over-

---

[82] *FRUS*, 1938, I, p. 85.
[83] *DGFP*, D, IV, no. 338. Bonnet tried to present this move to his Cabinet as a German initiative; see Philippe Henriot (ed.), *Les Carnets de Jean Zay* (Paris, 1942), pp. 168–70. This was also the impression created by the selected documents in the *Livre Jaune Français* (Paris, 1939), no. 18, and by François-Poncet in his memoirs, pp. 344–5. In his *Défense de la Paix*, II, pp. 23–4, however, Bonnet attributed the idea to François-Poncet, while the German Ambassador in Paris reported at the time that Bonnet had claimed the initiative as his own; *DGFP*, D, IV, no. 351.

ture, and the agreement would have been signed early in November had it not been for the assassination of the Counsellor of the German Embassy in Paris, von Rath. The Counsellor was killed by a Jewish refugee from Germany and the German government used the incident as a pretext to start a violent persecution of Jews in the Reich. These events delayed the agreement, particularly since it was to be signed during Ribbentrop's visit to Paris.

The forthcoming Franco-German agreement was intimately bound up with the question whether France should maintain her most important alliance in East Central Europe, the alliance with Poland. At the end of October, ambassador Léon Noël wrote a long letter to Bonnet analysing the Franco-Polish alliance and advising radical modifications. Noël warned that a change in Hitler's policy towards Poland was possible and that this could take the form of a demand for the cession of the Corridor. Poland, thought Noël, might be allowed to keep Gdynia and the railway connecting it with the hinterland, together with the use of the Vistula and of the port of Danzig. He also noted that an exchange of population in the Corridor, Western Pomerania, Poznania, and even Upper Silesia might be demanded by Germany. Poland, wrote the ambassador, would never accept such demands. Everything should therefore be done to prevent the situation from developing into another Munich, especially since French public opinion would not support any military action on this issue. Col. Beck himself had drawn Noël's attention to the French press campaign under the slogan, 'We will not fight for Danzig.' The ambassador proposed to Bonnet that the obligation of automatic military assistance should be abrogated, so that the French government could retain its freedom of action and the alliance attain some of the flexibility of the old Franco-Russian pact. He counselled, however, against a complete break of relations with Poland for she would then be left with a choice of partition or vassalage to Germany. On these grounds, he proposed a revision of the Military Convention of 1921, on the lines of the French efforts which had been made to this end in 1924, 1928, 1934, and 1936. This attempt, he wrote, should be taken up again and the existing agreements replaced by a 'pacte d'amitié et de consultation', complemented by a military agreement equally limited in scope. He also suggested that the negotiations should be used to put pressure on Poland to make her more 'loyal' to France, and that they could begin on the basis of the Polish memorandum of 26 May 1938.[84]

When Noël discussed the project with Bonnet in Paris in November, the latter told him that he had examined the alliance with Poland 'under a magnifying glass', and had decided that, even as it stood, it provided sufficient loopholes to prevent France from being drawn into a war. At the same time, he seemed anxious to abrogate all French agreements in East Central and Eastern Europe, including the alliance with Poland and the mutual assistance pact with the Soviet Union. However, Noël, probably aided by the military, persuaded Bonnet not to throw away the potential support of the Polish Army,[85] though General Gamelin agreed on the necessity of revising the Franco-Polish Military Convention of 1921.[86]

Bonnet's vacillations were reflected in the French press, which openly questioned the continuation of the alliance, and in the debates in the Chamber of Deputies. The Counsellor of the Polish Embassy in Paris, Anatol Muhlstein, told Szembek in mid-October that the alliance had, in fact, 'morally' ceased to exist.[87] The right wing in the Chamber had split into the 'Munichois' and 'Antimunichois', with the defenders of Munich in the majority. Among the latter, Etienne Flandin was prominent in suggesting that Germany be given a free hand in East Central Europe, and, in November, the Congress of his party, the 'Alliance Démocratique', voted overwhelmingly in favour of this

[84] Noël, *L'Agression Allemande contre la Pologne*, pp. 248–57. Noël referred to Beck's instruction of 24 May 1938. The Ambassador noted in his book that extracts of his report of 28 October 1938 were to have been published in the *Livre Jaune Français* but were omitted by 'error'.

[85] Noël, p. 259.

[86] According to Gamelin, Noël's reasons for revising the Military Convention were different from those which the Ambassador gave in his book. To Gamelin, Noël stressed the dangers of an alliance with an 'impulsive' nation and of Polish intransigence towards the Soviet Union which, he asserted, was an 'embarrassment' to France; Gamelin, *Servir*, II, p. 380. It is noteworthy that there is no record of the French General Staff's having seriously considered military co-operation with the Soviet Union in 1938.

[87] Szembek, *Journal*, 15 October 1938, p. 355.

policy.[88] Flandin and his supporters preached the abandonment of Poland on the plea that, by this means, France could improve her position in Europe.[89] The semi-official *Temps*, regarded as the mouthpiece of the Quai d'Orsay, published an article stating that in view of the new state of affairs in Central Europe the interest of the Western Powers in East European conflicts must, of necessity, be considerably more limited than before.[90] The Polish ambassador in Brussels reported that he had heard from the Belgian Ministry of Foreign Affairs that the Quai d'Orsay was considering the abrogation of the alliances with Poland and the Soviet Union.[91]

The Franco-German agreement was finally signed on 6 December 1938. The text of the declaration itself[92] did not indicate any abandonment of French alliances, but neither did it expressly confirm them; clause three merely stipulated consultation between France and Germany on all questions of mutual interest while reserving their relations with third Powers. Léon Blum had a point when he asked why the word 'relations' was used instead of pacts, alliances, or even agreements.[93] There is no record of any express declaration of French withdrawal from East Central Europe, as Ribbentrop later asserted,[94] but the only existing document of the Paris conversations leaves little doubt that this was Bonnet's intention. When the German Foreign Minister remarked that France should recognize Eastern Europe as a German sphere of influence and should abolish the remaining French alliances there, Bonnet made no protest. On the contrary, he remarked that France's relations in that part of the world had since Munich been 'fundamentally altered in this respect'.[95]

[88] See René Rémond, *La Droite en France de 1815 à nos Jours: Continuité et Diversité d'une Tradition Politique* (Paris, 1954), p. 225.

[89] Flandin maintained this view even after World War II. In his book on French policy, he wrote that France should have profited from Munich to denounce the Polish alliance and so have her hands free to redress her position in Europe; *Politique Française, 1919–1940* (Paris, 1947), p. 283.

[90] *Le Temps*, 28 November 1938.   [91] Roos, *Polen und Europa*, p. 377.

[92] *Livre Jaune Français*, no. 28.

[93] Léon Blum, *L'Histoire Jugera* (Montreal, 1943), p. 212.

[94] See *Livre Jaune Français*, no. 163.

[95] *DGFP*, D, IV, no. 370. In the record of this conversation, which took place on 6 December, Ambassador Welczeck, the Secretary of the Quai d'Orsay, Alexis Léger, and Paul Schmidt, the German interpreter, are listed as present. Paul

Confirmation of Bonnet's intention to liberate himself from
French commitments in East Central Europe is provided by the
comments of André François-Poncet and Robert Coulondre on
German policy on the one hand, and by the Foreign Minister's
attitude to Poland on the other. André François-Poncet commented that Hitler wanted peace but that he was at the same
time determined to split the Anglo-French bloc and to stabilize
the situation in the West so that he could have 'a free hand in the
East'. The question was only whether Russia or Poland was the
intended victim.[96] François-Poncet's successor in Berlin, Robert
Coulondre, reported in December, nine days after the signature
of the Franco-German declaration, that German renunciation
of conquest in the West was a corollary to expansion in the East,
and that this was the gist of many conversations which he had
had with important personages in Berlin.[97] A similar interpretation of the agreement of 6 December was given by the
German press, according to which France was expected to
recognize Germany's 'natural' position in Europe, and this
recognition justified and obliged the latter to pursue a con-
structive policy in East Central Europe.[98]

Bonnet's attitude to Poland was well known in Warsaw, thanks
to the French press and the reports of ambassador Łukasiewicz.
The ambassador painted a pessimistic but correct picture in his
report on French foreign policy after Munich, and on Ribbentrop's visit to Paris. On the basis of information which he had
received from Bonnet himself, Łukasiewicz estimated that
Ribbentrop had obtained an assurance that France would not
resist German expansion in the Danube Basin, and that he must

---

Schmidt confirms this version of the conversation in his book, *Statist auf Diplo-
matischer Bühne* (Bonn, 1949), pp. 423–4. Bonnet, however, asserts that only one
conversation took place, at which Schmidt was not present, *Défense de la Paix*, II,
p. 26. For an analysis of the documents showing that at least two conversations took
place of which the conversation on 6 December was one, see Jan Przewłocki,
'Jeszcze Raz o Rozmowach Bonnet-Ribbentrop' (Once Again on the Bonnet-
Ribbentrop Conversations), *Studia z Najnowszych Dziejów Powszechnych* (Warsaw,
1963), vol. 5, pp. 213–23. For a discussion of the significance of the agreement, see
Zbigniew Kulak, 'Spotkanie Ribbentrop-Bonnet z 6go grudnia 1938 roku' (The
Ribbentrop-Bonnet Meeting of 6 December 1938), *Przegląd Zachodni* (Poznań,
1957), no. 3, pp. 1–17.
[96] François-Poncet, *Souvenirs*, p. 348; *Livre Jaune Français*, no. 18.
[97] *Livre Jaune Français*, no. 33.   [98] *Frankfurter Zeitung*, 7 December 1938.

also have carried away from Paris the impression that France would not oppose any expansion of German political influence in this region.[99] The declaration of 6 December meant, in fact, a 'free hand' for Germany in East Central Europe, not only with regard to the Danube Basin or to German plans for a Great Ukraine[100] but also with respect to Poland. The ambassador reported that there was no lack of signs that if, for some reason, France found herself faced with the problem of carrying out her obligations to Poland, she would make every effort to extricate herself. This attitude resulted from the French estimate of the international situation. France, he observed, was too weak either to cancel her obligations or to face up to them; her only policy, therefore, was one of resignation and of a defeatist attitude towards everything that took place in Central and Eastern Europe. The only factor which France could oppose to the Axis was her alliance with Great Britain, and in this partnership she played a passive role. The alliances with Poland and the Soviet Union were not considered as having any significance and, what is more, they were even resented as a burden. Łukasiewicz thought that a change in French policy could only take place in one of three situations. In the first case, France might, under British influence, undertake an offensive policy towards Italy and Germany; in the second, she might change her policy, if events proved that Poland could offer an effective resistance to Germany, and thus influence the attitude of other countries in Central and Eastern Europe. Another possibility for a change of policy might arise if France were forced to be more active, even without British support, on the Italian sector. She would then, thought Lukasiewicz, bring her continental alliances into play, but only in an accessory role and never on a level of equality with the British connection.[101] Thus, in the state of Polish-French relations after Munich, the situation was extremely uncertain, and Warsaw had to face the growing likelihood of French desertion. The greatest danger which threatened Poland now

[99] Łukasiewicz to Foreign Minister, 17 December 1938, Political Report, *PD*, I.

[100] In his defence of French policy at this time, André Schérer makes the interesting statement that there never was any question of French support for Germany, but merely of letting her do as she pleased; 'Les Mains Libres à l'Est,' *Revue de l'Histoire de la Seconde Guerre Mondiale*, vol. 8 (1958), no. 32, p. 23.

[101] Łukasiewicz, *PD*, I, 17 December 1938.

was that she might be the next victim of a 'peaceful settlement' between the major Powers.[102]

In these circumstances, Beck's plans for a Third Europe had little chance of success. He had hoped for Italian support, but had been disappointed. The opportunity for co-ordinated action with Hungary had not been utilized during the last stages of the Czechoslovak crisis, because, until the last moment, Beck had taken into account the possibility of a European war over Czechoslovakia and in such a war Poland could not fight on the side of Germany. When action could have been taken, after the crisis, it was apparent that neither Poland nor Hungary felt strong enough to take the initiative. Budapest did not want to risk a conflict with Rumania or Yugoslavia, and, in particular, it did not wish to cross Berlin. Beck did not feel that in Poland's exposed position and cool relations with France he could afford to strain relations with Hitler. Finally, he failed to win over the Rumanian government, nervous as always of any strengthening of Hungary, to the concept of a common frontier between Hungary and Poland.

Yet the Third Europe concept could have had some interesting results if it had been given some effective support from the outside. That it might have fulfilled the role assigned to it by Beck of stemming further German expansion in Eastern Europe[103] is borne out by the determined opposition which it encountered in Berlin precisely on those grounds. It is interesting to note that the Soviet Ambassador in Berlin told Ambassador Lipski in October that the USSR favoured the creation of a Polish-Hungarian frontier, an attitude presumably dictated by the dislike it shared with Poland of the prospect of an independent Subcarpathian Ruthenia and its effect on their Ukrainian populations,[104] but also perhaps by the realization

---

[102] The U.S. Ambassador in Poland to the Secretary of State on 5 November 1938, *FRUS*, I, 1938, p. 731.

[103] Wojciechowski interprets Beck's Third Europe concept as being essentially anti-Soviet, although he cites Soviet support for a common Polish-Hungarian frontier and gives Beck's failure to attain his objectives in Polish-German relations as one of the motives for the project; *Stosunki Polsko-Niemieckie*, pp. 504, 508. Kozeński calls the Third Europe concept unrealistic but thinks that its implementation would have barred the way to further German expansion eastward; *Czechostowacja w Polskiej Polityce Zagranicznej*, p. 289.

[104] Wojciechowski, p. 508.

that a new bloc of states opposed to Germany would be in the Soviet interest. The Soviet attitude could, however, hardly be expected to go beyond a lack of diplomatic protest, whereas what was needed was the support of a Great Power able and willing to intervene in Eastern Europe. Italy had an interest in preventing the spread of German domination over the Balkans, but Ciano's idea of a 'Rome-Budapest-Bucharest-Warsaw Axis' could not have been realized without the support of France and Britain. Neither Chamberlain nor Bonnet, despite all their desire of detaching Mussolini from Hitler, ever seriously considered the possibilities of such a policy. Such a course of action was excluded by the assumption which then lay at the base of French and British policy, the desire to reach an agreement with Hitler even at the cost of further German aggrandizement in the East.[105] A few months later, in March and April 1939, British diplomacy was to attempt the creation of a bloc of East European states backed by its guarantees, but by that time it was too late.

[105] This was in particular the attitude of Bonnet, despite his denials in *Défense de la Paix*, II, chap. I. In glaring contradiction to this book, he claims that the Franco-German declaration of 6 December 1938 could have been the first step towards a 'United States of Europe', and that Hitler could have later obtained ample satisfaction for his Danzig and Corridor claims from a new conference, if only he had waited; see G. Bonnet, *Le Quai d'Orsay sous Trois Républiques* (Paris, 1961), pp. 240–43.

VI

DANZIG AND THE CORRIDOR: INTERLUDE BEFORE THE STORM

THE period from 24 October 1938 until 15 March 1939 constituted in Polish-German relations an interlude between uneasy friendship and open hostility. The attitude of France and Great Britain towards East Central Europe after Munich, and particularly the policy of France, encouraged Hitler in the belief that Poland, having no support from the West, was bound to accept the best terms that she could. But the Führer was not yet willing to exercise pressure on Warsaw and attempted to gain his ends by persuasion; thus German policy at this time was one of advances and retreats. Col. Beck, on the other hand, played a consummate waiting-game. Without breaking off conversations with Berlin, he tried to maintain good relations and had some hope of a reasonable agreement on Danzig which would safeguard Polish rights in the Free City. At the same time, he strove to avoid any decision on Danzig by the League of Nations which would be detrimental to Poland and sought British agreement to his request that this question should not be settled without Polish participation. It is a measure of Beck's success that he attained the last two objectives and that, by the time of the German occupation of Prague on 15 March 1939, the ground had been prepared for an official British commitment to Poland.

In October 1938, with the Franco-German declaration in the

offing, Hitler took up Stresemann's old policy of peace in the West and revision in the East. The first warning signals of German intentions had already appeared in the Hitler-Lipski conversation on 20 September in Berchtesgaden, when the Führer had countered Lipski's demands for an agreement on Danzig and an extension of the Declaration of Non-Aggression with a proposal for an extra-territorial highway linking Germany and East Prussia. Hitler's intention seems, at that time, to have been to checkmate Polish demands on Danzig and the common frontier with Hungary, rather than to initiate pressure on Poland. It appears that after Munich Hitler thought in terms of a future reorganization of East Central Europe which would be sanctioned by an international guarantee. 'Trial balloons' on the Danzig and Corridor issues were launched in the French and British press with the aim of sounding out the attitude of those governments. Nevertheless, from the treatment of this problem and other questions in Polish-German relations by Berlin, it was evident that Hitler did not consider the time ripe for putting Poland's back to the wall, and that he thought he could gain his ends by persuasion.

German soundings of Polish and Western reactions on the subject of Danzig and the Corridor took the form of hints in a diplomatic conversation[1] and of rumours 'leaked', principally to British newspapers in the first half of October. On 12 October, the *Daily Express*, and on the next day the *News Chronicle*, carried almost identical reports of a Polish-German agreement on German sovereignty over Danzig, an exchange of populations, and a highway connecting Germany and East Prussia. Two days later, the *Daily Express* reported rumours that in return for Danzig, Hitler would give up German claims to the Corridor. Ambassador Lipski evaluated these reports as German 'ballons d'essai', and recommended a formal *démenti* by the Polish Embassy in London.[2] It is typical of German tactics that an

[1] The German Minister of Trade, Walther Funk, spoke to the Polish Ambassador in Ankara, Michał Sokolnicki, at the beginning of October about Germany's need for a land connection with East Prussia and mentioned a 'Corridor through the Corridor' hinting at compensation for Poland in Soviet territory; see M. Sokolnicki, 'Na rozdrożu Czasów' (The Parting of the Ways, *Kultura*, no. 1/2, 111–12, Paris, 1957).

[2] Lipski to Foreign Minister, 14 October 1938, cypher telegram no. 24 APEL, Cyphers, 1938.

official denial of these rumours was published by the *Angriff* in Berlin on 15 October, along the lines of the denial issued by the Polish embassy in London. Ribbentrop was apparently willing to see Col. Beck on the subject, for on 22 October the Polish Foreign Minister informed Lipski that such a meeting could only take place if there was a prospect of extending the 1934 agreement or of obtaining a declaration on the Polish-German frontier, or of a regulation of the Danzig question.[3] The Polish attitude was thus diametrically opposed to the German.

It seems that Hitler, at this time, was thinking of changes in Danzig and the Corridor within the framework of an internationally guaranteed Polish-German frontier. In a conversation with the Inspector General for German Highways at the end of October, the Führer expressed the opinion that if there was to be any international guarantee for Polish Pomerania, Germany would have to be granted a 'traffic corridor' through the existing Corridor for a highway and possibly a railway line as well. Nothing could be more effective, Hitler said, in lending force to a guarantee for the Polish Corridor than the elimination, by means of such a highway, of the economic disadvantages which the Corridor involved for Germany.[4]

The tactics used to further German aims were those of persuasion and particular care was taken not to ruffle Polish feelings unduly on other questions, such as the German minority in Poland and the Ukrainian broadcasts from Vienna, and instructions were issued to avoid the impression of co-operation between official German agencies and the Ukrainians.[5] Likewise, the German government took no notice of complaints by the *Volksdeutsche Mittelstelle* as to the alleged mistreatment of Germans in Trans-Olza,[6] except to register a routine diplomatic

[3] Beck to Lipski, 22 October 1938, cypher telegram, MFA (London), P–G, 1938.

[4] In reporting this conversation to Ribbentrop on 27 October, Todt, General Inspector of Highways, wrote that there were two possible courses for the highway: (*a*) an approach from Bütow to Elbing, via Praust, running about 40 km. through the Polish Corridor and 75 km. through Danzig territory; (*b*) between Schlochau and Marienwerder, running about 85 km. through Polish territory (see Map I). Todt claimed that the Polish military preferred the latter; *DGFP*, D, V, no. 86. There is no evidence that any such opinion had been given by the Poles.

[5] Schliep, 22 October 1938, Office of the State Secretary, 147 PGD, Hoover.

[6] The Head of the *Volksdeutsche Mittelstelle*, Werner Lorenz, complained to Ribbentrop at the beginning of November that the German press had not taken a

protest.[7] Hitler confirmed, on 11 October, instructions for the press to release nothing unfavourable on the German minority in Poland.[8] The only incident which created a certain amount of friction between the two governments at this time concerned Polish Jews living in Germany. The Polish government decreed, at the beginning of October, that Polish passports and passes would be valid only if ratified by Polish consulates by the end of the month. On 28 October, the Gestapo organized a mass transport of Polish Jews to the Polish frontier. The Polish government protested against their dispossession and threatened retaliatory measures against Germans living in Poland. Finally, an agreement was completed in January 1939, whereby a certain number of Polish citizens were allowed to return to Germany to settle their affairs and bring their families to Poland.[9] The matter was not publicized by either government and its settlement showed, as did the German handling of other problems, that Berlin was not disposed to put any undue pressure on Poland.

The clearest evidence of the fact that Germany did not intend to press the matter of Danzig and the highway to an immediate issue can be seen from the manner in which the first formulation of official demands was made and in the later development of conversations on this subject between October 1938 and January 1939. On 24 October, Ribbentrop proposed a 'Gesamtlösung' (total solution) involving the return of Danzig to Germany, an extra-territorial highway, and a multiple-track railway line through the Corridor. Poland was to receive guarantees for a market for her goods in Danzig, a recognition of

stand on the mistreatment of Germans in Trans-Olza and that this encouraged the exodus of Germans from the region. He suggested that Hitler take the matter up with the Polish Ambassador, that the provincial press be allowed to report 'incidents', and that the Bund Deutscher Osten, as a 'private organization', be allowed to attack Polish policy without attacking the Polish government; Leader of the *Volksdeutsche Mittelstelle* to Foreign Minister, 5 November 1938, FOL, 147/78694–99.

[7] Szembek, *Journal*, 27 October 1938, p. 364.

[8] *DGFP*, D, V, no. 70.

[9] 'Aufzeichnung', 11, 15 November 1938, 147, PDG, Hoover, also FOL, 147/78708–28. This was probably in answer to the Foreign Minister's request for a memorandum on the state of negotiations; *DGFP*, D, V, no. 97. Also Szembek, *Journal*, 17 November 1938, p. 374. Documents and correspondence on the problem are in the archives of the Polish Ministry of Foreign Affairs, Warsaw.

her eastern frontier and an extension of the Declaration of Non-Aggression of 1934 for twenty-five years. Ribbentrop also proposed that Poland should accede to the Anti-Comintern Pact,[10] thus holding out by implication the old prospect of territorial compensation in the East at the expense of Russia.[11] Although the proposals made by Ribbentrop presaged a radical change of policy on the Danzig and Corridor questions, they should be viewed in the context in which they were made. Ribbentrop put forward his proposals at a time when Lipski wished to discuss the Polish-Hungarian frontier and Poland's participation in an eventual German-Italian arbitration of the dispute between Hungary and Czechoslovakia.[12] Moreover, the German Foreign Minister was in no hurry to obtain an answer and wished to keep the conversation secret. He asked Lipski to repeat his proposals orally to Col. Beck, and extended an invitation to the Polish Foreign Minister to discuss the question with him in the coming month. When Lipski told him that he did not consider the cession of Danzig to Germany possible, if only for domestic reasons, Ribbentrop hastened to assure him that he did not want an immediate answer.[13]

When the Polish response to the German proposals turned out to be negative, the reaction of Berlin was extraordinarily mild. Beck made his position clear in an interview with Mr William Hillman, a correspondent of the Hearst papers, at the end of October. He stated that all rumours of Polish-German negotiations for a return of Danzig to Germany, and for a German right of transit through the Corridor, were false.[14] On 31 October, the Polish Foreign Minister instructed Lipski to communicate a categorical rejection of the German proposals on Danzig, and indicated that while he favoured the replacement of the League of Nations mandate by a bilateral Polish-German agreement,

[10] *DGFP*, D, V, no. 81.

[11] In a conversation with Burckhardt on 17 December 1938, Ribbentrop told him that the 'small solution' involving the annexation of Memel and Danzig to Germany was favoured by Forster, while the 'great solution' envisaging the annexation of Danzig, Toruń and Poznań in return for territorial compensation for Poland in the East was favoured at that time by Göring and apparently by Hitler also; Burckhardt, *Meine Danziger Mission*, p. 201.

[12] See also *supra*, chap. V., pp. 162–63.

[13] *DGFP*, D, V, no. 81.

[14] Beck, *Przemówienia*, pp. 390–4; *Detroit Sunday Times*, 30 October 1938.

this would have to guarantee the existence of the Free City with all Polish rights therein. He made his attitude quite plain by warning that

> notwithstanding the complications involved in such a system, the Polish Government must state that any other solution, and in particular any attempt to incorporate the Free City into the Reich, must inevitably lead to a conflict.[15]

While the rumours of an impending Polish-German agreement on Danzig continued, accompanied by conjectures on eventual compensation for Poland in Lithuania and Russia,[16] and Lipski waited impatiently to communicate Beck's answer to Ribbentrop, the latter seemed curiously uninterested in seeing the Polish Ambassador and hearing the Polish reply to his proposals. On 12 November, Lipski reported that the German Foreign Minister was inaccessible and surmised that perhaps he wished negotiations with Poland to take place only after an understanding with France had been reached.[17] It was not until 19 November—almost a month after he had put forward his demands—that Ribbentrop finally granted the Ambassador an interview. Surprisingly enough, far from being angered by the communication of Beck's refusal, Ribbentrop seemed to beat a retreat. He emphasized his desire for good Polish-German relations, and stressed the fact that he had discussed their stabilization with the Chancellor only in very general terms. He also said that his suggestions of 24 October had been put forward on his own initiative; he thus dissociated Hitler from the proposals and gave them only a semi-official status. At the same time, he expressed regret that Beck had given a press interview on Danzig without first consulting Germany. Beck, on the other hand, used the highway project as a tactical manœuvre to keep the door open for negotiations. When Ribbentrop asked Lipski about Polish reactions to his highway proposal, he received a vague reply that this might be possible to arrange.[18] Three days later, Ambassador Moltke told Beck, on the occasion of transmitting a copy of the German memorandum to Budapest, that

---

[15] *PWB*, no. 45.   [16] *DBFP*, 3, III, no. 298.

[17] Lipski to Foreign Minister, 12 November 1938, MFA (London), P-G, 1938.

[18] *PWB*, no. 46; Lipski to Foreign Minister, 19 November 1938, MFA (London), P-G, 1938; *DGFP*, D, V, no. 101.

Ribbentrop continued to attach the greatest importance to good Polish-German relations and considered that the solution of the problems in hand could be found on 'another level'. Moltke concluded by emphasizing that in a matter like Danzig, which was of such lively interest to German public opinion, the German government had decided to act only in accordance with the general principles of Polish-German policy.[19] It is significant that these assurances were given in connection with a discussion of Hungarian claims to Subcarpathian Ruthenia and with a German note to Budapest requesting it to refrain from armed action for the time being.[20] The decisive element in Hitler's strategy was the confident belief that Beck was isolated and that Polish agreement to German demands was only a matter of time.

The German Foreign Minister showed equal broadmindedness in his reaction to the Polish-Soviet declaration of 27 November, which marked the end of the tension existing between Poland and the USSR since the exchange of notes on 23 September.[22] The declaration confirmed all the existing agreements between Poland and the Soviet Union, including the Non-Aggression Pact of 1932. Both governments declared themselves in favour of an extension of commercial relations and of disposing of recent frontier incidents.[23] Negotiations immediately began for a trade agreement. The French press hailed the declaration as the beginning of a new orientation in Polish foreign policy. Some German observers saw in this move a Soviet attempt to draw Poland away from co-operation with Germany, while others commented that Col. Beck wished to demonstrate the independence of Polish foreign policy in view of the forth-

---

[19] *PWB*, no. 47; Conversation of Minister Beck with Ambassador von Moltke, 22 November 1938, MFA (London), P-G, 1938. The German version does not mention Danzig; *DGFP*, D, V, no. 104; Moltke's remarks, recorded in *PWB*, may have been personal.

[20] See *supra* chap. V, pp. 167.

[21] In December, Weizsäcker told Burckhardt that after the Polish rejection of the German October proposals conversations were put on a 'vaster' plane, and that Warsaw would give in because it was isolated; *DBFP*, 3, III, appendix VI, pp. 657 ff.

[22] Wojciechowski ascribes the improvement in Polish-Soviet relations primarily to Soviet aversion to an independent Subcarpathian Ruthenia which would constitute a Ukrainian 'Piedmont', unwelcome both to Poland and the USSR; *Stosunki Polsko-Niemieckie*, p. 508.　　　　[23] *PWB*, no. 160.

coming Franco-German agreement.[24] While the initiative was Polish, the step only demonstrated Beck's fundamental principle of maintaining a position of equilibrium without commitment to either of Poland's mighty neighbours.

Although the Polish-Soviet agreement was not welcome in Berlin, the German press did not interpret it as hostile to Germany. Ribbentrop, in an interview with Lipski on 2 December, expressed understanding for the agreement, although he regretted that he had not been informed beforehand. He also emphasized that it was in Germany's interest that Poland should constitute a potential dam against Bolshevism[25]—a statement which the Germans were fond of making when they wanted to stress the need for good relations with Warsaw and were not prepared to make any concessions of a concrete nature.

In the first week of December, Beck came to the conclusion that Polish-German relations had reached an *impasse*, and that conversations would have to take place. He therefore decided to invite Ribbentrop to Warsaw, taking up a suggestion which Lipski had made after his conversation with the German Foreign Minister on 19 November.[26] On 8 December, the Polish Foreign Minister sent the Ambassador instructions to transmit the invitation to Ribbentrop. He stated that his aim in such conversations would be to obtain a confirmation of Hitler's declaration of November 1937 to the effect that the Free City could not be a source of conflict between Poland and Germany. As for the highway, Lipski was instructed to show a favourable attitude, but only 'à titre officiel', that is, without any discussion of commitments.[27] Lipski, however, seems to have discouraged the idea of conversations at that time, and two days later Beck told him to suspend the execution of his instruction, except for the extension of the invitation to Ribbentrop. Lipski was recalled to Warsaw for further discussions on the subject,[28] and the project for an immediate 'basic discussion' in Berlin was post-

[24] See the comments of the German ambassadors in Moscow and Warsaw, *DGFP*, D, V, no. 108 and no. 105; for a discussion of the agreement, see also B. Budurowycz, *Polish-Soviet Relations*, pp. 127–33.

[25] Lipski to Foreign Minister, 3 December 1938, MFA (London), P–G, 1938.

[26] Szembek, *Journal*, 22 November 1938, p. 380.

[27] *Ibid.*, 7 December 1938, p. 385.

[28] Beck to Lipski, 10 December 1938, Telephonogram, MFA (London), P–G, 1938.

poned.[29] It is clear that this decision was the result of Lipski's advice, for he considered that Polish-German conversations at this time would be premature.[30]

The Polish Ambassador finally extended the invitation to Ribbentrop on 15 December. The German Foreign Minister accepted, but, although he had himself suggested a meeting with Beck, he now stated that he would have to discuss the matter with the Chancellor before a date was finally agreed upon. He put great emphasis on the need for diplomatic preparations for the visit and asked what subjects would be discussed. Lipski vaguely mentioned the Danube basin, the East, and the Baltic States. When Ribbentrop asked about Polish-German relations and the highway, Lipski merely said that the highway project was being considered but could only be discussed within the framework of a 'general solution'. To a question on Danzig, the Ambassador answered by referring to the complaints of the Polish Commissioner General and by protesting against German support for the Ukrainian independence movement. Ribbentrop, for his part, retaliated with protests against the alleged mistreatment of the German minority in Teschen. He also intimated the existence of German plans for the annexation of Memel, stating that it was a German city, but that Polish economic interests there would be taken into consideration.

Despite the altercation which took place between the Ambassador and the Minister, it was significant that Ribbentrop expressed sorrow that his intentions in the Berchtesgaden conversation of 24 October had been 'misunderstood' by Col. Beck. Towards the end of his interview with Lipski on 15 December, he emphasized that, if Poland continued the policy of Marshal Piłsudski and of Hitler, Polish-German agreement was possible, but that this depended also, in his opinion, on whether Poland wished to understand 'certain principles of German policy'[31].

[29] Beck to Lipski, 11 December 1938, *ibid*.

[30] On 12 December, Beck complained to Szembek that Lipski 'refused' to talk to Ribbentrop; *Journal*, p. 387. Two days later Lipski told Szembek that he had judged it impossible to carry out Beck's instructions as they stood since several conversations had already taken place with the German government and since he was convinced that the ground should be first prepared for Ribbentrop's visit to Warsaw (p. 389).

[31] Lipski to Foreign Minister, 15 December 1938, MFA (London), P–G, 1938; *DGFP*, D, V, no. 112.

It was finally agreed to postpone the discussion of arrangements for the visit until 10 January 1939.

The Polish Foreign Minister was not satisfied with the results of the Ribbentrop-Lipski conversation and decided to see Hitler himself. The Führer had, in any case, indicated a desire to see him,[32] and Beck told Ambassador Moltke that he wished to see Hitler on his way back from Monte Carlo on 5 or 6 January 1939.[33] The Polish Foreign Minister hoped to ascertain whether the Chancellor really supported the demands put forward by Ribbentrop, whom he suspected of responsibility for the *impasse* in German-Polish relations.[34] The situation, in view of Ribbentrop's retreat in November, and of the secrecy in which the Polish-German conversations were shrouded,[35] was indeed far from clear. The demand for the return of Danzig was not publicized, although the highway proposal was reported, Polish consent to it being considered as likely. Hitler mentioned it to King Carol of Rumania when the latter visited Berlin, but he did not speak of the Free City.[36]

The 'wait and see' strategy which Hitler pursued in connection with Ribbentrop's October proposals to Lipski was reflected in the Danzig situation. The promulgation there of anti-Jewish racial decrees for 'the protection of German blood and German honour' on 23 November again brought up the possibility of a withdrawal of the League of Nations mandate from the Free City and confronted Hitler with the unwelcome prospect of carrying out his promise of taking the City back into the Reich before he had obtained Polish assent. The Director of the Foreign Affairs Department of the Danzig Senate, Dr. Böttcher, had warned against the implementation of the laws, reminding the authorities of his promise to Lord Halifax that no changes should be undertaken in Danzig without consulting Great Britain.[37] Great Britain was, indeed, disturbed. Two days before the

[32] Szembek, *Journal*, 14 December 1938, p. 389.
[33] *DGFP*, D, V, no. 115.
[34] Szembek, *Journal*, 7 December 1938, pp. 383–4.
[35] On 24 November, in informing Senator Schimmel of Danzig of the Polish rejection of Ribbentrop's proposals, State Secretary Woermann asked that the matter be kept strictly secret and that no one should be told except Gauleiter Forster and President Greiser; FOL, 97/108295.
[36] *DGFP*, D, V, no. 254.   [37] *Ibid.*, no. 77.

publication of the decrees, Burckhardt had told Böttcher that Ambassador Kennard had condemned the anti-Jewish incidents in Danzig and had declared that his government would not tolerate such a state of affairs. The High Commissioner quoted Kennard as saying that if the incidents continued, the Committee of Three on Danzig in the League of Nations' Council would have to be convened, and that Burckhardt would be relieved of his office. The High Commissioner tempered this warning by telling Böttcher that he had managed to persuade Kennard not to send such a report to London. In private, however, Burckhardt and Kennard agreed on this occasion 'that if the Committee of Three should be dissolved and the League mandate withdrawn some other basis for Polish and German collaboration might be found and the danger of the League and ourselves being faced with a humiliating situation might be obviated'.[38]

The question now arose whether the withdrawal of the High Commissioner from Danzig could not lead to a German move in this sector, and whether Polish interests might not be sacrificed by London and Paris to the cause of peace. Before the passing of the anti-Jewish decrees, Great Britain had resisted French proposals that the solution of the Danzig problem should be precipitated by the resignation of the High Commissioner,[39] but the proclamation impelled London to reconsider its attitude. Public opinion in England had reacted with indignation against the wave of violent persecution of the Jews in Germany in the first half of November; to maintain the League of Nations mandate after the Danzig constitution had been so flagrantly violated seemed a risk of British prestige. The British government began, therefore, to consider again the old plan of completely withdrawing League responsibility for the Free City, with the possible sequel of a German annexation of Danzig.

In a situation fraught with danger for Poland, Beck received aid from an unexpected quarter. It appeared that the possibility of a withdrawal of the League from Danzig was, for the time being at least, just as distasteful to Berlin as to Warsaw, though, of course, for different reasons. The German government was not yet ready to put pressure on Poland. At the end of November,

---

[38] *DBFP*, 3, III, no. 319.   [39] *Ibid.*, no. 321.

therefore, Gauleiter Forster changed his tone considerably from the offensive attitude which he had adopted after Munich. While he had then told Burckhardt that Poland had disappointed the Reich by her policy in the Czechoslovak crisis, and that 'she would shortly get the bill',[40] he now declared that he did not wish Danzig to be the cause of Polish-German conflict. The population, he asserted, wished to return to the Reich but it was willing to bear sacrifices and wait for a better solution in the course of time.[41] When the British reaction to the passing of the anti-Jewish decrees became known, Ribbentrop called the High Commissioner to Berlin where Burckhardt had conversations with the Foreign Minister and with Weizsäcker. From the conversation which Burckhardt had with Ribbentrop, it was clear that the latter was anxious to avoid any discussion of Danzig at Geneva. He told the High Commissioner that he would instruct Forster to follow the Commissioner's suggestion that the Senate declare its willingness to legalize the violations of the constitution by having the offending decrees approved by a normally elected *Volkstag* (Parliament). Although Ribbentrop stated that the best solution of the problem would be the annexation of Danzig and Memel to Germany, he also said that he was in no hurry to adopt such measures. On the contrary, he expressed the hope that Burckhardt would be able to continue his co-operation in maintaining good relations between Germany and Poland.[42] As a result of his Berlin conversations, Burckhardt was able to inform the Deputy Secretary of the League, Mr Walters, that although he had always been in favour of the liquidation of the post of High Commissioner, he did not think that anything should be done to precipitate the issue.[43]

Circumstances seemed auspicious for a discussion of the Danzig and highway questions when Beck stopped on his way

[40] Report of M. Carl Burckhardt, High Commissioner of the League of Nations at Danzig, *League of Nations Official Journal*, no. C. 42, M. 38, 1940, vol. VII, p. 8; Burckhardt, *Meine Danziger Mission*, p. 190.

[41] Interview with *Paris-Midi*, published in the *Danziger Vorposten*, 29 November 1938.

[42] So reported the Polish Commissioner General in Danzig on the basis of a conversation with Burckhardt; Commissioner General to Foreign Minister, 21 December 1938, APEL, Gdańsk, 1938. These assurances only reflected the temporizing policy of Berlin; see n. 21, above.

[43] *DBFP*, 3, III, appendix VI.

home from a vacation in Monte Carlo for conversations with Hitler and Ribbentrop. On 5 January 1939, the Polish Foreign Minister discussed Polish-German relations with the Führer at Berchtesgaden. For the first time since the agreement of 1934, Hitler himself, in discussing a definitive settlement between the two countries, raised the question of the return of Danzig to Germany. He also mentioned the desirability of a connection between Germany and East Prussia through the Polish Corridor. In return, he offered guarantees for Polish rights in the Free City and for Poland's Western frontier. Moreover, as often before, he hinted broadly at Polish-German military co-operation against Russia and prospects of future Polish gains in the Ukraine.

To these overtures the Polish Foreign Minister replied that he did not see in the Chancellor's suggestions any 'equivalent' for Danzig, and that Polish opinion was particularly sensitive on the subject of the Free City.[44] It is significant that Hitler, for his part, put forward his demands in a very restrained manner, and that he took pains to assure Beck that there would be no *faits accomplis* in Danzig.[45] In discussing a solution to the Danzig problem, the Führer mentioned the possibility of creating a 'new organism', which he termed a 'Körperschaft' (corporation), to safeguard both Polish and German interests in the City. This suggestion may have been intended as a hint that Berlin would welcome some form of *condominium* with Warsaw on the territory of the Free City.

On 6 January, the Polish Foreign Minister had a conversation with Ribbentrop in Munich. Beck did not conceal his critical attitude to Hitler's proposals of the previous day. He warned the German Foreign Minister that he considered Danzig to be the touchstone of Polish-German relations, and that any *faits accomplis* would force Poland to take a firm stand. In view of Hitler's express promise on this subject, Beck's statement to Ribbentrop may be interpreted in the light of his belief that a difference of attitude existed between the Führer and his Foreign

[44] *PWB*, no. 48; Szembek, *Journal*, 8 January 1939, pp. 405–6. According to the German version, Beck saw 'great difficulties' in the German demands and wished to think them over at leisure, *DGFP*, D, V, no. 119.
[45] *PWB*, no. 48.

Minister.[46] Beck also warned Ribbentrop that a withdrawal of the League mandate from Danzig would compel Poland and Germany to deal with the problem themselves—a fact of which Ribbentrop was well aware. The German Minister tried to tempt Beck again with perspectives of territorial gains in the Ukraine and asked whether Poland would be prepared to join the Anti-Comintern Pact, to which Beck, as always, gave a negative answer.[47] The Polish Foreign Minister would not be deflected by these overtures from giving Ribbentrop a solemn warning. He asked the German Minister to inform the Chancellor that after all his conversations with German statesmen in the past, he was, for the first time, 'in a pessimistic mood' and saw no possibility of agreement. To this, Ribbentrop gave the reassuring answer that Germany did not seek a violent solution, and that she desired to maintain friendly relations with Poland. In these circumstances, said the German Foreign Minister, a settlement should be sought which would respect the rights and interests of both parties.[48]

The comments which Beck made to his collaborators on his conversations in Germany were not as pessimistic as his statement to Ribbentrop might imply. He did, it is true, see his interview with Hitler as the 'decisive moment' in Polish-German relations,[49] but the door to negotiations had not been shut and Hitler had not pressed for an immediate answer. After his return to Warsaw, Beck decided to work for closer relations with France and Great Britain,[50] but he simultaneously meditated on ways of continuing conversations with Germany so as to avoid an open break. Immediately upon his return to Warsaw, after a conference at the royal castle at which the President, the Premier, and Marshal Śmigły-Rydz were present, Beck gave an instruction to Łubieński. He told his Chef de Cabinet to find some means of arriving at a compromise with Germany over Danzig. He felt that there might still be room for such an arrangement without sacrificing any existing Polish rights in the Free

[46] Beck, *Dernier Rapport*, p. 182.
[47] *DGFP*, D, V, no. 120. Polish version in *PWB*, no. 49, and Szembek, *Journal*, 8 January 1939, pp. 404–7.
[48] *Journal, ibid., PWB*, no. 49; this passage does not appear in the German version, *DGFP*, D, V, no. 120.
[49] Beck, *Dernier Rapport*, p. 182.   [50] Szembek, *Journal*, p. 407.

City. Łubieński thereupon had a conversation with Ambassador Moltke in which he put forward a project for agreement. The main points were the abolition of the League mandate and its replacement by a Polish-German *condominium* with a guarantee for all Polish economic rights and privileges. The inhabitants were to have the option of deciding whether to live under Polish or German rule. Thus Poland would preserve her rights while Hitler would be able to realize his promise of returning Danzig to the Reich. Finally, by this means, the Polish-German conflict would be postponed at least for the time being.[51]

The radical innovation which Łubieński's project introduced to Polish policy on Danzig was the abandonment of the former attitude that any new agreement would have to preserve the statute of the Free City. It was obvious by this time that the League of Nations could not be counted on to provide any protection in case of a German *putsch* and that Poland was isolated. Nevertheless, it is not clear whether Beck was ready to agree to a change of Statute in Danzig, or whether he was playing for time. He wrote to the Polish ambassador in London that, if Danzig were to be the subject of concrete discussion with Berlin, Poland would still have time to reach an understanding with Great Britain.[52] In any case, two days later, Łubieński's project was abandoned.[53] After another conference at the castle, Beck instructed Łubieński to drop the conversations. It had been decided that if Germany were to pursue her demands for Danzig and the highway, these should be interpreted as pretexts for a serious conflict with Poland and that in such a case any hesitation could lead to the loss of Poland's independence and vassalage to Germany. Whether the Germans were bluffing or not, it was

[51] Michał Łubieński, 'Ostatnie Negocjacje w Sprawie Gdańska' (Last Negotiations on Danzig), *Dziennik Polski i Dziennik Żołnierza* (London, 3 December 1953); see also Szembek, *Journal*, 10 January 1939, pp. 407–8. The *Condominium* was to have consisted of a mixed commission of Polish and German representatives which would have directed the administration of the City; letter from M. Łubieński to the author, London, 27 April 1959.

[52] Beck to Raczyński, 11 January 1939, cypher telegram, APEL, Cyphers, 1939. It is not clear from this brief sentence whether Beck had in mind a British guarantee of Polish interests in the Polish-German *Condominium* envisaged in the Łubieński project, or whether he was referring to his attempts to obtain British support for his demand that the League should not dispose of Danzig without Polish consent.

[53] Łubieński, 'Ostatnie Negocjacje'.

decided that Poland should adopt a firm policy and draw a line of no retreat.[54] When Moltke took up the subject again, evidently on the instructions of the Wilhelmstrasse, Łubieński beat a graceful retreat and the matter was dropped.[55] The final upshot of the Berchtesgaden conversations was, therefore, a decision by the Polish government to make no concessions whatever to the German demands on Danzig, and not to begin any conversations on this subject even for tactical reasons.

It is characteristic of this phase of Polish-German relations that the January conversations were kept strictly secret on both sides, though, of course, from entirely different motives. Berlin wished to avoid an open break with Poland because it believed that sooner or later she would accept the German demands, while Warsaw desired to avoid a break because it hoped to gain time. The semi-official press in Poland stressed that the Foreign Minister's visit to the German Chancellor and the conversations held there had shown that there were no insuperable difficulties which could lead to a change in the policy followed by the two countries towards each other over the past five years.[56] Col. Beck adopted the same tone in reporting his conversations to the Polish diplomatic missions abroad,[57] and to the ambassadors of Great Britain and France in Warsaw. He informed Ambassador Kennard that there was no change in Polish-German relations, that there had been no detailed discussion on Danzig and that he did not expect any German 'surprises' in this sector.[58]

The same policy was followed in Berlin. The State Secretary assured the Swedish Minister that Polish-German relations remained unchanged.[59] The only information, and it was unofficial, of Hitler's proposals to Beck was transmitted by

[54] Beck, *Dernier Rapport*, pp. 183–4.

[55] Łubieński, 'Ostatnie Negocjacje'. Beck does not mention the project in his book nor is there any record of it in German documents. It can be surmised that Beck's first instruction to Łubieński was based on a policy decision which did not have the whole-hearted support of all the participants of the castle conference. Szembek's opposition to any such project may be indicative of a division of opinion; *Journal*, p. 408.

[56] *Gazeta Polska*, 8 January 1939.

[57] Beck, Circular, 10 January 1939, MFA (London), P–G, 1939.

[58] *DBFP*, 3, III, no. 531; Beck to Raczyński, 11 January 1939, cypher Letter, APEL, Cyphers, 1939.

[59] Office of the State Secretary, 13 January 1939, PGD, Hoover; see also the State Secretary's circular to German missions, *DGFP*, D, V, no. 121.

Weizsäcker to Burckhardt.[60] Weizsäcker took care to emphasize that though Hitler had raised the subject of Danzig he had seemed to retreat in the face of Beck's reaction, and the High Commissioner on this good authority informed the British and French representatives in Geneva that no German action was likely in Danzig for a long time, perhaps for a year.[61] At the end of January, Dr. Böttcher told the British Consul in Danzig that the situation had changed. He had anticipated, he said, that Danzig would finally be incorporated in the Reich, but it was desirable that this should take place by peaceful means and the choice of the moment would depend on the Führer; the Danzigers would therefore have to be patient.[62] It was evident that Hitler did not wish to press the issue after his conversation with Beck, and the impending session of the League of Nations was a further inducement to restraint on the part of Germany. A withdrawal of the League mandate from the Free City would face Hitler with the unwelcome task of implementing his promise for the return of Danzig to the Reich before an agreement with Poland had been reached. The League Council meeting turned out to be favourable to both Polish and German hopes since the Committee of Three decided—in view of the Polish-German conversations of which it was informed—to defer the study of the Danzig situation to another meeting which was to take place before the next session of the Council.[63]

While Berlin was as pleased as Warsaw that the League Council had made no decisions on the Free City, it did not relinquish its efforts to persuade Col. Beck to take a more favourable attitude on the Danzig and Corridor question. An opportunity for the Germans to press their point came on the occasion of Ribbentrop's visit to Warsaw at the end of January. Although the German Foreign Minister did not by this time set out with the aim of obtaining Beck's immediate agreement to his postulates,[64] he did cherish the hope that some progress might be

---

[60] Burckhardt, *Meine Danziger Mission*, p. 256. Burckhardt writes that the conversations were known only in the most intimate National Socialist circles (p. 257); see also *DBFP*, 3, III, no. 538.

[61] Burckhardt, *ibid.*   [62] *DBFP*, 3, IV, no. 47.

[63] For a fuller discussion of the deliberations of the Committee of Three at this time, see pp. 204–05 of this chapter.

[64] The United Kingdom delegate in Geneva wrote that, according to Burck-

made. His visit coincided with the fifth anniversary of the Polish-German Declaration of Non-Aggression and was commented on in this light by the Polish press. Ribbentrop himself emphasized the existing friendship between the two countries. At a banquet given in his honour on 25 January, he said:

> In accordance with the resolute will of the German national leader, the continual progress and consolidation of friendly relations between Germany and Poland, based upon the existing Agreement between us, constitute an essential element in German foreign policy. The political foresight, and the principles of true statesmanship, which induced both sides to take the momentous decision of 1934, provide a guarantee that all other problems arising in the course of the future evolution of events will also be solved in the same spirit, with due respect and understanding of the rightful interests of both sides....[65]

The conversations which took place between Beck and Ribbentrop between 25 and 27 January were conducted in a conciliatory spirit. Ribbentrop brought up the subject of Danzig and the highway more in the manner of sounding out the Polish attitude than as demands. He linked these problems with a proposal for a joint Polish-German attack on Russia and the prospect of a satisfying solution of the question of Subcarpathian Ruthenia. In both cases his advances were firmly repulsed by Beck, who stated that he failed to see any signs of Soviet disintegration, which, he declared, would be a necessary precondition for any changes in the Soviet Ukraine, and declared that if Subcarpathian Ruthenia proved to be troublesome, Poland would find the means of dealing with it.[66] On the subject of Danzig, the Polish Foreign Minister stressed the fact that the strongest political opposition was to be expected in Poland to any proposed return of the city to Germany, and that he could not, therefore, be optimistic as to the outcome of discussions on this question. He also drew Ribbentrop's attention to the fact that Poland could not make any concessions with

---

hardt, Ribbentrop was going to Warsaw but 'no longer with the object of signing a final agreement'; *DBFP*, 3, III, no. 538. Weizsäcker noted on 22 January that after the conversations with Col. Beck at the beginning of the month, 'any more fruitful discussions of certain questions with him will hardly be possible'; *DGFP*, D, V, no. 125. [65] *PWB*, no. 50. [66] Szembek, *Journal*, 1 February 1939, p. 414.

regard to the Free City, 'for we could not part with tangible rights in exchange for mere guarantees'.[67]

The fact that the conversations did not lead to any open break was due to the German policy of not forcing the issue, and to Beck's tactic of stating his case in such a manner as not to exclude the possibility of further discussion. The German policy of patient waiting was demonstrated by the conclusion of a 'Gentlemen's Agreement' between the two Foreign ministers whereby it was stipulated that, in case of a sudden withdrawal of the League mandate from Danzig, a joint Polish-German statement should be issued within twenty-four hours. It was agreed that the statement should stipulate the maintenance of the existing state of affairs in the Free City until some other solution was reached.[68] Ribbentrop, moreover, reassured Beck that there would be no surprises in Danzig.[69] Beck categorically rejected the principle of the extra-territoriality of the highway through the Polish Corridor, but expressed willingness to begin conversations on the subject of greater transit facilities for Germany.[70] Despite the negative results of his mission, Ribbentrop demonstrated Germany's friendly attitude by making an almost official declaration to President Mościcki and Marshal Śmigły-Rydz on behalf of the Chancellor. He stated that Germany counted upon the continuation of good relations with Poland, and that there were no difficulties which could not be solved by co-operation between Col. Beck and himself.[71] On leaving Poland, he sent a friendly telegram from the frontier, expressing his thanks for Polish hospitality.

Ribbentrop's visit to Warsaw marked the high-water mark in Hitler's policy of patience and persuasion towards Poland, although relations remained officially good for a few weeks to come. Both capitals continued their policy of silence on the questions in dispute and strove to create a good impression abroad. The official Polish *communiqué* on the visit stated that the two Foreign ministers had discussed 'all problems directly con-

---

[67] Szembek, *ibid.*, *PWB*, no. 53. According to the German account of the conversations, Col. Beck promised to give the matter his 'careful consideration'; *DGFP*, D, V, no. 126.

[68] *PWB*, no. 53.

[69] *DGFP*, D, V, no. 126.

[70] *PWB*, no. 53; Szembek, *Journal*, p. 414.

[71] *PWB*, no. 51.

cerning the two neighbouring states', as well as the international situation. The *communiqué* asserted that the conversations were based on the policy begun in 1934 and 'revealed a unanimity of view that both current and future problems concerning the two states should be studied and solved with due regard to the legitimate interests of both nations'.[72] The Wilhelmstrasse followed a similar policy, even with regard to German diplomatic missions abroad.[73] Hitler himself, in his speech of 30 January, devoted a friendly passage to the good relations existing between Germany and Poland. It seemed, at the end of January, as if the Führer really believed in the necessity of a long period of peace and perhaps intended to realize his aims in Danzig and the Corridor by political and economic pressure without the use of force.[74]

Polish-German relations proceeded outwardly on a harmonious note, despite such minor irritants as the Polish agrarian reform towards which was protested by Berlin as discriminating against German landowners in western Poland,[75] and friction between Polish and German students in Danzig. On 24 February, anti-German demonstrations took place in Warsaw as a consequence of the rough treatment of Polish students in the Free City. Despite this, ambassador Moltke spoke to the British ambassador in a mood of restrained optimism. He told Kennard that it had been agreed between Poland and Germany that Danzig must eventually be the object of a thorough discussion, but that for the time being the situation had best remain as it was. He described the 'eventual' German demands as the incorporation of Danzig and an extra-territorial highway through the Corridor. He stressed the fact, however, that the German government wished to attain these objectives not by force but by peaceful negotiations and the situation was not likely to change

---

[72] *PWB*, no. 54.

[73] In a circular dated 30 January 1939, Weizsäcker stated that the Ribbentrop visit to Warsaw manifested the solidarity of German-Polish relations and gave the German Foreign Minister the opportunity of pursuing the discussions begun at Munich. The next phrase, 'in which the problems of Danzig and the Polish attitude towards the Soviet Union', was struck out of the draft of the circular; PGD, Hoover, Pol. V, 228.

[74] Lipski to Foreign Minister, 7 February 1939, MFA (London), P–G, 1939.

[75] Moltke to Foreign Minister, 17 February 1939, telegram no. 13, Pol. V, PGD Hoover.

in the near future.[76] There was only one sphere in which the German 'war of nerves' was active against Poland, and that was in the Ukrainian question. Despite German agitation in Eastern Poland,[77] Col. Beck did not take up the matter with Ribbentrop and the question was not treated as one of major importance by either side. In the field of foreign relations even the Polish-Soviet Trade Agreement of 19 February 1939[78] failed to evoke any criticism from Germany.

Although Berlin refrained from putting pressure on Warsaw at the beginning of March 1939, Beck was well aware that the situation could change from one day to the next. Poland would then have to seek the support of the Western Democracies and her chances of obtaining it did not look encouraging. There were disturbing signs, moreover, of a forthcoming withdrawal of the League mandate from Danzig or at least of a desire to abolish the League guarantee for the constitution.[79] Ambassador Kennard gave an apt description of Beck's dilemma when he wrote of the Polish Foreign Minister: 'he is undoubtedly in rather a hole . . . He knows full well that Danzig is his Achilles' heel and that at any moment Germany may put on the screw with painful and even disastrous results.'[80]

[76] *DBFP*, 3, IV, no. 144.

[77] At the end of January, Polish observers noted great activity among the anti-Polish Ukrainian organizations in Germany, particularly the OUN. Frequent trips to south-eastern Poland were recorded on the part of Dr. Hans Koch, Director of the Institut für den Osten at the University of Königsberg, of Dr. Theodor Oberlaender of the same University, and of Dr. Heinz Seraphim, Director of the University's Institut für Ostdeutsche Wirtschaft, MFA (Warsaw). Note on German Activities in Poland in Ukrainian Affairs, Warsaw, 25 January 1939. It is noteworthy that both Seraphim and Oberlaender have been employed as experts on Eastern Europe by the German federal government. In 1960 Oberlaender resigned from his post as Federal Minister for refugees in Adenauer's government when he was accused by the Polish government of directing the mass murder of Polish intellectuals at Lwów (Lvov) in 1941.

[78] *PWB*, no. 162. Negotiations for a trade agreement had begun in November 1938, and preliminary talks took place in mid-December; see B. Budurowycz, *Polish-Soviet Relations*, pp. 138–40. The Poles were unsuccessful in their aim to obtain Soviet agreement to the transit of goods through the USSR for which they had striven in view of the increasing danger from Germany.

[79] The German Consul General in Geneva reported in February that Burckhardt foresaw such a development and that he intended to propose the abolition of the post of High Commissioner at the May meeting of the League Council; *DGFP*, D, V, no. 129, footnote 1, 133.

[80] *DBFP*, 3, IV, no. 187.

While France and Britain seemed inclined to leave Danzig to its fate, the attitude of Italy also proved to be discouraging to the Poles. Whatever hopes Beck had nourished of active Italian support against Germany were dissipated by Ciano's visit to Warsaw between 25 February and 3 March 1939. In a letter written three months later to the Polish ambassador in Rome, Beck admitted that he had, in the face of German demands, considered the possibility of seeking support against Berlin within the Axis. Ciano, however, 'was afraid of his own shadow whenever there was talk of a policy to be pursued towards Germany in Eastern Europe', and during his visit he had not put forward any new ideas.[81] The fact was that in the case of Poland, as in that of Hungary, Mussolini followed a policy of wavering and ambiguous encouragement which he never had the courage to implement against the wishes of Berlin. Ciano himself fully expected that Poland would adopt a policy of appeasement toward Germany, although he thought that she would take her time in making the final decision and would consult her own interests.[82] His visit to Warsaw also convinced Beck that he could not rely on Italy.

There were more encouraging signs for Poland in France despite her continued appeasement of Germany. In the face of undisguised Italian ambitions in North Africa and the Mediterranean, symbolized by the cries of 'Tunis, Corsica, Nice' in the Italian Chamber of Deputies on 30 November 1938, there was some revival of public interest in France's alliances in Eastern Europe. The Italian challenge reunited the French Right—which had been split on the issue of Munich—at least as far as Italy was concerned, and it awoke the nationalism of the Left.[83]

[81] Letter of Minister Beck to Ambassador Wieniawa-Długoszowski, 10 May 1939, *ŻH*, 6, no. XXVI.

[82] He observed that 'it would be dangerous to affirm lightly—as is done in certain German circles—that Poland is a country which has been won over to the system of the Axis and the Triangle, but it would also be unjust to describe Poland as an enemy country. When the great crisis arises, Poland will for long remain with her arms at rest, and only when the outcome has been decided, will she throw in her lot with the conqueror'; *Ciano's Diplomatic Papers*, pp. 274–5; see also *Ciano's Diary 1939–1943* (ed. Malcolm Muggeridge, London, 1947), 27 February 1938, p. 36.

[83] So observed the Italian ambassador in Paris, Raffaele Guariglia, *La Diplomatie Difficile: Mémoires 1922–1946* (Paris, 1955), p. 91.

Bonnet was criticized in the press for not making any attempt to see Col. Beck during the latter's brief vacation in Monte Carlo, prior to his visit to Berchtesgaden. The fact that Bonnet did not meet the Polish Foreign Minister was due at least in part to the opposition of ambassador Noël who knew that Beck wished to speak with Bonnet. Noël feared that such a meeting might impede his cherished aim of revising the Franco-Polish alliance.[84]

The pressure of public opinion on Bonnet was great enough to elicit a confirmation of the validity of France's alliances with Poland and the Soviet Union. In a speech in the Chamber of Deputies on 25 January 1939, Bonnet specifically denied the charge that his policy had led to the abandonment of French engagements to the two countries. Premier Daladier seconded Bonnet in declaring that these agreements would be maintained. Despite the fact that the French ministers had made these declarations under political pressure,[85] the reaffirmation of the Franco-Polish alliance was a welcome sign for Warsaw. It also had the consequence of leaving aside, at least for the time being, the realization of Noël's proposals for the revision of the alliance of 1921. Bonnet told his Ambassador to Poland, during the latter's visit to Paris at the end of January, that it was too soon after Ribbentrop's visit to proceed with this task.[86] Ambassador Łukasiewicz was able to report from Paris at the beginning of February that the French attitude to Poland had undergone a considerable change for the better. He tempered this information, however, by the warning that, if a situation arose in which France should make an active attempt to reach a more definite stabilization in Europe, Poland would have to defend her own interests as best she could. He foresaw that, if a final agreement should be reached between Germany and the Democracies, Poland would be isolated.[87]

[84] Noël justifies his opposition to such a meeting by the paradoxical contention that Bonnet might either have reaffirmed the Franco-Polish alliance integrally, or have given Beck the impression that France would abandon Poland to her fate; Noël, *L'Agression Allemande contre la Pologne*, p. 283–4.
[85] Bonnet told the German ambassador that they had been made for 'internal consumption'; *DGFP*, D, IV, no. 387.
[86] Noël, pp. 289–90.
[87] Łukasiewicz to Foreign Minister, Political Report, 1 February 1939, *PD* I, no. 8.

In Great Britain two trends of policy were becoming discernible at the beginning of 1939: on the one hand was the Prime Minister's continued striving for an agreement with Germany based on appeasement, and on the other the attitude of Lord Halifax, who did not share Chamberlain's optimism and had begun to show some interest in, and sympathy for, Poland. The right-wing press in Britain continued to voice the opinion that London had no interest in opposing German expansion towards the east or south-east,[88] and the German Embassy in London was under the impression that Chamberlain would accept German expansion in Eastern Europe.[89] The Prime Minister believed that the ground for a final settlement could be laid by drawing Italy into an agreement with the Democracies, then by a trade agreement with Germany, and finally by a settlement of the colonial question.[90] He failed, however, both in his attempts to draw Italy away from her close dependence on Berlin, and in his efforts to tempt Germany into dependence on Great Britain by extending the bait of economic aid. His visit to Rome in January 1939 merely convinced Mussolini that Britain was weak and that the Triple Alliance proposed by Ribbentrop would enable Italy to obtain whatever she wished.[91] The Italian Dictator therefore intensified his attacks on France, despite Bonnet's attempts to begin secret negotiations.[92] The British mission to Berlin in February, headed by Frank Ashton-Gwatkin of the Foreign Office, also failed to obtain the desired results. On the contrary, Ashton-Gwatkin reported warnings that Britain should not meddle in the affairs of Eastern Europe and indications that Berlin would not modify its plans on the receipt of British economic aid.[93] Despite these rebuffs, further

[88] Raczyński to Foreign Minister, 8 February 1939, APEL, P–GB, 1939.

[89] See the 'Political Report on the British Attitude towards the East European Question,' London, 4 January 1939, *DGFP*, D, IV, no. 287.

[90] See *DBFP*, 3, IV, appendix I (iii).

[91] *Ciano's Diary 1939–1943*, 10 January 1939, p. 10.

[92] Bonnet used the industrialist, Paul Beaudoin, as his intermediary with Rome, while he sent Ferdinand de Brinon, a prominent figure in Franco-German cultural relations, to plead for German support in Berlin; *Ciano's Diary 1939–1943*, pp. 17, 23, *DGFP*, D, IV, no. 384.

[93] Ashton-Gwatkin reported: 'Herr von Ribbentrop gave me to understand that there was some further task for Germany to do in Central Europe—"where England must not mix herself in"—and also some further stage to reach in her

trade conversations were planned in Berlin for mid-March and a visit to England by Göring was scheduled for the autumn, to be followed by agreement on the limitation of armaments and a settlement of the colonial question.[94]

Chamberlain's hopes for an agreement with Germany did not portend any good for Poland. Sir Nevile Henderson, who stood very near to the Prime Minister's way of thinking, deduced the logical consequences of 'economic co-operation' between London and Berlin. On 9 March, he wrote to Lord Halifax:

> I realize that such co-operation, quite apart from the expense, means acquiescing to a certain extent in Germany's aims in South-Eastern Europe . . .
>
> It seems inevitable that in the course of time Memel and Danzig, and even, possibly, some minor fringes will be re-attached on the basis of self-determination to the Reich. The most that we can hope for is that this will happen without sabre-rattling and by means of constitutional forms or peaceful negotiations.

Henderson also foresaw Czechoslovakia's complete subordination to Germany and commented, 'We may dislike the latter, but geographically speaking, it is inevitable.' He did not believe that Germany aimed at world domination for that was 'a thing of the past', but he consoled himself that in any case 'Germany's continental future lies eastward and it is probably not un-

---

Four Year Plan policy before the moment for Anglo-German conversations or co-operation had been reached.' The Financial Adviser to the British Embassy reported: 'The things we want—particularly arms limitation and to some extent, the freeing of the exchange—are not in reality practical politics. But the German mouth is wide open for concessions on debts, trade, etc., which would in reality merely serve to strengthen their rearmament position. There may perhaps somewhere be some scope for an understanding; but we have listened *ad nauseam* to what the Germans want, and it is perhaps time that we told them again in plain terms what we want'; *DBFP*, 3, IV, appendix II (i), (iii).

[94] The Parliamentary Under-Secretary for Foreign Trade, Mr. Robert S. Hudson, told Ambassador Raczyński on 9 March that, due to the difficult economic situation of Germany, the British government saw an opportunity to reach a trade agreement which would abolish the German bilateral exchange system. Britain, for her part, would not question the German primacy in certain markets which was justified by her natural and geographical position; Raczyński to Foreign Minister, Political Report, 9 March 1939, APEL, P–GB, 1939. It is difficult to see how such an arrangement could have made Germany dependent on Great Britain and increased the latter's influence on German foreign policy.

fortunate for us that it should be so'.[95] If such were the implications of British 'co-operation' with Germany, then Poland's prospects were bleak indeed.

In this apparently hopeless situation, aid was to come from two quarters: the growing interest of Lord Halifax in Poland's attitude on Danzig, and the unexpected German aggression against Czechoslovakia on 15 March 1939.

Despite the policy of Chamberlain, there was some hope for Poland in the fact that Lord Halifax did not share the Prime Minister's complete unconcern with East Central Europe. Immediately after the Munich Conference, Beck made great efforts to establish closer relations with Great Britain and these had been well received by the Foreign Secretary. On 17 October 1938, Raczyński had transmitted to Halifax Beck's message that 'Polish policy would never willingly diverge on great issues from that of Great Britain, unless, as he hoped would never be the case, Great Britain was to take the line of wholly disinteresting herself from the affairs of the European continent'.[96] The Polish Foreign Minister also succeeded in averting any British initiative or support for the withdrawal of the League mandate from Danzig. After the passing of the anti-Jewish decrees in the Free City in November 1938, the British government began to think of such a project. At the beginning of December, Mr. Strang informed Ambassador Raczyński of the British intention to discuss the Danzig problem at the forthcoming meeting of the League Council, with the object of liquidating the post of the League High Commissioner in the Free City. Raczyński lodged a strong protest[97] but Beck was privately pessimistic about the chances of Polish opposition to the British project.[98] He obtained, however, a promise of great significance for the future of the Danzig question and of Polish-British relations. He instructed Raczyński to propose to Halifax the conclusion of a 'friendly agreement' between Great Britain and Poland on certain appropriate matters, such as Danzig and the problem of Jewish emigration

[95] *DBFP*, 3, IV, no. 195 (p. 216).
[96] *DBFP*, 3, III, no. 213; Raczyński to Foreign Minister, 18 October 1938, cypher telegram no. 96, APEL, Cyphers, 1938.
[97] Raczyński to Foreign Minister, 9 December 1938, cypher telegram no. 106, APEL, Cyphers, 1938.
[98] Szembek, *Journal*, 19 December 1938, p. 387.

from Poland.[99] The Foreign Secretary welcomed this proposal and assured the Polish Ambassador on 14 December that no final decision on Danzig had been reached and that this would not be done without consulting Poland. He also expressed the desire to receive Polish proposals on the matter.[100]

The favourable attitude of Lord Halifax towards Poland was confirmed in an official *aide-mémoire* transmitted to Col. Beck on 15 December 1938. Although the *aide-mémoire* stated the British intention to recommend a termination of the League's guarantee for the Danzig constitution and the conferment of the post of High Commissioner on a person proposed by Poland or Germany, it included a solemn confirmation of the promise made by the Foreign Secretary to Raczyński that 'His Majesty's government would not wish to take any decision in Danzig matters without full consultation with the Polish government and would therefore welcome a frank statement of their views'.[101] Beck could now hope that the Danzig problem would not be settled without his participation. The British promise to consult Warsaw proved to be of great significance for the future.

The Polish Foreign Minister took advantage of the British suggestion that he state his views on the matter of discussing Danzig at the forthcoming League of Nations Council. He told Ambassador Kennard that he saw two possible solutions: either the League Council would settle the matter definitively at its January meeting, in which case it would do so on its own account and Poland would do nothing to facilitate its task, or Lord Halifax could postpone the calling of the Committee of Three without setting a definite date for its meeting. In the second case, Beck expressed willingness to advise the Foreign Secretary ahead of time on the progress of Polish-German conversations and facilitate the presentation of the problem in the Committee of Three. Finally, he tentatively suggested his own participation

[99] In view of her large Jewish population (*c.* 3,000,000), Poland was anxious to obtain a special contingent of entry certificates to Palestine.

[100] For Beck's instruction to Raczyński, see Note based on the oral instruction given to Ambassador E. Raczyński by the Foreign Minister in Warsaw, 29 November 1938, APEL, P–GB, 1938. Raczyński reported his conversation with Halifax on the day it took place; Raczyński to Foreign Minister, London, 14 December 1938, cypher telegram no. 108, APEL Cyphers, 1938; see also *DBFP*, 3, III, no. 430.

[101] *DBFP*, 3, III, no. 504, enclosure I: *aide-mémoire*.

in the next meeting of the Committee and told Kennard that he would be willing to come to London if it were to be held there.[102]

Beck's suggestions were welcomed by Halifax and it was decided that Great Britain should direct her policy at the January meeting of the League Council accordingly. In choosing such a course, the Foreign Secretary had first to overcome the objections of France. The French Ambassador in London transmitted a note stating that neither Britain nor France had any interest in maintaining the *status quo* in Danzig during the Polish-German negotiations, and that Col. Beck's suggestions involved the risk of embarrassing the League, London, and Paris by some *fait accompli*. The French government even suggested that the Committee of Three should meet a few days before the League Council, in order to prevent the discussion of the Danzig problem in the presence of the Polish delegate to the League of Nations.[103] Halifax, however, informed Paris that the British government was in favour of encouraging the Committee of Three to 'go slow' at Geneva, and possibly adjust its action to the situation as it developed. In a highly significant passage of his reply to the French government, Halifax motivated his attitude by stating that it would be undesirable to annoy the Polish Foreign Minister 'when we might in certain circumstances want Col. Beck's assistance in a much graver situation'.[104] In pursuance of this policy, Great Britain pronounced herself in favour of a settlement between Poland and Germany, and of maintaining the High Commissioner in Danzig for the time being.[105] It thus came about that the final *communiqué* of the Committee was based largely on Polish suggestions.[106] The *communiqué* stated that in order to facilitate the consideration of all aspects of the Danzig problem, and in view of the conversations taking place on the subject, the Committee thought it advisable to defer the final study of the situation, and would discuss the developments at another session to be held before the

[102] Łubieński to Raczyński, 21 December 1938, cypher telegram no. 125, APEL, Cyphers, 1938.

[103] *DBFP*, 3, III, no. 508, annex.

[104] *Ibid.*, no. 519.   [105] *Ibid.*, no. 548.

[106] For this question and the Polish attitude on Danzig, see 'Danzig Affairs during the 104th Session of the League of Nations Council', T. Komarnicki, Geneva, 19 January 1939, APEL, Gdańsk, 1939.

forthcoming session of the League Council. The High Commissioner was to retain his post, but he was to take a leave of absence.[107]

The one hundred and fourth session of the League of Nations Council had a further and much more important result for Poland. Lord Halifax clearly intimated to the Polish delegate in Geneva, Dr. Tytus Komarnicki, that he would like to see Col. Beck in London. He asked whether he could have a formal assurance that the League would not be faced with a *fait accompli* in the shape of a surprise Polish-German agreement. Komarnicki could not give such an assurance but said that Poland reserved to herself the possibility of consultation with the members of the Committee. Halifax thereupon expressed the wish that the next meeting of the Committee of Three should take place in London and noted that this would be a good occasion for the British government to establish contact with Col. Beck, thus taking up a suggestion made by the Polish Foreign Minister in December.[108] Mr. R. A. Butler, Parliamentary Under-Secretary of State for Foreign Affairs, confirmed the wish of the Foreign Secretary to see Col. Beck in London, saying that this would be a good occasion for an exchange of views on other subjects besides Danzig. Thus, owing to the support of Lord Halifax, Beck's wish that the League should make no decisions on Danzig prevailed, and an invitation was extended to the Polish Foreign Minister to visit London.

At the end of January, Halifax took up the subject of the visit and told Raczyński that he wished to see Col. Beck before the next meeting of the Committee of Three; the Foreign Secretary suggested that the Polish Foreign Minister should come to London at the beginning of March.[109] About two weeks later, Beck replied through his Ambassador that he welcomed the opportunity of renewing contact with the British government, but that he would prefer to visit London without any formal connection with the Committee of Three.[110] At the end of February, Halifax told the Polish Ambassador that the next

[107] *DBFP*, 3, III, no. 556, encl. II.   [108] See *supra*, p. 204.
[109] Raczyński to Foreign Minister, 25 January 1939, cypher telegram APEL Cyphers, 1939; also *DBFP*, 3, IV, no. 10.
[110] Beck to Raczyński, 10 February 1939, cypher telegram no. 18, APEL, Cyphers, 1939.

meeting of the Committee might take place at the beginning of April, and suggested that Beck should visit London in the last week of March or the first week of April.[111] Beck accepted the proposed date and emphasized to Kennard that he wished to discuss the general situation with the British Foreign Secretary, 'especially since Polish and British aims in Northern Europe seem to more or less coincide'.[112] The Polish Foreign Minister thus hinted that he would wish to take up the subject of Polish-British co-operation in the Baltic which he had unsuccessfully proposed to Duff Cooper in August 1938.[113] It was finally agreed that Beck should visit London in the first week of April. The British government was aware of the motives impelling Col. Beck to make the visit, and so was Berlin. Ambassador Moltke reported that '. . . it is becoming increasingly apparent that Poland desires to get into closer touch with the Western Democracies'.[114] In this way, Col. Beck's projected visit to Great Britain, which had originated in his suggestion that he might participate at a meeting of the Committee of Three, assumed at the beginning of March a much broader scope. It was to take on a still greater significance under the impact of new German aggression in East Central Europe.

[111] *DBFP*, 3, IV, no. 141.
[113] See *supra*, Ch. III, pp. 87.

[112] *Ibid.*, no. 148.
[114] *DGFP*, D, V, no. 130.

VII

THE PARTING OF THE WAYS:
THE BRITISH GUARANTEE
TO POLAND

WHEN the German occupation of Prague shattered the Munich agreement, Poland appeared to be the one country on which the eastern wing of a diplomatic 'containment' of Germany could be based. This was the result of Col. Beck's patient efforts to obtain British support for the Polish policy on Danzig, and his success in convincing Lord Halifax that Poland could play an important role in an attempt to check further German aggression. These factors, combined with the pressure of public opinion in Great Britain and growing political opposition to Chamberlain's policy of appeasement, led to the British guarantee to Poland and to the agreement of 6 April, which was, in all but name, an alliance between the two countries. Despite Chamberlain's persistent hope for an agreement with Germany, the Anglo-Polish accord meant that a German attack on Poland would not be an act of condoned aggression, but would almost certainly lead to the outbreak of a world war.

Hitler's brutal move against Prague on 15 March 1939 did not come as a complete surprise to France and Britain. In fact, both had long been reconciled to the final absorption of Czechoslovakia by Germany but hoped it would be a peaceful one. On 13 March, Chamberlain stated in the House of Commons that Britain did not regard her guarantee to Czechoslovakia as binding. This was interpreted in Berlin as an encouragement to aggression. Upon the German occupation of Prague, both London and Paris sent protests to Berlin, but, as Weizsäcker observed, the British note lacked the statement that Britain did not recognize the new state of affairs.[1] The French government did refuse to 'recognize' the new situation,[2] but it was clear that this language was designed to meet internal pressures. Chamberlain did not give up hope of reaching a final agreement with Germany and the British note reflected his policy,[3] as did his declaration in Parliament that his government did not, in view of the events in Czechoslovakia, hold itself bound by its guarantee to that country.[4] The chief difficulty which Hitler's new move posed for the policy of appeasement was succinctly stated by Ambassador Henderson when he wrote:

> What distresses me more than anything else is the handle which it will give to the critics of Munich. Not that I did not always realize that the complete subservience of the Czechs to Germany was inevitable . . . But I did not foresee the lightning turn which events would take, nor in justice to myself, did anyone else. . . .[5]

From the Polish point of view, the complete absorption of Czechoslovakia by Germany was fraught with great danger. The new status of Slovakia as an 'independent' country under the protection of Berlin was most unwelcome to Warsaw, and the German occupation of Memel which soon followed raised Polish fears of a sudden annexation of Danzig. Finally, the liquidation of the Czechoslovak state left Poland as the next victim, and she was soon confronted with a restatement of German demands for Danzig and a highway through the Polish Corridor.

In view of these events, the establishment of a common Polish-Hungarian frontier through the Hungarian occupation of Subcarpathian Ruthenia could no longer serve as the nucleus of a possible anti-German bloc in East Central Europe.[6] The

[1] *DGFP*, D, VI, no. 25.

[2] *Livre Jaune Français*, no. 76; *DBFP*, 3, IV, no. 278, annex II.

[3] The note stated that 'His Majesty's Government have no desire to interfere unnecessarily in a matter with which other Governments may be more directly concerned than this country'. The strongest words used were an intimation that Great Britain 'cannot but regard the events of the past few days as a complete repudiation of the Munich Agreement'; *DBFP*, *ibid.*, no. 247.

[4] *Parl. Deb. H. C.*, 5th ser., vol. 345, col. 437.

[5] *DBFP*, 3, IV, appendix I (viii), p. 395.

[6] As Kennard observed to Halifax on 15 March 1939; *DBFP*, 3, IV, no. 269.

advantages which accrued to Poland with regard to her Ukrainian problem through the collapse of the Republic of Subcarpathian Ukraine were far outweighed by the disadvantage of a German-controlled Slovakia on her southern flank. On 17 March, Ambassador Lipski protested very sharply to Göring against the 'surprise' solution of the Czechoslovak question. The Field-Marshal at first asserted that he had been surprised himself, but then tried to justify German action by saying that Hitler had been aggrieved over the anti-German demonstrations in Warsaw at the end of February.[7] He promised, however, to draw Hitler's attention to the interests of Poland and declared that no German garrisons would be stationed in Central or Eastern Slovakia.[8] This promise, like so many others, was soon to be broken.[9]

Hitler did not think of checking German expansion after the fall of Czechoslovakia but pressed on with his plans in the Baltic region. At first, it seems as if both Danzig and Memel were included in his plans for immediate annexation,[10] but the Polish attitude towards the Free City as well as his own hope of reaching an agreement with Warsaw once more convinced him that he should wait. Lithuania was told on 19 March to hand over Memel 'graciously'[11] and two days later Ribbentrop put the German demands again to Ambassador Lipski. The German Foreign Minister told the Ambassador that an early visit by Col. Beck would be welcomed in Berlin. He made the purpose of this invitation clear by saying that Poland must realize that she could only remain a national state if she worked for a 'reasonable relationship' with Germany; the only other alternative, asserted Ribbentrop, was for her to become Marxist. After these pre-

[7] Lipski to Foreign Minister, 17 March 1939, FOL, *PD* II.

[8] Lipski to Foreign Minister, 17 March 1939, telephonogram no. 54, MFA (London), P–G, 1939.

[9] The German-Slovak agreement of 23 March stipulated that German garrisons would be stationed on Slovakia's eastern and western frontiers; *DGFP*, D, VI, no. 40.

[10] On 13 March, Weizsäcker warned Dr Burckhardt that Danzig and Memel would be threatened and advised him not to return to the Free City. When the High Commissioner did return, the President of the Senate, Greiser, told him that Hitler had declared that 'If the Poles behave nicely, we will put off a little dealing with Danzig and Memel; if not, they will learn who is the master'; *DBFP*, 3, IV, no. 419.

[11] *Ibid.*, no. 441.

liminary remarks the Foreign Minister repeated his former demands for the return of Danzig and for an extra-territorial highway linking Germany with East Prussia. He also raised the question of Polish adherence to the Anti-Comintern Pact. In return, he offered German recognition of Poland's western frontier, including the Corridor, intimating the possibility of a satisfactory solution of the Slovak question and hinted again at Polish territorial gains in the Ukraine.[12] After this conversation Lipski was pessimistic about further developments, and predicted the possibility of a German ultimatum.[13]

In this difficult situation, Col. Beck received support from Great Britain where a shift in policy took place as a result of the pressure of public opinion and fear of German domination over Rumania. Public reaction to German aggression against Czechoslovakia was so strong that Chamberlain was forced, two days after his conciliatory note to Berlin and his statement in the House of Commons, to adopt a firmer tone. In a speech delivered on 17 March, in his home town of Birmingham, the Prime Minister reaffirmed his opposition to any British commitments in East Central Europe, but at the same time warned Germany against further aggression. He then said:

> I feel bound to repeat that, while I am not prepared to engage this country by new and unspecified commitments operating under conditions which cannot now be foreseen, yet no greater mistake can be made than to suppose that . . . this nation has so lost its fibre that it will not take part to the utmost of its power in resisting such a challenge if it ever were made.[14]

It is difficult to say whether the British government would have taken any definite steps to implement its warnings to Germany if there had not been new and alarming rumours of a German threat to Rumania. On 16 March, Vioril Tilea, the Rumanian Minister in London, told Lord Halifax that Berlin had demanded that Bucharest agree to a German monopoly of

[12] *DGFP*, D, VI, no. 561; *PWB*, no. 61.
[13] Szembek, *Journal*, 22 March 1939, p. 433.
[14] Speech by the Prime Minister at Birmingham, 17 March 1939, *Documents concerning German-Polish Relations and the Outbreak of Hostilities between Great Britain and Germany on September 3rd, 1939*, London, His Majesty's Stationery Office, 1939, Command Paper no. 6106, doc. no. 9.

Rumanian exports and accept certain demands in the running of Rumanian industry. In return, Germany offered to guarantee the frontiers of Rumania. In view of this situation, Tilea asked whether the British government would indicate what its position would be in case Rumania became the victim of German aggression. As a counter-move to the threat of German expansion, Tilea proposed a bloc of East European and Balkan states which would be supported by France and Britain. In this connection, the Rumanian minister inquired whether Great Britain would find it easier to define her position if Poland and Rumania agreed to make their alliance clearly applicable to Germany,[15] and if the states of the Balkan Entente proclaimed their joint determination to guarantee one another's frontiers. Finally, Tilea inquired as to the possibility of a British loan to Rumania for the purchase of war materials.

It is indicative of the pressure felt by the British Cabinet, and perhaps of the influence of Lord Halifax in particular, that on the evening of Tilea's conversation with the Foreign Secretary British diplomatic missions in Paris, Warsaw, Athens, Ankara, and Belgrade were instructed to question the Foreign Ministers of those states on their attitude towards Rumania if it should be the object of German aggression.[16] The answers to this question were negative with one exception. All the Foreign Ministers asked, except the French, expressed doubts that Rumania was threatened. Only the French government replied that it would be ready to assist Rumania. The Soviet government, on the other hand, proposed on 19 March that a conference should be held in Bucharest between representatives of Great Britain, France, Poland, Rumania, and Turkey to discuss common action. The Rumanian government itself officially denied that there had been any German ultimatum. Col. Beck told Ambassador Kennard that he had received no information of such a threat.[17]

In view of the official denial by the Rumanian government that any German ultimatum had been presented, Tilea's *démarche* in London should be seen in the light of Rumania's fear of Hungary. Although the new Rumanian Foreign Minister,

[15] The Polish-Rumanian alliance of 1921 was limited to defensive co-operation against Soviet aggression.

[16] *DBFP*, 3, IV, nos. 390, 395.   [17] *Ibid.*, no. 400.

Grigoire Gafencu, who had succeeded Petresco-Comnène early in the year, was more amenable to a Hungarian annexation of Subcarpathian Ruthenia, no arrangement had been worked out by 15 March. This was largely due to Hungarian opposition to any territorial concessions to Bucharest in that region. Gafencu had obtained Beck's support in this matter during his visit to Warsaw on 5 – 6 March, but the Hungarians gave no answer to Polish or Rumanian requests. When the Hungarian troops advanced into Subcarpathian Ruthenia on 15 March, the Rumanians were afraid to move without Polish help and thus lost any chance of compensation. Moreover, it looked as if the Hungarians might also try to reclaim some of the territories lost to Rumania in 1919. The Rumanians reacted to this situation by proclaiming a partial mobilization and seeking support in the West by spreading rumours of a German ultimatum.[18] Tilea told Raczyński that Lord Halifax had asked him whether Rumania could count on Polish military aid in case of a direct German threat, thus attributing his own question to the Foreign Secretary. What is more, he said that if the Polish answer were positive, Col. Beck should immediately inform Bucharest because the government there was 'defeatist'.[19]

Tilea's proposal to Lord Halifax, that the Polish-Rumanian alliance should be modified to include aid against a German threat of aggression, was in direct contradiction to the agreement which had been reached between Warsaw and Bucharest. During his visit to Warsaw in March, Grigoire Gafencu had agreed with Col. Beck that there was no need to extend the mutual assistance clause of the pact to cover German aggression.[20] It was soon apparent what use Bonnet could make of this situation. France declared her readiness to aid Rumania, but conditioned her own aid to Poland on the extension of a Polish guarantee to Bucharest. On 18 March, Ambassador Phipps reported from Paris that Daladier had told him of an inquiry made by the Polish government as to whether France would help Poland in

[18] For a detailed discussion of this phase of Rumanian-Hungarian relations, see Macartney, *October Fifteenth*, I, pp. 333–40.

[19] Raczyński to Foreign Minister, 17 March 1939, cypher telegram no. 30, APEL, Cyphers, 1939; for the German Economic Mission in Rumania, see *DGFP*, D, V, nos. 257, 279, 282, 284, 293, 294, 298, 306, *passim*.

[20] Beck, circular, 6 March 1939, MFA (London), P–G, 1939.

case of a German attack on Danzig. Daladier had answered in the affirmative, but on the condition that Poland should conclude a defensive alliance with Rumania against Germany.[21] As a matter of fact, no such direct question had been put by Poland, but soundings had been made and these had been eagerly seized on in Paris[22] in order to link the two issues together and to induce Poland to declare herself against Germany. Thus Tilea's proposal of an alliance between Poland and Rumania against Berlin was used by Paris as a pretext to make unacceptable demands on Poland, the rejection of which could justify, if necessary, an official abrogation of the Franco-Polish alliance.

Although the British government soon realized that its anxiety for Rumania was premature, further steps were taken to implement a more active policy and this led to the support of Poland's attitude on the Danzig question. Lord Halifax, who had for some time already been favourably inclined to Poland in this matter, was the moving spirit in the construction of a diplomatic front to check German expansion. On 20 March, he informed the British Ambassador in Paris that, despite doubts as to the accuracy of the reports on the German ultimatum to Rumania, the absorption of Czechoslovakia indicated the German government's determination to go beyond the aim of consolidating the German race. In view of this development, Halifax felt that an organization for mutual support should be set up, including all those who wished to prevent further violations of the laws of international society. As a first step, it was proposed that France, Poland, Great Britain, and the Soviet Union—whose proposal of 19 March had been rejected as premature—should join in signing and in publishing a formal declaration as follows:

We the undersigned, duly authorized to that effect, hereby declare that, inasmuch as peace and security in Europe are matters of

[21] *DBFP*, 3, IV, no. 402.
[22] Ambassador Łukasiewicz told Ambassador Bullitt that he would have to ask the French government about French aid to Poland in case of a German attack on Danzig. Bullitt 'by chance' put the question to Daladier who answered in the affirmative but on the condition that a Polish guarantee was given to Rumania; 'Pamiętniki Amb. Łukasiewicza; Wspomnienia i Uwagi: (1) Po Zajęciu Pragi' (The Diaries of Ambassador Łukasiewicz; Memories and Remarks: (1) After the Occupation of Prague), *Dziennik Polski* (London, 20 February 1947, no. 44).

common interest, and since European peace and security may be affected by any action which constitutes a threat to the political independence of any European State, our respective Governments hereby undertake immediately to consult together as to what steps should be taken to offer joint resistance to any such action.[23]

Although Chamberlain did not yet believe that a radical change of policy was necessary,[24] the sending of the proposal to Paris, Warsaw, and Moscow, on 20 March, constituted an important development in the international situation.

On 21 and 22 March, Anglo-French conversations took place in London. The French Foreign Minister's main object was to convince the British of the necessity of persuading or inducing Poland to give a guarantee of assistance to Rumania in case of a German attack. Despite the fact that he knew of Beck's objections to such a course of action,[25] Bonnet wished that Poland be brought to collaborate actively with Bucharest. He proposed that France and Great Britain should ask Poland outright what she would do if Germany attacked Rumania; if the question were put in this way, he thought that it would be difficult for Poland to give a negative answer.[26]

Bonnet found that in his attitude to Poland he did not have the support of Lord Halifax. The Foreign Secretary expressed the opinion that a firm policy was needed to check German aggression. If the Democracies were to ask Poland for aid to Rumania, they should give her 'a private undertaking' that in return for such aid they would also help her. Thus Halifax, unlike Bonnet, saw the need of offering Poland some guarantee of support in return for a policy which would most likely lead to a conflict

[23] *DBFP*, 3, IV, no. 446.

[24] In a letter to his sister on 19 March, Chamberlain wrote: '. . . I have an idea it won't bring us to an acute crisis, at any rate at once. As always, I want to gain time for I never accept the view that war is inevitable'; Feiling, *Neville Chamberlain*, p. 401.

[25] Col. Beck had instructed Łukasiewicz to tell Bonnet that he did not see any likelihood of German aggression against Rumania and that, in any case, this could only take place with Hungarian participation. In view of this fact, Beck assured Bonnet that Poland would use all her influence to secure peace and better relations between Hungary and Rumania. He reminded Bonnet that the Polish-Rumanian alliance was directed against Soviet aggression and noted that Rumania had not asked for further guarantees; Beck to Łukasiewicz, 20 March 1939, cypher telegram no. 46, APEL, Cyphers, 1939.

[26] *DBFP*, 3, IV, no. 484, (p. 458).

between Warsaw and Berlin. A fact of even greater importance for Poland was that the Foreign Secretary was prepared to consider a German threat to Polish independence 'as a grave question which was of concern to all'.[27]

It is of interest to note that Halifax had made up his mind on the subject of Danzig by 19 March at the latest. He had then told the Soviet ambassador, Ivan Maisky, that Britain would welcome a German-Polish agreement on the Free City but if 'out of the Danzig question emerged a threat to Polish independence, that would at once, in my view, constitute a question of interest to us all'.[28] He had been even more explicit with Ambassador Raczyński. On the morning of 21 March, before the Anglo-French conversations began, Halifax told the Ambassador that if a Polish-German agreement on Danzig proved unattainable, the British offer in the Four Power Declaration would also hold good for German aggression against Danzig, provided this threatened Polish independence. He even envisaged the extension of protection to Lithuania if German demands should prove too high for Kaunas. During the course of the conversation the Foreign Secretary asked Raczyński whether, in view of the Polish-German Declaration of 1934, Poland would eventually be able to enter into armed conflict with Germany and how far Polish alliance guarantees extended to Rumania. The Polish Ambassador answered that the 1934 agreement recognized Poland's previous obligations to third parties, and that the Polish-Rumanian alliance was oriented against Soviet aggression. He added that Poland was making great efforts to ameliorate Hungarian-Rumanian relations.[29] From the Halifax-Raczyński conversation of 21 March it seemed that the Foreign Secretary now considered the possibility of supporting Poland on Danzig, though this was put forward in a very cautious and tentative manner. Nevertheless, his attitude was more hopeful for Poland than that of Paris. The Secretary General of the Quai d'Orsay, Alexis Léger, told the British Ambassador that, as far as Danzig

---

[27] *Ibid.*, no. 458, p. 424.　　　　[28] *Ibid.*, no. 432.

[29] Raczyński to Foreign Minister, 21 March 1939, cypher telegram no. 35, APEL, Cyphers, 1939; also *DBFP*, no. 471. Two days later, Beck expressly warned the Hungarian government through Ambassador Orłowski that, in his opinion, a conflict between Hungary and Rumania would precipitate a general war; Beck to Ambassador Orłowski, 23 March 1939, cypher telegram no. 33, APEL.

and Memel were concerned, 'Their return to Germany was a foregone conclusion, and there was no reason for France and Great Britain to take action to prevent it.'[30] The attitude of the French Foreign Office towards Poland was nowhere more apparent than in Léger's interpretation of the Polish Foreign Minister's intentions with regard to Great Britain. He told Ambassador Phipps that Beck would ask Britain for an alliance with the sole object of obtaining a refusal, and thus acquire an excuse to support Germany even at the cost of becoming her vassal. 'Mr Beck,' said he, 'was entirely cynical and false.'[31] It is hard to see whether this analysis stemmed from a misunderstanding of Poland's vital interests or from Bonnet's determination to avoid any possibility of war; whatever the case may be, France directed her efforts to secure a Polish guarantee for Rumania which Poland was bound to refuse without an assurance of French aid, and this Bonnet was determined not to give.

Col. Beck received the proposal of the Four Power Declaration on 21 March, the day on which Ribbentrop confronted Lipski once more with the demand for Danzig and the highway. In studying the British proposal, the Polish Foreign Minister had to take into account the fact that though Berlin had not yet put its demands in the form of an ultimatum it might soon do so, and that, without a clear guarantee of aid against Germany, Poland could not afford to risk a conflict with her. Beck's objective was, therefore, to obtain the support of Great Britain while avoiding, at the same time, any worsening of his relations with Berlin. As ambassador Kennard put it, the proposed declaration faced Beck with 'a parting of the ways', for its acceptance carried the risk of an immediate hostile reaction on the part of the German government. The Ambassador also noted that Polish officials were reluctant to consider collective guarantees except in the case of immediate danger, and then only if they were accompanied by military commitments.[32]

As a way out of his predicament, and as an alternative to the projected declaration—which Beck claimed would put him in the Soviet camp as far as Berlin was concerned[33]—he suggested a

---

[30] *DBFP*, 3, IV, no. 418, encl.
[31] Phipps to Halifax, 18 March 1939; *ibid.*, no. 405.
[32] *DBFP*, 3, IV, no. 465.   [33] *Ibid.*, no. 479.

secret bilateral agreement on consultation between Great Britain and Poland.[34] From the Polish point of view, such a solution had the advantage of leaving out France and the USSR and thus avoiding the appearance of any 'encirclement' of Germany.[35] In a commentary on Col. Beck's instruction to Ambassador Raczyński, Józef Potocki, the Head of the Western Department in the Polish Ministry of Foreign Affairs, elaborated the motives of the Minister. He wrote that the idea of a secret agreement had actually been mentioned by ambassador Kennard, so that the concept was not new to the British government, a comment borne out by the fact that Halifax himself had suggested a secret undertaking of aid to Poland in the Franco-British conversations of 21 – 22 March.[36] Potocki wrote that Poland would be willing to consider a bilateral agreement providing for British support, especially in the case of Danzig, in return for which she would undertake to consult with Great Britain. He stressed that such an agreement could be realized at the same time as German-Polish negotiations on Danzig, while, on the other hand, such negotiations would be impossible if Poland should take a stand against Germany together with the Soviet Union. Poland would also prefer a bilateral agreement with Great Britain because a tripartite agreement, which would include France, would offend the USSR.[37]

Ambassador Raczyński delivered Beck's counter-proposal to Lord Halifax on 24 March. The Foreign Secretary told the ambassador that he interpreted the Polish Foreign Minister's suggestions as a 'gentlemen's agreement' between Great Britain and Poland to consult with each other if Polish independence should be threatened. Raczyński, speaking in the light of Potocki's commentary, said he thought that Col. Beck had something more in mind. He said the Polish Foreign Minister envisaged not only consultation in case of a threat to Rumania or some other country, but also British aid if the Danzig question should develop into a threat to Polish independence. In return

[34] *Ibid.*, no. 485.   [35] Szembek, *Journal*, 22 March 1938, p. 434.
[36] *DBFP*, 3, IV, no. 458 (p. 424).
[37] Potocki to Raczyński, 23 March 1938, 'Top Secret', and Łubieński to Raczyński, 23 March 1938, APEL, P–GB, 1939; this was also Kennard's view; *DBFP*, 3, IV, no. 485. The text of Beck's instruction to Raczyński as printed in *PWB*, no. 66, omits the adjective 'secret' from the bilateral agreement proposed.

for a promise of such aid, Poland would undertake to consult with Great Britain. Halifax thereupon asked whether Beck envisaged assistance in case the independence of *either* country were threatened, that is, whether it was to be reciprocal. Raczyński gave a negative answer. After clarifying this issue, it was agreed that the first stage of the agreement would be a confidential bilateral accord on consultation, which would presumably be followed later in the second stage by an accord on joint action in case of attack on either country by a third state. The significance of the conversation lay in the fact that the British Foreign Secretary seemed to consider an alliance between Poland and Britain as a distinct possibility.[38] At the same time, it was clear that Warsaw could now hope for British support in the Danzig question.

The conversations between Warsaw and London take on a deeper significance in the light of the events of 22 March 1939, and their consequences. The German occupation of Memel on that day gave rise to fears that Danzig might also be seized. Whatever the German plans may have been, the Polish attitude on this issue was firm and clear. The Polish Commissioner General declared that any *coup* would be met with armed force.[39] Poland carried out troop concentrations in the Corridor and a number of trains to Danzig were cancelled. In Warsaw, on 24 March, Beck told his closest collaborators that the situation had to be examined anew since Germany had lost 'all sense of responsibility'. The Polish line of conduct, said the Foreign Minister, was fixed; the limits of possible concessions had been determined and beyond that line lay the Polish *non possumus*— 'Poland would simply fight.' She could not, said Beck, accept a unilateral solution of the Danzig question and he expressed the hope that if Hitler met with a determined attitude he would recover his sense of proportion.[40] It is not possible to determine whether the Polish Foreign Minister had been informed of the Raczyński-Halifax conversation of that day before he announced his policy, but, in any case, hopeful though it was for Poland, it still did not constitute a guarantee of aid. It must be assumed that

[38] *DBFP*, 3, IV, no. 518.   [39] *Ibid.*, V, no. 6.
[40] Szembek, *Journal*, 24 March 1939, pp. 434–7. Szembek makes no mention of the Raczyński-Halifax conversations of 21 and 24 March.

Beck decided to refuse the German demands on the hypothesis that firmness would both deter Hitler from any aggression and encourage Britain to support Poland. On the same day, 24 March, Szembek told ambassador Moltke that Poland could not accept the demands for an extra-territorial highway and that, in order to avoid a conflict between Poland and Germany, Danzig would have to remain a Free City.[41] This amounted to a refusal of the demands put forward by Ribbentrop on 21 March.

Despite the determined Polish reaction to the threat of German aggression against Danzig, Hitler still had no wish at this time to precipitate a crisis in Polish-German relations. In fact, knowing that Szembek had already communicated a refusal of the German demands to Moltke on 24 March, the Führer was anxious to give the Poles time to change their minds. In a military directive of 25 March, Hitler stated that he was leaving Berlin because he expected Lipski to return from Warsaw on that day and did not wish to see him. He directed that, 'For the present, R[ibbentrop] is to conduct the negotiations. The Führer does not wish to solve the Danzig problem by force, however. He does not wish to drive Poland into the arms of Britain by this.' A military occupation of Danzig was to be con-templated only if Lipski indicated that the Polish government was unable to justify to its people a voluntary cession of the Free City and that a *fait accompli* would ease the situation. 'For the present, the Führer does not intend to solve the Polish question. However, it must be worked upon.'[42] The fate of Poland when the time came was grim, and shows that German policy on this question had already been outlined by the spring of 1939. If the preconditions were favourable, Poland was to be so 'beaten down' that she would not be taken into account as a political factor for several decades. An advanced German frontier was envisaged, extending from the eastern tip of East Prussia to the eastern tip of Silesia—that is, roughly the frontier of 1914. The Polish population of these regions was to be evacuated and re-settled.[43] For the moment, however, Hitler was willing to bide

---

[41] *Ibid.*, pp. 438–9.   [42] *DGFP*, D, VI, no. 99.
[43] By disregarding this part of Hitler's instruction, A. J. P. Taylor was able to conclude that 'Hitler's objective was alliance with Poland, not her destruction'; *The Origins of the Second World War* (London, 1961), p. 210.

his time. The restraining influence was his desire to prevent a *rapprochement* between Poland and Great Britain.

On 26 March, Lipski delivered the official Polish reply to Ribbentrop's demands of 21 March. In accordance with his instruction, the ambassador stated that Poland was willing to study with the German government the possibility of further simplifying and increasing facilities in rail and road communication between Germany and East Prussia, but that an extra-territorial highway could not be considered. The Polish government estimated that it should be possible to 'find a solution based on a joint Polish-German guarantee' of the Free City of Danzig which would have 'to meet the aspirations of the German population on the one hand, and to safeguard Polish interests on the other'. On this question the Polish government considered it advisable to have a preliminary discussion of 'political principles' between the two governments in order that the interests of both sides be respected. With regard to the German invitation for Col. Beck to visit Berlin, Lipski stated that the Polish Foreign Minister felt that the above questions should first be clarified.[44]

Ribbentrop received Lipski's declaration with evident disappointment, but showed anxiety to give the Polish government more time for a definite answer. He asked the ambassador whether Poland would not reconsider the German proposals, to which Lipski replied that his government would study them further and that it was willing to do everything possible to reach an agreement. The German Foreign Minister repeated his former proposals of recognizing the priority of Polish interests in the Ukraine and the possibility of a satisfactory solution of the Slovak question. He warned Lipski, however, that on the basis of his reply the Chancellor might conclude that it was impossible to reach an understanding with Poland; the Führer, he said, wished to avoid having to reach such a conclusion.[45] The Polish answer amounted to a rejection of the two basic German demands: the return of Danzig to the Reich and the extra-territorial highway through the Polish Corridor. The Polish government, however, kept the door to negotiations open by expressing its willingness to discuss a settlement of the Danzig

[44] *PWB*, nos. 62, 63.   [45] *DGFP*, D, VI, no. 101: *PWB*, no. 63.

question and of communications through the Corridor on a basis in harmony with its own interests.

While doing everything possible to conceal the deadlock in Polish-German relations—a policy which was also followed by Germany—Beck maintained a very firm attitude towards Berlin. He was no doubt encouraged in this policy by the results of the Halifax-Raczyński conversations and by reports that a determined stand augured the best prospect for British aid.[46] On 29 March, in reply to Ribbentrop's statement that any Polish *coup* in Danzig would be considered by Berlin as aggression against Germany, Beck warned Moltke that 'if any attempt should be made by Germany to alter the status of the Free City unilaterally, Poland would regard this as a *casus belli*'. He also told the German Ambassador that the same would apply in case the Danzig Senate should be guilty of a breach of the Versailles Treaty—an allusion to a possible declaration by the Senate of the union of the Free City with the Reich. After this very direct warning, Beck said that he still hoped for a friendly solution of the problem but that he was under the impression 'that we have come to a turning-point in German-Polish relations', and that the decision now rested with Berlin.[47]

Such a determined attitude, coupled with Hitler's unwillingness to push Poland into closer relations with Great Britain, had tangible results. Weizsäcker wrote to the President of the Danzig Senate that he did not consider it advisable 'to provoke Poland in any way through Danzig' and Ribbentrop commanded that the Free City adopt 'a sphinx-like attitude' towards Poland.[48] A sudden calm followed, and the Polish Commissioner General reported a disorientation in party circles due to definite orders from Berlin forbidding any local *putsch*.[49] This state of affairs

[46] Raczyński reported that, according to the United States ambassador in London, Joseph Kennedy, if Poland offered resistance to German aggression against Danzig, Great Britain would, though unenthusiastically, stand by her; Raczyński to Foreign Minister, 28 March 1939, cypher telegram no. 48, APEL, Cyphers, 1939. Ambassador Kennedy telephoned this message to Ambassador Biddle in Warsaw.
[47] *DGFP*, D, VI, no. 118.   [48] *Ibid.*, nos. 124, 126.
[49] Commissioner General to Foreign Minister, Danzig, 11 May 1939, APEL, Gdańsk, 1939. The Polish minister in Stockholm also reported that, according to the Swedish Foreign Minister, Greiser had been ordered to 'behave quietly'; Potworowski to Foreign Minister, Stockholm, 6 April 1939, *ibid.*

did not mean, however, that Berlin was ready to let the matter rest for any considerable length of time. Weizsäcker told President Greiser:

> I thought it now possible to conduct a kind of policy of attrition towards Poland in order to make the Government more disposed to the solution we aimed at for certain German-Polish questions, including also the Danzig question.[50]

The State Secretary thought that Polish consent to German demands was only a matter of time. On 30 March, he told the Italian Ambassador in Berlin that the Poles were still 'hard of hearing' but that they would become more yielding, particularly on Danzig. He did not envisage the possibility of a dangerous situation arising between Poland and Germany.[51]

While, virtually unknown to the outside world, Polish-German conversations had reached a deadlock, the British Cabinet reconsidered its proposal for a Four Power Declaration. The firm Polish attitude on Danzig, as displayed on 23 March, was no doubt a factor in the drawing up of the new project, though the decisive point was the negative attitude of Poland and Rumania towards entering any alignment to which the Soviet Union would be a party. The Polish argument that the inclusion of the USSR in the declaration would antagonize Germany found understanding in London, all the more since the Prime Minister did not wish to provoke Hitler. Moreover, Lord Halifax had no desire to drive Poland and Rumania into the arms of Germany by any hasty agreement with the USSR. The Foreign Secretary wrote to Kennard on 27 March that 'our attempts to consolidate the situation will be frustrated if the Soviet Union is openly associated with the initiation of the scheme'. Since the inclusion of Poland and Rumania was considered to be of prime importance, Halifax instructed Kennard that it had been decided to make two parallel sets of proposals: one was to be communicated to both Warsaw and Bucharest, and the second to Warsaw only. In the first instance Britain and France would ask the states concerned whether they would be ready to assist one another if threatened by Germany. If the answer was positive,

[50] Memorandum by State Secretary, *DGFP*, D, VI, no. 124.
[51] FOL, 97/108331.

Great Britain would be prepared to come to the help of the threatened state; in return, both would expect Poland and Rumania to keep them informed of any developments which might threaten their independence. The assurance of British aid would in this case be conditioned on Polish help to Rumania. This proposal was therefore modelled on the earlier French project of securing Polish assistance for Bucharest. The second proposal, which was to be communicated to Warsaw only, was that France and Britain would help Poland if she were threatened by Germany; in return, Poland was to promise aid to London and Paris if they had to resist German aggression either in Western Europe or against Yugoslavia. Halifax added that the proposal to Poland was to be kept secret, although it would be necessary to make a statement of assurance to Poland in Parliament.[52]

The British project of 27 March constituted a compromise between the French efforts to condition aid to Poland on a Polish guarantee for Rumania, and Lord Halifax's attitude that Poland should be promised aid if threatened by Germany. It was a great advance over the previous proposed declaration in that it envisaged a secret agreement between Poland and the two Western Powers and thus constituted an important step toward an alliance between Warsaw and London. While Kennard was discussing the new British proposals with Col. Beck on 30 March, he received another urgent message from London which accelerated the realization of the new project. The Ambassador was instructed to request the Polish Foreign Minister's agreement to a declaration which Chamberlain was to make in Parliament on the following day. This declaration would be nothing more or less than an offer on the part of Great Britain to guarantee Poland against German aggression. Without a moment's hesitation, Col. Beck agreed to the proposed text of the guarantee.[53] On 31 March, the Prime Minister of Great Britain was able to announce in the House of Commons that, though the British government favoured the adjustment of Polish-German differences by free negotiation, nevertheless,

[52] *DBFP*, 3, IV, no. 538 (pp. 516–17).
[53] Kennard suggested that the word 'unprovoked' should be used to qualify German aggression. Halifax decided against this suggestion on the ground that it

In order to make perfectly clear the position of His Majesty's Government in the meantime before these consultations are concluded, I have to inform the House that, during that period, in the event of any action which clearly threatened Polish independence, and which the Polish Government accordingly considered it vital to resist with their national forces, His Majesty's Government would feel themselves bound at once to lend the Polish Government all support in their power. They have given the Polish Government assurance to that effect.

I may add that the French Government have authorized me to make it plain that they stand in the same position in this matter as do His Majesty's Government.[54]

Col. Beck could now congratulate himself on having achieved a long-cherished object of Polish displomacy—the commitment of Great Britain to the maintenance of Polish independence. He could not afford to be over-confident, however. The guarantee was but a fragile instrument if Hitler should decide on aggression; it provided only the foundation on which an alliance could be built and there were many difficulties to overcome before this aim could be reached.

The guarantee to Poland marked a departure from Great Britain's former lack of interest in East Central Europe but it did not commit her to an irreversible policy. Chamberlain viewed the guarantee as a diplomatic deterrent which was to bring Hitler to his senses, and also as a limited commitment of a temporary nature whose extent and application would be decided by the British Cabinet. In order to gauge the real nature of the declaration of 31 March, it should be seen in the light of its origins and of the significance which it had for Chamberlain and his closest associates.

In view of the absence of any official confirmation of the rumours of an imminent German attack on Poland,[55] it is clear

would give Germany an advantage; *ibid.*, nos. 573, 584. These documents should be compared with Bonnet's distorted version of the origin of the British guarantee to Poland; *Défense de la Paix*, II, pp. 155–6 and *Le Quai d'Orsay*, p. 261.

[54] *Parl. Deb. H. C.*, 5th ser., vol. 345, col. 2415. The consultations referred to were those proceeding on the proposals outlined in Halifax's instruction of 27 March.

[55] The United States ambassador in Poland, Drexel J. Biddle, reported such rumours, as did the Berlin correspondent of the *News Chronicle* on 29 March; see

that the decision to grant Warsaw a guarantee of British protection was due to other reasons. Three factors decided the
British government to take this new step: the pressure of public
opinion, the pressure of the 'anti-Munich' faction of the Conservative Party, and the interest of Lord Halifax in supporting
Poland as part of the policy of diplomatic deterrent.[56] The
growing interest of the Foreign Secretary in Polish affairs dated
from the period after Munich and had manifested itself in
willingness to keep in touch with the Poles over Danzig. Public
opinion in Britain had reacted strongly to Hitler's move against
Czechoslovakia on 15 March, and demanded a stronger policy.
Most dangerous of all to the government was the rebel faction of
Conservatives, led by Churchill, which threatened to undermine
Chamberlain's majority in the House of Commons and thus
overthrow his Cabinet. On 28 March, Churchill and thirty other
members of the Conservative Party set down a resolution calling
for a national government and a more active policy. On the same
day, Chamberlain was pointedly asked in the House whether it
had been 'made clear to Poland that His Majesty's Government
would be willing, in conjunction with other Powers, to come to
Poland's assistance if she is to be the next victim of German
aggression'. To this, the Prime Minister gave the evasive reply
that he still had to maintain 'a certain reserve' on the matter.[57]
There may have been a division of opinion on this subject in the
Cabinet, for, despite the fact that Halifax had already, on
27 March, mentioned an assurance for Poland to be given in
Parliament,[58] Raczyński was told on the morning of 30 March
that no public announcement would be made unless 'the
situation were suddenly to deteriorate and there was reason to
fear that Germany might be contemplating immediate action'.[59]
Yet it was later in the same day that Kennard was directed in all

---

Feiling, *Neville Chamberlain*, p. 493. These reports were not confirmed by Kennard
or G. Ogilvie-Forbes; *DBFP*, 3, IV, nos. 564, 572, *passim*.

[56] Halifax's view of British guarantees is stated in an unpublished memorandum
written after the outbreak of the war, in which he stated that neither Poland nor
Rumania had any illusions about any concrete help from Great Britain in the event
of war; for all parties concerned, the guarantees 'were the best chance, and indeed
the only chance, of warning him [Hitler] off that decision'; cited by the Earl of
Birkenhead, *The Life of Lord Halifax*, p. 437.

[57] *Parl. Deb. H. C.*, 5th Ser., vol. 345, col. 1884-5.

[58] See *supra* n. 52.   [59] *DBFP*, 3, V, no. 5.

haste to obtain Beck's agreement to the declaration which was to be made on 31 March. What is more, Sir Orme Sargent told the Polish ambassador that a speedy Polish reply to the British proposal was essential because of increasing attacks on Chamberlain for his lack of initiative in the face of German aggression.[60] Thus it is clear that the guarantee was more the result of political pressure on Chamberlain than of any fear of immediate German attack on Poland.

The Prime Minister and his closest advisers did not see the guarantee as a radical change of policy or as a commitment to defend the *status quo* in East Central Europe. The Conservative press immediately seized upon the ambiguities of the declaration and asserted that Chamberlain's statement was not an engagement to defend the territorial integrity of Poland. Lord Beaverbrook's paper, the *Evening Standard*, suggested on 31 March, the day of the announcement, that the guarantee did not apply to changes in Danzig or the Corridor. When ambassador Raczyński lodged a protest against this assertion, the diplomatic correspondent of the paper telephoned the Polish Embassy and explained that the offending article had been written by Lord Beaverbrook himself, who claimed that he had this information from circles closest to the Prime Minister.[61] The same interpretation was given on 1 April by *The Times*, which declared:

> Mr. Chamberlain's statement involves no blind acceptance of the status quo. On the contrary, his repeated references to free negotiations imply that he thinks that there are problems in which adjustments are still necessary. The new obligation does not bind Great Britain to defend every inch of the present frontier of Poland. The key word is not Integrity but Independence.

After an official Polish protest against these reports had been made, and after Col. Beck had threatened to cancel his forthcoming visit to London, an official denial was issued by the Foreign Office and published in *The Times* on 3 April, the day of Beck's arrival in the British capital.[62]

[60] Raczyński to Foreign Minister, 30 March 1939, APEL, P–GB, 1939.
[61] Raczyński to Foreign Minister, 1 April 1939, *ibid.*
[62] For Beck's threat to cancel his visit, see Edward Raczyński, *In Allied London: The Wartime Diaries of Count Edward Raczynski* (London, 1962), p. 14. Raczyński thinks that the articles were inspired by Sir Horace Wilson, special adviser to Chamberlain, Sir John Simon, and perhaps Sir Samuel Hoare.

Notwithstanding the official denial of the reports in the *Evening Standard* and *The Times*, these papers did indeed express the thoughts of Chamberlain and his 'inner Cabinet'.[63] The Prime Minister himself wrote privately at this time that 'what we are concerned with, is not the boundaries of states, but attacks on their independence'.[64] Sir Samuel Hoare, later Viscount Templewood, claims that the decision to interpret and implement the guarantee rested entirely with the British Cabinet:

> The two conditions under which we undertook to intervene were, firstly a clear threat to Polish independence which we should ourselves define, and secondly, Polish armed resistance to aggression. The decision as to whether or not we should take part in a war was retained in our own hands.[65]

The guarantee was neither a rigid commitment to Poland, nor was it conceived to imply any possibility of direct military aid. At best, it was seen as a diplomatic deterrent. On the eve of Beck's arrival in London, Raczyński made soundings as to the possibility of immediate 'technical' talks. He was told that such conversations belonged to a later stage which had not yet been considered.[66] On the British side, there was, in fact, no consideration of financial, material, or military aid to Poland to implement the guarantee. According to Air Vice-Marshal Slessor, the Combined Chiefs of Staffs were concerned at this juncture with gaining time to improve their defences and to build up a heavy bomber force. Writing of this time, he says:

> Partly for this reason, we were unenthusiastic about the guarantees to Poland, Rumania and Greece; we had no delusions that we should not have to fight if any of them were attacked, but the vague term 'all support in our power' really meant nothing because it was not in our power to give them any support—as opposed to eventually liberating them and avenging them.[67]

Both the French and the British General Staffs agreed, 'That in

---

[63] This name was given to the group formed by Chamberlain, Halifax, Hoare, and Simon; see Lord Strang, *Home and Abroad*, p. 124.

[64] Feiling, *Neville Chamberlain*, p. 403.

[65] Viscount Templewood, *Nine Troubled Years* (London, 1954), p. 349.

[66] Raczyński to Foreign Minister, 30 March 1939, APEL, P–GB, 1939.

[67] Sir John Slessor, *The Central Blue: Recollections and Reflections* (London, 1956), p. 214.

fact, there was nothing that either of us could do to save Poland'[68] —a conclusion reminiscent of their attitude towards Czecho- slovakia in 1938. It appears that, in both cases, the two General Staffs did not believe in the necessity of a French offensive against Germany which would involve the latter in a two-front war. The British government doubled the size of the Territorial Army from thirteen to twenty-six divisions, but it did not mobilize the entire industrial and financial strength of the country until after the fall of France in 1940. In such circumstances, it is not surprising that in the spring of 1939; the possibilities of helping Poland seemed *nil*; they were not even seriously considered.

As far as Poland was concerned, the acceptance of the British guarantee involved the risk of immediate conflict with Ger- many.[69] The Polish government considered that a German *coup* in Danzig could take place even during the Polish Foreign Minister's visit to London. On the eve of Beck's departure, therefore, a conference was held to lay down the line of action if

[68] *Ibid.*, p. 350. This attitude was confirmed by the Chiefs of Staff in July when they warned the Committee on Imperial Defence that the fate of Poland must depend on the ultimate outcome of the war. This would depend on allied ability to defeat Germany in the long run and not to relieve Poland at the outset. Indirect aid by bombing Germany was put in doubt owing to the risk of retaliation against France and to the French inferiority in the air; see J. R. M. Butler, *History of the Second World War: Grand Strategy*, vol. II, September 1939—June 1940 (London, 1957), p. 56.

[69] Soviet historians interpret Beck's acceptance of the British guarantee as motivated by his hopes of still reaching agreement with Hitler; see *Istoriia Velikoi Otechestvennoi Voiny*, vol. I., p. 163, where Beck's statement that the door to negotiations with Germany was still open is quoted without his qualification that he had no illusions about any success on this score; *Dernier Rapport*, p. 199. H. Batowski admits that the guarantee was a great success for Beck's policy of avoiding a multilateral agreement and above all co-operation with the USSR; the author claims that Beck's success must be attributed to the fact that his anti-Soviet attitude was fully understood by Chamberlain; *Kryzys Dyplomatyczny w Europie*, p. 283. According to K. Lapter, Chamberlain's aim in giving the British guarantee to Poland was to provoke Hitler to attack that country and then to march against the USSR; K. Lapter, 'Angielskie Gwarancje dla Polski w 1939r' (English Guarantees to Poland in 1939), *Sprawy Międzynarodowe* (Warsaw, 1959), no. 6, pp. 3–31. For a criticism of this thesis, see Anna M. Cienciala, 'O Polityce Angiel- skiej w 1939r' (On English Policy in 1939), *Bellona* (London, 1959), III, pp. 297– 301. Władysław Gomułka expressed the official attitude of his government on this subject by saying that instead of choosing the only real and effective alliance, i.e., with the USSR, the Polish government in 1939 chose the 'mythical' alliance with France and Great Britain; *Pravda*, 22 July 1959, cited in *Istoriia*, p. 159. This is also the theme stressed by Batowski.

such an event should occur. Besides the Foreign Minister, the participants at the meeting were General W. Stachiewicz, Chief of the General Staff, Michał Łubieński, Beck's Chef de Cabinet, Tadeusz Kobylański, Head of the Eastern Department of the Ministry of Foreign Affairs, and Mirosław Arciszewski, Second Deputy Foreign Minister. Beck opened the discussion by saying that, although he did not think that Poland would immediately face a decisive conflict over Danzig, she should be prepared for such an eventuality and have in readiness some 'compromise between military and diplomatic action'. Several possible courses of action were outlined and were to be applied according to the circumstances. If a local *putsch* should take place on the formal initiative of the Senate or the Party, Poland was to react on the diplomatic level by lodging a protest against Danzig. In case of a political declaration of union with the Reich, Poland would treat it as diplomatic incident and protest to Berlin against the irresponsibility of the Danzig authorities. Recognition of such a declaration by Berlin would constitute a Polish-German incident and Polish reaction would be the same as in the case of entry of German troops, that is, all privileged transport through the Corridor would be cancelled and this measure would be supplemented by mobilization decrees in Poland. In short, the principle laid down by Beck was that Poland should try to keep any incident on the local level as long as possible and that any transfer of the matter to the plane of Polish-German relations should take place on German initiative. However, no German ultimatum could be accepted and Poland would act in case of a German *coup*. Finally, it was agreed that if any of the above incidents should take place, Beck would interrupt his visit and immediately return to Warsaw.[70] The conference of 1 April thus reflected the Polish Foreign Minister's just estimate of the fragility of the British guarantee and of the risks which he had incurred by accepting it. Moreover, he had to take into account British warnings that he must avoid an uncompromising or provocative attitude towards Berlin.[71]

[70] Note by the Chef de Cabinet, 1 April 1939, MFA (London), P–G, 1939.
[71] On 31 March, Halifax wrote to Kennard warning that the Polish government must take particular care to avoid an uncompromising attitude or any provocative action in their dealings with Germany and to keep in touch with us'; *DBFP*, 3, IV, no. 584.

Col. Beck set out for London on 2 April with the hope of concluding a bilateral agreement with Great Britain. Such an alliance, or at least co-operation, had been the great desire of Marshal Piłsudski from the earliest days of the Polish republic and, in particular, since it had become obvious that France would do nothing in international affairs without the support of Britain. From 1936 onwards, Beck himself had repeatedly declared his readiness to co-operate with London. Once the alliance had become a distinct possibility, the Polish Foreign Minister's attitude towards it evolved considerably within a short time. Before the offer of the guarantee he had thought in terms of a vague, general, public agreement, which would be complemented by a secret accord, perhaps between the two General Staffs.[72] After the declaration of 31 March, Beck came to feel that a more extensive and durable arrangement, perhaps a bilateral alliance, could be envisaged, although, on the eve of his trip to London, he was still undecided as to the extent to which such an agreement should be made public.[73] Whatever form the agreement should finally take, the basic aim of the Polish Foreign Minister was to emerge from his position of dangerous isolation with respect to Germany. He hoped that a permanent agreement with Great Britain would modify the German attitude on the Free City. If, on the other hand, war should prove unavoidable, Poland would have a powerful ally by her side. Finally, he intended to use the accord with Great Britain in order to obtain a satisfactory understanding with France on the interpretation of the Franco-Polish alliance.[74]

On the British side, the aims were not only more limited but also diverged from those of Beck. Chamberlain, though desirous of obtaining Polish co-operation in a multilateral agreement, did not yet entertain any thought of a bilateral accord with Poland; furthermore, he had set himself certain objectives in the forthcoming talks which were not attractive to Beck. First of all, the British Cabinet was anxious to learn the precise stage which had been reached in Polish-German conversations; second, it

[72] Beck, *Dernier Rapport*, p. 189.
[73] It was apparently at this time that Beck proposed to Marshal Śmigły-Rydz and President Mościcki that the unilateral British guarantee should be transformed into a bilateral agreement, and obtained their consent; *ibid.*, pp. 189–90.
[74] *Ibid.*, pp. 190–91.

wished to obtain a Polish guarantee for Rumania and, if possible, a promise of Polish aid for the Western Democracies against German aggression in Western or South-Eastern Europe. Finally, the British ministers hoped for some agreement between Poland and the USSR. Col. Beck's ability to obtain the transformation of the temporary and ambiguous guarantee into a binding agreement illustrates his diplomatic skill and the value which the British government now put on Polish co-operation.

The most insistent British probing on Danzig brought forth from Col. Beck only very guarded statements, though these had the virtue of being literally true. The British government, for its part, had plenty of indirect information on the Berlin-Warsaw conversations but was not satisfied with the reports of Kennard on the subject.[75] Beck replied to queries in London that he saw no danger of military action, and that the question of Danzig was not yet in a negotiable shape. As far as he was concerned, that was indeed the state of affairs, since the Polish attitude was that negotiations could not take place on the basis of the German proposals as they stood. To further questions the Polish Foreign Minister answered that conversations, rather than negotiations, had taken place, and he added that Poland would not accept a *fait accompli*.[76] He outlined the Polish conditions for a Danzig settlement: a bilateral agreement guaranteeing free government for the local population and safeguarding Polish rights in the Free City. He rejected the possibility of an extra-territorial highway. Finally, he emphasized the fact that Poland would oppose any unilateral solution, and that Danzig had become 'a kind of symbol' for his nation.[77] All these statements were literally true but for obvious reasons Beck tried to avoid giving the impression that conversations with Germany had reached a deadlock.

Beck has been accused by some historians of evasiveness on the subject of German-Polish relations, and even of a lack of frankness on this score during the London talks.[78] Such an accusation

---

[75] Kennard wrote on 2 April that he had been unable to secure any 'straightforward statement' and suggested that Beck be urged to tell the British government 'frankly' what had passed and what concessions Poland would be willing to make; *DBFP*, 3, IV, no. 605.

[76] *DBFP*, 3, V, nos. 1, 2, pp. 3, 17.   [77] *Ibid.*, no. 2, pp. 17–18.

[78] '... the discussions were hampered to a considerable extent by Beck's habitual

misreads the actual state of affairs. The British government was
well informed of the German objectives and of the Polish attitude
towards them.[79] What the British ministers wished to know was
whether there was any possibility of agreement. Here it was in
Beck's interest not to reveal that a stalemate had been reached.
He may well have feared, in view of the past sympathy in Britain
and France toward the German claims to Danzig, and in view of
Chamberlain's continued hope for an agreement with Germany,
that the revelation of the complete deadlock existing between
Warsaw and Berlin might discourage the Prime Minister from
extending his commitments to Poland. In particular, he had in
mind the comments of the British right-wing press on the nature
of the guarantee of 31 March.

The Polish Foreign Minister also resisted the British request
for a Polish guarantee to Rumania on the grounds that he wished
to avoid throwing the Hungarians into the arms of Germany.[80]
In his view, a German attack on Rumania would either have to
pass through Hungary, or be carried out by the Hungarians
themselves. He therefore held that any Polish promise of aid to
Rumania would be seen by Budapest as a recognition of
Rumanian claims in the territorial dispute between the two
countries and would impel the Hungarians towards an alliance
with Berlin. Beck qualified his rejection of the British request
with the statement that if Rumania actually resisted an attack by
Germany, Poland would then help her. He avoided giving a
direct commitment on Polish aid, however, by saying that he
would first have to consult the Rumanian government.[81] He was

secretiveness and evasiveness, which could only increase the British Ministers'
lack of confidence in him'; Arnold J. Toynbee and Veronica Toynbee (eds.), *The
Eve of War, 1939*, Royal Institute of International Affairs (London, 1959), p. 96.

[79] Burckhardt informed Mr. Walters, the Secretary General of the League
Council, of all his talks with Weizsäcker so that the British government was aware
of the Hitler-Beck and Beck-Ribbentrop conversations of 5 and 6 January 1939.
Kennard was informed of the German demands of 21 March and of the Polish
attitude towards them; see *DBFP*, 3, IV, no. 547. On 1 April, Kennard reported
that Beck had confirmed the information that the German government had
declared it would consider any Polish occupation of Danzig as a *casus belli*', and
that he had taken the same attitude; *ibid.*, no. 595.

[80] *DBFP*, 3, V, no. 1 p. 2.

[81] *Ibid.*, no. 2, p. 15. At this time the Polish government was working toward a
non-aggression pact between Rumania and Hungary and territorial concessions
by the former to the latter, Hungarian ambassador in Warsaw to the Foreign

indirectly aided in his stand by the reluctance of Bucharest to commit itself to any agreements which would make it difficult to preserve Rumanian neutrality, and by the fact that the Rumanian government did not want the Western guarantee for Rumania to be conditional on Polish aid.[82]

The British spokesmen showed considerable interest in the matter of Polish-Soviet relations. Chamberlain asked Beck whether, in case of war, Poland would welcome Soviet aid in war materials. The Polish Foreign Minister replied that he was in no position to accept any agreement which would have the effect, even indirectly, of linking Poland with the USSR.[83] His position was that Poland was ready to 'improve' her relations with her eastern neighbour, but not to 'extend' them.[84] The British did not press the matter, all the more so because their own attitude towards Russia was one of distrust.[85] Their inquiries as to the possible Polish acceptance of Soviet aid, or of British aid through the Soviet Union, were indicative, however, of their attitude towards the problem of aiding Poland in case of war and of plans to negotiate with the USSR.

The most important aspect of the London conversations concerned the nature of Poland's relations with Britain. Beck had left for London with full powers to sign a secret bilateral agreement but he took it upon himself to extend his mandate. Already at the first meeting, when he indicated his readiness to accept reciprocity, he made no mention of secrecy. What had led him

---

Minister, 30 March 1939; see Júhasz Gyula ed., *Magyarország Külpolitikája, a* II, *Világháború Kitörésének Időszakbán 1939–1940* (Hungarian Foreign Policy. At the Outbreak of the Second World War, 1939–1940, Budapest, 1962), vol. IV, document no. 42.

[82] *DBFP*, 3, IV, no. 601.

[83] *DBFP*, 3, V, no. 2, p. 12.

[84] *Ibid.*, no. 1, p. 7.

[85] Chamberlain distrusted Soviet Russia's motives and did not believe in her ability to launch an effective offensive action; Feiling, *Neville Chamberlain*, p. 403. This latter opinion was shared by British General Staff. Viscount Templewood writes that the prevalent opinion in government and military circles was that negotiations with the USSR would take time and were unlikely to succeed; *Nine Troubled Years*, p. 347. The opinion of the British Embassy in Moscow was that '. . . in the event of a European war, there is every reason to suppose that the attitude of the Soviet Government would . . . be one of nervous neutrality and that the principal aim of Soviet policy would be to prevent the Soviet Union from itself becoming involved'; *DBFP*, 3, V, appendix III (pp. 611–12).

to this decision was the realization that now or never was the occasion to obtain a firm British commitment to Poland and that he had more chance of obtaining it if the accord were to be public.[86] He succeeded in persuading the British ministers of the advantage of a bilateral agreement with Poland by offering Polish aid to Britain on the condition of a bilateral accord between the two countries. In reply to a question put by Chamberlain, whether Poland would support Britain in case of war arising from a German attack on Belgium, Holland, or Switzerland, Beck answered, 'if Great Britain and Poland reached a permanent binding agreement, the Polish government would not exclude friendly discussion on these points. If the principle of permanent collaboration was accepted, Poland would be willing to discuss them.' This statement by the Polish Foreign Minister finally elicited from the Prime Minister the declaration that 'that principle had been accepted by His Majesty's Government'.[87]

Chamberlain had not envisaged such an outcome of the conversations. He described his original aims in the course of the third meeting which took place on 5 April, by saying that

the conversations appeared to him to be tending towards a result different from that which public opinion was expecting, namely, towards a bilateral Anglo-Polish agreement, whereas what was hoped for was an arrangement by which a number of states would band themselves round Great Britain, France and Poland as a nucleus.[88]

His efforts to return to this objective were of no avail. Beck, for his part, avoided a direct answer to Chamberlain's request for a Polish commitment to aid Britain in defending other countries in Western Europe, by stating that his instructions were to treat the question by stages, but that he was sure his government would examine the matter further and also give favourable consideration to the Rumanian question. Upon this basis the bargain was struck. In return for the Polish Foreign Minister's agreement to the principle of reciprocity, Great Britain prom-

[86] Beck admitted that he took personal responsibility to overstep his powers; *Dernier Rapport*, p. 190.
[87] *DBFP*, 3, V, no. 2, pp. 13–14.
[88] *DBFP*, 3, V, no. 10, p. 30.

ised to aid Poland if her independence should be threatened. Decision in this matter was left expressly in the hands of the Polish government. Both governments were to keep each other informed of any developments threatening the independence of either. In the 'Summary of Conclusions' embodying this agreement which was drawn up on 6 April, it was stated:

> As an earnest of their intention to enter into a formal agreement to render assistance to Poland in the circumstances contemplated above, His Majesty's Government in the United Kingdom have informed the Polish Government, and have stated publicly, that during the period required for the conclusion of the formal agreement outlined in paragraph 2 above, in the event of any action which clearly threatened Polish independence, and which the Polish Government accordingly considered it vital to resist with their national forces, His Majesty's Government would feel themselves bound at once to lend the Polish Government all the support in their power.[89]

In contrast with the ambiguities of the guarantee of 31 March, the interpretation of what constituted a threat to Polish independence was extremely liberal and flexible, and was left entirely to the discretion of Warsaw. If Germany attempted to undermine Polish independence by economic penetration, 'or in any other way', Britain would support Poland in her resistance. Moreover, 'In the event of other action by Germany which clearly threatened Polish independence, and was of such a nature that the Polish Government considered it vital to resist with their national forces, His Majesty's Government would at once come to the help of Poland.' This all-embracing guarantee was the result of Polish fears of a German annexation of Danzig and Beck's insistence that this possibility should be provided for.[90]

[89] *Ibid.*, no. 16, point 3, p. 48.
[90] *Ibid.*, point 2b, p. 47. Raczyński reported that to cover the contingency of a German annexation of Danzig, the Under-Secretary of State, Sir Alexander Cadogan, had called in a legal adviser, Mr. Malkin, who drafted the appropriate paragraph; Note by Raczyński, 6 April 1939, APEL, P–GB, 1939. A Foreign Office memorandum of the previous day put the case for Danzig very strongly, saying that Germany's aim was to 'use Danzig and the Corridor to secure the neutralization and ultimately, perhaps, a further partition of Poland'. Ambassador Henderson protested that such a formulation of the Danzig-Corridor question did not consider the German position. He was in favour of an arrangement whereby

The conclusion of a formal alliance was made contingent on the settlement of points dealing with Polish aid to Britain in case of German aggression against certain countries in Western Europe, the granting of a Polish guarantee to Rumania if the latter should be threatened, and an agreement with the French government for its acceptance of the same obligations towards Poland as those undertaken by Great Britain. The British government also declared its intention of continuing its conversations with Rumania and of initiating conversations with other members of the Balkan Entente; furthermore, it expressed the wish to obtain better relations with the USSR. The Polish government, for its part, declared that if Britain assumed any further obligations in Eastern Europe these should not extend the commitments of Poland; this was a reference to the USSR. It also emphasized the importance of taking into consideration the position of the Baltic States in any attempt to develop co-operation in this region.[91]

The Polish Foreign Minister had scored a great diplomatic success with the agreement of 6 April 1939. On the unsteady ground of the ambiguous and provisional guarantee of 31 March he had built a *de facto* bilateral alliance, and this despite Chamberlain's original aim of concluding merely a vague multilateral agreement. By offering a public and reciprocal agreement Beck succeeded in transforming the British project for a general arrangement between several parties into an agreement between Poland and Great Britain, accompanied by a provision for British support whenever the Polish government should consider its independence to be threatened. Poland was no longer an isolated potential victim of German aggression; an attack on her would, in all likelihood, launch a world war.

The Anglo-Polish Agreement of 6 April 1939 was an alliance in all but name—it was to be formalized by the signing of a treaty on 25 August. It was the result of Col. Beck's long efforts to establish close relations between Poland and Britain, and of the

---

Poland would exchange its control over Danzig foreign policy for a German undertaking not to militarize Danzig. He thought it preferable to wait for such a German-Polish agreement before guaranteeing Polish independence; see *DBFP*, 3, V, appendix XII, pp. 814, 817.

[91] *Ibid.*, points 5, 6, p. 48.

British government's realization, under the pressure of public opinion and political opposition, that the time had come to present a united front against Germany, even if that front were only a diplomatic one. Lord Halifax had greatly contributed to the *rapprochement* by his sympathy with the Polish attitude on Danzig and his belief that Poland should be granted a promise of help in return for her co-operation with London and Paris against Germany. Beck's policy of gaining time by a skilful direction of conversations with Berlin and of simultaneously presenting a firm attitude made it possible for the British government to regard Poland as the key to any organization of states which could be set up to check German expansion.[92] It seemed at last as if, after evading the issue for twenty years, the British government had recognized the fact that Europe was strategically an indivisible whole and that the independence of every country was therefore its vital interest.

[92] Viscount Templewood, *Nine Troubled Years*, p. 347.

EPILOGUE

THE British guarantee to Poland and the subsequent Anglo-Polish Agreements of 6 April did not make the outbreak of a world war inevitable, nor were they viewed in this light by the parties involved. In the spring of 1939, neither Col. Beck nor Neville Chamberlain expected the Führer to proceed immediately with his aggressive designs. On the contrary, both statesmen thought that the new link between Great Britain and Poland would act as a deterrent to Germany. There was, however, an essential difference of view between the two men as to the ultimate objective of the deterrent. The British Prime Minister still hoped for a settlement which would satisfy German ambitions in Eastern Europe, provided this was accomplished by peaceful means. The Polish Foreign Minister, for his part, assumed that Poland was no longer isolated in case of German attack; at the same time there was a glimmer of hope that Poland's new tie with Britain might induce Hitler to drop or modify his demands. Still, in view of Chamberlain's attitude, it was not out of the question that Beck might be forced to accept them in time. It was Hitler's impatience and greed, backed by his success in negotiating an alliance with the Soviet Union, which ultimately precipitated the Second World War.

In the first few weeks after the London agreement Col. Beck believed that Hitler would be deterred from pressing his demands on Poland.[1] At first he seemed to be right. The German press avoided an all-out attack on Warsaw, and Hitler issued orders that the Polish question should be left entirely to himself. By the end of April, however, he had made up his mind. In his Reichstag

[1] See *DBFP*, 3, V, no. 11; *FRUS*, 1939, I, p. 118; J. Łukasiewicz, 'Uwagi i Wspomnienia: 3. Rozbudowa Gwarancji' (Remarks and Reminiscences: 3. The Extension of the Guarantee), *Dziennik Polski* (London, 26 February 1947).

speech of 28 April, he repeated and elaborated his earlier offers to recognize the Polish-German frontier, to extend the Declaration of Non-Aggression and to guarantee Poland's economic rights in Danzig. He also proposed a joint German-Polish-Hungarian guarantee for the independence of Slovakia. In return, he demanded the inclusion of Danzig as a Free City in the Reich and an extra-territorial highway and railway through the Corridor.[2] He held the door open to negotiations on these terms.

Though it can certainly be said that Hitler's demands were moderate when compared with those of his predecessors, it was nevertheless clear to the Polish government that their acceptance would not only cut Poland off from direct access to the sea but that it would also make the British guarantee inoperative and would leave Poland completely at the mercy of Hitler. Col. Beck made a courageous and dignified reply in his speech to the Sejm on 5 May. After analysing the new situation and rejecting both German grievances and demands as unjustified, he expressed his readiness to hold conversations, provided the Reich manifested its peaceful intentions and adopted peaceful methods of procedure. He concluded his speech with the famous statement that while Poland wanted peace she did not believe in peace at any price. 'There is only one thing in the life of men, nations and states which is without price, and that is honour.'[3]

Beck's declaration was not a romantic gesture made without regard for the consequences. The acceptance of Hitler's terms would have led to renewed isolation and to the eventual absorption of Poland; at the same time, many observers, including Beck, thought it unlikely that Germany would risk a world war. Even if it came, however, Poland's alliances would be a guarantee of ultimate victory. But these considerations did not mean that Beck gave up all hope of averting war by a settlement based on some reasonable and honourable compromise. He made at least two attempts to reopen conversations with Berlin but did not press the issue when he found the Germans unreceptive. Ambassador Moltke reported on 23 May that Deputy Foreign Minister Arciszewski had assured him of Beck's chagrin

[2] *PWB*, no. 75; N. H. Baynes, *The Speeches of Adolf Hitler*, vol. II, p. 1631.
[3] *PWB*, no. 77.

at having to give up his former policy of good relations with Germany. Arciszewski said that the Foreign Minister had done so under pressure from public opinion and military circles but that he still hoped to reach an understanding with Berlin. Such a settlement, however, would have to be in the nature of a compromise, not a capitulation.[4] Arciszewski's statement that Beck had changed his policy under pressure should not be taken at its face value. It is true that Beck grieved over the failure of his hopes that the Anglo-Polish tie would act as a deterrent to Hitler, but he also believed that Poland could not accept Hitler's terms of 28 April. Arciszewski's comments should be seen as a variation on a theme often used by Polish diplomacy with regard to Berlin, namely, that Beck was the only Polish statesman moderate enough to come to terms with Germany and that excessive pressure on the part of the latter would make any agreement impossible.

One more attempt to open conversations was made a few weeks later when Count Łubieński, Beck's Chef de Cabinet, flew to Berlin in the hopes of seeing Göring and using the Marshal's declared peaceful intentions and animosity towards Ribbentrop to counter the latter's pressure for war. Łubieński was an advocate of delaying war in view of Poland's military weakness by a compromise on Danzig. At this time he apparently hoped to broach once more the project which he had outlined to Moltke in January but which had then been dropped. This plan envisaged a plebiscite in Danzig for union with either Poland or Germany the result of which was obviously a foregone conclusion; but it also projected a Polish-German commission to govern the city. There was no inclination to concede full German political or military control in Danzig nor the extra-territorial highway and railway. Łubieński was, however, unable to see Göring and only spoke to his secretary; thus the project never reached the stage of a formal proposal.[5] Since there was no German reaction then or

---

[4] *DGFP*, D, VI, no. 429.

[5] Letter of Count Łubieński to the author, London, 27 April 1959. In an article discussing Polish prewar policy, Jan Gawroński, former Polish Minister to Vienna, stated that on Beck's request he travelled to Berlin about 20 May 1939, to meet von Papen who came up especially from Turkey to try to re-establish Lipski's contacts with the leaders of the Reich. However, Gawroński and von Papen were told that it was too late; see Jan Gawroński, 'Polityka Pałacu Brühla Widziana od

later, it may be assumed that Hitler was not willing to accept an arrangement on these lines. It is clear that Beck did what he could to prevent a war with Germany short of signing away Polish independence.

The Polish Foreign Minister's efforts to preserve both peace and independence ultimately met with failure owing to Hitler's intransigence, the ambiguous attitude of the British government, and, finally, the conclusion of an alliance between Germany and the Soviet Union.

Chamberlain's hope of reaching a settlement on Hitler's demands in Eastern Europe was partly responsible for British reluctance to grant Poland financial aid or to undertake any military commitments to that country, and for extreme caution over the Danzig question. Poland asked for a loan of £20,000,000, but she was offered only £8,000,000, and this was accompanied by requests for changes in her monetary policy and coal exports. Agreement was finally reached on supplies of military equipment, notably planes, but at so late a date that these never reached Poland. It is true, of course, that the British government faced very great difficulties in extending such aid at a time when its own resources were strained to the utmost. Nevertheless, the protracted negotiations and the difficulties encountered by the Polish government[6] were known in Berlin and contributed to Hitler's conviction that Chamberlain was not wholeheartedly committed to the support of that country. Even

Loursa' (The Policy of the Brühl palace seen from Lours), *Kierunki* (Warsaw, 12 January 1958). It is not clear whether or not this effort was made concurrently with that of Łubieński. There were rumours of Polish readiness to reach a compromise by partitioning the territory of the Free City, but no such project reached the stage of Polish proposals to Berlin; see G. L. Weinberg, 'A Proposed Compromise over Danzig in 1939?' *JCEA*, vol. XIV, no. 4 (1955), pp. 334–8. In the period from 1 April to the end of July, the Hungarian ambassador in Warsaw reported Polish readiness to listen to 'reasonable' German proposals. Warsaw was prepared to discuss a change of the status of Danzig which would guarantee Polish rights and put the city under a Polish-German *condominium*. In the month of August, however, the attitude reported was that of resolution to fight if need be, and of belief that France and Britain would come in and aid Poland; see *Magyarország Külpolitikája*, vol. IV, nos. 54, 76, 96, 106, 108, 202, 210, 217.

[6] For a brief statement on the negotiations, see Count Edward Raczyński, *The British-Polish Alliance: Its Origin and Meaning* (London, 1948), General Sikorski Historical Institute, pp. 19–20. For British records, see *DBFP*, 3, V, VI, documents for May, June, July, *passim*; Polish records, APEL, P–GB, 1939.

greater reservations were displayed as far as military commitments were concerned, although this was understandable in view of Britain's own military situation. The British Military Mission which visited Poland in May could only give the Polish General Staff a qualified assurance that air attacks would be launched against Germany if the latter bombed Poland. The mission would not undertake any discussions on the provision of air bases for British planes in Poland or for naval action in the Baltic.[7]

In the case of Danzig, the constant British pleas for moderation and prior consultation, made during the summer months, were principally motivated by Chamberlain's hope for an agreement which would satisfy Hitler. The Prime Minister told General Sir Edmund Ironside, Chief of the Imperial General Staff, on the eve of the latter's visit to Poland in July, that he envisaged the annexation of the Free City by Germany with some kind of international guarantee for Polish rights.[8] Ironside's task was to discover Polish intentions and plans in case of German aggression in this sector. Under the British General's prodding questions Marshal Śmigły-Rydz went as far as he could to accommodate Chamberlain's wishes but, as the British Chargé d'Affaires in Warsaw remarked,

> . . . I think that it is impossible to get the Polish Government to give a binding pledge that they will in no circumstances take military action if challenged by Germany, without first consulting us. . . . I believe that in fact they will do anything possible to let us know if they see a combustion point approaching. Can they say more than that?[9]

General Ironside, for his part, spoke very highly of the Polish military effort and recommended that Britain grant Poland financial aid without many conditions attached; the General thought that this would convince Hitler of the seriousness of British intentions.[10]

---

[7] See *Protocols of the Polish-British General Staffs Conference in Warsaw, May, 1939* (London, 1958), General Sikorski Historical Institute, offprint from *Bellona*, 1957, no. III–IV (texts in French).

[8] Col. R. Macleod and D. Kelly (eds.), *The Ironside Diaries, 1937–1940* (London, 1952), p. 77.

[9] *DBFP*, 3, VI, no. 397. [10] *Ironside Diaries*, pp. 81–2.

Chamberlain, however, still hoped to reopen negotiations with Hitler on the old lines of a settlement in Eastern Europe complemented by one in the colonies. Unfortunately, this attitude was read in Berlin as a willingness to tolerate even forceful German expansion in Eastern Europe. It must be said that the confidential conversations which took place in the summer months facilitated a German misunderstanding of British intentions. Adam von Trott zu Solz, a former Rhodes scholar with connections in British political circles, visited England in June with the task of exploring the government's attitude towards Germany. At the Astors' Cliveden manor he discussed this matter with Lord Halifax, Lord Lothian, and Sir Thomas Inskip. According to his report, Lord Lothian assured him that British opposition to German expansion in Eastern Europe would cease if Germany 'led' but did not dominate the area. Lothian suggested that this could be achieved if Bohemia and Moravia were given full independence. The Danzig and Polish questions would find their own solution as soon as Poland could no longer justifiably assert that an increased economic and geographic dependence on Germany was equivalent to subjection to Berlin. In a later conversation with Chamberlain, von Trott zu Solz heard that the new obligations had been forced on the Prime Minister by Hitler.[11]

The greatest damage to the deterrent value of Britain's commitments in Eastern Europe was probably done by the declarations of Sir Horace Wilson, Chamberlain's closest adviser, and Mr. R. S. Hudson, Secretary of the Department of Overseas Trade, in their conversations with Dr. Helmuth Wohlthat, an official of the German Four Year Plan who visited London in July. According to Wohlthat, Sir Horace Wilson suggested that an Anglo-German declaration ruling out aggression as an instrument of policy would make the British guarantees to Poland and Rumania superfluous.[12] Mr. Hudson, speaking of

[11] *DGFP*, D, VI, no. 497. For a commentary on the visit of Adam von Trott zu Solz, see A. L. Rowse, *All Souls and Appeasement* (London, 1961), pp. 91–101.

[12] *DGFP*, D, VI, no. 716. This statement is not included in the British record of the conversation, *DBFP*, 3, VI, no. 354, but in the account of a conversation Wilson had with Ambassador Dirksen on 3 August, he is recorded as saying: '. . . all our commitments were entirely defensive and if it was once made clear by the German Government that there was henceforth to be no aggression on their

Danzig, said that the Free City in a Europe mobilized for war was one thing, but that in a Europe disarmed and committed to economic collaboration, it would be another.[13] He also reverted to the previous British suggestions for giving Germany some share in Africa. These conversations could not but confirm Hitler in his belief that Britain was not seriously committed to her guarantees in Eastern Europe. Finally, in August the Swedish businessman Dahlerus attempted to bring about negotiations by using his friendship with Göring. He was in constant touch with Lord Halifax but Hitler's ultimatum to Poland ended these efforts.

While the Polish government encountered difficulties in its relations with Great Britain, its efforts to reach a clarification of the Franco-Polish alliance also met with obstruction and delay. Since Polish hopes and plans for successfully resisting a German attack were based on a French offensive in the West, it was imperative to secure a revised military convention to supersede the one signed in 1921. According to the military protocols signed in Paris on 19 May by General Gamelin, Chief of the French General Staff, and General Kasprzycki, Polish Minister for War, the French Air Force was to begin action against Germany immediately on the outbreak of war, while the French Army was to begin offensive action on the fifteenth day.[14] Foreign Minister Bonnet, however, made the validity of the military convention dependent on the signature of a new political agreement.[15] This he delayed on the official plea that Polish demands for considering German aggression against Danzig as a *casus belli* had not been included in the London agreement of 6 April. The truth of the matter was that, while the secret clauses of the agreement were broad enough to embrace German aggression in any form, the British government was unwilling to commit itself *expressis verbis* on this question. Thus Bonnet was able to delay the

part, the policy of guarantees to potential victims *ipso facto* became inoperative'; *ibid.*, no. 533.

[13] *Ibid.*, no. 370.

[14] *Protocols of the Polish-French General Staffs Conferences in Paris, May 1939* (London, 1958), General Sikorski Historical Institute, pp. 12–13, offprint from *Bellona*, 1958, no. II (texts in French).

[15] Bonnet, *Défense de la Paix*, II, pp. 222–3.

signature of the political agreement until 4 September.[16] More-over, the French Foreign Minister hoped that another con-ference, similar to the Munich Conference, would be called and would grant Hitler all he wanted without war.[17] Gamelin, for his part, had no intention to implement the French commitments made in the military convention. When General Faury was sent to Warsaw in the latter part of August as head of the French Military Mission, he was told that no date could be given for a French offensive, that the French Army was in no state to attack, and that Poland would have to hold out as best she could. His mission was to see to it that the Poles would fight.[18] It is strange that Bonnet apparently knew nothing of the conditions on which the military convention had been signed,[19] but if this was indeed so, the French General Staff apparently acted on the grounds that unaided Polish resistance would give it the advantage of time. General Ironside commented in July, 'The French have lied to the Poles in saying they are going to attack. There is no idea of it.'[20]

The final factor which rendered the Polish situation desperate was the conclusion of the Ribbentrop-Molotov Pact on 23 August. During the tense summer months there seemed to be a possibility of averting war by means of an alliance between the Western Democracies and the Soviet Union. However, the negotiations dragged, owing to the divergent aims of the prospec-tive partners. The most desirable arrangement for Britain would have been a general declaration of assistance in case of war; the

[16] For an account of the Franco-Polish negotiations, see J. Łukasiewicz, 'Uwagi i Wspomnienia', no. 3 (see *supra* n. 1), and no. 6, 'Interpretacja Sojuszu z Francją' (Interpretation of the Alliance with France', *Dziennik Polski* (London, 10 March, 1947); also no. 7, 'Wahania Ministra Bonnet' (The Waverings of Minister Bonnet, 14 March 1947); no. 8, 'Misja Generała Kasprzyckiego' (The Mission of General Kasprzycki, 24 March 1947); no. 9, 'Rokowania o Pożyczkę Francuzką' (Negoti-ations for a French Loan, 8 April 1947); no. 10, 'Warunki Angielskie' (The English Conditions, 14 April 1947); no. 11, 'Sprawa Gdańska' (The Danzig Question, 22 April 1947). Documents on the negotiations in MFA (London), P–F, 1939.

[17] See Bonnet, *Le Quai d'Orsay sous Trois Républiques*, pp. 249–50.

[18] General Faury, 'La Pologne Terrassée', *Revue Historique de l'Armée*, vol. IX, no. 1 (Paris, 1953), pp. 132–6. For a discussion of French obligations to Poland by the former head of the Polish General Staff, see W. Stachiewicz, 'L'Offensive pour la Pologne', *Kultura* (Paris, 1951), no. 2–3 (40–41), pp. 128–60.

[19] Bonnet, *Le Quai d'Orsay*, pp. 267–8.

[20] *Ironside Diaries*, p. 85.

Soviet Union would then have been expected to give material aid to her western neighbours. The USSR, for its part, seemed concerned with averting the danger of a sudden German attack through the Baltic States, perhaps with their consent or submission. The Soviet negotiators, therefore, pressed for what was virtually a free hand in the south-east Baltic area; they also demanded that a military convention should precede a political agreement. Chamberlain was unwilling to grant the Soviet demands, partly because he feared that precipitate Soviet action in the Baltic States might lead to war,[21] but mainly because he still hoped to reach an agreement with Hitler.

Polish reluctance to accept a Soviet guarantee and automatic Soviet aid was a minor consideration in the breakdown of the negotiations. In the context of Chamberlain's hopes for a settlement with Hitler, the Polish attitude provided a welcome pretext for drawing out the negotiations. As far as the Soviet Union was concerned, Poland provided an excellent scapegoat for the failure to conclude an alliance with the West and a plausible excuse for the pact with Hitler. Poland was not the decisive factor in the breakdown of negotiations between the Western Democracies and the USSR. The Soviet Union, in fact, conducted two parallel sets of negotiations, one with the Western Democracies and the other with Germany. It is difficult to say at what moment Stalin made up his mind to accept an alliance with Hitler, if, indeed, he had not considered this possibility all along. It should be borne in mind that Soviet proposals for closer relations with Germany were recorded all through the era of propaganda warfare and of Litvinov's policy of collective security. As late as January 1937, Stalin himself had made a proposal for negotiations to Berlin. Whatever the case may be, Britain's procrastination certainly gave the Soviet government ample reason to doubt her good intentions. It was clear to Ambassador Maisky, at least by 12 June, that the British government was not seriously considering the conclusion of an alliance with Moscow. On that day Maisky informally asked Lord Halifax

[21] Lord Strang, then the British negotiator in Moscow, commented in his memoirs that Great Britain 'did not wish to be involved in a war with Germany, as a result of what might be a reckless or provocative Soviet reaction to the mere possibility of a threat from Germany through one of the Baltic States'; *Home and Abroad*, p. 172.

whether he would be interested in travelling to the Soviet capital in order to negotiate an alliance. Halifax avoided an immediate answer and, according to Maisky, never gave one. Eden's offer that he should go was ignored,[22] and Strang went to Moscow instead. It may not have been accidental that two days later the Soviet Chargé d'Affaires in Berlin, Astakhov, told the Bulgarian ambassador that the USSR hesitated between three possible courses of action: the conclusion of a pact with England, a further dilatory treatment of the pact negotiations, and a *rapprochement* with Germany. He indicated that the Soviet Union inclined towards the third possibility and stated that if Germany declared she would not attack the Soviet Union or that she would conclude a Non-Aggression Pact with her, Moscow would probably refrain from concluding a treaty with Great Britain.[23] These interesting remarks, duly reported by the Bulgarian ambassador to the German Foreign Ministry, fore-shadowed the conclusion of the negotiations two months later.

As far as Poland was concerned, it was only on 14 August, when Hitler's readiness to sign was already known in Moscow, that Marshal Voroshilov confronted the French and British Military Missions with the demand that Soviet troops be given the right of passage through Polish and Rumanian territory. Beck's attitude towards this proposal was, of course, negative since he considered his assent to be tantamount to the loss not only of Poland's eastern territories but also of her independence. He would have had no choice, however, but to accept if his allies had decided to grant the Soviet demand. Indeed, General Doumenc told Marshal Voroshilov on 22 August that he had full authority to sign the military convention on Soviet terms. The Soviet Marshal then declared that he would have to obtain the direct assent of the parties involved, although he had earlier rejected suggestions that the USSR should approach Poland and Rumania on the plea that his country did not have military conventions with the two states and that France and Britain should do so. On the following day, the news of the Soviet-German Pact ended all possibility of further negotiations.[24]

---

[22] Ivan Maisky, *Who Helped Hitler?* (London, 1964), pp. 141–4.
[23] *DGFP*, D, VI, no. 529.
[24] For a detailed discussion of Poland's attitude toward the British-Soviet

In response to the Soviet-German Pact, Great Britain formalized her agreement with Poland by an alliance signed on 25 August. Nevertheless, even at this late date hopes were entertained in Paris and London that a conference could still settle the Polish-German quarrel. The British and French governments pleaded with Warsaw, despite the fact that Danzig was already a German armed camp, not to mobilize the Army; the result was that when the German attack came the Polish forces were only partly mobilized. Hitler's last terms to Poland, read hastily by Ribbentrop to Ambassador Henderson on 29 August, were intended only for propaganda use and were, in fact, an ultimatum, since Hitler demanded the presence of a Polish plenipotentiary in Berlin on 30 August. According to these terms, Danzig was to return to Germany, while a plebiscite would be held to decide the fate of the Corridor; moreover, only those Germans and Poles resident there in 1918 could vote. Whichever state received the Corridor would allow the other free transit. A commission of inquiry was to be set up to investigate minority problems.[25] While the British government transmitted these demands to Poland, it did not feel that it could press its ally to capitulate. The French attitude, on the other hand, was to countenance all concessions in order to avert war. Whereas the German invasion of Poland began on the morning of 1 September, France and Britain did not declare war till 3 September owing to Bonnet's efforts to arrange a conference through the mediation of Mussolini. The British Cabinet too was willing to envisage this solution, but only if Hitler withdrew his armies from Poland.[26] This he refused to do.

When the war broke out, the full weight of the German military machine was hurled against Poland with disastrous effects. Facing a concentric attack from the north, west, and

negotiations and a summary of the German-Soviet negotiations, see B. Budurowycz, *Polish-Soviet Relations*, chap. VII, *passim*. A selection of Polish documents was printed in *Polish Diplomatic Documents concerning Negotiations between Great Britain, France and the Soviet Union before the Outbreak of the Second World War* (in Polish), General Sikorski Historical Institute (London, 1955). Selected documents dealing with Polish-Soviet relations in 1939, most of them reprinted from published sources, are to be found in St. Biegański (ed.), *Documents on Polish-Soviet Relations 1939–1945* (London, 1961), vol. I, pp. 24–42.

[25] *DGFP*, D, VII, no. 458.
[26] Bonnet, *Le Quai d'Orsay*, pp. 293–303; *DBFP*, 3, VII, no. 652.

south-west, the partially mobilized and greatly inferior Polish Army could only hope to hold out if part of the German forces were drawn off by French action on the western front. However, the long established defensive plans of the French High Command, the reluctance to violate the neutrality of Belgium, and the fear of German retaliation to air attacks limited French action to manning the Maginot Line. And yet the Polish campaign, though it lasted barely three weeks, created a weak position on the German western front which could have been exploited. Commenting sadly on the fall of Poland, General Ironside wrote:

> Militarily we ought to have gone all out against the German the minute he invaded Poland. . . . We did not. There were many reasons. We were to prepare for a long war. The French Air Force was so bad that it might be annihilated like the Polish Air Force. We were expanding rapidly in our industry. The British army was crossing to France and passing up to the front. All was to our advantage to wait. And so we missed the strategical advantage of the Germans being engaged in the east. We thought completely defensively and of ourselves. We had to subordinate our strategy to that of the French and so didn't let our Air Force in. We missed a great opportunity.[27]

At the Nuremberg Trials, General Milch stated that in 1939 Germany had an inadequate supply of bombs and an air force too small to fight a world war. General Jodl declared that the German Army was unable to fully garrison the Siegfried Line and had only twenty-three divisions on the western front.[28] The brief but heroic stand of the Polish Army in 1939 caused Hitler to lose military equipment equivalent to eight months of production as well as about fifty thousand casualties in dead and wounded.[29] This was in itself a considerable contribution to

[27] *Ironside Diaries*, pp. 113–14. In a memorandum to the President of the Council and the Minister of National Defence and War, dated 1 September 1939, Gen. Gamelin suggested that the only way to help Poland was to extend the front to the area between the Moselle and Meuse rivers and to make use of Belgium for bombing the lower Rhine; see *Die Geheimakten des Französischen Generalstabes* (Berlin, 1941), p. 173. The suggestion was not followed.

[28] *International Military Tribunal*, vol. XV, p. 350. General Keitel stated there were only five German divisions on the western front; vol. X, p. 519.

[29] The German casualties in the Polish campaign were equivalent to half the

Poland's western allies, both in terms of armaments and of time gained for their own preparations.

On 17 September, the Soviet attack on Poland eliminated whatever slim possibility still existed of reconstructing a front in eastern Poland. It is curious that, despite all German appeals, the USSR did not launch its offensive until the French mobilization was complete and, possibly, until the likelihood of action in the West was no longer entertained in Moscow. A few days later Poland ceased to exist as an independent state and entered a long nightmare of savage extermination and destruction unparalleled even in her long history of wars and occupations.

----

total German losses in the period 1 September 1939 to 21 June 1941; see Zbigniew Załuski, *Przepustka do Historii* (A Passport to History, Warsaw, 1964), pp. 234–5.

CONCLUSION

A POLICY which fails is always subject to severe criticism and if its failure is accompanied by a national catastrophe a long time must elapse before it can be evaluated with any degree of objectivity. The very dimensions of the Polish tragedy, itself part of a world-wide holocaust, have tended to obscure the real problems which Polish diplomacy had to face in the years preceding the outbreak of the war. The shock and disillusionment of patriots, the linguistic and psychological difficulties which hamper outside observers, and, finally, the need for historical justification experienced by the new political system of postwar Poland have all contributed to the picture of a calamitous or at least unintelligible policy directed by one mysterious man, Col. Beck. Yet, if the circumstances which led to the formulation of Polish policy are taken into account and when that policy is studied in the context of the international situation, its objectives become comprehensible and its failures can be seen as due more to the conditions of the time than to the mistakes and misconceptions of its leaders.

If the unique prerequisite of successful diplomacy is the freedom of multiple choices,[1] the question which must be answered is whether Poland had any real, and not merely theoretical, choice of policy. The alternate policies which have been suggested by various critics include an accommodation with Germany, an alliance with the USSR, or an alliance with Czechoslovakia together with close co-operation with France within the framework of the Franco-Polish alliance. These suggestions must be considered in the light of two criteria: with regard to Germany and the USSR, it must be asked whether an alliance with either

[1] J. Korbel, *Poland between East and West*, p. 180.

of these powers would have allowed Poland to maintain her independence or at least to avert the great biological and material losses incurred by the war, and, with regard to France and Czechoslovakia, whether any such policy could have been realized in the circumstances prevailing at the time.

It has been suggested that Poland could have been spared her tragic fate if Beck had accepted a compromise with Hitler over Danzig and the Corridor. The Polish Foreign Minister did, in fact, consider the possibility of a German-Polish *condominium* in Danzig, but he could not voluntarily accept its outright cession to the Reich nor the extra-territorial highway and railway through the Corridor. In any case, if Hitler had been really interested in a compromise in the Free City, he could either have pressed his other demands in due time by the threat of force, or received them from the Great Powers at another conference. Beck had these possibilities in mind when he remarked on 3 September 1939 that he was glad he had concluded an alliance with Great Britain and had not entered into any 'conversations' with the Germans. In such a case, he thought, war might have been delayed for a few months but it would have come in the spring and Poland would have been isolated.[2]

A voluntary acceptance of Hitler's demands in October 1938, or March 1939, would have meant the end of Polish independence and would not have spared Poland or guaranteed her national resurgence at a later time. Moreover, Hitler could have used Poland's capitulation in order to move immediately against the Soviet Union, and would then most probably have scored an initial victory in seizing the key industrial centres of Western Russia including Moscow. He would most probably have proceeded then or later to carry out the policy of resettling the population of Western Poland in the eastern territories; this was a plan already announced in his military directive of 25 March 1939, but it was also implicit in Göring's *Gesamtlösung* and had a precedent in the projects discussed by the Imperial German government during the First World War.[3] If, on the

[2] Szembek MSS, 3 September 1939.
[3] *DGFP*, D, VI, no. 99. Plans involving the deportation of Poles and Jews from certain regions of Western Poland were discussed in 1915 as part of the project of constructing a defensive frontier in the East and of isolating the Prussian Poles

other hand, the Führer had immediately struck at France, her fall might have been even swifter than it was in 1940, while Great Britain would have faced much greater odds than she did in that same year. In this case, too, Hitler would have been able to implement his plans in Poland. These measures would have met with resistance which in turn would have led to the same policy of extermination as that used against the Polish people during the Second World War. In either case, Poland's capitulation would have given the Führer the great advantage of striking at his enemies earlier than he eventually did, with incalculable consequences for Western Europe as well as the USSR. At the same time, Poland would not only have suffered the same fate but, if and when the Soviet Union had recovered her strength, she also might well have become another Soviet Republic.

Did Poland really have the alternative of an alliance with the USSR? There is no documentary evidence that the Soviet government ever proposed such an alliance to Poland[4] but there

from those in Congress Poland; see Fritz Fischer, *Griff nach der Weltmacht: die Kriegszielpolitik der kaiserlichen Deutschland 1919–18* (2nd edition; Düsseldorf, 1962), pp. 340–1. A detailed discussion of the Polish problem in German war policy in 1914–18 is to be found in Immanuel Geiss, *Der polnische Grenzstreifen: Ein Beitrag zur deutschen Kriegszielpolitik im Ersten Weltkrieg* (Lübeck, Hamburg, 1960), and Werner Conze, *Polnische Nation und Deutsche Politik im Ersten Weltkrieg* (Köln, Graz, 1958).

[4] In 1933, the Soviet government made two attempts to interest Poland in a Soviet-Polish guarantee of the Baltic States, but the Polish government refused to discuss the matter; see B. Budurowycz, *Polish-Soviet Relations, 1932–1939*, pp. 32, 39–40. Boguslaw Miedziński, then editor of *Gazeta Polska*, relates that during his visit to Poland in July 1933, Radek proposed a Polish-Soviet defensive alliance against Germany. He claims that he transmitted the proposal to Piłsudski who answered that he would take the matter into consideration but that at the moment the proposition was premature; B. Miedziński, 'Pakty Wilanowskie' (Wilanów Pacts), *Kultura*, no. 7/8 (Paris, 1963), pp. 113–33. There is no other mention of this proposal in Polish sources. The only recorded intimation of Soviet interest in an alliance with Poland in 1938 is a report of the proposals of the Soviet Attaché Militaire in Kaunas, Major Korotkikh. In a conversation with his Polish colleague after Munich, he implied that the Soviet Union might be willing to conclude an alliance with Poland and the Western Powers if Poland agreed to Soviet occupation of the Baltic States and to the passage of Soviet troops through the regions of Wilno and Lwów; see Leon Mitkiewicz, 'Czy był możliwy Front antyniemiecki?' (Was an Anti-German Front Possible? *Kultura*, Paris, 1959), no. 12/146, pp. 102–7; also the letter of Tadeusz Pełczyński, former head of Polish Military Intelligence, to the editor, *Kultura* (1960), no. 4/150, pp. 155–7. No formal or informal Soviet proposal made directly to the Polish government for an alliance either on these or any other terms has been discovered.

is evidence in the German documents that, while calling for collective security, the Soviet leaders never abandoned the hope of restoring close relations with Berlin.[5] It has been argued that the realization of the Eastern Locarno project of 1934 might have provided a safeguard for peace or that a Polish-Czecho-slovak-Soviet alliance in 1938 might have checked Hitler even if France and Britain had carried on their policy of appeasement. It is difficult to see, however, why the Soviet Union should have accepted the risk of a war with Germany even if Eastern Europe had become a zone of Soviet influence. Without a corresponding firmness from France and Britain, Hitler's rearmament would have proceeded at the same pace and in 1938–39 the USSR would have faced the choice of war with Germany's superior military forces, or an agreement over Eastern Europe. It could be argued that, in accepting such a war in 1938 or 1939, Stalin would have courted the same disaster as that which met Tsarist Russia in 1917. Eastern Europe in such a situation, even if under Soviet hegemony, would have been more useful to Moscow as a bargaining counter with Germany than as a motive for war. Western determination to stop Hitler by force if necessary might have decided Stalin to co-operate, at a price of course, but even this cannot be a certainty. The Soviet leader had to think of gaining as much time for his country as he could; moreover, a conflict between capitalist states which would lead to their mutual exhaustion might have been seen as both a gain of time for the Soviet Union and an advantage for the cause of revolution. In any case, whether Moscow would have been prepared to fight for Eastern Europe or not, Poland was still in the tragic position of lying athwart both German and Soviet ambitions. From the point of view of biological survival, the situation would not have been much better than it was in the case of an alliance with Germany. Though the Soviet government declared itself sympathetic to the Polish people, this sympathy did not extend very far in 1939–40 or in 1944–45. In the first period almost 2,000,000 Poles were deported from the eastern territories, most of them to die in Soviet labour camps; the second period saw the tragedy of the Warsaw Rising and the use

[5] See *supra* 'The Background', pp. 19–20, and n. 46.

of terror in imposing a Communist government. The establishment of a Polish-Russian community of interests against Germany, which Dmowski had foreseen and advocated in 1909,[6] did not come about until the Potsdam Conference which partitioned Germany and gave *de facto* recognition to the Oder-Neisse Line. That such a common interest now links Poland and the USSR should not blind historians to the fact that objective conditions for it were almost non-existent in the period 1918–39, not only on the Polish but also on the Soviet side.

Perhaps the commonest criticism of Polish foreign policy during the period in question is that it contributed to the fall of Czechoslovakia in 1938 and therefore sealed the fate of Poland in 1939. While the supporters of the concept of the Polish-Czechoslovak-Soviet alliance claim that such a move would have checked Hitler even if France and Britain had continued their policy of appeasement,[7] the advocates of the Polish-Czechoslovak alliance claim, that at least in 1935–36, the two countries, together with a strengthening of the Franco-Polish alliance, could have weakened or delayed Hitler's expansion despite the Franco-Soviet alliance and even if France had continued her weak policy towards Germany.[8] Alternatively, it is suggested that if Poland and her neighbours had united their forces, even without French support, they could have played a role in international affairs far beyond their individual capacties.[9] From the point of view of Polish and Czechoslovak interests, an alliance, or at least a close co-operation, would undoubtedly have been the best solution, but the possibility for a logical solution of any problem depends on whether existing conditions allow its realization at any given time.

The evolution of Polish-Czechoslovak relations up to 1933 did not augur well for the future.[10] Up to and including that year, it must be said that the Poles had made efforts to solve existing disputes and obtain an alliance with Czechoslovakia. Beneš himself declared in March 1933 that he had rejected an offer of

[6] R. Dmowski, *La Question Polonaise* (Paris, 1909), *passim*, especially chap. VII.

[7] S. Stanisławska, *Wielka i Mała Polityka Józefa Becka*, pp. 209–10.

[8] Hans Roos, *Polen und Europa*, p. 400.

[9] B. Budurowycz, *Polish-Soviet Relations*, p. 196.

[10] See *supra* 'The Background', pp. 13–15.

alliance against Germany made by Beck earlier that year, and previous Polish attempts had also failed.[11] Beck never seriously considered the possibility of co-operation with Czechoslovakia after 1933, but it must be noted that, while Beneš tried to improve relations between the two countries, he did not think an alliance with Poland to be desirable. The axiom of his policy was that Czechoslovakia stood no chance in a conflict with Germany without the aid of France; if France was unwilling to support her ally, Poland could not ensure a Czechoslovak victory. Even in the Soviet-Czechoslovak alliance of 1935, there was a clause to the effect that the USSR should only help Czechoslovakia if France simultaneously came to her aid. Beck, on the other hand, did not want to strain his relations with Germany and pursued a policy towards Czechoslovakia similar to that of Masaryk and Beneš towards Poland in the 1920's, when the Czechoslovak government avoided involvement in the German-Polish dispute and considered a revision of the Polish-German frontier as inevitable. The Polish Foreign Minister was, however, ready to change his policy and to stand by Prague if France had manifested willingness to support Czechoslovakia to the point of war. Polish policy in 1938 could only have contributed to the fall of Czechoslovakia if Beneš had been willing to ally himself with Poland, regardless of France, or if France and Britain had been willing to guarantee Czechoslovak independence—but this was not the case. It is ironic that the only point on which Beck and Beneš were fully agreed was that neither country could risk a conflict with Germany without the support of France. Thus the key to Polish-Czechoslovak co-operation in 1938, and earlier, lay in a guarantee of French aid to Prague, and by the same token, to Poland. The dominant factor in the failure of Poland and Czechoslovakia to co-operate against their common enemy was the absence of a real commitment on the part of France, backed by Britain, to the maintenance of an independent Eastern Europe.

Close Franco-Polish co-operation was, of course, imperative for the interests of both countries but it is difficult to see how it

[11] See *supra* 'The Background', pp. 14–15. Beck claims that Skrzyński had tried and failed to obtain an alliance in 1925; see *Dernier Rapport*, p. 108, cf. Wandycz, *France and her Eastern Allies*, pp. 344–6.

could have been implemented after the Locarno treaties of 1925. The key to an effective alliance lay in French determination to support Poland as well as Czechoslovakia as a counterweight to Germany. France's retreat from this policy began in 1925, continued with the building of the Maginot Line and flowered into appeasement. By 1933–34, the French alliance system was a policy without content. Without the necessary rearmament and strategic planning, the alliances with Poland and Czechoslovakia became a diplomatic burden which grew increasingly inconvenient for Paris, in proportion as its dependence on Great Britain grew more apparent. In 1936, France resigned herself to the loss of the demilitarized zone in the Rhineland because she knew that Britain would not support her in a war with Germany on this issue. Daladier's efforts to obtain British consent for a guarantee to Czechoslovakia failed both in the spring of 1938 and at Munich; yet he realized that only such a guarantee would have induced Poland and even Yugoslavia to stand by Prague. Finally, Bonnet's temporizing tactics with regard to the clarification of the Franco-Polish alliance in 1939 showed that French doubts as to the extent of the British guarantee carried more weight in Paris than Polish readiness to stand up to Germany.

At best, it can be assumed that a Polish government composed of National Democrats, Socialists, and Populists might not have signed the Declaration of Non-Aggression with Germany, or might have abrogated it had they come to power after 1934. However, this would have given Hitler the choice of pressing for the revision of the Polish-German frontier rather than for the incorporation of Austria and the Sudetenland. The declaration of 1934 had the effect of turning his attention to the south-east and of postponing the dispute with Poland. Had there been no Declaration of Non-Aggression, it is more than likely, especially in view of the prevalent British sympathy for German claims, that the Munich Conference or its equivalent, would have given Hitler Danzig, the Corridor and Upper Silesia.

The Polish Foreign Minister cannot be absolved of all criticism. He did not believe that an independent Czechoslovakia was vital to Polish security. He assumed that Hitler would require a great deal of time to digest his conquests and that he would not risk a world war. On these counts it must be admitted that Beck failed to recognize the real interests of Poland. This charge cannot, however, be made without certain important qualifications. First, it is impossible to say whether he could have achieved any modification of Czechoslovak policy had his beliefs been different; it should be borne in mind that his predecessors' attempts to establish closer relations with Prague had failed, and so had his one attempt in 1933. Second, few statesmen at the time failed to underestimate Hitler. Third, Beck was ready, in case of a general war, to stand automatically by Czechoslovakia. Finally, his axiom that Poland could not fight Germany without a guarantee of French aid was fully shared by Beneš in the analogous case of Czechoslovakia. Thus, Polish foreign policy was part of a general picture and not peculiar to Beck alone.

The negative image of Polish foreign policy which prevailed in Western Europe, Czechoslovakia, and the Soviet Union was due to the widespread opinion that Beck pursued a policy of co-operation with Hitler. Such an impression is easily understandable. The cool relations prevailing between Warsaw and Prague and Warsaw and Moscow visibly contrasted with those existing between Warsaw and Berlin. France officially declared her opposition to German expansion in Eastern Europe and Beneš affirmed that his efforts at co-operation with Poland were rejected. The Soviet government loudly called for collective security. In the face of all this the Polish Foreign Minister maintained a negative attitude towards Czechoslovakia and the USSR and friendly relations with Hitler; finally, Polish troops occupied a part of Czechoslovak territory in 1938.

The other side of the coin was not so easily visible and has emerged only after a part of the documentation has become available. Western public opinion did not suspect that the French statesmen who called for Polish-Czechoslovak co-operation against Germany were determined not to commit France to a war without British support, and that they knew such support would not be forthcoming. Bonnet did not publicize the fact that he accepted Chamberlain's policy of a peaceful amputation of Czechoslovakia, but pictured Beck as the man who prevented Franco-Polish co-operation to save that country.

France exerted pressure on Beneš towards the end of the crisis to cede Teschen Silesia in return for Polish neutrality, but condemned the Polish occupation of the area after the Munich Conference had deprived Czechoslovakia of territory vital to her independent existence. Finally, French statesmen saw the root of all evil in the Polish-German Declaration of Non-Aggression, although they and their predecessors had long before that resigned themselves to the eventual abandonment of Poland through a revision of the Polish-German frontier.

Beneš desire for better relations with Poland never went as far as a desire for an alliance and, according to all available sources, the only offer of this type was made by Warsaw and not Prague. While the Soviet government called for collective security, it did not omit efforts to improve relations with Germany and finally concluded a Non-Aggression Pact with that country which also entailed the partition of Poland and the annexation of Latvia, Estonia, and part of Lithuania. Public opinion in Western Europe widely accepted the Soviet thesis that Stalin had no other choice, since the policy of appeasement persuaded him he could expect no help from the Democracies. However, this argument has rarely been applied to justify Polish-German relations in the period 1934–38. To this day, Soviet historiography pictures Beck as a pro-German statesman who was only deterred from an alliance with Hitler and a joint attack on the USSR by the heroism of the Polish people. It is interesting that Polish historiography since 1956 has modified these charges to a criticism of Beck for his anti-Russian complex and for following a policy parallel to that of Germany. At the same time, Polish historians have pointed out the impact of appeasement on Polish diplomacy in this period.

Perhaps a compromise between the divergent views of Polish foreign policy may be found in the thesis that, while Beck's assumptions on the dispensability of Czechoslovakia and the timing of Hitler's further plans proved mistaken, they did not exert a decisive influence on the course of events. Seen against the background of Franco-British policy, the diplomacy of Col. Beck was not a factor in the disintegration of the peace settlement but a reflection of this process. In this sense it can be said that 'the responsibility for Eastern Europe ultimately rested with the victorious powers of the first world war.'[12] The tragedy was that France and Britain refused to recognize this responsibility until it was too late. An English historian, writing of the interwar period, aptly summed up the dilemma:

> The Anglo-French entente and the Eastern alliances did not supplement each other; they cancelled out. France could act offensively, to aid Poland and Czechoslovakia, but only with British support; but this support would be given only if she acted defensively, to protect herself, not distant countries in Eastern Europe. This deadlock was not created by changed conditions in the nineteen-thirties. It existed implicitly from the first moment, and no one, either British or French, ever found a way round it.[13]

There was, of course, a way round it but it was rejected out of hand by Great Britain without whose support France did not feel strong enough to maintain her commitments to Poland and Czechoslovakia. The only solution to the problem would have been an assumption by Great Britain of co-responsibility with France for the peace settlement in Eastern Europe. It could have taken the form suggested by James Headlam-Morley, historical adviser to the Foreign Office, when he advocated a general guarantee for all the postwar frontiers in Europe. In 1924, he wrote:

> What is it that the smaller states really want? Surely it is confidence that in the case of a serious crisis they could look forward to active and effective support, especially from this country. . . . As far as this country is concerned, we should not leave the world in this state of uncertainty and should in some way or another clearly state that we are interested in the maintenance of the new system in Europe, that we could not regard with equanimity the forcible overthrow of any of the new states, and that if a grave crisis arose, we could be depended on to carry out the obligations into which we have entered.[14]

Headlam-Morley also warned that a pact with France and a declaration of British interests in Belgium or on the Rhine would not be sufficient:

[12] See Henry L. Roberts, 'The Diplomacy of Col. Beck' in Craig and Gilbert (eds.), *The Diplomats*, p. 593.

[13] A. J. P. Taylor, *The Origins of the Second World War*, p. 38.

[14] James Headlam-Morley, *Studies in Diplomatic History*, p. 185.

As everyone knows, the danger point in Europe is not the Rhine, but the Vistula, not Alsace-Lorraine, but the Polish Corridor and Upper Silesia. . . . The whole contention is that we cannot dissociate ourselves from responsibility in regard to what happened in Eastern and Central Europe.[15]

Such a general guarantee, whether in treaty form, or, as Headlam-Morley suggested, in the shape of a statement by the Foreign Secretary in Parliament,[16] would have meant the adoption of a policy of 'containment' towards Germany. In Britain, however, such a course faced serious obstacles. The first was the traditional view of British diplomacy that Eastern Europe was a zone of German and/or Russian interests and that the area of vital British interests was confined to Western Europe. The second was deep pacifism together with wide-spread sympathy for German territorial revindications. The third obstacle was the reluctance of the Dominions, especially in 1938, to follow Britain into a European war. Finally, Britain was not prepared for a major war. It is difficult and perhaps impossible to determine which of these factors had the greatest impact on Chamberlain's policy of appeasement,[17] but they certainly all gave it considerable support. Chamberlain cannot, however, bear the entire burden for the failure to stop Hitler. The policy which he implemented in 1938 can certainly be explained in military terms but it had been implicitly accepted by previous British governments. At least as early as December 1935, long before Hitler's armed strength had become over-powering, Great Britain had already made the choice between buying peace and waging war, and part of the price of peace was agreement to the peaceful revision of the 1919 settlement in Eastern Europe.[18]

The problem of maintaining peace in the interwar period resolved itself into a vicious circle: without a long period of

---

[15] *Ibid.*, pp. 182, 185.   [16] *Ibid.*, p. 186.

[17] For an evaluation of the role of the Dominions in British foreign policy in 1938, see D. C. Watt, *Personalities and Politics*, Essay 8, pp. 159–74. After a quotation from the South-African General, Hertzog, the author notes that the British Cabinet and the Dominions were already prepared for German demands in the Sudetenland in 1937, p. 165; for the penetration of German views in England, see Essay 6, pp. 117–35.

[18] See *supra* 'The Background', n. 53.

peace, the countries of Eastern Europe could not hope to surmount their economic backwardness and disputes, but a long period of peace could only be obtained if the Western Powers were determined to impose it by force if necessary. Germany, whether democratic or Nazi, was capable of making another attempt to impose her hegemony on Europe. The differences between Hitler and Stresemann lay in statesmanship and the extent of their objectives. Stresemann was willing to wait for a revision of Germany's eastern frontiers by an agreement with France and Britain. His aims were restricted to the recon-struction of a modified Bismarckian Germany. Hitler, on the other hand, was willing to make use of Western diplomatic support only as long as he did not feel strong enough to use force, and his aim was the domination of Europe. In either case, con-cessions to German demands in Eastern Europe would have meant German domination of that area and would have provided a base for a later attack against France, or Russia, or both.

If the history of the period 1919–39, and of 1938–39 in particular, can be said to prove anything it is that the European continent could not be divided into spheres of 'vital' and 'non-vital' interests, either as far as the Western Democracies were concerned or for the good of Europe as a whole. Ultimately, French and British passivity towards the resurgence of Germany as a military power and their willingness to dismantle the eastern wing of the peace settlement led to German hegemony over the continent. This hegemony had to be destroyed at an immense cost in lives, property, and cultural heritage. The organic unity of the continent was confirmed once again when the imposition of Soviet domination over Eastern Europe placed the USSR in possession of East Germany and created the 'Berlin problem'. The question whether this situation could have been avoided is not relevant here but it is relevant to note that a Western policy of containment averted the establishment of Soviet domination over the whole of Germany, as well as Greece, Iran, and Turkey. It is true, of course, that the Second World War could not have been won, nor the postwar situation stabilized, without the military participation of the United States. But it is also true that the containment of Germany, at least until 1936, if not until

1939, was not beyond the military strength of France and Britain.

The generations which have lived through the era of crisis since 1945 have largely accepted the fact that peace can only be maintained by adequate armaments, that aggressive powers must be contained, and that the loss of a small state in a remote area may alter the balance of power in the world as a whole. These principles were also applicable to Eastern Europe in the period between the two world wars, but the containment of Germany, and thus commitment to the support of Eastern Europe, was as alien to the tradition of British foreign policy as to British public opinion. France, with a very different tradition of interest in the area, subordinated herself to Great Britain. These factors, whether inevitable or not, were decisive not only for the fate of Poland, but, with it, for the fate of Europe.

BIBLIOGRAPHICAL ESSAY

I. BIBLIOGRAPHIES

The most comprehensive bibliographies on Polish foreign policy in 1938–39 are to be found in HANS ROOS, *Polen und Europa: Studien zur polnischen Aussenpolitik 1931–1939* (Tübingen, 1957), and BOHDAN BUDUROWYCZ, *Polish-Soviet Relations, 1932–1939* (New York, 1963). A short selective bibliography is given by ROMAN DEBICKI, *Foreign Policy of Poland, 1919–1939* (New York, 1962).

JAN KOWALIK has published *Polonica Niemieckie za Czas od 1go Września 1939 do 31 Grudnia 1948 roku* (German Polonica for the Period 1 September 1939 to 31 December 1948, Paris, 1952), and *Polska w Bibliografii Niemieckiej, 1953–1956* (Poland in German Bibliography, 1953–1956) with a supplement for 1945–53 (Paris, 1958). Older German bibliographies are largely outdated but useful from a historiographical and political point of view. Among these the following are of interest: *Bibliographie zur Aussenpolitik der Republik Polen, 1919–1939* (Stuttgart, 1943), and *Bibliographie zur Geschichte der deutsch-polnische Beziehungen und Grenzlandfragen, 1919–1939* (Stuttgart, 1942).

Material on Poland is to be found in American bibliographies dealing specifically with Eastern Europe: JIRINA SZTACHOVA (ed.), *Mid-Europe: A Selective Bibliography* (New York, 1953); ROBERT BYRNES (ed.), *Bibliography of American Publications on East Central Europe, 1945–1957* (Bloomington, Ind., 1958); and *The American Bibliography of Slavic and East European Studies*, which has been published at Bloomington, Ind., annually since 1959.

The standard bibliography for contemporary history is the *Foreign Affairs Bibliography*, vol. I, 1919–32, ed. W. L. LANGER and H. F. ARMSTRONG (New York, 1933); vol. II, 1932–42, ed. R. G. WOOLBERT (New York, 1945); vol. III, 1942–52, ed. H. L. ROBERTS (New York, 1955), vol. IV, 1952–62, ed. H. L. ROBERTS (New York, 1964).

Finally, the bibliographies in journals dealing with Eastern Europe should also be consulted (see section V, 1).

II. GENERAL WORKS, SURVEYS

A balanced and informative survey of the period is given by J. DUROSELLE in his *Histoire de la Diplomatie de 1919 à nos Jours* (2nd ed., Paris, 1953). G. M. GATHORNE-HARDY gives a good but very general introduction to the subject in the *Short History of International Affairs 1920–1939* (4th ed., London, 1952). PIERRE RENOUVIN surveys the period in *Les Crises du XXème Siècle: Histoire des Relations Internationales*, vols. VII, VIII (Paris, 1957, 1958). MAURICE BEAUMONT's two-volume study, *La Faillite de la Paix, 1918–1939: Peuples et Civilisations*, vols. XX, XXI (2nd ed., Paris, 1951), is somewhat disappointing, particularly for East Central Europe, and was published too early to make any extensive use of the British and German documents. A. J. P. TAYLOR's *The Origins of the Second World War* (London, 1961) is a controversial but very stimulating study which seeks to prove that Hitler had no precise plans of aggression but crystallized them by using the opportunities afforded him by Western statesmen.

General surveys for each year are to be found in the *Surveys of International Affairs*, published under the auspices of the Royal Institute of International Affairs, London. The volumes dealing with the Czechoslovak crisis and the post-Munich period have the advantage of being published after the war and thus of access to some of the published documents. These include R. G. D. LAFFAN's *The Crisis over Czechoslovakia, January–September 1938, Survey of International Affairs, 1938* (ed. ARNOLD TOYNBEE), vol. II (Oxford, 1951), and his study of Polish-Czechoslovak relations in *Survey of International Affairs, 1938*, vol. III (Oxford, 1953). The year 1939 is studied in *The World in March 1939* (ed. ARNOLD TOYNBEE) and *The Eve of War 1939* (eds. ARNOLD and VERONICA TOYNBEE), in the same series (Oxford, 1957, 1958). LEWIS NAMIER's *The Diplomatic Prelude, 1938–1939* (London, 1948), summarizes the information available at that date but is still useful as an introductory survey. The Polish Institute of International Affairs has compiled a most useful chronology of Poland's international relations of which the following have been consulted in this work: MARIA SAFIANOWSKA (ed.), *Chronologia Stosunków Międzynarodowych Polski 1938* (Warsaw, 1962) and JÓZEF CHUDEK (ed.), *Chronologia Stosunków Międzynarodowych Polski, Styczeń-Sierpień 1939* (Warsaw, 1963, both in roneotype).

III. MONOGRAPHS AND SPECIAL STUDIES

I. POLISH FOREIGN POLICY

(a) In English, German, and French

A concise, documented, survey of Polish foreign policy in the inter-war period is to be found in ROMAN DEBICKI's *Foreign Policy of Poland, 1919–1939*. Mr. Debicki was formerly in the Polish Ministry of Foreign Affairs and in the diplomatic service. This book provides an excellent introductory study of the subject. The most exhaustive work published so far on this aspect of the interwar period is HANS ROOS (Meissner), *Polen und Europa: Studien zur Polnischen Aussenpolitik 1931–1939*. He does not, however, carry the story beyond January 1939. The book is based mainly on published British and German sources but also makes use of material published in the Polish *émigré* press in London and Paris. Aside from German translations of captured Polish documents, the 'M-Akten', the author did not utilize unpublished Polish sources. A short English-language study which is of great interest is H. L. ROBERTS's monograph 'The Diplomacy of Col. Beck,' in G. CRAIG and F. GILBERT (eds.), *The Diplomats, 1919–1939* (Princeton, 1953). Basing his study on material available at that time, Dr. Roberts presented as balanced a verdict as his sources allowed and showed great insight into the problems confronting the Polish Foreign Minister and an appreciation of the influence of French and British policy on that of Poland. BOHDAN BUDUROWYCZ's *Polish-Soviet Relations, 1932–1939* is an excellent and extensively documented survey of this aspect of Polish foreign policy. MARIAN K. DZIEWANOW-SKI's *The Communist Party of Poland: An Outline of History* (Harvard, 1959), part II, deals with the history of the party in 1919–39. The book of ADAM C. ROSÉ, former Under-Secretary of State for Industry, *La Politique Polonaise entre les Deux Guerres: Un Aspect du Problème Européen* (Neuchâtel, 1945?), is of particular interest for economic problems but is also an interesting attempt to interpret Polish policy as a whole. STANISŁAW MACKIEWICZ is very critical of Col. Beck in *Colonel Beck and his Policy* (London, 1944).

JOSEF KORBEL's *Poland between East and West: Soviet and German Diplomacy toward Poland, 1919–1933* (Princeton, 1963) deals with an earlier period and, as the subtitle indicates, does not study Polish foreign policy. Despite his lack of sympathy for Poland, Korbel provides an excellent picture of the precarious nature of her existence between two predatory neighbours and gives an intelligible background to Polish-German and Polish-Soviet relations after 1934. PIOTR WANDYCZ in his study, *France and her Eastern Allies, 1919–1925: French-Czechoslovak-Polish Relations from the Paris Peace Conference to Locarno* (Minneapolis, 1962), provides invaluable information without which Poland's later relations with France and Cechoslovakia are unintelligible. TYTUS KOMARNICKI's *Rebirth of the Polish Republic: A Study in the Diplomatic History of Europe, 1914–1920* (London, 1957), offers an exhaustively documented study of the shaping of Polish independence and of problems which were to confront Polish foreign policy in the interwar period.

Several articles published by Polish scholars in the United States on the earlier period also contribute to the understanding of later developments. These include: M. K. DZIEWANOWSKI, 'Pilsudski's Federal Policy 1919–1921', *Journal of Central European Affairs*, vol. X (July–October, 1950), pp. 113–28, 271–87; Z. J. GĄSIOROWSKI, 'Stresemann and Poland before Locarno' and 'Stresemann and Poland after Locarno', based on unpublished German documents, *JCEA*, vol. XVIII (1958), no. 1, pp. 25–47, no. 3, pp. 292–317; 'Polish-Czechoslovak Relations 1918–1922' and 'Polish-Czechoslovak Relations 1922–1926', *Slavonic and East European Review*, vol. XXXV (December 1956, June 1957), pp. 173–93, 473–504. GĄSIOROWSKI's two articles on Piłsudski's policy in 1933–34 are valuable but may be criticized in the case of the Declaration of Non-Aggression, which is sometimes termed a 'Pact', for insufficient attention to the role of Western appeasement in Piłsudski's decisions: 'Did Pilsudski Attempt to Initiate a Preventive War in 1933?' *Journal of Modern History*, vol. XXVII (June 1955), pp. 135–51; 'The German-Polish Nonaggression Pact of 1934', *JCEA*, vol. XV (1955), no. 1, pp. 3–29. His article on 'The Russian Overture to Germany of December 1924', *Journal of Modern History*, vol. XXX (1958), no. 2, pp. 99–117, discusses unpublished German documents on this subject.

(b) *In Polish*

(i) *Prewar and Emigré Studies.* Three prewar studies on Polish foreign policy are of interest for the period. WŁADYSŁAW STUDNICKI's *Polen im Politischen System Europas* (Berlin, 1936), is a German translation of the Polish original published in 1935. STUDNICKI was a wholehearted supporter of alliance between Germany and Poland and his book sets forth the thesis of German-Polish co-operation as the nucleus of an anti-Soviet bloc of East European states. ADOLF BOCHEŃSKI follows the same lines in his *Między Niemcami a Rosją* (Between Germany and Russia, Warsaw, 1937). JULIUSZ ŁUKASIEWICZ, then Ambassador to Paris, in his *Polska jest Mocarstwem* (Poland is a Power, Warsaw, 1939), sets out the programme of Piłsudski's foreign policy and defends Polish policy in the Munich crisis. The book approaches closest to an official apologia of the Piłsudski-Beck policy but it should be borne in mind that it was written in October 1938, and its somewhat strident tone can be attributed both to the criticism to which Poland was then subjected and to the resentment felt by Beck's entourage against the disregard of Polish interests at the Munich Conference. A more balanced assessment is provided in the author's *Polska w Polityce Józefa Piłsudskiego* (Poland in the Policy of Józef Piłsudski, London, 1944).

The most interesting study of Polish foreign policy by an *émigré* writer after the war is J. GIERTYCH's *Pół Wieku Polskiej Polityki: Uwagi o polityce Dmowskiego i polityce polskiej lat 1919–1939 i 1939–1947* (Half a Century of Polish Policy: Remarks on the Policy of Dmowski and of Poland in 1919–1939 and 1939–1947, 1st ed., Author's publishing rights, West Germany, 1947). Giertych, a National Democrat, writes from a party point of view though he is also critical of the Party leadership in 1938.

The books of Stanisław Mackiewicz, former editor of the Wilno paper Słowo, *Historia Polski od 11 listopada 1918r. do 17 września 1939r* (The History of Poland from November 11, 1918 to September 17, 1939, London, 1941), *Klucz do Piłsudskiego* (A Key to Piłsudski, London, 1942) and *Polityka Becka* (London, 1942), published in an English version as *Col. Beck and his Policy* (London, 1944), are written with journalistic verve but have a literary and psychological rather than a historical value. Mackiewicz had consistently supported close relations between Poland and Germany and later blamed Beck for incompetence in being unable to maintain them or to obtain vital concessions from Hitler. After returning to Poland in the later 1950's, Mackiewicz wrote many articles accusing Polish prewar policy of *naïveté* and incompetence and Great Britain of a machiavellian plot to provoke a Polish-German war in order to turn Hitler eastwards against the USSR.

Some information on Polish foreign policy is to be found in WŁADYSŁAW POBÓG-MALINOWSKI's *Najnowsza Historia Polityczna Polski, 1864–1945* (Contemporary Political History of Poland, 1864–1945), vol. I (Paris, 1953); vol. II, part I (London, 1956); vol. II, part II (London, 1960). This work is, however, most valuable for the light it sheds on internal political history. The author was a devoted follower of Marshal Piłsudski. A survey of foreign policy for the whole interwar period is to be found in w. STARZEWSKI's *Polska Polityka Zagraniczna, 1919–1939* (Polish Foreign Policy, 1919–1939, mimeograph, London, n.d.). This work is not so much an interpretation as a chronological study prepared for the use of candidates studying for the Polish diplomatic service during the Second World War. It is, however, a mine of information and is based on documentary sources available to the author. TADEUSZ KUNICKI discusses Polish-German relations in a long article, 'Problemy Polsko-Niemieckie 1920-1939', *Niepodległość*, vol. IV (Józef Piłsudski Institute, London, 1952; this is a continuation of the prewar periodical). TYTUS KOMARNICKI's 'Piłsudski a Polityka Wielkich Mocarstw Zachodnich' (Piłsudski and the Policy of the Great Western Powers), *ibid.*, is a perceptive study of this subject.

Two former ambassadors have made important contributions on the basis of materials in their possession and their own reminiscences. JULIUSZ ŁUKASIEWICZ recounted the course of Franco-Polish negotiations and relations in 1919 in a series of articles published in the Polish-language London daily, *Dziennik Polski i Dziennik Żołnierza* nos. 44, 49, 59, 63, 71, 87, 94 (February, March and April 1947). JÓZEF LIPSKI, former Ambassador to Berlin, wrote an excellent study of the genesis of the Polish-German Declaration of Non-Aggression of 1934, in which he played an important role. His monograph, 'Przyczynki do polsko-niemieckiej deklaracji of Nieagresji' (Contributions to the Polish-German Declaration on Non-Aggression), *Bellona*, nos. III–IV (London, 1951), is based on his own documents and is of paramount importance not only for the Declaration itself but also for the understanding of later Polish foreign policy.

Some general information on Polish foreign policy and the most authoritative data on Polish prewar armaments and military planning are to be found in *Polskie Siły Zbrojne*, Tom I, Cześć I, *Kampania Wrześniowa 1939* (Polish Armed Forces in the Second World War, vol. I, part I, 'The September Campaign 1939', London, 1951).

(ii) In Poland. Writers in postwar Poland necessarily view the period 1919–39 differently from Poles writing abroad. While the latter are for the most part concerned with explaining and justifying Polish policy before 1939, the former are, in the context of Poland's political situation after 1945, motivated by the desire to show that the policy of Piłsudski and Beck was responsible for the great catastrophe. Their chief argument is the known aversion of both Piłsudski and Beck to close relations with the Soviet Union. Historians writing in postwar Poland almost uniformly declare that this attitude was a

BIBLIOGRAPHICAL ESSAY

great political mistake since only a Polish-Soviet alliance could have saved the country from disaster. Before October 1956, Beck was frequently pictured as an agent of Hitler whose policy was primarily dictated by the desire to join Germany in an attack on the USSR, see, for example, STEFAN ARSKI's *Przeklęte Lata* (The Accursed Years, 2nd ed., Warsaw, 1953), and M. STANIEWICZ's *Kęlska Wrześniowa na tle Stosunków Międzynarodowych, 1919–1939* (The September Catastrophe in the Light of International Relations, 1919–1939, Warsaw, 1952). Recent studies published in Poland take a more sophisticated approach to the problem.

No full-length study has yet appeared dealing with Polish foreign policy as a whole for the period 1919–39, but some important studies have been published on various aspects and periods. HENRYK BATOWSKI discusses Polish foreign policy in 1938–39 in the context of the international situation as a whole in his *Kryzys Dyplomatyczny w Europie: Jesień 1938–Wiosna 1939* (The Diplomatic Crisis in Europe: Autumn 1938–Spring 1939, Warsaw, 1962). The author is highly critical of Beck and of the Western Powers but the book is, nevertheless, the most exhaustive and broadly documented study of international relations between the wars to have appeared on this subject not only in Poland but in Eastern Europe and Soviet Russia. It also supersedes K. PIWARSKI's earlier and narrower study, *Polityka Europejska w Okresie Po-Monachijskim, X. 1938 III. 1939* (European Policy in the Post-Munich Period, Warsaw, 1960). BATOWSKI's *Ostatni Tydzień Pokoju* (The Last Week of Peace, Warsaw, 1964), deals, as its title indicates, with the last days before the outbreak of war. He has also written several articles, the most important of which are 'Rumuńska Podróz Becka w Pażdzierniku 1938 roku' (Beck's Rumanian Journey in October 1938), *Kwartalnik Historyczny* (Warsaw, 1958), no. 2, translated into French as 'Le Voyage de Joseph Beck en Roumanie en Octobre 1938' (Tirage à part de l'Annuaire polonais des affaires internationales, Warsaw, 1959–60), and 'Środkowoeuropejska Polityka Polski w Latach 1932–1939' (The Central European Policy of Poland in the Years 1932–1939), *Historia Najnowsza Polski*, VIII Powszechny Zjazd Historyków Polskich (Warsaw, 1960), pp. 265–77.

The most important and the most scholarly work on Polish foreign policy in the period 1933–38 is MARIAN WOJCIECHOWSKI's book on Polish-German relations in this period, *Stosunki Polsko-Niemieckie 1933–1938* (Poznań, 1965). It is not limited to Polish-German relations but deals with Polish foreign policy in general and its relation to the policy of the Western Democracies and the USSR. WOJCIECHOWSKI had access not only to Polish archives but also to German

270

documents in Bonn. Although he condemns Polish foreign policy for its anti-Soviet 'complex' and Beck for his attitude to Czechoslovakia, his book is, nevertheless, the most balanced and thoroughly documented study of the period and subject to have appeared so far in Poland.

Several other books deserve mention although they deal either with an earlier period or only with a particular aspect of Polish foreign policy. KAREL LAPTER's *Pakt Piłsudski-Hitler, 1934* (The Piłsudski-Hitler Pact, 1934, Warsaw, 1962) is a study of the genesis of the Declaration of Non-Aggression of 1934. Lapter attempts to prove that Piłsudski's anti-Soviet bias was responsible for the 'pact' and dismisses any interpretation which stresses the importance of French and British appeasement of Germany in Piłsudski's decisions as an 'unfounded and reactionary thesis' (p. 204). According to the author, Piłsudski and Beck rejected the only alternative open to Poland because of their 'class-hatred' of the USSR. The author's article 'Polityka Józefa Becks' (The Policy of Józef Beck), *Sprawy Międzynarodowe*, vol. XI (Warsaw, 1958), no. 5, pp. 47–69 follows the same lines. Jarosław Jurkiewicz in his *Pakt Wschodni: Z Historii Stosunków Międzynarodowych w Latach 1934–1935* (The Eastern Pact: From the History of International Relations in the Years 1934–1935, Warsaw, 1963) studies the fate of the proposed Eastern Locarno and blames Poland's negative attitude for the failure of the project. STEFANIA STANISŁAWSKA's *Polska a Monachium* (Poland and Munich, Warsaw, 1967), appeared too late to be consulted in this work.

2. GERMAN FOREIGN POLICY AND POLISH-GERMAN RELATIONS

No adequate study of German foreign policy has appeared to date in Germany to supersede the work of A. VON FREYTAGH-LORINGHOVEN *Deutschlands Aussenpolitik, 1933–1941* (Berlin, 1942).

A brief but well-documented English study is to be found in E. M. ROBERTSON, *Hitler's Pre-War Policy and Military Plans, 1933–1939* (London, 1963).

An authoritative work on Polish-German relations is H. ROOS's study on Polish foreign policy, though it has been superseded in documentation by WOJCIECHOWSKI. R. BREYER's *Das Deutsche Reich und Polen, 1932–1937: Aussenpolitik und Volksgruppenfragen* (Würzburg, 1955) deals with the role of minority questions in relations between the two countries.

Polish-German relations in the years 1912–32 have been the subject of a scholarly study by JERZY KRASUSKI in his two volumes, *Stosunki*

Polsko-Niemieckie 1919–1925 and *Stosunki Polsko-Niemieckie 1926–1932* (Poznań, 1962, 1964). The author was unfortunately either unable or unwilling to make use of the archives in Bonn but found important material in the archives of the German Democratic Republic.

3. THE CZECHOSLOVAK CRISIS OF 1938 AND POLISH-CZECHOSLOVAK RELATIONS

(a) In Western Europe and the United States

The most exhaustive studies of the crisis published in the Western World are BORIS CELOVSKY's *Das Münchener Abkommen von 1938* (Stuttgart, 1958) and KEITH EUBANK's *Munich* (Norman, Oklahoma, 1963). Based on published German and British documents, articles, memoirs and other studies, these books supersede WHEELER BENNET's *Munich: Prelude to Tragedy* (London, 1948), and R. G. D. LAFFAN's account in the *Survey for International Affairs, 1938*, vol. II (Oxford, 1951). HUBERT RIPKA's *Munich: Before and After* (London, 1939) is still valuable for the light it sheds on Czechoslovak foreign policy in the making of which Ripka took part. The most important work from the Czechoslovak point of view is EDUARD BENEŠ's *Mnichovské Dny* (Munich Days, ed. JAN SMUTNY, mimeograph 2nd ed., London, Ustav Dra. Edvarda Beneše, 1958). This is both a study of the crisis and a memoir written by PRESIDENT BENEŠ in London during the Second World War. He intended to publish it but never did so. An interesting analysis of Beneš's foreign policy is to be found in EDWARD TABORSKY's 'The Triumph and Disaster of Edouard Benes,' *Foreign Affairs*, vol. 36 (1958), no. 4.

The works of SIR LEWIS NAMIER are still useful, mainly owing to his access to Polish and Czechoslovak documents. In his *Europe in Decay* (London, 1950) he included translations of documents on Polish-Czechoslovak relations in 1938 which he had obtained from President Beneš. In his later book, *In the Nazi Era* (London, 1952), he made use of an article by former Ambassador JULIUSZ ŠUKASIEWICZ, 'Sprawa Czechosłowacka w r.1938 na tle Stosunków polsko-francuskich' (The Czechoslovak Question in 1938 against the Background of Polish-French Relations), *Sprawy Międzynarodowe* (London, 1948), no. 2–3, 6–7, which included the text of Col. Beck's instruction to Łukasiewicz of 24 May 1938.

C. A. MACARTNEY in his *October Fifteenth: A History of Modern Hungary 1929–1945*, part I (2nd ed., Edinburgh, 1961) gives a valuable analysis of Hungarian policy in the crisis and makes use of private, unpublished documents.

(b) In Poland

Two outstanding studies on Polish-Czechoslovak relations have been published since 1956. JERZY KOZEŃSKI's *Czechosłowacja w Polskiej Polityce Zagranicznej w Latach 1932–1938* (Czechoslovakia in Polish Foreign Policy in the Years 1932–1938, Poznań, 1964) is a work of great importance based on the archives of Warsaw and Prague. Though by no means condoning Beck's policy, Kozeński points out that Beck's predecessors and Beck himself were interested in an alliance with Czechoslovakia and that the attitude of the Prague government was negative. He emphasizes the decisive role of French appeasement in Polish policy during the Munich crisis and considers it to have been responsible for the ultimate collapse of both Czechoslovakia and Poland. He has also published articles on Polish-Czechoslovak relations, 'Rokowania polsko-czechosłowackie na Tle Niebezpieczeństwa Niemieckiego w Latach 1932–1933' (Polish-Czechoslovak Negotiations in the Face of German Danger in the Years 1932–1933) *Przegląd Zachodni* (Poznań, 1962), no. 2, pp. 253–75, and 'Wpływ Deklaracji polsko-niemieckiej o Nieagresji na Kształtowanie się Stosunków polsko-czechosłowackich w 1934r' (The Influence of the Polish-German Declaration of Non-Aggression on the Shaping of Polish-Czechoslovak Relations in 1934) *Przegląd Zachodni* (1963), no. 2, pp. 218–36.

STEFANIA STANISŁAWSKA in *Wielka i Mała Polityka Józefa Becka* (The Great and Small Policy of Józef Beck, Warsaw, 1962) deals with Polish-Czechoslovak relations in the period March–May 1938. Although she, like most other historians writing in Poland, believes that the only solution for Poland was an alliance with the USSR, she also shows understanding of the difficulties which Beck was facing, particularly in his relations with France. The book is based, like Kozeński's, on the archives of the Polish and Czechoslovak Ministries of Foreign Affairs.

The prevalent view is summed up by JÓZEF CHUDEK in 'Polska wobec wrześniowego Kryzysu czechosłowackiego 1938r' (Poland in the face of the Czechoslovak Crisis of September 1938), *Sprawy Międzynarodowe* (Warsaw, 1958), no. 4. His thesis is that, although there was no formal agreement between Poland and Germany, there was an understanding on common action against Czechoslovakia. It can be noted that even the documents of Jósef Lipski, edited by Chudek in *ZH*, 7, hardly bear out this contention. Chudek condemns Beck's policy and blames it for the breakdown of collective security and for sealing the doom of Poland.

(c) In Czechoslovakia

The official interpretation of prewar history follows on similar lines to postwar Poland with the difference that Beneš is criticized for sabotaging the Soviet-Czechoslovak alliance which he himself had brought about. In 1956, a collective work appeared in Prague edited by VLADIMIR SOJÁK O Československé Zahraniční Politice w Letech 1919–1938: Sbornik Stati (On Czechoslovak Foreign Policy in the Years 1919–1939: A Collection of Articles). Despite the usual criticism of Beneš's policy, this is a valuable work and documents from the archives of the Ministry of Foreign Affairs are cited. A good summary of official views, based on archive material, is to be found in VÁCLAV KRÁL's article 'Československo a Mnichov' (Czechoslovakia and Munich) Československý Časopis Historicky, vol. VII (1959), no. 1. The result of a historical symposium on the subject was published in a French translation, Contributions à l'Histoire de Munich (Prague, 1959). The pamphlet is an excellent summary of the views which prevailed in 1958–59, and which are still prevalent in Eastern European publications.

4. FRENCH FOREIGN POLICY AND FRANCO-POLISH RELATIONS

No full-length scholarly study on either subject has appeared to date. PIERRE-ETIENNE FLANDIN, Foreign Minister at the time of the Rhineland crisis, published a study of French foreign policy containing an apologia for his own views on limiting French interests to Western Europe and the colonies, Politique Française, 1919–1940 (Paris, 1947). GEORGES BONNET, Foreign Minister from April 1938 to September 1939, wrote a study of the subject in memoir form with documentary appendices, defending his policy of peace at all costs in La Défense de la Paix, 2 vols. (Geneva, 1947–49). The author gives a considerable amount of information on Franco-Polish relations but a comparison of his data and interpretation with both published and unpublished documents shows that he often distorts information to suit his purpose. He confirms his views in Le Quai d'Orsay sous Trois Républiques (Paris, 1961), in the chapters dealing with the period 1938–39.

The work of TADEUSZ KUŹMIŃSKI, Polska, Francja, Niemcy, 1933–1935 (Poland, France, Germany, 1933–1935, Warsaw, 1963), is a valuable contribution on the subject of the Franco-Polish alliance in the period of the 'preventive war' scare and the Polish-German Declaration of Non-Aggression. It is based on Polish archives. Chapter II, on the problem of the preventive war, is reprinted from his article published in *Najnowsze Dzieje Polski. Materiały i Studia z Okresu 1914–1939* (Warsaw, 1960), vol. III, pp. 5–49.

5. BRITISH FOREIGN POLICY, 1938–1939: THE BRITISH GUARANTEE TO POLAND AND THE AGREEMENT OF 6 APRIL 1939

There is no really satisfactory study of British foreign policy in the interwar period. W. N. MEDLICOTT's book *British Foreign Policy since Versailles* (London, 1940) is interesting but somewhat outdated, and his study 'The Coming of the War', in *From Metternich to Hitler: Aspects of British and Foreign History, 1914–1939* (New York, 1963), is only a brief sketch. P. A. REYNOLDS's *British Foreign Policy in the Interwar Years* (London, 1954) is rather superficial. Some unorthodox views on the scope of British interests and obligations in the early years is provided by Sir James Headlam-Morley's posthumous book *Studies in Diplomatic History* (London, 1930). The study by MARTIN GILBERT and RICHARD GOTT, *The Appeasers* (London, 1963), is a useful guide to the documents for the period and a summary of Chamberlain's policy. MARTIN GILBERT, in *Roots of Appeasement* (London, 1966), attempts an analysis of the historical and psychological factors involved.

Some interesting light is shed on policy-making by the *History of The Times* (London, 1952), vol. IV, part II, which deals critically with the ideas and influence of the editor-in-chief, GEOFFREY DAWSON, a close friend of Neville Chamberlain. A. L. ROWSE's *All Souls and Appeasement* (London, 1961) is a stimulating but acidulous sketch of the Cabinet members and of Geoffrey Dawson, who often gathered at All Souls to discuss current politics. LORD STRANG's book *Home and Abroad* (London, 1956) is not, as he himself states in the Foreword, either an autobiography or a volume of memoirs. Written by an experienced member of the Foreign Office who took part in the Czechoslovak crisis and the negotiations with the Soviet Union in 1939, it contains a most valuable and somewhat critical account of British policy in those years. His chapters on the same period in a later book, *Britain in World Affairs: A Survey of the Fluctuations in British Power and Influence from Henry VIII to Elizabeth II* (London, 1961), tend to be less critical of Chamberlain. D. C. WATT, in his *Personalities and Policies: Studies in the Formulation of British Foreign Policy in the Twentieth Century* (London, 1965), has two relevant and interesting essays dealing with the 1930's Essay: 6, 'Influence from Without: German Influence on British Opinion, 1933–38, and Attempts to Counter it', and Essay 8, 'The Influence of the Commonwealth on British Foreign Policy: The Case of the Munich Crisis'. A. J. P. TAYLOR's *The Trouble-Makers: Dissent over Foreign Policy, 1792–1939* (London, 1957) gives an interesting analysis of left-wing attitudes towards Germany in the interwar period.

Two English-language studies have been published on the British guarantee to Poland and the agreement of 6 April 1939. In 1948, the former Polish Ambassador in London, COUNT EDWARD RACZYŃSKI, published a pamphlet, *The British-Polish Alliance: Its Origin and Meaning* (General Sikorski Historical Institute). Although only a brief study, it is based on the Ambassador's own papers and personal participation in those events. PROFESSOR T. DESMOND WILLIAMS's study, 'Negotiations leading to the Anglo-Polish Agreement of 31st March, 1939,' *Irish Historical Studies*, vol. X (1956), nos. 37, 38, gives a good summary of the documents in *DBFP*, 3, V, and also includes the April negotiations. The subject receives a rather summary treatment in ARNOLD and VERONICA TOYNBEE (eds.), *The Eve of War, 1939*, published in the series *Surveys of International Affairs* (Oxford, 1958).

The only study of the British guarantee written in Poland which was available at the time of writing was KAROL LAPTER's article 'Angielskie Gwarancje dla Polski w r.1939' (English Guarantees for Poland), *Sprawy Międzynarodowe* (Warsaw, 1959), no. 6, pp. 3–31. Professor Lapter's view, that the chief aim of British policy was to provoke Hitler into attacking Poland and then the USSR, is supported neither by the documents published in the *DBFP*, 3, V, nor by the Polish documents in the General Sikorski Historical Institute, London.

6. SOVIET FOREIGN POLICY AND POLISH-SOVIET RELATIONS

(a) In Western Europe, United States, Poland

The best account is given by MAX BELOFF in *The Foreign Policy of Soviet Russia, 1929–1941*, 2 vols. (Oxford, 1949, 1952), which has, however, the disadvantage of having appeared too early to make use of all the British and German documents published for the period. E. H. CARR's *German-Soviet Relations between the Two World Wars, 1919–1939* (Baltimore, 1951), is a stimulating but somewhat superficial study. J. BOUVIER and J. GAÇON in *La Vérité sur 1939: La Politique Extérieure de l'U.R.S.S. d'octobre 1938 à juin 1941* (Paris, 1953) present the official Soviet views on the subject. G. HILGER and A. G. MEYER (eds.), *The Incompatible Allies: A Memoir-History of German-Soviet Relations, 1918–*

1941 (New York, 1953), is very useful for the extensive memoir literature involved. G. L. WEINBERG's *Germany and the Soviet Union, 1939–1941* (London, 1954) is an exhaustively documented study of the period.

The best work on Polish-Soviet relations is by BOHDAN BUDUROWYCZ (see section 1). W. P. and Z. K. COATES, *Six Centuries of Russo-Polish Relations* (London, 1948), is a cavalier study of the subject and reproduces official Soviet views for the interwar period. KONOVALOV's *Russo-Polish Relations* (Princeton, 1941) is a brief study somewhat biased in favour of Russia. H. L. ROBERTS's study on Maxim Litvinov in *The Diplomats*, CRAIG and GILBERT (eds.), is imaginative and stimulating. JOHN ERICKSON's monumental study *The Soviet High Command: A Military-Political History, 1918–1941* (London, 1962) includes some very interesting information on foreign policy, particularly Stalin's advances to Hitler in 1936–37.

In Poland, K. LAPTER has published *Zarys Stosunków polsko-radzieckich w latach 1917–1960* (An Outline of Polish-Soviet Relations in the Years 1917–1960), part I (Warsaw, 1961). The book follows the official line of interpretation.

(b) In the U.S.S.R.

The first study of any length to appear on Soviet foreign policy is contained in vol. III of *Istoriia Diplomatii*, edited by the former Deputy Foreign Minister V. P. POTEMKIN, published in three volumes in Moscow in 1945. A French translation by XENIA PAMPHILOVA and MICHEL ERISTOV was published in Paris in 1947 as *Histoire de la Diplomatie*. The most serious study to date is to be found in *Istoriia Velikoi Otechestvennoi Voiny Sovetskovo Soiuza, 1941–1945* (History of the Great Fatherland War of the Soviet Union, 1941–1945), vol. I, edited by P. N. POSPELOV and published in Moscow in 1960. Part I, chapters II, III, and IV, deal with the foreign policy of the Soviet Union during the 1930's. The authors make use of much documentary and memoir material published in the West with sparse references to the Archives of the Foreign and Defence Ministries of the USSR. These materials are presented in such a way as to prove that the Western Democracies and Poland followed a pro-German policy aimed at launching a joint attack on the Soviet Union. The leading motive for Polish foreign policy is given as the desire to co-operate 'even with the devil himself' if only against Soviet Russia. The fact that Poland finally resisted Germany is explained as the result of the patriotism of the Polish people (pp. 155, 159).

Many popular studies have also appeared, particularly since 1960, for example, G. L. ROZANOV, *Germaniia pod Vlastiu Fashizma, 1933–1939* (Germany under Fascist Government, 1933–1939, Moscow, 1961); A. M. NEKRICH, *Vneshnaia Politika Anglii, 1939–1941* (The Foreign Policy of England, 1939–1941, Moscow, 1963); Z. S. BELOUSOVA, *Frantsuzkaia Diplomatiia Nakanune Miunkhena* (French Diplomacy on the Eve of Munich, Moscow, 1964). None of these works contributes anything new to the knowledge of Soviet foreign policy or differs from the official interpretation. Worthy of note is the study of English policy towards Soviet Russia written in the form of memoirs by IVAN MAISKY, former Ambassador to London, *Kto Pomagal Gitleru?* (Who Helped Hitler?, Moscow, 1961), translated into English by ANDREW ROTHSTEIN and published under that title in London, 1964.

IV. MEMOIRS, BIOGRAPHIES, AUTOBIOGRAPHIES, DIARIES

1. POLISH

The key sources in this category are the memoirs of COL. JÓZEF BECK and the papers of the Under-Secretary of State for Foreign Affairs, COUNT JAN SZEMBEK. The Polish Foreign Minister dictated his *Dernier Rapport: Politique Polonaise, 1926–1939* (Neuchâtel, 1951), translated into English and published as *Final Report* (New York, 1957), while in exile in Rumania where he died in 1944. The work was edited by MRS. J. BECK, MICHAŁ ŁUBIEŃSKI, WŁADYSŁAW POBÓG-MALINOWSKI, and T. SCHAETZEL. Although it must be borne in mind that the author naturally sought to explain and justify his own policy and that much was omitted since he dictated from memory, his book is a most important source since it gives his personal interpretation, fresh after the great catastrophe, of the motives and evolution of Polish foreign policy from 1926 until the outbreak of war.

JAN SZEMBEK'S *Journal, 1933–1939* (Paris, 1952), edited by LÉON NOËL, former French Ambassador to Poland, consists of selected passages from the original MSS. The extracts are not always dated correctly, nor is it clear where passages have been omitted. The published diary deals mainly with Poland's relations with the Great Powers and leaves out much of interest with respect to other countries, particularly Hungary. Despite these drawbacks, the *Journal* is still a valuable source of information to readers who do not have a knowledge of Polish. JÓZEF CHUDEK edited a Polish version for the years 1933–35, based on archival material in the Polish Foreign Ministry, under the title, *Fragmenty Dziennika Szembeka, 1933–1935* (Fragments of Szembek's Diary, 1933–1935, mimeograph, Polish Institute of International Affairs, Warsaw, 1956). The first volume of the definitive Polish edition, edited by T. KOMARNICKI, *Diariusz i Teki Jana Szembeka* (Diary and Papers of Jan Szembek), vol. I (London, 1964), includes a long and extensively documented introduction covering the years 1933–34 and the diary for 1935. Volume II, which appeared in 1965, covers the year 1936. (For the original MSS, see section VII).

The memoirs of COUNT EDWARD RACZYŃSKI, former Ambassador to London, *W Sojuszniczym Londynie: Dziennik Ambassadora Edwarda Raczyńskiego, 1939–1945* (London, 1960), translated: *In Allied London: The Wartime Diaries of the Polish Ambassador Count Edward Raczynski* (London, 1962), deal with wartime years but include a few remarks of interest on the negotiations of 1939.

ANTONI SZYMAŃSKI's *Zły Sąsiad. Niemcy, 1932–1939 w Oświetleniu polskiego Attaché wojskowego w Berlinie* (The Bad Neighbour: Germany, 1932–1939 as seen by the Polish Attaché Militaire in Berlin, London, 1962) gives some interesting information on the Attaché's conversations and observations at his post. The memoirs of GENERAL LEON BERBECKI, published as *Pamiętniki Generała Broni L. Berbeckiego* (Katowice, 1959), are of interest for Polish military policy in the face of German danger but are written in a vein of undiluted criticism.

2. CZECHOSLOVAK

PRESIDENT BENEŠ's *Mnichovské Dny* (Munich Days, London, 1958) is essentially a study of Czechoslovak policy during the Munich crisis but should be mentioned here since it is written on the basis of the President's reminiscences (see section III, 3).

For a different point of view on the subject, the reader may turn to the memoirs of the former Czechoslovak Ambassador to Moscow and later member of the Czechoslovak Communist government, ZDENEK FIERLINGER. The first volume of *Ve Službách ČSR* (In the Service of the Czechoslovak Republic, Prague, 1951) deals extensively with the crisis of 1938 and is very critical of President Beneš.

An important source for the period are the memoirs of DR JURAJ SLÁVIK, former Czechoslovak Minister in Warsaw. They appeared in serial form in the *New Yorsky Dennik* (New York Daily), a Slovak paper, during 1958. Since the memoirs are based on the Minister's papers, which are often cited, these memoirs should also be considered as a documentary source. Many of the documents cited by Slávik are also referred to by STEFANIA STANISŁAWSKA in her

Wielka i Mała Polityka Józefa Becka, who consulted them in the archives of the Foreign Ministry in Prague (see section III, 3).

3. GERMAN AND AUSTRIAN

Although many memoirs, biographies, and autobiographies have appeared in Germany since the Second World War, they are in general of little value for Polish-German relations.

Of this vast literature, only a few books have any relevance to Poland. HANS VON DIRKSEN's *Moskau-Tokio-London* (Stuttgart, 1949) sheds some indirect light on Polish questions in the account of German-British relations in 1939, when the author was ambassador in London. ERNST VON WEIZSÄCKER's *Erinnerungen* (Munich, Leipzig, Freiburg, 1950), is an astute defence of the author's role as State Secretary under Ribbentrop. His plea that he stayed at his post in order to preserve peace is warmly corroborated by his old friend, the last League of Nations High Commissioner in the Free City of Danzig, Dr. Carl J. Burckhardt. BURCKHARDT, *Meine Danziger Mission, 1937–1939* (Munich, 1960), may be mentioned here since it is written in German. BURCKHARDT's book gives some interesting information on the attitudes of Hitler, Ribbentrop, Göring and others toward Poland and is a valuable record of the High Commissioner's own role as an intermediary, sometimes self-appointed, between Warsaw and Berlin and his contacts with the British delegation in Geneva.

4. ITALIAN

The most relevant sources for the period 1938–39 are the diaries of the Italian Foreign Minister, COUNT GALEAZZO CIANO. They have been published in two parts: *Ciano's Diary, 1937–1938*, translated and edited by ANDREAS MAYOR (London, 1952), and *Ciano's Diary, 1939–1943*, translated by V. UMBERTO COLETTI-PERUCCA and edited by MALCOLM MUGGERIDGE (London, 1947). These give a valuable insight into the vacillating policy of Mussolini and Ciano's vague projects for an Italian-supported 'Axis' in Eastern Europe.

5. FRENCH

The memoirs which contain the most information on Polish-French relations in this period are those of LÉON NOËL, ambassador to Poland from 1935 to 1939, GEORGES BONNET, Foreign Minister from April 1938 to September 1939, and GENERAL MAURICE GAMELIN, Chief of the French General Staff, 1935–40. NOËL's account of his embassy, *L'Aggression Allemande contre la Pologne: Une Ambassade à Varsovie, 1935–1939* (Paris, 1946), is valuable for the light it throws on Bonnet's policy towards Poland. The book is not, however, a reliable interpretation of Polish foreign policy owing to NOËL's misunderstanding of its motives and problems as well as the ambassador's personal antipathy toward Beck. BONNET's memoirs and study of French foreign policy are described in section III, 4. GENERAL MAURICE GAMELIN in his memoirs, *Servir*, 2 vols. (Paris, 1946–49), provides a considerable amount of information on the attitude of the French General Staff towards Poland. He also gives an interesting account of his visit there in 1936, of the visit of Śmigły-Rydz to France in the same year, and of military relations in 1938–39.

The memoir literature which does not deal directly with Franco-Polish relations is useful for the information it provides for French policy as a whole. ANDRÉ FRANÇOIS-PONCET in his *Souvenirs d'une Ambassade à Berlin, 1931–1938* (Paris, 1946) testifies, if sometimes unwittingly, to Bonnet's policy of appeasement at any price. ROBERT COULONDRE, ambassador to Moscow in 1936–38, and successor to FRANÇOIS-PONCET in Berlin in 1938–39, had a clear appreciation of Hitler's policy, if not of Stalin's. His book, *De Staline à Hitler: Souvenirs de deux Ambassades, 1936–1939* (Paris, 1950) contains some interesting though scanty information on French policy towards Poland during the Czechoslovak crisis. PAUL REYNAUD, member of Daladier's Cabinet and loyal friend of Czechoslovakia, gives some insight into Bonnet's methods as Foreign Minister and of the conflicts within the Cabinet. In *Au Cœur de la Mêlée, 1930–1945* (Paris, 1951), he revised his earlier study, *La France a sauvée l'Europe*, 2 vols. (Paris, 1947), and also included his memoirs. JEAN ZAY, another member of Daladier's Cabinet, was murdered by the Germans. His notebooks were edited by PHILIPPE HENRIOT and published posthumously as *Les Carnets de Jean Zay* (Paris, 1942) with the aim of condemning him as a warmonger. The book contains some information on the Czechoslovak crisis.

6. BRITISH

A source of paramount importance for Neville Chamberlain's attitude toward Germany, Poland, and Eastern Europe is KEITH FEILING's biography *Neville Chamberlain* (London, 1946), which includes extracts from the Prime Minister's diaries and letters to his sisters. IAN MACLEOD's *Neville Chamberlain* (London, 1961) is a sympathetic biography but adds no new information.

The best illustration of the attitude toward Germany and Eastern Europe which prevailed among men in government circles, their friends and the right-wing press is to be found in THOMAS JONES's *A Diary with Letters, 1931–1950* (London, 1954). Thomas Jones, a former private secretary to Prime Minister Stanley Baldwin, was a member of the so-called 'Cliveden Set', a distinguished group which included Cabinet ministers, men of letters, newspaper editors, and politicians, who met occasionally at the Astors' manor. The book gives a faithful picture of the strength of appeasement in British governing circles.

LORD TEMPLEWOOD (formerly Sir Samuel Hoare) provides interesting information on the British guarantee to Poland and the agreements of 6 April 1939. His *Nine Troubled Years* (London, 1954) is valuable since he was a member of the 'inner circle' of ministers consulted by Chamberlain, but is not always reliable. *The Memoirs of Anthony Eden: Facing the Dictators* (London, 1962) describes Eden's political career from 1923 to his resignation in February 1938. They are of interest in demonstrating Eden's fruitless efforts to oppose the policy of appeasing the dictators and testify eloquently to Chamberlain's tactics of bypassing his Foreign Secretary. LORD STRANG's memoirs *Home and Abroad* (London, 1956) are valuable for their information on British policy towards Germany, Eastern Europe, and the USSR, particularly for the period during which Strang was Head of the Central Department of the Foreign Office (1937–39). He shared that institution's reservations about the policy of Chamberlain (see section III, 5). DUFF COOPER's memoirs, *Old Men Forget* (London, 1957), contain a few pages of interest on his visit to Gdynia and Danzig as First Lord of the Admiralty in August 1938, though he does not recount his conversations with Col. Beck.

AIR VICE-MARSHAL SLESSOR, Director of Plans in the Air Ministry from 1937 to 1941, gives some information on British aircraft production and plans and also on the attitude of the Chiefs of Staff towards Poland and Czechoslovakia in 1938–39 in his memoirs, *The Central Blue: Recollections and Reflections* (London, 1956). The *Ironside Diaries, 1937–1940*, edited by COL. R. MACLEOD and D. KELLY (London, 1962) give extracts from the diaries of GENERAL SIR EDMUND IRONSIDE, Chief of the Imperial General Staff in 1938–40. Of particular interest here is IRONSIDE's account of his visit to Poland in July 1939.

The first volume of SIR WINSTON CHURCHILL's History of the Second World War, *The Gathering Storm* (Boston, London, 1948) gives an account of his efforts to awaken the government to a sense of urgency in rearmament but there is little directly relevant to Polish affairs. The memoirs of LORD HALIFAX, *The Fullness of Days* (London, 1957), and those of SIR NEVILE HENDERSON, *The Failure of a Mission, Berlin, 1937–*

1939 (London, 1940), are useful for British foreign policy but have no direct bearing on Poland. LORD BIRKENHEAD in his *Halifax: The Life of Lord Halifax* (London, 1965) devotes part III of the book to Halifax's role in foreign affairs both before and during his tenure of the Foreign Office. The author had access to family papers and to the unpublished diary of SIR ALEXANDER CADOGAN, Deputy Under-Secretary of State in the Foreign Office, 1936–7, and Permanent Under-Secretary in 1938–46. Both sources throw some interesting light on Halifax's attitude at the height of the Munich crisis and after.

7. RUMANIAN

The memoirs of the former Rumanian Foreign Minister, E. PETRESCO-COMNÈNE, *Preludi del Grande Dramma* (Rome, 1947), give a detailed account of his policy during the Czechoslovak crisis and of Col. Beck's visit to Galati in October 1938. Comnène's personal antipathy to Col. Beck colours his description of Polish-Rumanian relations at this period. Comn`ne's successor, GRIGOIRE GAFENCU, in his *Last Days of Peace* (New Haven, 1948), gives a highly coloured and unreliable account of his conversation with Col. Beck in April 1939.

8. SOVIET

The only memoirs to have appeared to date which deal with the period are those of IVAN MAISKY, *Kto Pomagal Gitleru?* (Moscow, 1961) translated by ANDREW ROTHSTEIN, *Who Helped Hitler?* (London, 1964). Maisky's book is a study, in memoir form, of Anglo-Soviet relations during his embassy in London during the years 1932–39 (see section III, 6).

V. NEWSPAPERS AND PERIODICALS

1. CONTEMPORARY

For opinion and comment on Poland published in the non-Polish press, the best guide is the weekly bulletin of the former Polish Ministry of Foreign Affairs, *Przegląd Prasy Zagranicznej* (Review of the Foreign Press), which the author consulted in the library of the Ministry in Warsaw. Foreign newspapers consulted in the original were only those reflecting official policy in France and Britain such as *The Times* and the Paris *Le Temps*.

A good survey of Polish press opinion during the Czechoslovak crisis is to be found in BARBARA RATYŃSKA's *Opinia Polska wobec*

Monachium w Świetle Prasy (Polish Opinion on Munich in the Light of the Press, roneotype, Polish Institute of International Affairs, Warsaw, 1959). The pro-government *Gazeta Polska* (Polish Gazette) was consulted for the whole period as was the *Polityka Narodów* (Policy of the Nations), a monthly publication equivalent to the western journals on foreign affairs.

2. AFTER 1939

The most useful Polish *émigré* publications are *Niepodległość* (Independence), published irregularly by the Józef Piłsudski Institute in London, a continuation of the prewar periodical; *Kultura* (Culture), a monthly journal with broad literary and political interest published in Paris; *Zeszyty Historyczne* (Historical Notebooks), published by the editors of *Kultura* in Paris since 1962; *Bellona*, a journal of military history published irregularly in London; *Wiadomości* (News), primarily a literary weekly, London; *Dziennik Polski i Dziennik Żołnierza* (Polish Daily and Soldiers' Daily), London.

There are two periodicals in Poland which specialize in recent and contemporary history. *Najnowsze Dzieje Polski. Materiały i Studia z Okresu 1914–1939* (The Most Recent History of Poland. Materials and Studies of the Period 1914–1939), published since 1958 as an annual by the Historical Institute of the Polish Academy of Sciences, and *Studia z Najnowszych Dziejów Powszechnych* (Studies in Contemporary History), published since 1960 by the Department of Contemporary History and International Relations of the Higher School of Social Studies attached to the Central Committee of the Polish United Workers' Party.

A number of articles on prewar Polish policy appeared in the years 1957–60 in the *Sprawy Międzynarodowe* (International Affairs), a monthly published by the Polish Institute for International Affairs in Warsaw. A number of interesting articles have also appeared in the *Przegląd Zachodni* (Western Review, 1944 ff.), and in *Polish Western Affairs* (1959 ff.), both published by the Instytut Zachodni (Western Institute) attached to the University of Poznań. The institute is devoted to the study of Polish-German relations. Occasional articles can also be found in the *Acta Poloniae Historica*, an annual French and English language publication of the Historical Institute of the Polish Academy of Sciences which has been appearing since 1957. The periodicals *Kwartalnik Historyczny* (Historical Quarterly) and *Przegląd Historyczny* (Historical Review) do not have many articles on recent and contemporary history.

On anniversaries relative to the war and occupation there are occasional articles dealing with prewar Polish foreign policy but few have any academic value. An interesting and lively discussion took place on this subject in the weekly press in 1957 but the articles are chiefly of interest because of the light they shed on the existence of a lively controversy on this matter in postwar Poland. A selection of the articles was published in roneotype by the Polish Institute of International Affairs under the title: *Dyskusja nad 1939r* (Discussion on 1939, Warsaw, 1957). It should be noted that no analogous discussion has taken place on this subject since that date.

Among American periodicals, articles on recent Polish and East European history and politics are to be found primarily in the *Journal of Central European Affairs* (Boulder, Colorado, discontinued, 1964); the *Slavic Review* (formerly the *American Slavic and East European Review*, Seattle, Washington); the *Journal of Modern History* (Chicago, Illinois), and *Foreign Affairs* (New York). Occasional articles of interest can be found in the *Polish Review* (New York).

In Western Europe, some German, French, and Italian periodicals are of great interest. The German periodical which deals with modern and contemporary history is the *Vierteljahrshefte für Zeitgeschichte*, published in Stuttgart. In France, articles of interest can be found in the *Revue d'Histoire de la Seconde Guerre Mondiale* and *Revue d'Histoire Moderne et Contemporaire* (Paris). The most useful Italian periodical is the *Rivista di Studi Politici Internazionali* (Milan).

In the USSR, the leading journal for recent history is the *Voprosy Istorii* (Historical Problems, Moscow). In Czechoslovakia, the most informative and scholarly historical journal is the *Československý Časopis Historický* (Czechoslovak Historical Review, Prague).

VI. PUBLISHED DOCUMENTS

1. POLISH

Some Polish documents were published in Western Europe during the Second World War, while some have appeared in the USSR and Poland since 1945. *The Polish White Book: Official Documents Concerning Polish-German and Polish-Soviet Relations, 1933–1939* was published by the Polish Government-in-Exile, first in a French version in Paris in 1940, then in English translation in London and New York. It is based on the archives of the Embassy in London, and the fragmentary collection of the archives of the Ministry of Foreign Affairs. Most of the material is given in the form of extracts.

A selection of the Polish documents found by the Germans in the

Ministry of Foreign Affairs was published under the title *Polnische Dokumente zur Vorgeschichte des Krieges*, Erste Folge (Berlin, 1940). Although the aim of the editors was to present the Polish government in an unfavourable light so as to make it appear responsible for the outbreak of the war, the collection is nonetheless valuable since it contains some documents no longer available elsewhere and all possibility of tampering is removed by the printing of photostats from the original documents side by side with the German translation. Some of the Polish documents captured by the Germans in 1939 fell into Soviet hands in 1945 and were incorporated in the collection *Documents and Materials Relating to the Eve of the Second World War*, 2 vols. (Moscow, 1948), published as a rejoinder to the *Nazi-Soviet Relations* (Washington D.C., 1948).

In postwar Poland, the period after October 1956 saw the publication by the Polish Institute of International Affairs of much valuable material. Particularly relevant are JÓZEF CHUDEK's selections from the correspondence between Col. Beck and the Polish ambassador in Rome 1938–39, General Bolesław Wieniawa Długoszowski, and the reports of ambassador JÓZEF LIPSKI, Berlin, ambassador EDWARD RACZYŃSKI, London, and ambassador JULIUSZ ŁUKASIEWICZ, Paris. These documents were published in mimeograph by the Historical Department of the Institute in the form of *Zeszyty Historyczne* (Historical Notebooks). Some of the material also appeared in the monthly journal of the institute, *Sprawy Międzynarodowe*.

2. CZECHOSLOVAK

The first documents published for this period appeared in a German collection edited by FRIEDRICH BERBER under the title *Europäische Politik im Spiegel der Prager Akten* (Essen, 1942). The selection is based on documents found in the Czechoslovak Ministry of Foreign Affairs. It is possible that some of the documents are incomplete and some may have been tampered with.

In Czechoslovakia, the twentieth anniversary of Munich led to the publication of two collections of documents. The *New Documents on the History of Munich* (Prague, 1958) are based on selections from the Czechoslovak and Soviet archives, edited by a mixed team of scholars from both countries. The book is slim but valuable since it contains many documents hitherto unknown or inaccessible. Another collection, *Mnichov v Dokumentech* (Munich in Documents), 2 vols. (Prague, 1958), includes, besides Soviet and Czechoslovak documents, French, British, and German material published in Western Europe.

The aim of both selections is to prove that only the USSR was a loyal friend and ally to Czechoslovakia in 1938.

3. GERMAN AND AUSTRIAN

The most extensive documentary basis for a study of the period is to be found in the *Documents on German Foreign Policy, 1918–1945*, series D, 1937–39; series C begins in January 1933 and covers the period until September 1937. The English translation, published simultaneously in Washington, D.C., and London in 1949–66, corresponds entirely with the German text as published in *Akten zur Deutschen Auswärtiges Politik, 1918–1945*, series D (Bonn, 1950). There is also a French edition. These documents can be supplemented by the *Trial of the Major War Criminals before the International Military Tribunal* (Nuremberg, 1947–49), vols. XLII. However, most of the material relevant to diplomatic history is contained in the *DGFP*. An excellent discussion of the captured German documents and problems of research involved is to be found in MARGARET LAMBERT's article 'Source Material Made Available to Historical Research as a Result of World War II', *International Affairs*, vol. XXXV (London, 1959), no. 2, pp. 188–96. The HON. MISS MARGARET LAMBERT is editor-in-chief, of *DGFP*.

The only Austrian documents published so far which have a bearing on the period are those concerning the trial of Dr. Guido Schmidt, former Foreign Minister, in *Der Hochverratsprozess gegen Dr. Guido Schmidt vor dem Wiener Volksgerichts* (Vienna, 1947). The trial contains important documents for the Anschluss, including some interesting testimony by FRITZ VON PAPEN, ambassador to Vienna in 1936–38. The statements made by Guido Schmidt and Papen should, however, be considered in the light of the trial as pleas for the defence.

4. BRITISH

The *Documents on British Foreign Policy 1919–1939* (eds. E. L. WOODWARD and R. BUTLER), 3rd series (London, 1948–53), cover the period March 1938–September 1939. Together with the *DGFP*, series D, they provide the most detailed documentary basis for a study of the diplomatic history of these years. The *DBFP*, 2nd series, and *DGFP*, series C, can be consulted for the earlier 1930's.

British parliamentary debates and pronouncements on Poland for the period March 1939–August 1941, are to be found in WACŁAW JĘDRZĘJEWICZ (ed.), *Poland in the British Parliament, 1939–1945*, vol. I (New York, 1946).

5. UNITED STATES

The *Papers Relating to the Foreign Relations of the United States*, 1938, vol. I, and 1939, vol. I (Washington, D.C., 1956, 1957), contain many interesting reports from the United States ambassador in Warsaw, J. DREXEL BIDDLE, and the ambassadors in Paris and London, JOHN W. BULLITT and JOSEPH P. KENNEDY respectively. Bullitt was President Roosevelt's most trusted diplomat in Europe and he was also a close friend of ambassador Juliusz Łukasiewicz. His information, though not always confirmed by other sources, reveals much of interest on the attitude of the French government toward Poland.

6. FRENCH

The French diplomatic documents for the interwar period had not yet reached the years 1938–39 at the time of writing. The first volume of the *Documents Diplomatiques Français*, second series, covering the period 1 January to 31 March 1936, was published in Paris in 1963.

The only official collection of documents available for 1938–39 was the *Livre Jaune Français* (Paris, 1939). The aim of the editors was to prove that the French government had done everything possible to prevent war.

Much information of interest is to be found in the reports of the French Parliamentary Inquiry into the events preceding the war, in which leading prewar politicians were questioned. The results of the inquiry were published in *Les Evénements survenus en France de 1933 à 1945: Témoignages et Documents recueillis par la Commission d'Enquête Parlementaire*, IX vols. (Paris, 1947–51). Some information on prewar policy is also to be found in the records of trials held by the Vichy government, an account of which is given by Maurice Ribet in *Le Procès de Riom* (Paris, 1945).

7. ITALIAN

The official Italian publication, *I Documenti Diplomatici Italiani*, 8th series, vols. XII, XIII (Rome, 1952–53), only covers the period from May to September 1939 and was therefore, of little use for the period concerned. *Ciano's Diplomatic Papers*, ed. MALCOLM MUGGERIDGE (London, 1948), was of interest for the Italian Foreign Minister's projects concerning Eastern Europe. *Ciano's Diaries* for 1938–39, and 1939–43, may also be considered as a documentary source (see section IV, 4).

8. SOVIET

The Soviet official series, *Dokumenty Vneshnei Politiki SSSR*, XI vols. (Moscow, 1957–66), had at the time of writing reached December 1928. *The Soviet Documents on Foreign Policy*, 3 vols. (London, 1951–53), ed. JANE DEGRAS, consist of official pronouncements and published diplomatic correspondence.

The only Soviet archival documents relevant to the period 1938–39 are contained in the *New Documents on the History of Munich* (Prague, 1958) (see section VI, 2).

9. HUNGARIAN

A volume of Hungarian diplomatic documents dealing with Hungarian foreign policy in the period 1936–1938 was published by the Historical Institute of the Hungarian Academy of Sciences in 1965. *A Müncheni Egyezmény Létrejötte Es Magyarország Külpolitikája, 1936–1938* (The Coming of the Munich Agreement and Hungarian Foreign Policy, 1936–1938), ADÁM MAGDA, ed., constitutes volume II of a series which will extend to 1945. The documents shed some light on Polish-Hungarian relations and on Italian support of the project for a common Polish-Hungarian frontier in 1938. The volume dealing with Hungarian foreign policy and the outbreak of World War II is interesting but contains no revelations; JUHÁSZ GYULA. ed., *Magyarország Külpolitikája a II. Világháború Kitörésének Időszakbán 1939–1940* (Budapest, 1962).

VII. UNPUBLISHED DOCUMENTS

1. POLISH

Polish diplomatic documents dealing with the interwar period are located in Great Britain, the United States, Canada, and Poland. The most comprehensive collection for the 1938–39 period is to be found in the General Sikorski Historical Institute, London, which has in its possession the archives of the former Polish Ministry of Foreign Affairs. The Embassy deposit consists of the correspondence of the Polish ambassador and staff with the Ministry in Warsaw in the form of reports, some instructions, and some correspondence between the ambassador in London and those in Berlin and Paris. The Cyphers include copies of important telegrams and letters exchanged between the Ministry and the Embassy as well as Polish Embassies in the major capitals of Europe. The Embassy deposit also includes copies of correspondence between the Polish Commissioner General in Danzig and the Ministry. The fragmentary collection of documents belonging to the Ministry of Foreign Affairs contains copies of reports and instructions exchanged between Warsaw and the Embassies in Paris and Berlin. Besides these documents, the Institute also possesses some interesting material in the form of personal reports made by certain diplomats, officials, and army officers to a commission set up to investigate the causes of Poland's defeat in 1939.

The Polish Research Centre in London possesses the entire MSS of the diary of COUNT JAN SZEMBEK, Polish Under-Secretary of State for Foreign Affairs (see section IV, 1). It also has a copy of an important collection of documents on the Czechoslovak crisis in roneo-type, 'Referat: Ślask Cieszyński,' Zeszyt II (Report on Teschen Silesia, Book II), prepared for the wartime government on the basis of documents found in the archives of the Embassy and the Ministry of Foreign Affairs.

In the United States, the most important collection of Polish diplomatic documents is to be found in the Hoover Institute and Library on War, Revolution, and Peace, Stanford University, California. The library has part of the archives of the prewar Polish Embassy in Washington deposited by the former ambassador, JAN CIECHANOWSKI. These documents deal mainly with the pre-1938–39 period, but contain some material for those years. They include an incomplete but sizable collection of Polska a Zagranica (Poland and Foreign Countries), a monthly bulletin compiled by the Ministry of Foreign Affairs on the basis of reports from Polish diplomatic missions. A complete set of this valuable guide to Polish foreign policy is located in the Polish Institute of Arts and Science, New York. A few documents of interest were found in the Józef Piłsudski Institute of America, New York, and some important documents have been deposited by the Polish Government-in-Exile in Montreal, Canada.

The author was permitted to consult the personal archives of DR TYTUS KOMARNICKI, former Polish Delegate to the League of Nations and present Research Advisor in the Polish Institute and Sikorski Museum, London. In the Foreign Office Library, London, the author was able to consult the microfilm copy of the unpublished 'Polnische Dokumente zur Vorgeschichte des Krieges', Zweite Folge, microfilm H1832.

In Poland, the documents which survived the holocaust of war have until recently been available to scholars in the archives of the Ministry of Foreign Affairs but are now being transferred to the Archiwum Akt Nowych (Archives for Contemporary Documents) in

Warsaw. Most of the documents consulted come from the archives of the Polish Embassy in Berlin, and the selected documents on Polish-German relations which constitute the most comprehensive collection. There are also fragments from the Embassies in Paris, Rome, London, the Balkans, and the Polish Ministry in Prague. Collections of the departments for Western and Eastern European affairs are also represented. There are documents dealing with Danzig but the main deposit for Danzig affairs is located in the Provincial State Archives, Gdańsk. The Ossolineum library in Wrocław possesses the typescript of the memoirs of ALFRED WYSOCKI, Ambassador to Berlin, 1931–33, and to Rome, 1933–38. These were of interest for the months preceding the Polish-German *communiqué* of 3 May 1933, and for accounts of conversations with Ciano and Mussolini in the later period.

2. GERMAN

Microfilms of unpublished German documents were consulted in the National Archives, Washington, D.C. Extensive collections of photostats made from these microfilms are available in Stanford, California, and in particular, in the British Foreign Office Library, London. The relevant documents are to be found mainly in the files of the offices of the Foreign Minister, the State Secretary, and of the German Embassy in Warsaw. Most of the important documents dealing with Polish-German relations have been published in the *DGFP*. The unmicrofilmed originals which are now in Bonn are mainly of interest for studies on special aspects of Polish-German relations.

3. THE UNITED STATES

Limited access was available to the author to the papers of the United States Embassy in Warsaw which also included relevant correspondence with other missions in Europe. The papers are deposited in Department of State files, the National Archives, Washington, D.C.

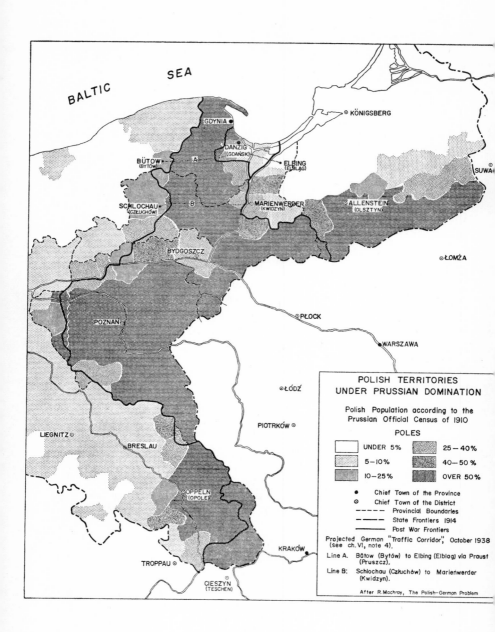

BALTIC SEA

○ KÖNIGSBERG

GDYNIA ●

DANZIG
(GDAŃSK)

BÜTÓW
(BYTÓW)

A

ELBING
(ELBLĄG)

SUWA

SCHLOCHAU
(CZŁUCHÓW)

B

MARIENWERDER
(KWIDZYŃ)

ALLENSTEIN
(OLSZTYN)

BYDGOSZCZ

○ ŁOMŻA

POZNAŃ ●

●PŁOCK

●WARSZAWA

○ ŁÓDŹ

PIOTRKÓW ○

LIEGNITZ ○

BRESLAU

OPPELN
(OPOLE)

KRAKÓW ●

TROPPAU ○

CIESZYN
(TESCHEN)

POLISH TERRITORIES
UNDER PRUSSIAN DOMINATION

Polish Population according to the
Prussian Official Census of 1910

POLES

	UNDER 5%		25—40%
	5—10%		40—50%
	10—25%		OVER 50%

●   Chief Town of the Province
⊙   Chief Town of the District
- - - - -   Provincial Boundaries
⸺⸺   State Frontiers 1914
▬▬   Post War Frontiers

Projected German "Traffic Corridor", October 1938
(see ch. VI, note 4).

Line A.   Bütow (Bytów) to Elbing (Elbląg) via Praust
           (Pruszcz).

Line B: Schlochau (Człuchów) to Marienwerder
           (Kwidzyn).

After R. Machray, The Polish–German Problem

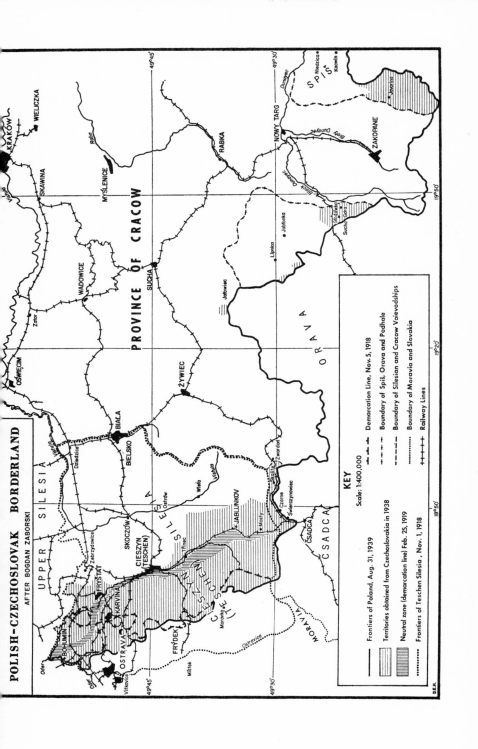

POLISH—CZECHOSLOVAK BORDERLAND

AFTER BOGDAN ZABORSKI

PROVINCE OF CRACOW

KEY

Scale: 1:400,000

	Frontiers of Poland, Aug. 31, 1939
	Territories obtained from Czechoslovakia in 1938
	Neutral zone (demarcation line) Feb. 25, 1919
	Frontiers of Teschen Silesia, Nov. 1, 1918
—··—··—	Demarcation Line, Nov. 5, 1918
—·—·—	Boundary of Spiš, Orava and Podhale
— — —	Boundary of Silesian and Cracow Voievodships
·······	Boundary of Moravia and Slovakia
┼┼┼┼┼	Railway Lines

D.B.K.

INDEX

ALEKSANDROVSKY, S., Soviet Minister in Prague 1938: asked by Beneš on Soviet help 19 Sept., reply, 116, n. 31; and 30 Sept., 139, n.103

Allenstein (Kwidzyń): plebiscite decision 1919, 1

Anschluss, chap. I, *passim*; *see also* Austria

Arciszewski, Mieczysław (1893–1963), Polish Deputy For. Minister, May 1938 to Sept. 1939: statement to Hory 19 Sept., 120, n. 37; at conference 1 April 1939, 229; conversation with Moltke, 23 May, 1939, 239–40

Astakhov, G., Soviet chargé d'affaires in Berlin 1939: on alternative for Soviet for. policy, 14 June 1939, 247

Austria: in Hitler–Halifax conversation, Nov. 1937, N. Chamberlain on, 23; independence 1919, St. Germain, Versailles Treaties, customs union with Germany prevented, 1931, Mussolini 1934, Stresa Conference 1935, 30; N. Chamberlain, British public opinion on, Dmowski view of 1917, 31; Piłsudski, Beck opinion on, 32–33; Beneš on 1937, 33–4; in Polish–German conversations, Jan. 1938, 38–9; Hitler reorganizes govt., 4 Feb. 1938, ultimatum 12 Feb., British, French reaction to, 43–4; *The Times*, 17 Feb., N. Chamberlain on, 45–6; German occupation 12 March, 48.

BALTIC: Polish policy in: Piłsudski, Bloc, Wilno, 6; Beck policy on, Lithuania, 49, n. 56, 57; ultimatum to Lithuania, 51; and Third Europe, Gt. Britain, Scandinavia, 86–7; USSR and, 1939, 246, n.21; in 1933, 253, n. 4

Barthou, Louis J. (1862–1934), French For. Minister 1934: proposes East Locarno, 18–19

Beck, Józef (1894–1944), Polish For. Minister Nov. 1932 to Sept. 1939: offers alliance to Beneš 1933, Girsa's opinion on, 14, n.

31; plan to visit Prague 1933 dropped, 14–15, n. 32; rejects alliance with Germany against USSR, signs extension of Polish–Soviet Non-Aggression Pact, 1934, 17; policy aims 1937, Danzig problem 1935–37, 23–6, 28 n. 70; declaration to France, 7 March 1936, 26 n. 66; conversations with Eden, French alliance, attitude to, 1936, 27–8; Austria, Czechoslovakia, view on Central Europe Jan. 1938, 33–4; Danzig and Austrian crisis 35–7; conversation with Eden, Jan. 1938, and Churchill, obligations to France, 40–2; with Göring 23 Feb. 1938, 47–8; Lithuania 49–52; criticism of, 53; policy in Czech. crisis and Third Europe, 54 n. 1, 55–6; on Polish minority in Czech. 7 Jan., March 1938, 60; Hungarian state visit, note to Czech., 22 March, 61; answer to French–British *démarches* 3 May, sees Slávik, 72; Bonnet proposal to 22 May and reply, 75–78 n. 53, 57; policy to June 1938, 78–80; refuses French request for statement on Czech., 83–4; Moltke on concessions to, June, 85; Baltic policy, 86–7 n. 18, 19; view of Slovakia, policy instruments in Czech., June, July, 89, n. 29; on Mussolini, Balkans, agreement with Ciano, March 1938, 90 n. 30; demands equal treatment of Polish minority in Czech., 92–3; instruction, and Lipski–Göring conversation 24 Aug., 97–9; diplomatic task mid-Sept., 107; agreement with Hungary 9 Sept., Polish minority 16–17 Sept., 110–11, n. 11; on Trans-Olza plebiscite 15 Sept., 112 n. 16; on Hungary, 19 Sept., 120 n. 37; answers French, British, Soviet protests on troop concentration 124–5; receives Franco-British note on Teschen 26 Sept., on Beneš' letter, 130–1; Polish maximum and minimum aims in Czech., 23 Sept., 135 n. 89; on Bohumin, 136; Munich, 139–40;

294

INDEX

Daladier (*cont.*)
of Nat. Defence and Dep.
Premier 1936–37, Premier and
Min. of War 1938–40: on
preventive war, 1933, 12 n. 24;
pleads for British guarantee of
Czech., April 1938, 65; agrees to
cession, opposes plebiscites, 18 to
19 Sept., 114–15; in Cabinet
crisis, 117; opposes plebiscites, on
Poland, Teschen, 25 Sept.,
127–8 n. 65; invited to Munich,
138; on Eastern European agreements, Jan. 1939, 199; on Polish–
Rumanian alliance and Danzig,
212–13

Danzig, Free City of, and Polish
Corridor: in 1919–20, 1–3, n. 3;
French advice on, 1932, French–
German conversations on, Jan.
1933, 10; Westerplatte, 6 March
1933, 11; Czech. attitude to,
14–15; Piłsudski's aims in, 1933–
34, 16; German influence in,
Nazification, relations with
Poland, 1933–34, 17; British
attitude to, 21–2, n. 52, 53; in
Hitler–Halifax conversation,
Nov. 1937, 23; problem for Beck,
Polish rights in 24, n. 58; Beck
policy in 1935–36, 25–6; Beck to
League of Nations Powers on,
1936, 1937, 28, n. 70; Beck on,
Dec. 1936, 34; Burckhardt's view
of, 1938, 35; tension with Poland,
1937–38, 35–6; Beck on, Jan.
1938, 36; Łubieński, Szembek on,
in Beck conversations Berlin,
Jan. 1938, 36–9; German For.
Minister to Army on 39; relations with Poland, Jan. 1938, at
League of Nations Council,
Delbos, Eden, 40–2; in Hitler
speech, 20 Feb., 47; in Polish
aims, early 1938, Śmigły-Rydz on,
48; in Beck policy, Czech. crisis,
55; Horthy advice on Feb., 61;
rumours denied, Ribbentrop to
Burckhardt on, Forster visit to
Poland, 62; Halifax on, May
1938, 87–8; Goebbels in Danzig,
Forster in London, June, July,
tension in, Aug., 94; Beck on
role of in Polish–German
relations, 94–5; Łubieński to
Lipski on, in Lipski–Göring
conversation 24 Aug., 97, 99;
Mackiewicz criticism of policy on,
102–3; in Lipski's Nuremberg
conversations 7–12 Sept., 105;
Göring to Lipski on, 16 Sept.,

113, n. 19; Hitler on, 20 Sept.,
119; and Southeast Silesia,
Göring on, 4 Oct., 151; Noël,
French press on, 170; Ribben-
trop to Lipski on, 24 Oct.,
162–3, 180–1; Halifax on, Oct.,
169; Bonnet on, 176, n. 105;
Beck policy on, Oct. 1938 to
March 1939, 177; Hitler, Funk
on, press rumours, 178–9, n. 1;
Beck rejects German proposals
on, 181–2; Moltke on, 182–3;
Beck, Lipski on, 184–5; German
secrecy on, 186, n. 35; anti-
Jewish decrees, Halifax, League
of Nations, British attitude to,
France on, Ribbentrop to
Burckhardt on, 186–8; Hitler,
Ribbentrop to Beck on, 5 to 6
Jan. 1939, 189–90; Łubieński
project, Polish decision on,
Beck to Kennard on, 190–2;
Weizsäcker on, Committee of
Three, Bötcher, 193; Ribbentrop
visit, agreement on, 25 to 27
Jan. 1939, 194–5; Moltke to
Kennard on, 196; Kennard on,
197; Henderson on, 201; Beck–
Halifax agreement on, Dec.
1938, 202–4; and Memel, 208;
Hitler plans, Greiser, Weizsäcker
on, 209, n. 10; Ribbentrop
demands to Lipski 21 March
1939, 209–10; Daladier on, and
Rumania, 212–13, n. 22;
Halifax on, 19, 21 March, 215;
French attitude on, 215–16; in
Beck proposal to Britain,
22 March, policy on, refusal of
German terms, 24, 26 March,
217, 220; Beck, Ribbentrop on
coup in, Weizsäcker, Ribbentrop
instructions to, 221–2; British
press on, and guarantee, 226;
Beck conference on 1 April,
228–9; in London talks, agreement on 321–2, 235 n. 90;
Hitler proposal, 28 April,
Polish attitude on, 239–40 n. 5;
Chamberlain on, July, 242;
Lothian, Hudson, Bonnet on,
243–4; Hitler demands, 29 Aug.,
248

Delbos, Yvon (1885–1956), French
For. Minister 1938: warned by
Beck on Danzig, 1936, 1937, 28,
n. 70; in Warsaw, Dec. 1937, 42;
to Frankowski on Austria, Feb.
1938, 44–5

Dmowski, Roman (1864–1939),
leader, National Democratic

298

INDEX

INDEX

Mackiewicz (*cont.*)
1966), journalist, writer: supports Polish–German co-operation against USSR, 31–2; criticizes Beck policy Aug. 1938, 102–3; on Czech., 123; on Polish failure, Munich, 143; books, 268

Marienwerder (Kwidzyń): plebiscite decision 1919, 1

Märisch–Ostrau: see Moravská Ostrava

Masaryk, Thomas G. (1850–1937), President of Czechoslovakia 1918–35: and Teschen 1918, 12–13; view of Polish–German frontier, 13–14

Memel: German preparations March 1938, 51; Halifax on, Oct., 169; Ribbentrop on, Dec., 185; Henderson on, 201; German occupation of, 208–9, and Danzig, 218

Místek: see Frýdek

Moltke, Hans A., von (1884–1943), German Minister, Ambassador in Warsaw 1931–39, conversation with Laroche on Polish Corridor, 1933, 10; analysis of Polish policy 1933, 11, n. 23; report on Beck policy, proposes concessions to, 1 July 1938, 85; Beck's Baltic policy, 86; on Polish claims in Czech., 135, n. 90; Beck warning to, 136; puts German demands to Szembek 6 Oct., 151–52; on Polish–Hungarian frontier, 154; Danzig, 183; Łubieński to, on Danzig, Jan. 1939, 190–1, n. 51; to Kennard, 196; on Polish policy March 1939, 206; refusal of German terms, 24 March, 219; Beck warning on Danzig, 221; conversation with Arciszewski on Beck 23 May, 239–40

Moravská Ostrava: Göring to Beck on, Feb. 1938, 47–8; incident 7 Sept., 101; Polish claim to, 23 Sept., 135, n. 89; decision on 28 Sept., 137; and Bohumin, South-east Silesia, Danzig, Göring on, 4 Oct., 151

Mościcki, Ignacy (1867–1946), President of Poland 1926–39; answers Beneš letter, 131; Ribbentrop declaration to 27 Jan. 1939, 195; Beck to, on Great Britain, 230, n. 73

Muhlstein, Anatol (1889–1958), Counsellor Polish Embassy Paris 1930–36: on French attitude to preventive war 1933, 12, n. 24;

on French-Polish alliance Oct. 1938, 171

Mukačevo (Munkatsch, Munkács) Užhorod (Ungvar): Hungarian report on Polish Gen. Staff decision 10 Oct. 1938, 154, n. 19; arbitration proposal on, 161; Ciano support for, Poland, 163–4; Vienna award, 165

Munich Conference: terms of, 138–9.

Mussolini, Benito (1883–1945), Dictator of Italy 1922–45: and Four Power Pact, March 1933, 10; Austria 1934, Abyssinia, Rome–Berlin Axis, 30; and Eden resignation, 1938, 46; and bulwark against Germany in Danube, Balkans, 90, n. 30; open letter to Runciman 15 Sept. 1938, 110; conference proposal, Munich, 138; vacillation on Polish–Hungarian frontier 156–8, 162, 166–7, n. 70; and Chamberlain visit Jan. 1939, 200; Bonnet conference attempt 1–2 Sept. 1939, 248

NATIONAL DEMOCRATIC PARTY: criticizes govt. March 1938, 53; attitude to Czech. April, 67; demands in Czech. crisis, 147; and alternative policy, 257

Neurath, Konstantin, von, Baron (1873–1956), German for. Minister 1932–38: conversation with Beck Jan. 1938, 37–8

Noel, Léon (b. 1888), French Ambassador in Warsaw 1935–39: Beck declaration to, 7 March 1936, 26; conversation with Szembek on Danzig 1938, 36–7; view on Czech., March, 63, n. 19; on French support to Slávik, 71; Beck, declaration to, on Czech., May 72; on French-Polish alliance and Czech., 77; Bonnet instruction to on, 83–4; on Beneš and Teschen, Śmigły-Rydz declaration, 126, n. 58; 129; on revision of French-Polish alliance 170–1; opposes Bonnet–Beck meeting Jan. 1939, 199, n. 84; memoirs, 281

ORAVA: see Spiš

PAPÉE, Kazimierz (b. 1889), Polish Commissioner General in Danzig 1932–36, Minister in Prague 1936–39: informed of Franco-British demands on Czech., 11 May 1938, 74; transmits

304

INDEX

dictators, 22; opinion on French–
British policy decision on Czech.,
April 1938, 66; on mission to
Prague, May, 91, n. 35; on
Runciman and Polish minority
in Czech., 93; on USSR, Baltic
States 1939, 246, n. 21; mission
to Moscow, 247; memoirs and
study, 275

Stresemann, Gustav (1878–1929),
German For. Minister 1923–29:
interpretation of Locarno, 8; and
Piłsudski, 10, n. 22; and Hitler,
262

Stroński, Stanisław (1882–1955),
Professor, publicist for National
Democrats, deputy to Sejm
1923–35, Minister of Information
Nov. 1939 to March 1943: on
Czech.–Soviet alliance, April
1938, 67; on Teschen, Spiš,
Orava, 122; on French–British
role in East-Central Europe, 143

Subcarpathian Ruthenia: see Poland,
relations with Hungary; with
Rumania; Hungary; Beck

Sudetendeutsche Partei, SDP: organized
by Henlein 1933, German support
for, programme of, 59–60,
and Czech. mobilization 20 May
1938, 74, n. 48; Henlein's
suggestions on solutions, 81–82

Szembek, Jan. Count (1881–1945),
Under Secr. For. Affairs, Nov.
1932 to Sept. 1939: diaries of,
5, n. 6; to Noël on Danzig 1936,
36–37; conversation with
Petresco-Comnène on Soviet
passage through Rumania July
1938, 89, n. 29; to Slávik on
Beneš letter, 129; conversation
with Moltke 7 Oct., 151–2; to
Moltke, refusal of German terms
24 March 1939, 219

Teschen (Cieszyn, Těšín): Polish–
Czech. dispute, Piłsudski–
Masaryk, Beneš, Spa Conference
1920, 12–13, n. 27; Polish
opposition parties on, April 1938,
67–9; French advice to Czech. on,
69, n. 30; Moltke proposal on,
July, 85; Lipski to Hitler on, 20
Sept., 119; Stroński on, 122;
Bonnet, Noël, on, 126, n. 58;
Daladier, Bonnet on cession of,
25 Sept., 128–9; French–British
offer of, for Polish neutrality,
Bullitt, Łukasiewicz, on, 130; in
Gamelin–Śmigły-Rydz letter, 132;
and Bohumin, Beneš on, 142;

Polish occupation of, press on,
143–4, n. 116; Churchill on, 145

Third Europe: Beck project for,
inspiration, formulation, 55–6;
Baltic policy, Scandinavia,
Great Britain, 86–7; Beck on
Italian interests in Balkans
March 1938, 90, n. 30; German
opposition to Polish–Hungarian
frontier, 154–5; Kennard on
Slovakia, Ukrainian problem,
Knox on frontier, 155–6; Ciano
promises support to Poland,
Mussolini on Hungary, 157;
French opposition to frontier
161, n. 49; failure, possibilities
of, 175–6

Trans–Olza (Zaolzie): see Poland,
relations with Czechoslovakia;
Teschen; Beck; Beneš

Ukrainian population in Poland,
4, n. 4; Kennard on, and Subcarpathian Ruthenia, 156;
UNDO resolution on autonomy,
Dec. 1938, 167; German interest
in, 197, n. 77

Upper Silesia: plebiscite 1919–20, 2,
n. 2; ethnic structure, 3, n. 3;
French–German conversations on,
Jan. 1933, 10; census in German
part delayed by Göring, April
1938, 62, n. 16; Noël on, 170; in
Hitler directive 25 March 1939,
219

USSR foreign policy: proposes
alliance to Germany 1925, 9, n.
17; and East Locarno, 18–19;
alliances with France, Czech.,
1935, approaches to Germany
1933–35, 19, n. 46; offer to
Germany Jan. 1937, 20; on
Polish ultimatum to Lithuania,
51–2, n. 66; proposes conference
on Czech., 18 March 1938, 64;
passage to Czech., 79–80, 89, n.
29; French General Staff on, 63;
Western opinion on Army,
Litvinov proposes staff talks,
Beneš, May, 80, n. 62; answers
Beneš on aid to, 20–21 Sept.,
116, n. 31; protest to Poland
23 Sept., Beneš appeal to, 126,
n. 56; offers military intervention, 132; aid to Czech. and
Poland, 147, n. 121; favours
Polish–Hungarian frontier, 175;
Polish–Soviet declaration 27
Nov., 183; proposes conference
on Rumania 19 March 1939, 211;
British attitude to, 233, n. 85;

309